Sword Fighting in
the *Star Wars* Universe

Sword Fighting in the *Star Wars* Universe

Historical Origins, Style and Philosophy

NICK JAMILLA

McFarland & Company, Inc., Publishers
Jefferson, North Carolina, and London

Library of Congress Cataloguing-in-Publication Data

Jamilla, Nick.
Sword fighting in the Star wars universe : historical origins, style and philosophy / Nick Jamilla.
p. cm.
Includes bibliographical references and index.

ISBN 978-0-7864-3461-9
softcover : 50# alkaline paper 

1. Star Wars films. 2. Swordplay in motion pictures. I. Title.
PN1995.9.S695J36 2008
791.43'75 — dc22 2008023053

British Library cataloguing data are available

Manufactured in the United States of America

McFarland & Company, Inc., Publishers
Box 611, Jefferson, North Carolina 28640
www.mcfarlandpub.com

For Brian Willis
and my parents

Table of Contents

Preface

In anticipation of the first prequel movie in 1999, I wrote three articles on Jedi sword fighting for EchoStation.com. These articles were so well received that I decided to seek a wider audience with which to share my knowledge of and experience with Western fencing and Japanese swordsmanship. Buoyed by so many gracious e-mails, I composed several query letters and soon had invitations to do bookstore talks/demonstrations and an offer to give a sword fight demonstration for the Washington, D.C., *Episode I* charity premiere that took place several days before the general release of the movie. The enthusiasm of my audience was so great that I decided to continue the dialog by writing a book titled *Shimmering Sword* that answers in part or in whole many of the questions that were asked of me during my public appearances. The book was quite successful but it was incomplete in that it only covered material from the first prequel movie—*The Phantom Menace.* Now that the saga is complete, this revised and expanded book looks at the Jedi Knights and their lightsaber from the perspective of all six episodes of the *Star Wars* saga.

It is against this background that I explore the world of the Jedi Knight, which finds its basis in the reality of human history. This book discusses swordsmanship as a way to better understand the Jedi Knights, an artistic expression of our own real-world existence. It focuses on the human activity surrounding the traditional weapon of the sword, which forces men to confront each other head to head. It is an exploration of the cultural conditions of men and women who find that there may be no choice but to resort to the use of force. The premise of this book is not "Could it happen?" but "How did it happen?" While it may seem a blatant form of artifice, all fiction asks the audience to suspend reality for a time. Whether that suspension of reality makes an impact on us is often a function of how transferable the fiction is to the real world. The more real it seems, the more enjoyable and profound the experience. It is therefore incumbent upon me to examine the historical precedents that have informed the development of the lightsaber in the *Star Wars* universe so that we might better understand ourselves.

Much of this book's content refers to historical examples as the basis of *Star Wars* lightsaber fencing, but my own history also affects the views and perspectives of swordsmanship, which do not, by any significant measure, reflect the general experience of fencers of the Western tradition. Students of Japanese martial arts will probably share many of my interpretations of the sword art and fighting, though modern arts have the tendency to become more competitive than life transforming. Knowing some of my experiences which serve as the lens through which I look at swordsmanship will help the reader evaluate the text.

I began my twenty years in the martial arts at the age of fifteen when I heard about a local fencing club in Fort Myers, Florida, on the radio. An avid player of Dungeons & Dragons, I was drawn to the club because I wanted to know what it must have been like to wield a sword. I had seen *Star Wars* earlier but never made much connection to the lightsaber fights until later. With the help of my dedicated instructor Tom Howson, I learned the basics quickly and was soon participating in local tournaments around the state and in national tournaments around the country.

I tried to find a university that had a competitive fencing team, but I opted instead to go to Georgetown for its program in international relations. My hope was that a city of Washington's size offered fencing somewhere in its locality. I did find a club, but I had to rely on mass transportation to get there. While I got to fence, I practiced without a regular coach and without a regular schedule.

Through of my studies in international affairs, I discovered that I was technically a Filipino citizen until the age of twenty-one. I had only one chance, so I contacted the national fencing organization in Manila and asked if they were sending fencers to the World Fencing Championships in Lausanne, Switzerland, that year. They said there was already one person going to be sent, but because each country was allowed three representatives, I was welcome to participate as long as I paid all my expenses getting there. They also invited me to participate at the World University Games, which were held in Zagreb, Yugoslavia.

I was overjoyed at the prospect of competing at the world level, but I performed miserably in a situation in which I had no teammates to practice with, I was fatigued from my travels, and I had little stability having to move from one hostel to another in the weeks and days preceding the competitions. While I did not rank in last place at either the World Championships or the World University Games, I was out of my league. My only consolation is the fact that I was probably one of the best fencers to have ever represented the Philippines.

I also had my first and only diplomatic experiences as the Head of Delegation at both competitions.

The experience profoundly affected my perspective on Western fencing. While my performance was lackluster, I did have a unique opportunity to observe the best fencers in action. What I found repulsed me. Instead of dignified and respectful swordsmen, world-class fencers were aloof, self-centered, and arrogant. The highest thing on their mind was winning, which created an atmosphere of unrivaled one-upmanship. This was, of course, competition, and winning medals depended on that state of mind, but something in my heart told me that if these were the people I was supposed to emulate as a fencer, I wanted nothing to do with it.

To this day I view the Olympics with a strong dose of cynicism. Despite the façade of peaceful competition, the Olympics are tainted by nationalistic pride, nepotism, outright corruption, and the worship of a technician who can accumulate the best statistics. The Olympics were originally a celebration of Greek culture, but they were also a demonstration of the Greeks' athletic prowess. It was a fillip to the face of barbarians who were not worthy of participating alongside the Hellenes. TV portrays the Olympics as a community of peaceful competition between nations, but underneath its nice veneer is a cutthroat network of big egos.

The one redeeming aspect of my world-class fencing experience was the reception of the Philippine delegation at the opening ceremonies. I was one of three representatives of the Philippines to walk out behind the flag of the nation of my parents' birth. Such small countries usually receive the token cheers of the crowd that awaits the largest delegations from the most powerful countries of Great Britain, the United States, and China. But just one year earlier, the Philippines had dominated the world press as Filipinos deposed their dictator Ferdinand Marcos. Croatians knew the yoke of oppression and they expressed their desire for more freedom by loudly cheering the Philippine delegation as we walked around the track. Many stood up from their seats in our honor, while others waved the pointer finger and thumb, making an "L" sign to symbolize the political party of Cory Aquino, who became president after Marcos fled the country. The loud chorus of cheers that followed us through the stadium was equal to that given to the United States. Their warm welcome of the Americans contrasted with the silence and cold stares given to the delegation of the Soviet Union. It was obvious the Yugoslavs still remembered the threatened invasion of the Soviet army in 1956. I will never forget the friends I made in Croatia and the welcome the city of Zagreb gave me during their opening ceremonies.

Once I returned to the States, I virtually gave up fencing until I met Martha Matthews, who was a clerk for Justice Harry A. Blackmun of the U.S. Supreme

Court. She introduced me to a curious martial art called aikido, which had at the heart and soul of its practice love for the enemies who might attack. You learned how to defend yourself, but you learned how to fight without doing permanent physical damage to your assailant. Suspicious at first, I finally joined the *dojo* after seeing classes in Japanese sword in which students used wooden practice swords called *bokken.* Aikido, which is predominantly an empty-handed fighting art, is basically the set of skills a samurai would use if he had lost his sword in battle.

Training under Shihan Mitsugi Saotome, I had the instruction of a world-renowned teacher who had trained directly under the founder of aikido, Morihei Ueshiba, who had derived his art from the martial techniques of an aiki-jujitsu style of fighting from Hokkaido. Saotome impressed me not only with a technical ability that stressed martial competence, but also by his philosophical interpretations of aikido. It was his influence that opened my mind to the fact that it was possible to pursue combative arts without the need to participate in competition.

After two years of aikido at Saotome's dojo in Washington, as well as training under the supervision of George Meyer who teaches aikido at the U.S. Naval Academy, I decided to go to Tokyo where I would train at the Aikikai Hombu Dojo, a kind of Mecca for aikido students the world over. For four years, I went to practice daily and quickly became a devoted follower of two generous instructors, Masuda Sensei and Endo Sensei, who taught me both the vigor and kindness of daily practice.

In Tokyo, I also decided to pursue my interest in kendo (the Japanese equivalent of Western fencing), which used bamboo swords called *shinai* instead of foils, epees, and sabres. Here, too, my instruction was deeply influenced by the kind and disciplined instruction of Kubo Sensei, headmaster of the Kyumeikan Kendo Dojo on the outskirts of Tokyo. Not only did his fluent English help me learn kendo (he lived in the United States for a year in his youth), but also his gentle yet tough spirit encouraged me to persevere in the most difficult of situations. Under his training, I also began my studies of *iaido* (the art of sword drawing), *jodo* (the art of short staff), and *naginatado* (the art of Japanese halberd).

When I wasn't doing martial arts or writing novels, I made a full-time living as a teacher. Starting first as a French conversation teacher in my senior year of college, I continued for four years teaching English as a second language in Japan. Upon my return to the States, I have pursued a career as a middle-school teacher. In addition, I have taught aikido and fencing at various times at private schools in the Washington, D.C., area, as well as the U.S. Naval Academy aikido club in Annapolis, Maryland.

Before moving to the body of this work, there are some points of clarification as well as basic expectations on the part of the reader that I must address.

It will be assumed that the reader is very familiar with the plots of the six films of the *Star Wars* saga. If there is some basic question about major characters, information can be most easily obtained by visiting the official Lucasfilm website at StarWars.com.

For the sake of brevity, I have used the episode numbers of the *Star Wars* films interchangeably with the titles of the movies.

Episode I *The Phantom Menace*
Episode II *Attack of the Clones*
Episode III *Revenge of the Sith*
Episode IV *A New Hope*
Episode V *The Empire Strikes Back*
Episode VI *Return of the Jedi*

Because of the plethora of *Star Wars* materials, I principally consider the original movies, their screenplays, and novelizations, which are considered, for the sake of argument, canon sources of information. No knowledge of the Expanded Universe (EU) is required, though some mention of it is made throughout the book and in the endnotes. The EU —found in Del Rey, Bantam Books, Dark Horse Comics, West End Games, and Wizards of the Coast publications— becomes so vast a collection novels, comic books, and graphic novels that it is now necessary to consult a detailed timeline to know where within the *Star Wars* universe a story takes place. Because plots are fleshed out by individual authors based on the needs of a particular time frame determined by editors at a publishing company licensed by Lucasfilm Ltd., it is easier for me to stick to the original films, which are both accessible to the general public and the work of George Lucas, the creator of the franchise.

Clarification is also necessary for the overlapping definitions of the martial arts discussed in this book. By "martial arts," I refer to all combative arts whether their professed purpose is battle or friendly competition. Competitive fencing, kendo, and aikido (the three arts I have practiced for twenty-five years) fall into this general category. "Sword arts," or more simply "swordsmanship," refers to combat with the intention of using a sword specifically for attack or defense in a battle or duel situation. If the focus of sword fighting is on the competition or the "way" of an art, I will specifically mention the art by name.

It should also be noted that in most instances I will use the terminology of the competitive arts (kendo and fencing) to express concepts, ideas, and movements in sword fighting used specifically for battle. It is my assertion that while the modern, competitive forms of the older "killing" swordplay are often exercises and games of tag that do not reflect real battlefield fighting, the essence of true swordsmanship used for that purpose can be learned and discovered if one's intention is to learn the "killing" aspect of the art. It follows, then, that the basics of classical *kenjutsu* (traditional Japanese sword fighting) can be learned by adapting modern kendo techniques. This is not to say that a modern foil fencer can pick up a small sword and will automatically become an expert in its use. The same goes for a kendo student picking up a *katana*, a live bladed Japanese curved sword. Practicing specifically with that weapon is still necessary for proficiency and eventual mastery.

When referring to the Jedi and their lightsabers, I have consciously and purposely refrained from using the self-created terms of "lightsaberist" and "lightsaber art." The Jedi, for the sake of linguistic style, will be referred to as "swordsmen" or the more cumbersome name of "lightsaber fighter." *Jedi* will be used to represent both its singular and plural usage.

For the sake of cultural differentiation, I will refer to European sword arts (broad sword, rapier, two-handed sword, etc.) as Western swordsmanship or more generally as Western fencing. On occasion, the new recreations of Western swordfighting as it was used for battlefield combat is referred to as Western martial arts. Eastern martial arts will include any and all Asian fighting arts, though many references are made specifically to Japanese martial arts.

For references and personal commentaries, footnotes have been included in many instances. Unfamiliar terms will be offset by italics and will be explained within the text. In the case of Japanese words that have in effect become indigenous English words when used within the context of a specific martial art, the word will be italicized in its first instance and then given in regular type thereafter. For those with a deeper, more academic interest, a bibliography is provided with the understanding that no bibliography is inclusive.

It will be quickly noted that my references to *Star Wars* lightsaber fighting are compared to Japanese martial arts exclusively. For reasons that will be explained later in the book, let it suffice at this point to say that lightsaber sword fighting is directly influenced by Japanese sword fighting arts, and more recently by the influence of Ray Park's Chinese martial arts training. While I may be criticized for limiting the scope of my comparisons to samurai arts, I would rather be accused of cultural myopia than being a charlatan expert in Chinese martial arts with which I have only cursory familiarity and incidental training. Perhaps this book will invite a fellow martial artist of the Chinese tradition to write a book similar to this one.

I have been influenced by my own experience and personal preferences, and from the many comments people have given me from my talks, there is a general acceptance for my particular perspective, which is undoubtedly biased toward Japanese martial arts. This prejudice cannot be stricken from my perspective, and it rests with the reader to consciously take my background into account when he or she judges this work according to his or her own intellect. I invite the reader to do so, and relish an informed discussion.

To experienced martial artists, much of this book will have the ring of simple common sense. Much is gleaned from the experiences I have had and conclusions I have come to over the past twenty-five years I have been doing and reflecting on the martial arts. Many of my seniors may recognize this enterprise as premature, but my intent is to make connections not for the experts in their own personal martial art, but to collect thoughts for those who would like to understand the sword fighting aspect of the *Star Wars* universe in comparison to the historical fencing tradition of two different and unique styles.

For librarians and parents, a quick warning about the contents of this book, which is recommended for high school students and older. The topic of sword fighting is a subject that, at its very heart, acknowledges the life and death of those that participated in the sword's use. No longer does the pursuit of the art of the sword as generally practiced in public have the goal of inflicting or advocating the infliction of harm to another person. Rather, its goal, if one can be given in the name of sword practitioners all over the world, is the improvement or entertainment of the person through an ancient art. Learning swordsmanship no more promotes the killing of another person than does the capture of a pawn by a queen in chess infer torture or execution. There are certain descriptions that do give specific detail of the uses of a sword, which often become an instrument of butchery, though the sword is more often used representatively as a symbol of peace through strength.

Lastly, it is imperative that all training in sword work should be done under the auspices of proper teachers. Anyone interested in learning the art of swordsmanship should inform and educate himself before participating in a critical dialog with any potential instructor, especially those bearing the title Master. One must know the goals and purposes of learning any martial art. Care must be exercised in the learning of skills that confer the power to coerce.

I want to thank Shane Ward for his creative inspiration, Robert B.K. Brown for his technical collaboration and the graphics, and Karl Austin for many *Star Wars* discussions. Gratitude also goes to Brian for his patience and support.

Sit Anima Tecum
Nick Jamilla

One

Jedi, Combat and Honor

Sword Culture: Understanding Fear

No phrase goes to the heart of swordsmanship so succinctly as Yoda's instruction to Anakin in Episode II: "Fear leads to anger; anger lead to hate; hate leads to suffering." Were it not for fear, there would have been no need for the elaborate codes of conduct that ruled behavior both in a civilized society as well as that on a battlefield. In the name of self-protection and self-preservation, swordsmen throughout history and across continents have always hidden their uncertainty and covered their trembling hearts behind the mask of bravado and a face-saving masculinity. It was this fear of embarrassment or failure, of loss of life or face that made warriors draw their swords, those crude but sharp instruments that make for a poor, but often effective substitute for a dull mind.

Swordsmen, however, like the Jedi, were not errant warriors with kind intentions. They were part of a culture that had established rules based on human fear and experiences from combat. While training to become the best swordsmen of the universe, the Jedi, like accomplished diplomats, the greatest leaders, and the most creative of individuals, did not need the brute force of strength. Instead, they became masters of wisdom and intelligence who had the skills of the sword at their disposal should words fail them.

Battlefield Experience

The fear of death is ultimately the most basic emotional urge a person can ever confront. This became even more prevalent in the minds of swordsmen. The basic drive for self-preservation during a surprise situation is instinctual: for men it more often instructs the body to stand and fight, for women the opposite. Life on the hunt became a testing ground for the best able to follow their instincts.

The battlefield, on the other hand, allowed more time for the brain to calculate the odds as opposing armies faced up in lines against each other. For individuals, there was the commanding thought that one person against an army of others could hardly make a difference. It was, therefore, the numbers and close proximity to other men in the same situation that made the individual desire to become part of the whole. The individual stood a better chance of survival in the group. Civilized cultures like Naboo, as well as their Gungan neighbors, realized that united and organized resistance was the best way to maximize the moral strength of any military force. Even the Jedi had a clear understanding that personal protection is different from fighting a war. It was also their motivation for taking control of the clone army as the threat to the Republic grew.

Rituals reassured individuals by shaping the psychology of the men so that they may better prepare for the final moments of their lives. The gathering of warriors into lines and ranks puts order into a situation that seems wild and chaotic. It gives the feeling that organization will be key to victory. Religious rites assured men that their cause was just in the eyes of God and sent the message that God was awaiting them if this were to be a person's last battle. The imbibing of wine, mead, or beer served as a final drink with one's comrades. It also had the intoxicating effects of dulling physical pain and reducing a person's natural inhibition to walk directly into the danger of combat. The presence of older, more experienced men behind the younger served as reassurance to green troops that others among them knew what to expect and what to do. Experienced soldiers also served as a deterrence to the coward who might flee the front line. Without preparations like this, the cohesion and resolve of the army would be seriously reduced.

Once the lines had been formed, men would be ordered forward and when lines met on the middle, the victorious army would be the one that pushed the enemy back without losing its own cohesion. Once a break in the enemy's line was created, men could push into the ranks, attacking the flanks of opponents who expected and desired to fight by pushing their own way through the enemy. Survival now became a question of ability, numbers, intensity, and tactics, all the while being thwarted by poor visibility, unfavorable ground, and the elements. Tactics were high in the mind of the swordsman slashing at his enemies, while a planned overall strategy was designed to make use of an army's strengths while limiting its weaknesses. Sometimes, as the Gungans know, victory was not necessarily guaranteed, but order in the face of an overwhelming adversary was still the best chance of success.

In the front lines, the sense of a successful attack depended on the continued momentum of a push forward and the feeling that fewer casualties were being taken than were being given out. As men moved forward, instincts took over, men automatically looking for opponents to engage until there were none left. Victory was assured when the whole company pushed forward and individuals at the periphery engaged in one-on-one exchanges. When the men on one side began to fall and the approach of enemies forced soldiers backward, the will to fight faltered and eventually the warrior had to either take a stand (and hope to come out victorious) or begin a retreat to save his own life. His withdrawal may have been organized and coordinated with his company who also sees the inevitability of defeat, or, more often, it became a self-interested every-man-for-himself mentality in which flight was the quickest and most direct route out of the battlefield.

When the enemy began to surrender or to flee, the moment of individual victory was at hand. But battles often took hours to fight, the complete victory being dependent on a series of successes, not one of a single company. When soldiers looked around and saw their side pushing the enemy back, he would be emboldened to continue the fight. When his compatriots lay sprawled on the ground dead or dying, he cowered and sought to retreat until he could find others on his side for solace and support.

The battlefield was both a training ground for the survivors in which their education was the pragmatic exchange of attacks and defenses. In the midst of the front line, there were no rules. It was each man for himself, and the desire for fair play was nonexistent when one's very survival was at stake. It was from this experience that the swordsman learned that survival was a brutal taskmaster.

Once an individual survived one battle, he became more convinced that he would be able to survive the next battle, being more prepared for the horrors that he was to experience. By virtue of his profession, the soldier became a pragmatist, understanding that the force of arms was the ultimate power in the universe. By defeating an enemy, the swordsman learned that victory only came to those who had the superior command of fighting skills, battle tactics, and strategy. The battlefield was the place where strength dominated and destroyed all the pleasantries, cultural refinement, and good intentions peaceful societies held in esteem. This was the reality of the swordsman — power came at the edge of his weapon.

Codes of Conduct

While survival was at the forefront of the soldier's thoughts during combat, it became evident after the clash that a favorable outcome was highly dependent on the training and preparation of the soldiers. Raw courage and determination were important traits of the warrior, but skills and preparation

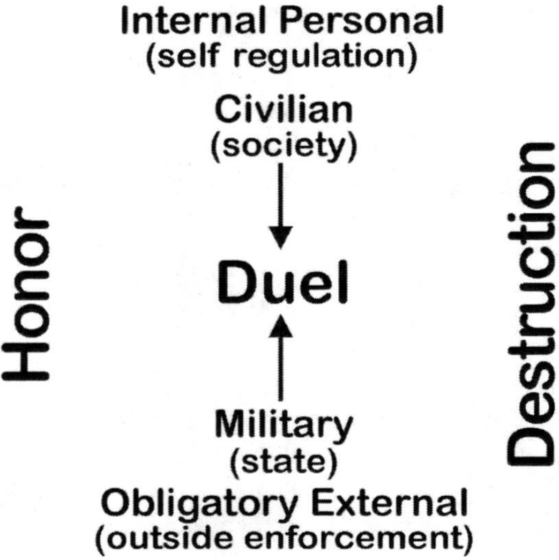

Protection of one's honor is preserved by the duel (center). Internal personal motivation for the duel stems from self-regulation and takes place in a nonmilitary situation among other civilians. Obligatory external motivation stems from the rules and pressure of a formal military institution (state). Whether a duel is fought for personal reasons or because of adherence to military obligations, there are ideally only two results: honor is preserved or death is inflicted.

guaranteed that the human spirit was not unnecessarily hamstrung before the battle had even begun. The experienced soldier realized that once the battlefield was left, there was another world in which he must live — that of civilized society. This was the world of the Jedi who served as protectors of the galactic universe.

In the heat of the battle or in the campaign of war, the most basic emotions of hate and anger came to dominate the swordsman's mind. As crude propaganda, vilification of the enemy gave troops simple reasons to fight as well as invectives to sling at their enemies. Swordsmen of the aristocracy, however, recognized that as men of value and worth, they shared a code of conduct that governed them even in the chaos of battle.

While battle was an act of last resort for civilized men, the reality of hand-to-hand warfare taught that when sword edge touched an opponent's flesh, men became one and the same, creatures of determination that kill in order to preserve their own life. When words failed and negotiation reached its limits, the swordsman, more than any other type of soldier, understood and recognized the destructive potential of a clash of arms. By staring into the brutish character of others forced into war, the swordsman was also reminded that his opponent was not simply some abstraction, but another being who bleeds, feels pain, and dies.

Without this understanding, there could be no hope for peace and the state of war would continue. Without high-minded leaders and diplomats, many of whom knew the harsh realities of war, there could be no less incentive to avoid war than by knowing firsthand its destructiveness. The repugnance of war did not only come from the hard experience of battle, however. Thoughtful martial artists too, because of the very nature of their discipline, can learn the lessons of war's horrors. The Jedi, too, who, at the time of Episode II, did not know of mass-scale battles, must have understood the nature of their sword art if they were to become active participants in the vast universe of galactic diplomacy. The Jedi must understand human and political motivations as well as the strengths and weaknesses of the people and aliens with whom he was to negotiate. Without this knowledge, the Jedi could not possibly understand his own position, nor that of his adversary. It was because melee combat was fought one-on-one, the Jedi understood that the power of coercion was the pragmatic reality of diplomacy, or "aggressive negotiations," as Anakin put it. The training of the lightsaber made the Jedi's outlook toward others highly personal.

Because combat began as confrontation between individuals, the combat between warriors at arm's length was seen as a heroic exploit that gave individuals, both commoners and elites, the opportunity to prove themselves in the severest form of masculine competition —combat. Contrast this with modern armies, which, because of the technology of the firearm, fight ideally from a distance under the protection of camouflage and natural or man-made barriers. The nature of warfare has changed, but there still exists the need to make modern wars into the heroic combat of the past. This is good in that the soldier will see the human side of the struggle of war, but it also has the potential of romanticizing the waste and carnage of human life.

The sword itself holds a particular meaning for human societies because it was the first weapon created specifically to take another human life. Like the lightsaber, it was not a tool, which implied some peaceful utility, nor was it a hunting weapon like the spear and the bow. And while the club was an easier man-to-man fighting instrument, the conscious invention of the sword demonstrated for the first time in societies that competition was no longer between bands of wandering humans, but of conflict between people who had less conflict with nature than they had with each other.

The sword found its origins in early knives, which were made of chipped flint. They were a flexible tool capable of cutting meat, stripping bone, puncturing hides, and could, in an emergency, be used for self-defense. As human skills evolved, the quality of the blade improved as well. Stone proved a poor substance out of which to fashion blades, but with improvements in metallurgy, society was transformed by the sword as profoundly as it was by newer, more complicated forms of organization and farming techniques. Early swords were made out of copper, bronze (a combination of copper and tin), iron, and finally steel. It was a simple object to create and construct (essentially a long knife), allowing cultures around the world to independently develop the sword, though with minor variations in size, shape, and style. Its inherent form remains either the single-sided or double-sided blade. Techniques of the sword evolved over thousands of years, the sword remaining the principal weapon of many societies until the technological achievement and preponderance of the firearm.

Warfare, however, was not the desired or total experience of either civilians or warriors. Much more of the soldier's time was spent honing skills, preparing defenses, or on the road marching from one battle to the next. It was a difficult life requiring discipline and a hardiness that civilians did not encounter with the same intensity. Barracks life has and always remains a disciplined and often difficult existence. Indeed, it was the soldier's very training that seemed contradictory to the life during peacetime. While being taught the art of war, the soldier was expected to behave in a civilized society. This cultural paradox is a reality with which all civilizations have had to come to grips. Even among the most cultivated and enlightened cultures, the need to resort to acts of war was sometimes necessary and even desirable.

Victor Davis Hanson's book on infantry battle (*The Western Way of War*) posits the credible theory that the battlefield was an effective and efficient method of deciding differences between rival city-states. Apart from wars of conquest and empire building, even the most democratic societies of Greece came to the conscious conclusion that questions of land rights and ownership were best settled by a single, decisive battle, rather than a long, extended campaign, which citizens in neighboring city-states neither sought nor desired.

What soldiers learned from the battlefield would become a source of enlightenment affecting forever the way armed men would interact. On the one hand, there was a simple recognition that in war all the basic rules of human interaction are dispensed with. On the other, there was a general recognition that the imposition of rules of engagement was useful to limit unbridled warfare.

Most civilizations have known periods in which no single authority predominated over another. In such situations, bands of soldiers laid waste to whatever land and possessions they could take for their own appetites. Control of violence and the men who could inflict violence became an issue of vital importance. Even the most savage commander must at some point recognize that the free rein of armed militants could not be allowed in either the military camp or the conquered town or village. Restrictions, in some form, had to be imposed. Either the spoils of war would be destroyed or the army would degenerate into self-destruction. Out of this evolved the iron discipline of military life, which eventually developed into a set of expected behaviors most commonly referred to among swordsmen as a code of honor.

Off the battlefield, the soldier presented as much a threat to society as he did to the enemies he conquered. It was easy for the swordsman to take his experiences on the battlefield and apply them to the civilian world. Business, politics, and even the arts were to be seen as the mere expression of competing interests that saw more value in their individual success than a more tempered and caring mode of behavior. Religion and civilian values had always placed a higher value on the benefits of peace than on the chaotic world of continual warfare. Societies, while often benefiting from the great technological and cultural leaps reaped from war (many countries achieved their very existence through revolution), there was no question that the benefits of societies that nurtured and cared for its citizens through peaceful regulation far surpassed the destructive changes brought about through war.

While the need for a soldiery was reluctantly deemed a necessity, rules that limited the power of swordsmen in society have always been seen as a necessary part of the swordsman's life, which was divided into two basic spheres of action — self-regulation and coercion.

Self-regulation corresponded to the public civility most reflected in the concept of honor, which acts as a public code of conduct that governed individuals who were given the privilege of carrying a sword.[1] Often, this state of civility and honor was referred to by swordsmen as point of honor. The other state of affairs was that of the battlefield in which a state of war existed between individuals and between civilizations, cultures, and countries. Point of honor was an ethical standard of behavior the swordsman had to follow in society, while the state of war was the coercive situation in which power and control were determined by the armed struggle. It required the swordsman to be an individual of two minds— one of peace and one of war. Where the two do not meet was often a source of post-traumatic battle syndrome, wherein a soldier cannot mentally separate the experience of one state of being from the other.

Throughout history, the soldier has always had to examine his relationship to the state because he served both as protector of it as well as its greatest threat. The swordsman was praised during times of war as the guarantor of freedom in his role as soldier, cavalryman, and knight, but reviled as dictator if he took control of the state for his personal aggrandizement. Society, therefore, has had a love-hate relationship with the military, for it must trust the swordsman to be a guardian, not a usurper. Society could trust the swordsman only if he were trained properly. In the *Star Wars* universe, the Jedi was not a usurper, but its guardian. That, too, however, would be called into question when Palpatine came to power.

Pragmatic Struggle

Ultimately, the proper swordsman had to respect not only the code of honor, which ruled his life from within, but also the law of the land, which were the rules of every citizen, including the swordsman. While there was no reason why the swordsman could not take power for himself, the principles inherent in the cult of honor tempered the swordsman and encouraged him to respect law of his own volition.

Honor as a public morality stemmed from the basic idea that a swordsman was part of an elite group that could impose restrictions on an individual who broke the code of the group. Knowing that the collective desired not to

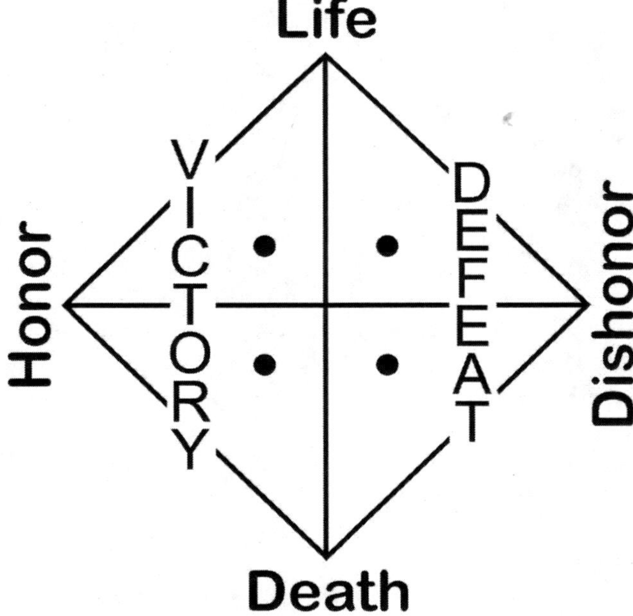

On the battlefield, there are four ideal states for a person's honor: life with honor, life with dishonor, death with honor, and death with dishonor. For the swordsman, victory is obtained through the preservation of honor through actual victory in combat, a heroic death, or an honorable surrender. Defeat occurs when one demonstrates cowardice by fleeing the battlefield and surviving or being killed during flight.

discipline a member publicly, the individual was encouraged to behave properly and according to the rules of the group. He had particular rights to challenge the group within the parameters of the rules, all the while being subject to verbal coercion and the threat of punitive measures. Since training with the sword was a long and difficult challenge, there was plenty of opportunity to create in the individual a pride in belonging to the group and a sense of obligation to it. Should these fail, men of honor could discipline both by fines and eventually through ostracism. Should those measures not prove sufficient in reining in the recalcitrant member, force of arms, for all the members are swordsmen, was the last recourse.

Implicit in this relationship was the assumption that power, being the final arbiter in the real world, would achieve a desired end in a civil society. It reflected the real state of the world and permitted regulation in what otherwise would have been a permanent state of war. Because the proponents of this form of "peaceful coercion" were the Europeans of the great continental nations, this mode of operation became the basis for the international organizations that would develop during the twentieth century. The concept of collective force disciplining a single defiant nation was at the heart of the League of Nations. This collectivist spirit hoped to be a supra-national organization in which mere alliance and regionalism in a state of international anarchy (which led to the conflict of World War I) could be prevented. States, however, while bowing to the ideas of Woodrow Wilson's proposal of a peace program (the Fourteen Points), did not act out of a belief in a greater, pan-national organization. They were still acting as self-interested nations who accepted war as a proper and sometimes necessary arm of national policy. Because of internal pressures and the rise of fascism, communism, and militarism, use of force was seen as a natural, if not inevitable, tool of the demagogue. Such ideologies attributed much of the inevitability of struggle — whether of ideas, class, or armaments — to the very state of human culture. Determinists — proponents of the belief that cultures, society, and past history predetermine future events — believed that human civilization was at a crossroad in its historical development. But when the swordsman drew his sword, he became an actor within the world who must change the world around him in order to survive, or die trying. The swordsman could not admit determinism without admitting the futility of his own profession.[2]

The League of Nations would ultimately fail because individual nations, including the United States, which did not even join the League of Nations, pursued an individual policy that had little concern for the general state of the world if it meant their own nation would suffer. In a world of political survival-of-the-fittest, there seemed to be a sense that the finite world of one country's gain meant another country's loss.

What the League of Nations lacked in its pragmatism, the United Nations made up in its commitment to idealism. Although acting within a world of inevitable unilateralism, the spirit of nations after the carnage of World War II was a commitment to a higher authority rather than the mere punishment of rogue nations. An emphasis was placed on the creative use of international standards of law as exemplified by the Nuremberg trials and the strengthening of international bodies like the World Court in which due process, fairness, and judgment according to high standards of conduct were respected. Law would not simply be the arbitrary will of the victor, as exemplified by the Treaty of Versailles.

The swordsman's code of honor went through a similar evolution. Recognizing the pragmatism of resorting to power, point of honor became as corrupt as the League of Nations. What worked on a personal level as a self-regulating honor system with a mechanism for disciplining defiant members became a rogue body of elitist oligarches. Under the short-sighted principle that courts of honor could rule in cases in which civil and criminal law had no jurisdiction, the court of honor became an alternate justice system that, in the end, could not regulate itself because individuals through their ability to manipulate the sword succeeded in thwarting the actions of the group. The point of honor system had its own courts made up of aristocratic swordsmen who, in the name of honor, defied the law of the land in which they lived.

The honor system simply gave individual swordsmen a framework to justify their own vigilantism. The honor system was envisioned as a code of behavior based on the premise that civilized people would refrain from the public staining of individual character — openly impugning a person's character or disparaging a person's behavior — because the recipient of such verbal abuse could challenge his accuser to a duel. However, instead of preventing public, uncivilized exchanges, such as calling an individual a liar, a cheat, or a coward, the honor system was used to bait weaker opponents into a situation that inevitably resulted in the defeat of the weaker swordsman. The arms race of developing better fencing skills was fueled as gentlemen of distinction fell into the trap of thinking the state of war would settle quarrels of perception and intellect.

Commoners aspiring to higher positions in society began to recognize the bloodthirsty futility of settling differences with the duel. At first they became reluctant participants as commoners entered the aristocratic world of knighthood, but as societies developed more refined ideas of democratic liberalism, the traditional point of honor system came to be understood as a sophist veil of unlawful and defiant aristocratic privilege. Not only did commoners lack the knowledge of elite rules of governance (a brotherhood of noblesse oblige), but they lacked the skills of swordsmanship, which were considered an important part of an aristocrat's upbringing. Commoners used logic, common sense, religion, and the developing tools of cannon and guns to wrest the privilege of exclusive point of honor away from swordsmen. In effect, the point of honor system became a separate court of law that distinguished itself apart from and superior to the laws of the nation.

The failure of point of honor lay in the arrogance of swordsmen who continued to act in civilian society as if they were still on the battlefield. Instead of esteeming the laws of the nation, they esteemed the laws of point of honor because it served their interest. The true goal of point of honor was a self-regulating system of conduct essentially based on trust of the judgment of individuals who belonged to the class of swordsmen.

Ever since civilizations first organized their earliest laws, there has always existed a concept that law was the best protector of people's interests. Replacing arbitrary whims, the codification of proper behavior became a way to equally protect and guarantee the rights and privilege of aristocrats and eventually the commoner as well. While not necessarily guaranteeing equality, it did allow for the peaceful intercourse with sovereigns (and its military) and important economic and privileged players in the country. Because laws had to be applied universally, the basis of most law systems found its roots not in power struggles, but in the concept of justice as expressed in standards of behavior that were considered correct and fair.

Jurists, knowing that simple enunciation of idealistic behavior was useless unless there was some form of enforcement, articulated the need for policemen to force individuals to conform. Usually this role fell to the executive branch of government (in most cases a sovereign king) who implicitly committed himself or herself to abiding by the laws when the military was used to defend national laws. When the sovereign was influential enough to command the military, the role of the swordsman and the law were in proper harmony. The swordsman could therefore feel reassured that his lawful behavior served not only his self-interest but that of justice as well. The sword became the symbol of justice.

Adjunct to the need of law to be enforced through the use of coercion was the concept that swordsmen came to have their privilege of exerting power because the sword was placed in their hands by a recognized authority. While that authority often came to the swordsman from a sovereign (the king, a state bureaucracy, divine representatives), the swordsman not only owed allegiance to his lord, but also to greater societal goods—nationhood, freedom, independence. There came to exist an assumption that since law was reflective of proper behavior, the swordsman too was bound by those laws. When the swordsman chose to disobey a law by virtue of his physical ability to do so, he ceased playing the role of power broker, statesman, soldier, and gentleman. Swordsmen became, instead, bullies, thugs, thieves, and murderers.

In the international arena of post–World War II geopolitics, the attempt to place the military in the service of international law has been a change that has met with relative success. While the Cold War depended highly on the self-interests of primarily the United States and the Soviet Union, a greater dependence has been successful in applying universal principles of law at the heart of governmental action. Where point of honor was once an expression of modes of proper behavior for the swordsman, the international legal system has titularly become the mode of proper behavior for sovereign states. When countries, especially the most powerful, begin to act out of a greater sense of concern for the public good, the success of international justice has a greater chance of being achieved. More than at any other period of history, the present international community of self-interested national governments has recognized the interdependence of both economic and political interests. Of even greater import is the more prevalent appreciation for the fact that pragmatic action can be exercised with deference to the idealism of justice.

The honor code of swordsmen as applied to the geopolitical state of the world (and in the case of *Star Wars*, to the universal state of the galactic republic) must resolve itself not in the idealistic vacuum of the court, but in the real world. A point of dispute often falls on the distinction of individual action and the need of the group. In many instances, the actual state of human politics often revolves around the needs of the minority and the needs of the majority.

Especially in nations where democracy and liberal freedom are held as principal assumptions of political organization, the question of a majority's tyranny still arises. Even if it is assumed that the majority is wise enough to properly manage the affairs of the whole, there will always exist the potential to use the swordsman (the military) to suppress the minority simply because it disagrees with the majority. The minority, if it is not stamped out through suppressive means, has two recourses: it can convince the majority to come over to its position, or it can raise an army of swordsmen to act on its behalf. Because the state of war will eventually judge the victor through the pure exercise of power, it is incumbent on those in positions to coerce others to have a proper respect for the law.

Because law holds justice as a standard for its norms, the swordsman, to properly remain the swordsman, must respect the law. Without the swordsman's support, there can be no effective justice. There are therefore two kinds of swordsmen — one who derives his power from the sword (state of war) and one who derives his power from the exercise of the sword in the name of justice (state of civility and honor). One is honorable because he strives to achieve justice, while the other loses his status as a guardian of society and becomes a common thug or dictator.

The enlightened swordsman, if properly trained, will submit himself to regulation. He will bow to proper authority, which in principle is submission to idealistic behaviors. He will be considered dishonorable if he defies the law and takes authority for his own. In the real world, however, the material exigencies of a nation may depend on the unlawful exercise of power. Take, for example, the case in which a swordsman disagrees with the law, one that he considers unjust.

The swordsman must feel compelled to act in accordance with justice, which, in this circumstance, does not conform to higher modes of behavior. His duty is, therefore, to fight against this law, creating a pragmatic struggle in which good behavior must be forced into the codification of law. Because the swordsman's resort to the state of war simply introduces a crude form of idealistic relativism, i.e., one person's preference of justice for another, there is another principle that governs the life and experience of the empowered swordsman — that of sacrifice.

When a minority, an individual or a group, breaks a just law, the swordsman has the moral imperative to exercise coercion in favor of the law. When that minority or majority breaks an unjust law, the swordsman must make a judgment on whether to enforce the law. Revolution is often justified in this latter category. If it is successful, and in accordance with just principles, the revolutionary swordsman gains not only de facto control of the country, he also reestablishes codes of behavior that are considered just. This recourse, because it is done in defiance of existing laws, must be accomplished with deliberate thought for fear of elevating a state of war without replacing it with a state of civility and honor. If honor is equated with self-interest, it results in personal preference — a dictatorship. If honor is equated with simply the judgment of a select few, it results in a larger form of personal preference — an oligarchy. For the state of civility and honor to take reign (a just society), the swordsman must eventually yield his power.

When the swordsman uses his sword to restore justice, his attempt is never considered a failure. By winning the pragmatic struggle, he installs a just regime. By losing, though he may not survive, he makes what is considered a noble and enlightened sacrifice. This tragic and romantic sacrifice may seem a futile exercise, but it still remains that the swordsman chose to use his power of coercion in the name of justice. Obi-Wan in Episode IV understands that sacrifice may be necessary if justice is to be achieved. As a Jedi in hiding, it may be necessary to stand up against the legal authority of the Empire when he knows its rule is unjust.

This willingness to give up his power (or sacrifice it) separates a Ferdinand Marcos from a George Washington. Both were men who struggled against what each believed were injustices in the system. Marcos, a lawyer by training, came up with an elaborate justification for installing himself as the de facto ruler of his country. But in subverting justice through the abolishment of the freedoms and rights of his own citizens when he refused to lift martial law, Marcos became a dictator. Washington, in his struggle, fought not only out of the self-interest of his fellow patriots, but in the name of justice against laws of a king and parliament that took away the freedoms and rights of its very own subjects. Washington, an honorable man, upon the attainment of a pragmatic struggle for justice, stepped down from his position as swordsman and let others rule on behalf of just laws, and not simply because they had the means to rule.

The Case of Japan

Examples of the pragmatic struggle (a just war) can be found in both the swordsmanship traditions of Western cultures as well as that of Japan, the two biggest influences on the Jedi of *Star Wars*—chivalry, principally a Christian ethic of warriors, and *bushido*, the samurai ethic that held honor as the highest social obligation.

In Japan, bushido, translated as the "way of Japanese warrior," reflected a fluid and evolving code of behavior. Unlike the point of honor system that found expression in legalistic treatises of European jurisprudence, bushido reflected general precepts that lacked specificity in details. Bushido was a military concept of honor that had a profound impact on the way samurai behaved in society. Today, bushido, like its Western counterpart, exists conceptually, having given way to the written rule of law.[3]

The Jedi of *Star Wars* were partially inspired by the samurai whom George Lucas encountered during his formative years studying film at the University of Southern California. Especially informative were the movies of Akira Kurosawa to whom Lucas readily admits a positive influence. The plot for Episode IV was borrowed directly from the Kurosawa movie *Hidden Fortress*, while sword fighting, by way of the two-handed manner Obi-Wan and Darth Vader fight in Episode IV, is indebted to samurai swordplay. The name of Lucas's Jedi Knights was derived from the Japanese samurai era of swordsmen called *jidai geki* (literally "the era of plays"), which refers to the samurai-inspired settings and themes of many Japanese books, plays, and movies based on that historical period.

Much of Japanese history was often dominated by the rise of the generalissimo called *shogun*. While at the outset the shogun, motivated primarily by self-interest and dynastic ambitions, does not fit neatly into the Western conception of an honorable swordsman who sets aside his sword in the name of justice, there were corollaries that demonstrated the existence of the pragmatic struggle within the context of Japanese history. Shoguns, realists and believers in the state of war, were ruled by a strong tradition that sought justification of their own authority according to principles and customs of Japanese law.

Despite the de facto elevation of military leaders to the highest level of rule in Japan, shoguns continually struggled to maintain the pretense that they ruled on behalf of the emperor, who was considered the divine ruler in whom proper authority rested. In the Heian Period (794–1190), it was the noble aristocracy (*kuge*) that looked down on the crude warrior whom they thought of as unsophisticated and barbarian. Their prerogatives rested, however, on the support of the military class, which was elevated in society as "protectors" of the aristocracy. As long as the army could be convinced to support the nobles, the *kuge* could maintain its cultural and military monopoly of the government. The court nobles asserted their authority for hundreds of years, but as the military learned the refinement of the court, they began to consider themselves equally capable of managing the culture and authority of the Japanese government, which expressed itself in the exalted position of the emperor. At this point, referred to as the Kamakura Period (1192–1333), the samurai class under Minamoto no Yoritomo established the first shogunate in which the military took over the country.

For three hundred years, the leadership of Japan rested with the shoguns who established their own hegemony through force of arms and the manipulation of the emperor who, while he held moral authority, was confined to rubber stamping the decisions of the reigning shogun. Ieyasu Tokugawa ushered in the Edo Period (1603–1867), a two-hundred-fifty-year dynasty of relative peace and stability in the country in which a new kind of samurai was to develop. Though the methods of the Tokugawa rulers would be considered authoritarian (if not draconian) by Western standards, this was the period when the role of the samurai evolved from one of simply warrior-servant to that of citizen-warrior.

Conscious of the threat the armed forces posed to his government, Ieyasu established a military state in which he controlled the countryside by establishing frontier posts to keep an eye on the movement of competing feudal lords, called *daimyo*. To further check the influence of enemy daimyo, Ieyasu formulated a complicated patronage system that required all important lords to maintain residences for part of the year in Edo, modern Tokyo. If a lord were to leave the capital, his family was required to stay in the city as a hostage should the lord conduct any affairs that went counter to the shogunate's interests.

The problems of recently unemployed samurai caused minor and even major consternations for the shogunate. Inequities between classes and within classes were a simple fact of life, and when masterless samurai, called *ronin*, or peasants felt they had an opportunity to gain some concession through open rebellion, the shogunate had to be quick in stamping out the insurrection, which could spark greater discontent among individuals and regions that chaffed under Tokugawa rule. So, in order to give new focus to samurai who no longer had wars to fight, laws were established that required samurai to behave as custodians of feudal domains and to pursue a life that imitated the graces of the imperial court. The samurai class was a disciplined and self-regulating military force. Now they were required to learn courtly skills such as refined behavior, and learning poetry and calligraphy; they began to develop an appreciation for *Noh* drama and other performing arts. Their martial skills, which were still necessary in case of challenges to the shogunate, were also transformed into less violent expressions.

During the Edo Period, schools of swordsmanship (*ryu*) trained samurai in the fighting arts of various weapons, the curved *katana* being the predominant weapon of the military class. Instead of training to fight on the battlefield, samurai were encouraged to demonstrate the superiority of their skills using protective gear that simulated the arms and armor of the samurai. The art of *kendo* (Japanese fencing) was born.

Kendo required the use of lighter armor and the use of a practice sword made of bamboo slats (*shinai*). Instead of tempering practice as they did with wooden practice swords called *bokken*, the new shinai allowed the samurai to engage in a more vigorous combat without the danger of using the bokken or live-blade katana. Though there were controversies on whether the new shinai style was indeed true Japanese swordsmanship, the prevailing consensus was that the new form of Japanese sword practice was soon to become a permanent fixture in the study of Japanese martial arts.

This peaceful era also led to the change in attitude toward the sword. Instead of using the sword as merely an instrument of power, practice of the sword was now used as a way to develop the spirit and martial ardor within the context of a less militant society. *Kenjutsu*, the use of the sword as a killing weapon, became kendo, a martial art used to develop personal spirit through training in swordsmanship. The state of civility and honor came to replace the perpetual state of war.

Kendo also came to be associated with Zen Buddhism, which taught that enlightenment could be attained by an epiphany that resulted from austere physical practices. Enlightenment, according to Zen philosophy, could be obtained by the tea ceremony, meditation, and even sword work. According to the philosopher Sato, Zen's disciplined simplicity suited a warrior's lifestyle. By contemplating and mastering his fear of death, the swordsman then became free to live a fulfilling good life; one that served the highest ends of Japanese culture itself.[4]

Mastering the Fear of Death

The refinement of both Western and Japanese swordsmanship was an idealized and relatively recent development in the cult of the sword. It played on a heroic tradition in which the swordsman could find the courage to suppress one's personal fears, allowing him to engage in the horrific melee of a clash of steel. The plain fact, however, was that the battlefield was really a stand of men together suppressing the natural urge to flee. Higher thoughts of country, justice, and honor did not enter the mind when self-preservation, that basest of human functions, seemed the only guiding principle.

It was only when given the moment to think — either during a lull in the battle or a period of civil peace — did the warrior contemplate lofty ideals. Loyalty to one's country spurred him forward, memories of family and thoughts of their protection exhorted the soldier to proceed, and love of justice drove the knight to bloody his sword so that he might then sheath it at the end of the battle. Peace and security from invasion tended to diminish the reliance on weapons, but in an emotional attempt to justify training with a sword, the soldier had to find a rational justification that redeemed his barbaric exercise, for war and battle when reflected upon became a romanticized abstraction that overshadowed the deadly violence for which the sword was most properly used.

Some swordsmen broke the self-justifying circle of violence — to make peace one must make war — by delving deeply into their own soul. The actions of their art led to a self-examination that questioned the very reliance on the sword as a means to an end. When this happened, swordsmanship then became a road toward a virtuous and compassionate life.

The paradox of religions professing doctrines of both peace and war were foreign to pacifists. But acts of terror, brutality, and inhumanity may sometimes convert the pacifist who becomes so disgusted by human atrocity that he can no longer tolerate the thought of inaction that would allow the continuance of unspeakable slaughter. Whether it was the slaying of innocent civilians, deliberate and planned genocide, or the injustice of subjugation, a man or woman might then be driven to right wrong and dispense justice personally.

His antithesis, by the very nature of his profession, was the warrior who had to act according to training and doctrine. Luck willing, there will have already been a higher authority that has tamed his mind and spirit away from the corruption and lure of power. Swordsmen by their very nature acted and reacted in the world, and it was by the laws of nature or by the laws of men that he kept his sword sheathed until the proper cause and proper authority released the stay on his gauntlet-covered hand.

Without justice, there was little reason to perpetuate the training with a sword. Thoughtful men and women used their training as a way to inform and enrich their lives. With the fragility of life and the body's permeability to violence, practice with the sword was preparation for death. Montaigne, crediting Cicero, said in his essay "That to Think as a Philosopher Is to Learn to Die":

> Foreknowledge of death is foreknowledge of liberty. He who has learned to die has unlearned servitude. To know how to die frees us from all subjection and compulsion. There is nothing evil in life for him who clearly understands that the loss of life is not an evil.[5]

Montaigne admonished the reader to train his soul and educate her to meet the force of the adversary of death.

The fencer was always an actor. He had the power to impose his will, but there was still the question of how to live one's life. Hamlet in his famous "To be or not to be" soliloquy pondered the struggle of mortality and man's natural fear of death. Was it better to bear the grief and suffering of life—"outrageous fortune"—or are we to take action to improve our existence by fighting against our miserable life? Hamlet knew that he could take the dagger into his own hands by slaying his father's murderer, effectively obliterating the passionate desire of a soul burning for revenge. He feared death—that "undiscovered country"—as well as the potential penalty of an agonizing hell as God's retribution for murder.

Because the swordsman, the actor, had the power to command, rule, and dole out death, he had to ask himself the question: How will he exercise his power? With the world offered on a platter, the will to a corrupt and decadent rule was a sweet dish easily tasted. This was the story of Anakin and Luke—both swordsmen with the power to shape the universe with the lightsaber. Would their rule be one of the good life or that of the corrupt and evil life? The lightsaber was the tool at their disposal, but in the end it was the heart and soul that was an even more powerful force.

As Anakin fell to the dark side of the Force, his hate and anger led him along a path that brought order to the universe but at the price of liberty and freedom. In his quest to make himself even more powerful, Vader then embraced the potential of his son who was both powerful and innocent. Luke knew of the destructiveness of the dark side of the Force, but could he resist his father's temptation? While Anakin was the chosen one who would bring balance to the Force, Luke was the "new hope" who harbored a burning faith in the goodness of his father. It was the son who would release the father from the slavery of wielding power with a lightsaber in hand.

In their climactic battle, Luke defeated Vader with the lightsaber, a weapon that brought him to the height of his glory. Seeing the reflection of himself in the dismembered stump of his father's hand, Luke realized that he was on the verge of becoming his father. Suddenly, the meaning of the test on Dagobah when he defeated the phantom Vader became clear. It was a test about life behind masks; masks that, according to Montaigne, scared innocent children.[6] Luke was no longer the child, and at the moment of his father's death, he removed the mask Anakin had worn since his fateful transformation into Vader in Episode III. Montaigne continued:

> We must remove the mask from things as from persons. When it is removed, we shall find underneath only the selfsame death that a man-servant or mere chambermaid met but now without fear.[7]

There is no longer any romantic notion of the sword, for when Luke sees his father's face for the first time there is solace in his soul. The lightsaber loses all value, for naked before Luke's eyes, Anakin has defeated death and can face it fearlessly. If Anakin can conquer death, to which all men are utterly defenseless, Luke, too, can begin to live life unfettered by a reliance on the lightsaber. He can face life as Anakin faced death — without fear.

Two

Jedi Culture: The Jedi Order, the Lightsaber, and the Force

The Jedi in the Politics, Society, and Military of Star Wars

When *Star Wars* debuted in 1977, George Lucas created an epic that turned the most fundamental technological change in history on its head — the superiority of the firearm over the sword. He blended the speculative world of science-fiction with the most ancient and epic tales. His was the universe of the Jedi and their lightsaber. Without them, there could be no *Star Wars.*

It was this world that defined the *Star Wars* universe. Around the basic story that Lucas envisioned, the Jedi Order was central to the theme of the fall and redemption of an individual who was destined to evolve and change, and forever leave a positive mark on society. Without having to resort to a claim to a Campbellian monomyth, Lucas's basic story resembles those of all stories that have captivated audiences. All great stories have a beginning, a middle, and an end. They revolve around the challenges of an individual and for the sake of the audience, this character must come to the brink of some peril, whether it be a simple act of error, an unconscious omission, or some unspeakable crime. There is both a challenge from the outside world, as well as an inner menace. It is this threat to the balance and harmony of existence that sets the stage for the drama, compelling an audience to listen and observe, to ponder and to think, to challenge and accept.

All things in the *Star Wars* universe serve to carry the story. As in all art forms, cinema is required to express itself within a limited and disciplined medium. There may be extraneous exposition, gratuitous action, or false philosophical underpinnings to the story. In small amounts, these do not harm the story; but it is through these criteria that good art is separated from self-indulgent expression.

This chapter focuses on the world of *Star Wars*; a vast place of immeasurable activity but of defined and limited scope. The characters in the saga travel around the cosmos, but the one institution that "binds the galaxy together" is the Jedi Order. Even in the Original Trilogy, Luke's story as well as that of his father is referenced to the values of the Jedi Knights, which were physically wiped away when the temple was destroyed. But what lived on in Episodes IV, V, and VI was the spirit of the Jedi Order, in particular, how Luke Skywalker had to relate to it. A common reading of the *Star Wars* epic popularizes the excitement of an entertaining thrill ride, but when one looks more deeply at the philosophical underpinnings of the saga, there is a profound moral message that actually contradicts the general interpretation of the franchise as a function of pure entertainment and unabashed consumerism.

Especially when considered in the actual chronological order of the movies—a trilogy created before its antecedent trilogy—the public and enterprising corporations affiliated with Lucasfilm focus more on the "coolness" factor than they do to the story being told. Metaphorically speaking, the audience pays less attention to the morality of the play, than they do to the bells and whistles of the production. As an artistic expression, the *Star Wars* saga can be viewed simply as a roller coaster wherein its riders care nothing about the mechanical genius of its construction. But *Star Wars* is a story, and this requires the observant audience to think more about the story and judge it among the pantheon of intellectual constructs of a person's experience. *Star Wars* is not the exemplar of excellent writing, nor a paragon of cinematic virtuosity. The franchise's impact on the world lies in its economic clout and technological advances in cinema. In addition, many people have had life-changing experiences due to the saga.

The popularity of *Star Wars* as a fad can be easily dismissed as a passing craze, but ever since the success of the *Shadows of the Empire* series (1996), the Prequel Trilogy, and the continuing production of two TV series (one animated; the other live-action), it has become clear to both the entertainment industry and academia that there is something about *Star Wars* that continues to draw an audience. It is not something on the surface that is popular, but something deeper—the culture of the Jedi Knight. It is a world of a futuristic but traditional warrior, his weapon, and a mystical spirit of the universe.

Civilian Institutions: Diplomats, Enforcers, Heroes

A general dichotomy in human endeavors has permeated the way societies have met the basic needs of the community—that of peace and war. If looked at in a pure form, the universe is essentially a Darwinian world in which each individual must compete for his or her basic survival. Communities since ancient times have developed very sophisticated societal rules (laws), which both control behavior and punish those who break the law. But especially in times in which an individual's survival, or that of the state, is at stake, the alternative is to prey on others. As reprehensible as this seems, there are any number of reasons for one group to physically bully, dominate, or conquer others. Some amount to a societal waging of war, as was known among the Vikings and the Spartans, but, according to Lorenzo Valla, a 15th century Italian humanist, "civilized" nations went to war for three reasons: greed, fear, and altruism.[1]

Despite the optimistic language of religion, society, and politics, Valla, who was a Christian apologist, was an intellectual who saw the world in terms of its reality. He acknowledged the religious element of Christ and his message of love, but Valla also looked at the world and commented on what he saw around him. Another scholar would have replaced the word *greed* with another, more positive expression, but Valla saw greed as the heart of two concepts that imply a high moral ground and a worthy endeavor: glory and enrichment. Like Lucas, Valla took a hard-nosed look at the world and determined that the personal desire for public recognition (honor) and material benefit (wealth) were both egoistic and self-serving enterprises. There was nothing wrong with honor, which, in its conceptual sense is one of the highest accolades an individual could ever hope to achieve, or a comfortable life, which requires a certain amount of accumulation and freedom from toil; but when it came to war, Valla saw that individuals desired both honor and wealth to such an extreme that there was no way to gloss over the negative effects of war on individuals and society. Humans openly waged war for honor and enterprise, but Valla recognized that their essential motivation was greed.

Valla's second motivation for war was fear, which he described as the "fear of incurring disaster later, if the strength of others is allowed to increase."[2] There is no shortage of examples to illustrate the human trait that finds endless justifications for the waging of war. Not only do street kids and ruffians find it natural that one should strike first to avoid being hit harder later, but intellectuals of every government have justified the necessity of war based on a fear of the future. This theme of fear is prominently expressed in Yoda's counsel that fear eventually leads to the greed and selfishness of the dark side of the Force. As will be seen with the concept of the chosen one and the balance of the Force later in this chapter, the concept of greed of both individuals and corporate institutions has had and will have negative consequences in society.

Valla's third reason for war was altruism. The very concept that war had beneficial consequences seems contradictory in the very least, but there is a logic that has been generally accepted among both moderate belligerents and centrist pacifists. One fights a war to punish the wrongdoer for on offense, as well as to impose some amends for it. The Christian idea to turn the other cheek is certainly a revolutionary one if carried out to the extreme that a pacifist would argue for. But governments, and certainly most individuals, would find it unacceptable to forgive an enemy that would enslave or slaughter them. The followers of Christian martyrs and Gandhi found in them examples of individuals willing to suffer extinction so that others might change their ways. The martyr was an example to Rome of the strength of faith in Christ. For protesters in India, the continuing brutality against a passive dissenter who offered up his body to be beaten had a demoralizing effect on the spirit of a human being. Under such conditions, to continue to wage violence became a testament to one's loss of status as a human being.

Valla was not the first to clearly state these primary motivations for war, but he, like Lucas, sought to comment on some of the darkest aspects of the human condition. It is one thing for a selfish person to seek to maximize joy and happiness in one's life, but it was also central to Lucas's worldview that despite the goodness found in each individual by the very nature of being human, it was possible that those with the best disposition, the best upbringing, and the best education could somehow become a person so hated in society that he is described as evil. For Lucas, Darth Vader was not the bad kid on the block predisposed (or predestined) to inflict suffering on others. The evil came from inside a person, manifesting itself in the choices a person made. Lucas spoke of the evil of the dark side not as power, as many mistakenly believe, but as "greed, self-centeredness, and fear."[3] For the Jedi Lucas created, fear led to the dark side of the Force. This is contrasted with Lucas's concept of the light side of the Force, which was "compassion, love, and helping other people."[4] For Valla, Lucas's concept of the light side of the Force would not be foreign.

Because of its scale, war has always been considered in a different category than murder — the killing of another individual without reasonable cause. The deliberateness in the fielding of a large army and then committing it to the violence of destruction and killing had a more devastating effect on society than gang violence. At least internal violence was limited and usually directed against particular individuals. War was not! Among the Greeks, there was little question about the morality of killing an enemy in battle. Concern was given to the conduct of battle and the proper justification of war in the interests of the state.[5] For the Confucian government in which the individual virtue of a leader assured a well-run society, war would not have been necessary.[6] For St. Augustine, a just, Christian war was designed to avenge wrongs, protect one's self and possession, and be waged only under a proper authority. A war was a remedy for sin, but also a way to chastise a transgressor.[7]

In Roman law, there existed a dual concept of *auctoritas* and *potestas*, which can be roughly translated as authority and power. *Authority* referred to the recognized legitimate ability of a person or institutional body to cause others to follow, while *power* referred to the ability to coerce others into compliance with one's will. The two went hand-in-hand, both being aspects of an organized society in which principles governed and legitimized the leaders of Rome. In a similar fashion, these two concepts could be applied to the Jedi Knights as they operated in the Galactic Republic. As representatives of the authority of the universe, the Jedi had both the authority and the physical ability to coerce others according to the law.

The development of law in societies has been considered critical in the stability of long standing cultures. The law was, and is, a social constant that organized and punished those who would destroy the order of society. While the common reference to *potestas* amounted to a limited form of coercion, it was not to be confused with *imperium*, which was military force — the greatest form of coercion. Just like Qui-Gon who said that he could only protect Queen Amidala, the Jedi possessed the *potestas* to maintain order within the universe as it existed under the Galactic Republic. The Jedi did not have *imperium*. Law in society acts as a limiting force. It prevents extreme action and hobbles complete freedom of action in favor of a greater good that goes beyond the individual. The greater good distinguishes killing for personal reasons from killing on behalf of the state.

Even though war between states encompasses complete freedom of action, there still seemed to be a general understanding between enemies that there were still rules by which armies had to abide. John A. Lynn (*Battle: A History of Combat and Culture*) offers a model that can be applied to the culture of warfare. On one side is the *reality of war*; the other is the *discourse on war*. The *reality of war* reflects the accepted conventions of war, the manner in which a war is generally fought. For example, it is almost universal that the armies of two enemies should first line up and then attack. The *discourse of war* represents the rules and customs of warfare, or beliefs among warriors that limit the devastation of a war. An example is the common acceptance that a herald should be permitted to approach unmolested.[8] These two concepts of war, the reality and discourse, worked to the benefit of most opponents because it allowed them to openly engage in a conflict knowing that a commitment and an outcome would be assured. One would be the victor.

This societal pull between order and disorder made the Jedi a unique kind of agent for the government. They were representatives of a civilized universe because they represented its law. And on that authority alone, they had the ability to coerce others out of their position and role in the general order. This can be most easily seen at the beginning of Episode I when Qui-Gon Jinn and Obi-Wan Kenobi were introduced as "ambassadors of the supreme chancellor."

As diplomats, their goal was direct contact, which, of course, contrasted with the Jedi's role as a warrior and peacekeeper. Their negotiation was abruptly ended before it had even started. Their starship and her crew were quickly destroyed. Diplomacy was over, and Qui-Gon and Obi-Wan were then caught in a string of events that prevented them from reporting directly to the chancellor that an actual invasion of Naboo had begun.

Qui-Gon and Obi-Wan's experience on the Neimoidian ship also illustrated another aspect of the Jedi that served them when diplomacy failed and their lives were placed in jeopardy. Failure in itself did not endanger the diplomat, but the mere fact that the Jedi were not without the means to protect themselves insulated them from many threats. In this sense, the Jedi had the *potestas* of an enforcer who wielded a limited ability to protect themselves. Their lightsaber gave them the means to fight not as a soldier, who fights as part of a group (often with an efficient distance weapon), but as a warrior who exerted physical strength to engage in combat one-on-one with an enemy. But the Jedi Knight was not an errant-knight released upon the world to correct injustice. The Jedi Knight served a master, the Galactic Senate, representing its authority like marshals did in the Wild West.

The word *marshal* is derived from the French word *maréchausée*. Marshals were originally house servants under early French kings charged with the care of a handful of horses.[9] The word *marshal* appears in the United States as a creation of the Judiciary Act of 1789. It is believed that the title *marshal* may have been coined as a result of a letter George Washington wrote to Frenchman Aeneas Lamont denying that he was Marshal of France. Perhaps Lamont's mistake goes back to the American Revolution when Washington actually created a unit of light dragoons (mounted soldiers) called the Marechaussee Corps, which acted as a military police for the army. They were a rear guard during a march, as well as a camp police who disciplined soldiers (but also acted on their behalf in contacts with civilian populations); at the battle of Yorktown they protected Washington's headquarters. The Marechaussee Corps was disbanded in 1783, but its duties are now performed by the Military Police Corps, which was created by the U.S. Army in 1941.

The marshal, however, is more widely known from cowboy westerns for the role they played in U.S. territories as the federal government's representative on the local level. In the early days of the American republic, many jurisdictions did not have a local police force to carry out governmental interests, but the U.S. marshal, of which one was originally appointed for each of thirteen districts, served as an enforcement wing of the federal judiciary. The U.S. Constitution clearly limited the role of government in local matters, but there were many issues that concerned the federal government. Marshals were used to capture and transport counterfeiters and criminals and fight local uprisings against the government. Sometimes the U.S. marshal was the only person who had the authority (and resources) to impose law. To assist them, the 1789 Judiciary Act gave marshals the power to create a posse by temporarily deputizing local police officials or even civilian citizens. The notoriety of the marshal in westerns was a clear precedent of the Jedi.

With the lawlessness of some corners of the universe, the Jedi had a particular role as the Supreme Chancellor's galactic agent. Operating for the Judicial Department under the office of the Supreme Chancellor of the Senate, the Jedi also acted like the agents of the International Criminal Police Organization (Interpol), which was originally established as the International Police Criminal Police Commission (IPCP) in 1923. Interpol is now organized under the office of the Secretary General in the United Nations. Unlike the Jedi, however, Interpol agents do not have any enforcement authority and depend on cooperation from the police institutions of its 186 members for their investigations. Headquartered in Lyons, France, their work includes intercommunicational support and consultative responsibilities combating international crime and terrorism.

The concept of a direct enforcer also goes back millennia to the literary concept of the hero. Not simply the protagonist of a plot, a hero from a historical-military perspective meant the direct participation of the individual leader in the battle, typically in the front ranks as inspiration to his troops. The hero was an individual who created his persona through his actual participation in combat. It confirmed masculine prowess and ennobled both aristocrat and democrat in the eyes of the troops they led titularly. It goes back to all epics and poems— the Iliad, Beowulf, Odysseus, Arjuna, and King Arthur — wherein the hero changes the world through a series of actions that involves active engagement in victorious battle. Alexander the Great suffered a punctured lung from fighting directly in front lines of battle; his father, Phillip II of Macedon, lost an eye in combat.

Other famous leader's participated directly in battle but many did not. Like most Roman generals,[10] Julius Caesar described battle in intimate detail because he was expected to remain behind the lines calling out orders directly to his men. He does not actually say that he fought directly in combat. Others, like Charlemagne, Kublai Khan, Darius, or Xerxes, were too important to risk losing in actual combat, while an individual like Tokugawa Ieyasu actually trained under particular sword instructors but refrained from combat because of his position and his obligations to his family line. King Francis I was reported to have physically fought his captors during the Battle of Pavia in 1525 before he was captured by the Imperial army of Charles V. King Leonidas of Sparta was probably the most famous person in Western history to engage in combat; at the battle of Thermopylae, he and his 299-man bodyguard died in heroic combat.

Today, the concept of heroic combat is openly frowned upon, if not ridiculed. Commentators on the state of today's military both support and refute the distinction between a warrior and a soldier. Max Boot (*War Made New*) emphasizes the discipline and cohesion of a soldier who fights efficiently as part of a group; each person like a cog in a huge machine. The warrior fights one-on-one with courage, honor, and a chivalresque spirit. Even in mass battle, Boot asserts the individual swordsman seeks out another individual to fight.[11] Robert D. Kaplan (*Warrior Politics*) explored how a pagan warrior ethos must necessarily permeate America's political culture.[12] Indeed, the military has gone to huge lengths to associate military soldiery with warrior culture. But the soldier on today's battlefield is not the hero in the romantic sense of literature because the soldiers do not, as a goal, put themselves into a proximity of immediate and sudden death.[13] With modern arms, warfare is simply too destructive for individuals to expose themselves except in moments of desperation. All contemporary militaries stress the superiority of group action and criticize any action that has any appearance of an individual desire for glory. The soldier may be awarded a medal for valor for service saving the lives of his comrades, but his glory comes out of concern for his fellow soldier, not for his personal glorification. Indeed, it has become passé to indulge in such self-aggrandizement except in recollection of distant service. Glorious battle neither serves the popular perception of battle to democratic constituencies, nor does it achieve the strategic objectives of any government.

As the creator of a literary work (*Star Wars* started as a script), however, Lucas is afforded the artist's prerogative of exploring military values without having to actually engage in the carnage. Lucas's concept of the Jedi Knight purposely prescribed individual combat. Obi-Wan fought against Darth Vader, Luke fought Darth Vader, and Qui-Gon fought Darth Maul. Lucas's story follows the long tradition of epics told throughout history. Contrary to public perception, *Star Wars* has less to do with myth (the archetype of Man versus the gods) or fairy tales and fables (Man versus Nature) than it has to do with a spiritual awakening of the inner spirit when confronted with utter and complete self-annihilation. The Death Star is representative of the folly of nuclear weapons, and not God's punishment by cataclysmic inundation. Nor is *Star Wars* a philosophical allegory or a religious parable. Rather, *Star Wars* takes an episodic look at the human condition in its polar extremes of goodness and evil. Most see this dichotomy of light and dark as two exclusive opposites, but Lucas's movies are profound examples of the gray area that is the balance of the outer fringes. Instead of a carefully delineated yin and yang, the two twisting orbs are more a confusion of light and its fading absence. While the Jedi may seem good and the Sith bad on a superficial level, there is, and always has been, a subtle subtext to *Star Wars* that says we humans live mostly, if not completely, in the gray.

Star Wars finds its fulfillment more as an epic in the ancient tradition, telling the tales of men and women as masters of their own destiny, even in the most dire of tragedies that illustrate how Man overcomes the Fates by accepting a tragic end instead of cowering to omnipotent beings such as the gods or the mightiest of goddesses—Mother Nature. Incidental interventions by the gods are simply that—incidental—when compared to the emboldening spirit of evolving writers who began to assert the inner strength of humans—fortitude, independence, free will, indomitability—than his supplication and submission to "greater beings."

Instead of the admission of spells and magic (powers borne of ignorant sentimentality), the modern person strikes a balance among the instincts to believe the unexplainable (magic equivalent to the heart), the fruit of his intellect (technology equivalent to the mind), and the determinism of his actions (ethics equivalent to the hand). Combining these three aspects, both Anakin and Luke find themselves in a most extreme, and often necessary, role—that of swordsman, the individual who must combine his inexplicable feelings for survival and self-preservation, the sword of his own creation, and a code of moral conduct that dispenses life and death at an instant's notice. Anakin/Vader is the contemporary person who finds fulfillment in the evil and nefarious ends of selfishness, while the other is a person who finds fulfillment in the pursuit of justice and peace.

The concept of a mythic hero has become part of common parlance when referring to the events that befall Anakin and Luke Skywalker. But as an outside observer, it is important to critique Lucas's own comments on *Star Wars* and myth.[14] Lucas has made numerous statements that he wanted to make a modern myth. It is even an unwritten corporate policy among writers associated with Lucasfilm to describe *Star Wars* as myth. The most easily referenced statement on Lucas's insistence that *Star Wars* is directly influenced by Joseph Campbell comes from a Bill Moyers interview in the April 26, 1999, issue of *Time* when Lucas said: "With *Star Wars* I consciously set about to re-create myths and the classic mythological motifs. I wanted to use those motifs to deal with issues that exist today. The more research I did, the more I realized that the issues are the same ones that existed 3,000 years ago. That we haven't come very far emotionally."[15] Michael Kaminski, in *The Secret History of* Star Wars, argues that the storyline of *Star Wars* evolved with each film and that a comprehensive mythic component did not formally exist as part of a master storyline in any of the early drafts of *Star Wars* or in any of Lucas's earlier notes. Indeed, the thesis of Kaminski's book is that there was never a completed story at the beginning when Lucas began writing the first draft of Episode IV, much less one with a deliberate mythic underpinning. Lucas's association with Joseph Campbell was an afterthought that took place after the completion of the Original Trilogy.

Undoubtedly, Lucas had read Campbell's *The Hero with a Thousand Faces* before he began his script for Episode IV in 1975, but there is scant evidence that *Star Wars* as a modern myth was the underpinning concept for the original treatment Lucas is fond of referencing in his many interviews since 1999. Lucas had not actually met Campbell until after the completion of Episode VI when someone had given him a tape of one of Campbell's lectures.[16] Joseph Campbell gained his greatest notoriety with the PBS broadcast of *The Power of Myth* and its companion book featuring a Campbell interview by Bill Moyers. A later George Lucas interview by Bill Moyers was subsequently published in the April 26, 1999, issue of *Time* magazine. In both interviews, Moyers's fascination with and respect for *Star Wars* has an almost worshipful tone. And while Lucas's notes have been the subject of several books on the making of the *Star Wars* saga, no evidence is cited for direct references to Campbell's monomyth. Many writers have gone to great lengths to pull characters out of the saga to fit them neatly into a Campbellian model. One writer even parallels the events of Lucas's own life as a monomyth.

An insight can be gleaned about the simplicity of *Star Wars* as the result of a basic storyline script. Because Episode III had already completed, Lucas began with new projects based on the *Star Wars* franchise. One product in development was The Force Unleashed, a video game about a secret Vader apprentice that takes place during the time between Episode III and Episode IV when Vader is hunting down survivors of the Jedi purge. Haden Blackman, the game's lead developer, says that Lucas wanted five basic characters: the protagonist (Sith Apprentice), a side-kick (a droid named Proxy), a mentor (a former Jedi general named Rahm Kota), a love interest (Juno Eclipse), and opponents (Maris Brood and Shaak Ti). From this, another story arc is being created, which again follows basic elements that move any storyline forward.[17]

One of the most compelling intellectual arguments for *Star Wars* as a mythic journey is made in James Lawler's Star Wars *and Philosophy* article "The Force Is with Us," which compares Hegel's philosophy of spirit with the prophecy of the chosen one. Nowhere in his writing, however, does Lucas make any mention of Hegel. Journalists, too, are especially uncritical in their acceptance of *Star Wars* as a new universal myth for contemporary times, perpetuating Lucas's post–Episode VI statements that the *Star Wars* story from the very beginning was mythic,[18] and not simply epic.

The protagonists of the *Star Wars* universe are basically flat characters who fit easily into very typical stereotypes and archetypes. There is a hero, a mentor, a sidekick, and a nemesis. They all fulfill roles necessary to the progress of the story. Informing these characters, however, was the Jedi Order, which serves as a reference for the Jedi Knights as diplomats, enforcers, and heroes. These are the practical functions of the Jedi as civilian representatives sent to travel through the universe on their particular assignments. On a more abstract level, though, the Jedi were also defined by their religious morality.

Religious Institutions: Force Users

The Order of Jedi Knights was not simply a military organization, but a religious institution whose adherents mastered a power called the Force. With the Force, Jedi were able to obtain and play a significant role in the institutional apparati of the galactic universe as "guardians" or "protectors" of the Republic. It is important to explore this aspect of the Jedi's religious background both within the *Star Wars* universe, as well as in the real world where the Force's religious content has had a perceptible, though minor, impact on *Star Wars* fans.

Traditionally, societies have often been marked by individuals in three critical roles—that of headman, shaman, and war leader—each of whom reflects the significant particulars of group societal organization. Their roles were not equivalent in power; often one's agenda was at odds with those of the others, representing a natural inclination to preserve and extend one's influence in society vis-à-vis the others. In *Star Wars*, the Emperor's conspiracy against the Jedi Order aimed to consolidate the political, religious, and military leader into one. Palpatine followed in a long history of ascendant political figures who, regardless of religious and ethical beliefs, had to subjugate these three critical aspects of society to their own will. This process of crushing opposition, however, was as easily accomplished as it is generally temporary and elusive. As Princess Leia put it, "The more you tighten your grip, Tarkin, the more star systems will slip through your fingers."

In *Star Wars*, as in the real world, religion matters. The 464 B.C. earthquake in Sparta was taken not as a tectonic event, but as a religious omen expressing the gods' displeasure with the Spartans. It was an opportunity for Spartan slaves—the helots—to take advantage of their masters' disunity in the aftermath, but the religious underpinnings were significant. The defilement of Hermes statues in Athens led to the recall of Alcibiades, which may have ultimately doomed the Sicilian expedition to Syracuse in 415 B.C. And in Mexico, the appearance of mounted conquistadores was initially taken as fulfillment of a prophecy that the gods would come down from heaven. More recently, Buddhist monks demonstrating in Burma in 2007 against the Than Shwe junta were as socially threatening to the political order as the religious monks of Japan called the sohei were to feudal military Japan. A religious institution like the Jedi Order had both religious and political repercussions on order and stability.

To many, the message gleaned from the Jedi is more of a personal and knightly tale, hardly a religious one. The fact that a Jedi religion (Jediism) has developed among *Star Wars* fans, however, is an indication that there is religious content in *Star Wars* if the lessons taught in the six films are extended further along philosophical lines. It shows how cultism has led many without strong conviction in present institutional religions to develop their own religion to meet their personal needs. As in many European adventure tales— such as *Ivanhoe* or *The Three Musketeers*—religion has a crucial impact on the morality of the story told by its authors because the religious outlook of the characters and time are entwined with the story's plot. In the case of *Star Wars*, numerous Christian apologists have expressed their concern that a concept like the Force alters the general public's perception of both spirituality and actual dogmatic teaching. It is therefore imperative that philosophical and moral issues in *Star Wars* be looked upon as religious issues and not amoral, secular civics.

Fritz Lang's *Metropolis* is typically acknowledged as a cinematic precursor to *Star Wars*, but it is almost never credited for its religious influence. Ralph McQuarrie, the conceptual designer for Episode IV, admits the physical inspiration of the female android in *Metropolis* on See Threepio, but *Metropolis*'s basic storyline and cinematic style have a richer impact on Lucas's literary and cinematic vocabulary. Visually, direct borrowings from Lang's film are evident,[19] but the story's plot contains characteristics that can undeniably be seen in both *THX-1138* and the *Star Wars* saga.

Metropolis begins with a simple line: The Mediator between heads and hands must be the heart. *Metropolis*'s twisting story is about Freder, the son of Johann "Joh" Fredersen who runs the futuristic city from which the movie takes its name. Freder goes through a story similar to that of Siddhartha Gautama (the Buddha) in which he discovers the pain and suffering, tedium and monotony of the underground workers who support the decadent society on the surface.[20] Freder's epiphany is a result of his infatuation for Maria who leads him down into the bowels of the earth where she is the religious head of an underground church. She serves the spiritual needs of the oppressed workers; her message is one of perseverance and the prophecy of a Mediator who will save them from their bondage. Because of his son's subterranean explorations, Fredersen realizes that the subversive underground church, like an opiate of the people, threatens to undermine his control over the workers. Fredersen engages the help of the inventor Rotwang who creates a mesmerizing android called the Machine-Man (Threepio's direct influence), which is transformed into Maria's beautiful female form in order to destroy the underground church and subvert future rebellion. The Inventor (obviously a reference to the mad scientist Frankenstein) is missing his right hand. In its place is a mechanical one. The android Maria is successful in destroying the underground church, but the workers become so angry that they flood the city below, destroying the machinery that supports Metropolis above. Fredersen's son is only able to quell the rioting mob when he kills the inventor whom he throws down from the above-ground cathedral,[21] while the living Maria is revealed. When society is on the brink of collapse, the prophetess Maria unites the hands of Fredersen (the head of society) with a representative of the workers (the hands). Between them is Freder, the Mediator, who, through his compassion for the worker's plight and his love for his father, fulfills the prophecy of a heart mediating between the head and the hands.

The parallels in the *Star Wars* saga are not coincidental. Images of the inventor, with his cyborg hand, can be seen in Darth Vader. Luke, like Fredersen's son, saves his father from the evil choices he has made. The inventor thrown down from the cathedral mimics the destruction of the Emperor in Episode VI. Maria, like Princess Leia, saves the world with her powerful command of the people and her stubborn persistence. *Metropolis* is also commentary on the rise of the bourgeoisie, communism, and authoritarianism, all elements common in pre–World War II cinema.

The Order of Jedi Knights, like the surface and subterranean churches, must be seen partially as an open religion which has impressed its own morality on the society around it. Religion, the organized and overt expression of spiritual values in a secular world, has a palpable, almost inseparable influence on society. Sometimes this influence is direct, as in the case of religious lands and territories where a religious government controls the economic and social life of its inhabitants. It then falls upon religious leaders to provide their own police and military units to maintain social order and to enforce religious regulations and even impose religious adherence, a situation which occurred in places like the Christian bishopric, a Buddhist monastery, or a Muslim mosque. While clerics and the religious would often try to avoid military service because of their sacred character, circumstances like threats of invasion or regular raiding forced many bishops to engage in war to ensure their very survival. It is reported that ten bishops died during battle in Germany in a fifty-year period during the late 800s; Bishop Bernard in 1000 fought with a lance as commander of Emperor Otto III's army.[22] Political leaders with religious vows might lead a campaign — Cardinal Richelieu and Pope Julius II both wore armor and sword on campaigns though they were not direct militants on the battlefield. Secular princes have forced clerics to go to war. In 1119, Louis VI instructed bishops to take Breteuil, France, with their diocesan militias.[23] Charlemagne expected the bishop of Metz, St. Eloi, and Noyon to accompany him on campaign to celebrate mass and carry sacred relics.[24] In a similar fashion, the backstory created by *Star Wars* writers included Senate legislation requiring Jedi to be generals in the clone army.[25]

The *Star Wars* saga was clearly marked by the role of the Jedi Knights who were inextricably linked to the concept of the Force, which is an energy field that is created by and pervades all living things. It can be manipulated by the Jedi in a physical way—telekinesis, mind control, clairvoyance, prescience, telepathy, the creation of Force lightning, an attunement to other Jedi—but it also partially controlled a Jedi's actions. And with the prequel movies, the Force was further divided into a living and unifying entity. The former is connected to the living essence of creatures in the present moment; the latter represents a broader sensitivity to the past and the future. Qui-Gon even insists to the Jedi Council that finding Anakin was the "will of the Force," which contradicts Han's negative inference that there is no "all-powerful force" that controls his destiny. Early drafts of Episode III included dialog in which Palpatine tells Anakin that he created Anakin by manipulating the midi-chlorians that created him.

The concept of the Force draws from a multitude of religious dogmas and practices as a way for Lucas to bring a religious element to his story: "When I wrote the first *Star Wars*, I had to come up with a whole cosmology: What do people believe in? I had to do something that was relevant, something that imitated a belief system that has been around for thousands of years, and that most people on the planet, one way or another, have some kind of connection to. I didn't want to invent a religion. I wanted to try to explain in a different way the religions that have already existed. I wanted to express it all."[26] Consequently, Lucas borrowed freely from religions of the world as a way to imbue his universe with a spiritual substance. He refrains from equating the Force with God.[27] Artistically, Lucas easily calls the Force a mystery that the Jedi attempt to master, even though the majority of the universe would be unable to truly fathom the religious doctrine. As on Earth, the failure of the public to embrace a religious life does not stop esoteric religious sects or cults from pursuing their religious path. Clearly, though, Lucas intended to separate the general population from those of the Force-wielding Jedi Knights.

In trying to understand the greater "mystery" of the Force, it helps to understand a key theme central to the story arc of the *Star Wars* saga—that of the problem of good and evil, which is a central conundrum all great religions must confront. To state it simply: if God is ultimately perfect and good, why would he "create" or "permit" evil in the world?

Taoism, which does not speak of a divine creator, avoids the question altogether. But it is clear that the teachings of taoism are present in the concept of the Force. The tao, which means the "way" (a mode of behavior likened to a path toward some objective), is clearly mentioned by Yoda when he tells Luke about the path to the dark side, which would forever consume him if he took it. The tao teaches that there is a natural manner of being that will lead you to your "destiny." Like water, to which the Tao is always compared, one's life requires that a person remain open to the universe in order to find the easiest and best path toward one's final end. Lucas's Force diverts from Taoism, in that the natural "end" of the path leads to a positive, beneficent conclusion, not just a harmony with the natural things of the universe. Ancient taoists believed that there was a finite energy to one's life. Once it was expended, a person would die. Taoist philosophy therefore taught that harmony with nature and the universe would maximize life by minimizing the expenditure of ki. Early drafts of *Star Wars* indicated that there was a limited amount of energy a Jedi was capable of wielding. In one draft, using the Force as a protective shield was so draining that at some point the shield would begin to falter as Force energy had been expended.

For Christianity, the problem of evil is really a question of free will. Again, the reference to the Force is apparent, especially when Lucas insists that the Force is about the choices we make. In this Christian answer, God gave each individual the free will to act in accordance with goodness or with what is not goodness (i.e., evil). The idea of theodicy asserts that God is still all-powerful and good regardless of the existence of evil. Goodness (which is the essence of God) is contrasted with evil, which is not the opposite of goodness, but its absence. To do evil means to *not* do good. To continue with Lucas's Force, it is ultimately love and compassion that defines the light side of the Force, and conversely — non-love is the dark side of the Force.

In Christian theology, Christ is the savior of humanity, a messiah who will bring believers into union with the goodness that is God. It is by Christ's example of complete love that God himself took human form and then sacrificed himself out of love for humanity, thereby removing the stain of original sin that hampers the fulfillment of a good life. It is in Christ's crucifixion that higher good is achieved, which also demonstrates the divine nature of Christ who was at one human, God, and the Holy Spirit — the trinity.[28] For Christians, love shown for others is not something that must be maintained in any kind of balance as is asserted in *Star Wars* with the Force. The example of Jesus Christ is one that Christians are called to follow. His appeal to turn the other cheek when struck by an enemy is an addendum to Talion's law that one should not do greater harm than that which was already inflicted. The Christian is called to love without hope of love's return. This unconditional love is the essence of God; as it is the fundamental essence of humanity. It is, however, an individual's choice to embrace the compassion of unconditional love, or to reject it.

The teaching of good behavior is a universal characteristic of every major religion. And in the Force, the concept of a light side reflects a major tenet of Buddhism and its conceptualization of the universe. For Buddhism, the universe is an endless cycle of birth and dying called the samsara. Through good works (compassion) and effort (wisdom), an individual is then able to depart the cycle of samsara and achieve Nirvana, which is the ultimate state of enlightenment. The Jedi religion does not make any claim to enlightenment (though Yoda does say the Force is used for "knowledge and wisdom"), but prequel assertions of attachment and suffering *(dukkha)* do reflect the Four Noble Truths that the Buddha taught, as well as the Eightfold path which leads to Nirvana.

The first Noble Truth is a statement that life is suffering. It is not a negative assertion that life is painful and bad in the Hobbesean sense, i.e., life is "solitary, poor, nasty, brutish, and short." For Buddhism, it is a simple fact that the experience of a person is pain of three forms: physical or mental pain, change, and rebirth. The second Truth is that suffering comes from desire *(tanha)*, which can also be expressed in terms of attachment. With attachment, the desire to hold on to things that are impermanent leads to the continuation of suffering. The third Truth says that suffering can be alleviated by getting rid of one's desire (i.e., one's attachment). Life is sustained by minimal and reasonable needs. Those needs can vary from one person to the next, and certainly the meager needs of a Buddhist ascetic contrast greatly with the cornucopia of material objects that are part of many modern lifestyles. The fourth Truth is termed the Eightfold path (*Ashtapatha*), which is a list of good behaviors stated as a positive exhortation: right view, right intent, right speech, right action, right livelihood, right effort, right mind, and right concentration. Also included in Buddhism (as well as in Hinduism) is the belief in dharma, which refers to a path of good behavior. If one acts in accordance with dharma, one creates good karma. If one behaves against dharma, bad karma results. One cannot transcend samsara without creating good karma.

In Episode II, Anakin was asked if a Jedi was permitted to love. He answered that attachment to people and things was forbidden because it prevented the Jedi to focus on service and love of others. He speaks of unconditional love — love that gives without the expectation of benefit or return — which encourages a Jedi to love. Why would it not be any other way? In the Buddhist tradition, attachment has the connotation of a distraction that prevents enlightenment, which is similar to Anakin's description of Jedi love. Attachment, for non–Buddhists, has sometimes been interpreted as a conscious refusal to give one's love — a love that understands another human through close interaction and even union. How can one truly love (and understand it) without having the experience of actually giving one's love to another? The distinction is one of physical love and conceptual love. In Christian traditions, there is a morality (a stigma) associated with physical love. This stigma is also present in Buddhism. In Hinduism, however, the conceptualization of physical love is reflected in a different way, which has led to the concept of *Kama Sutra*. The concept of the unconditional love of the Jedi is not without example in the Christian or Buddhist world where a priest or a monk elects sexual abstinence in his pursuit of service to God (and humanity) or to facilitate the achievement of enlightenment.

Another interpretation of the Force is posited by Dale Pollock, who says that the power of the Force is one of addictive exuberance.[29] The power of the Force can be used for good or bad purposes, but its extended use will eventually lead to one's doom. Yoda's comment that once the path of the dark side is taken, "forever will it dominate your destiny." Indeed, Yoda is wrong about Vader. It does not dominate Anakin forever. If one is to conceive of the light side of the Force as doing good, there is no limit to its utility unless one wants to argue that it may drive a person to a negative extreme of goodness. In any event, Lucas asserts the dark side is greed, selfishness, and fear, which is in turn corroborated by Yoda's claim that the dark side is "anger, fear, aggression."

For many, there is a huge emphasis on the power of the Force, especially in Yoda's claim that the dark side is not more powerful than the light side, but more seductive and quicker to manifest itself during a fight. An argument is made that the Force does give a person the enhanced ability to dominate an opponent because anger and the dark side give Luke the added power to defeat Vader at the end of Episode VI. While an argument regarding the psycho-physicality of anger during a sword fight is discussed later, the validity of the power of the dark side should also be examined in terms of the philosophical-religious aspect.

For Lucas, the Force is represented not by a religious spirituality, but by its physical manifestation. The very medium of cinema lends itself to this form of expression, if not requiring it. The Force is physically demonstrated on screen before our very eyes, starting with Luke's first experimentations on the *Millennium Falcon* with remote practice. The physical barrier of a blast shield covering the eyes was meant to show how the Force helped one "see" the remote beams in order to deflect them with the lightsaber. It was this ability to manipulate the Force that gave the Jedi knight his power. The problem for the Jedi was not its use, but its manner of use, which was an expression of Lucas's thematic assertion that choice has a consequence. Do you use the physical manifestations of the Force (vaulting, speed-running, moving objects) for good purposes, or for the accumulation of wealth and power?

In the basic sense of the concept, the physical manifestations of the Force (i.e., the Force divested of its concept of a light and dark side) amount to the classic convention of a comic book superpower. In tradition tales, the Force has magic. In classical stories, the Force is demi-god status.[30] And in more modern expressions, the Force is a super-ability created by scientific enhancement (a concoction) or mutation (radiation). From a literary point of view, the power of Superman is the same as Hercules is the same as Merlin. The convention is compelling historically; super-strength humans dominate literature, legends, and myths the world over.

The concept of the Force has a parallel on Earth in the Chinese concept of chi (ki in Japanese, prana in Sanskrit), which has only found recent, but limited, acceptance in the West despite the fact that it has been believed and developed in the East for millennia. Often translated in English as a "life force," chi is often described as a function of breath. The European concept of ghosts stealing the breath of children (their life force) falls into this same conceptual framework. In Hinduism, the path (goal) toward oneness with Brahman (the ultimate etherealness of the universe) can be enhanced through Yogic practices. Today in popular culture the exact opposite is true. Yoga is practiced as a form of physical exercise, not an ascetic practice of Yogi gurus toward oneness with the Brahman. Those who practice the martial arts of qi gong, tai chi, aikido, and hapkido are exposed to a long tradition in which the concept of a life energy is at the heart of their martial skills. Ascetic practices ranging from chanting, exposure, and martial training are designed to enhance one's life force energy for both self-defense and personal development. Mastering ki was a key component in many Japanese styles of swordsmanship.[31]

The Japanese school of swordsmanship called the Tenshin Shoden Katori Shinto Ryu, located near Narita, Japan, integrated Buddhism, Taoism, and Shinto into their martial arts training regime. The concept of ki as an energy force to be harnessed as power behind their techniques is accepted in most Japanese sword arts, but there are also physical expressions of the religious aspects of their curriculum. Mikkyo (esoteric) Buddhism includes practices that express the Buddha nature: mudras (hand gestures), mantras (chanting), and contemplation as a way to focus their training as well as achieve the Buddha nature of Nirvana through imitation.[32] It is this physical aspect that helps relate the spiritual application to their training. Master Otake, in the early 1980s, recollected an incident when the powers he developed helped him exorcise the spirit of a fox from a young man.[33] Esoteric Buddhism of the Katori Ryu was influenced by the Shingon school of Buddhism, which was itself influenced by Indian and Tibetan Tantra practice, which emphasizes physical energy.

A more passive form of religious action is meditation, which is not to be confused with Western contemplation. Western contemplation and prayer emphasize a focused peaceful quietude characterized by reflection and a direct communication with God. Meditation, however, takes many forms, often with a more formal posture and deliberate responsibilities during the activity. Hindu meditation seeks to identify the true self in order to overcome the ignorance that keeps the individual out of the Brahman. The goal of Buddhist meditation is to achieve Nirvana. There are two principal Buddhist traditions: Mahayana and Therevada. Therevada emphasizes two types: a tranquility meditation *(samatha)* and mindfulness meditation *(vipassana). Vipassana* stresses the breath during meditation which will focus on one's impermanence *(anicca)*, suffering *(dukkha)* or no-soulness *(anatta)*.[34] Inklings of meditation can be seen in *Star Wars* when the Jedi sit in a cross-legged position, as well as the moment of waiting when Qui-Gon drops into *seiza*, the formal Japanese sitting posture, just before he begins his duel again with Darth Maul.

Leaving the manifestations, there is one other physical aspect of the Force — midi-chlorians, which, as Qui-Gon says in Episode I, are a "microscopic life form which resides within all living cells and communicates with the Force." It caused a large outcry among *Star Wars* fans because it destroyed the idea of a spiritual and ethereal Force associated with Obi-Wan's description in Episode IV. No longer was the Force a spirit-like power, it was a physical "thing" found in the cells of the body; countable through examination of one's blood. The idea of a blood-link to Jedi Knighthood dashed the generally accepted concept that normal individuals could aspire to the ranks of the Jedi Order. Immediately after the release of Episode I, a flurry of diatribes against the midi-chlorians was written.

Most outspoken was science-fiction writer David Brin, who equated midi-chlorians with genetic elitism. To Brin, *Star Trek*, with its democratic Federation starships, portrayed an egalitarian utopia, while the midi-chlorian-count Jedi of *Star Wars* were remnants of an entitled upper class. One counter-argument to Brin's thesis included the idea that even in a democratic society, not all individuals are created equal — some are more endowed with intellect or strength than others— but still lived within an operative democratic society. Another counter argument asserted that the idea of midi-chlorians was a "metaphor" Lucas created to tie in the concept of symbiosis— a dependence of living creatures on other living creatures.

The idea was raised in Episode I as a way to emphasize the symbiosis between the Gungans and the Naboo, as well as a contrast between Obi-Wan and Qui-Gon, who, in his spirit of independence, sought guidance in the unifying Force, which was a larger perspective of the universe through time and space. Obi-Wan, in his reliance on the living Force, looked at creatures in the present, often with an aloofness which disparaged Jar Jar Binks as a "local," and then Anakin as "another pathetic life-form."[35] If Lucas's concept of the midi-chlorians is taken as a metaphor for mitochondria found in every living cell, the concept of Anakin with a midi-chlorian count higher than that of Yoda leaves plenty of possibilities for the future of the young boy with great Force-potential. As Lucas has always maintained, potential is defined by the choices a person makes. Still, the remnant idea of Darth Vader being more machine than human, as well as the inability of Vader to use Sith lightning because he has artificial limbs, leaves a suspicious taste that Lucas always did conceive of the Force as being reserved for the genetically lucky few. Of course, that idea is contrasted with Palpatine's assertion that a Sith is able to cause the midi-chlorians to conceive life; an idea that was poorly developed and never completely explained.

The pivotal religious aspect in the *Star Wars* saga concerning the Force was the prophecy of the chosen one — the appearance of someone who would destroy the Sith by bringing balance to the Force. Christian influence of a virgin birth (Lucas says it was common to many religions) is the clearest real-world connection. Early on, before the completion of the Prequel Trilogy, the lingering question was whether the chosen one was Luke or Anakin. Lucas states categorically in the "Chosen One" documentary that Anakin brings balance to the Force by destroying the evil Sith when Vader killed the Emperor.[36] Here again, Lucas remains consistent in his duality of the Force with the prophecy that the expunging of evil leads to the proper equilibrium of the universe. It remains in line with the Christian concept that a universe absent of evil is by definition the perfect union and goodness of God.

The last significant aspect of the Force as a spiritual force is that of an afterlife. Or, as Obi-Wan says in Episode IV, "I shall become more powerful than you can possibly imagine." An interesting contrast is the fact that the ability to become ethereal is surely intended as a slap in the face of the Sith who would arrogate the power to be able to prevent death. Given the idea that there is no expressed goal for Jedi religious study — no Nirvana, oneness with the Brahman, union with God — the question must be asked of the purpose of the Jedi Netherworld — that state of shimmering etherealness that constitutes Obi-Wan in Episode V, and Yoda and Vader (and Anakin the younger) in Episode VI. An early draft of the Original Trilogy included Ben appearing to Vader from the Netherworld. Ben warned Vader that if he embraced the dark side he would disappear forever and lose his identity. If he came back to the light side, when he died Vader would first go to the Netherworld where Ben would rescue him before he became one with the Force.[37] Is the Netherworld of the Force an allegory of Christ's resurrection? If it is, then logically the Jedi Council becomes a committee of Pharisees (unbelievers in the Messiah) and the unbelieving masses. Qui-Gon enters heaven to be followed by other true believers of Obi-Wan, Yoda, and Anakin. The comparison seems disingenuous (Christian apologists would say heretical) because the idea of Christ being compared to the evil character of Darth Vader is at the very least untenable. Lucas admits that he never intended Vader to be the pure embodiment of evil that characterized him in the Original Trilogy — Lucas sees Vader as both a hero and a victim.[38]

A strong case for the Christ-Anakin allegory has been made by James

Lawler, a professor of philosophy at the University of Buffalo, in his article "The Force Is With *Us:* Hegel's Philosophy of Spirit Strikes Back at the Empire,"[39] in which he uses Hegel's interpretation of Christ having to endure a descent into the world of evil. Jesus becomes human in an imperfect, and therefore evil, world. Jesus' separation from the perfection of God constitutes the evil of the world. His descent is followed by an ascent into perfection through love, which reconnects Jesus with his divine nature. Not only does Lawler clearly summarize Hegel's critique of the Christology of Jesus's experience on Earth, his essay is an elegant argument for the power of love in the redemption of Vader-cum-Anakin.

Many writers have identified *Star Wars* as a monomyth, a term coined by Joseph Campbell (1904–1987), a professor of mythology who is widely considered the primary influence on the *Star Wars* saga. The monomyth is the synthesis of a broad story outline that, according to Campbell, explains the similarities of the tales told in cultures around the world at various times in history. While interesting in terms of comparative cultural studies, the monomyth is so broad and general that it is very easy to apply details of particular tales and legends to its format. And where Campbell attempts to synthesize cultural creativities, the monomyth can also be criticized for what it leaves out in terms of iconic or plot elements. The monomyth works because it expresses the basic plot ideas that make all stories successful and complete. The idea of a figure who faces adversity and then conquers it by creating some solution is fundamental to all storytelling. In one sense, it is good that humanity can be seen as universal in their experiences, but the uniqueness and individuality of each culture and its traditional stories can be lost in such loose and broad comparisons. The story of Christ is profoundly different from that of Arjuna or Siddhartha. The creation story of the Bible differs in scope and texture from those of the Cherokee or the Sumerians. To lump origin myths together is an interesting task for comparative religious studies, but in another sense it is insulting that the uniqueness of particular cultures are agglomerated and made to conform to a neat and orderly arrangement.

Critics of the religious elements in *Star Wars* assert that there is no profound message to the saga, which contains, at best, only commonsense platitudes that people should be good.[40] And indeed, the religious borrowings in *Star Wars* are better described as trappings of religious iconography than the deep-rooted heart of any particular religious tradition. The very eclectic borrowing of language, behaviors, and clothing (attachment, prophecy, seated lotus position, a Franciscan habit, etc.) form a mish-mash of traditions that some Christian traditionalists find offensive. While many theological tenets can be shared — Western religions share the concept of a single Godhead, Shinto practices combine easily with Buddhist traditions, for example — many deep concepts from great religions cannot be philosophically syncretized. Buddhism rejects the dualism of a heaven and hell. Reincarnation of Hinduism and Buddhism was declared heretical in the Christian Church by the Council of Constantinople in 533. Taoism, as a philosophy, would reject the manipulation of the Force by the Jedi.

There is also the institutional tendency for canon literature to reflect the prevailing Campbellian influence on *Star Wars. The Magic of Myth* companion book may synthesize Luke into the hero monomyth, but it cannot do so with Anakin/Vader's story. Indeed, the strength of this book is its comparisons of real-world influences. Recent scientific exhibitions and memorabilia also tout the mythic connection of *Star Wars*. Greater emphasis should be made with the serial movies Lucas saw as a kid: Flash Gordon, Buck Rogers, the Western, and the swashbuckler movie. The subject of B-movies is not as academically intellectual as the myth, but at least it would be a more authentic study of the influences on the *Star Wars* saga.

The concept of the Force is clearly a significant aspect of the *Star Wars* franchise. It goes to the very heart of the Jedi Knight Order, which, without its religious content, would simply be a pure children's tale. But because of its popularity, the religious elements of the saga have taken a life of its own — a life that should not be dismissed, nor unduly elevated. As an artist, Lucas is within his rights to change, alter, or remove concepts of the Force, but he also suffers when he takes the luxury of espousing two extremes— myth and child's tale — at his own convenience. With the Original Trilogy, Lucas captured the audience with the more abstract nature of the Force but with added refinements of the concept, a reluctant ambivalence has set in among fans regarding the Force. The Force is so important a concept to the franchise, and yet so hard to find a clear expression that not even the databank at Starwars.com has the "Force" as an entry.

Lucas's intention from the very start was to get the audience to contemplate the mysteries of religiosity. Some quarters have done that with the Force and espoused a religious cult called Jediism. This unorganized and vague sect bears no threat to any organized religion, however. The 2001 religion census in Commonwealth nations was widely regarded as a joke both for the seriousness of the study's creators to rail against including Jediism as a "serious" creed, but also for the ease in making such a simple, unconfirmed declaration. It shows the weakness of a study that relies on a simple accounting of a person's religious declaration and the disingenuousness of its creators to skew the study according to their own personal preferences. While any true formation of a Jedi religion is dubious, the declaration of over 500,000 people in Australia, Canada, England and Wales attests to the impact the *Star Wars* franchise has had on world culture.

Consequently, because the moral impact of the Force has been so confused and misunderstood during its continued elaboration in the prequel movies, the Force's influence on the real world has been superficial at best. No one goes around exhorting others to "use the Force" (except as a joke). And while Lucas's insistence of *Star Wars* as a monomyth is virtually a religious tenet in the official canon of *Star Wars*–associated projects like the many touring *Star Wars* exhibitions, there has been virtually no serious academic discussion on the profound effect of the Force on religious or popular culture.[41] There is a huge line between a faith and belief in a greater divinity, which is an authentic aspect of a true religious institution. *Star Wars* remains a "cool" franchise, but not a religiously inspired one.

Military Institutions

As a religious institution, the Jedi Order had certain moral claims that helped maintain its authority in a secular world, but it must also be remembered that there was a military aspect exerting its actual power in the universe. For Lucas, the Jedi Order was the example of a moral extreme — the epitome of the good knight revered in Christendom, a *miles* (Latin for "knight") whose tales were recounted by troubadours in the great halls of European princes. The Jedi was an ideal like the knight. He was an example to the duke who came into his power when the centralization of the Roman empire began to recede from outlying regions. The knight was also a cultural propaganda tool that served the interests of feudal lords by lifting the prerogatives of rulership above the commoner to the established noble class, which was itself consolidated through force of arms. Once constituted and legitimized as a sovereign (a power with authority; *potestas* and *auctoritas*), it was in the interest of the prince to maintain the status quo.

History, however, has shown that religious influence has had the vibrancy and resiliency to challenge secular claims to authority. In Europe, Pope Gregory VII attempted to place the Church over the secular king in response to the growing influence of the Benedictine monastic houses. The investiture controversy of the 11th and 12th centuries was a struggle between the pope and kings of Europe like King Henry IV of Germany or King John of England. The popes had a religious authority, but they also had the two powers — excommunication and the interdict — to undermine the ruler's authority with his own people. The excommunication denied the sovereign ruler sacraments vital to salvation. The interdict denied sacraments to the people of a region and absolved them of moral obligations to their lord. In Japan, the strength of Tendai Buddhist monasteries influenced the Ikko-ikki movement to raise military forces in their struggle against the Nichiren sect. When the Ikko-ikki allied themselves with the rivals of Shogun Oda Nobunaga, an army was sent to destroy their temple complex on Mount Hiei northeast of Kyoto in 1571. The Shaolin Temple in Henan Province, China, was destroyed in 1732 by the Qing government, partially because the military expertise of its monks was seen as a latent threat.

The political nature of acquiring and asserting power has had an ebb-and-flow effect on religious institutions. So it was for the Jedi Order. What is lacking, however, are details regarding the establishment and history of the Jedi Order. The Episode I novelization asserted that they were established first as a study group that later abandoned isolated meditation for outward service to society and the galactic government.[42] Subsequent attempts to flesh out the *Star Wars* universe, however, have revealed huge contradictions in the *Star Wars* time line. The Episode IV novelization asserts that the Jedi were existent for a thousand generations. Expanded Universe novels, comics, and games insist that the Sith once attacked Coruscant and nearly destroyed the Jedi Order 4,000 years before the rise of Palpatine. And even if one were to accept these huge story arcs as true, we still do not know how the Jedi Order or the Galactic Senate evolved as political entities. We only know what can be immediately gleaned from the events portrayed in the six movies of the saga and the novelizations, especially the prequel novels, which have done an excellent job of giving logical and consistent details about the evolution of the political intrigue that led to the destruction of the Jedi Order and the rise of the Galactic Empire.

A good parallel for the preeminence of the Jedi is Plato's *Republic*. In her essay "The Aspiring Jedi's Handbook of Virtue"[43] in Star Wars *and Philosophy*, Judith Barad makes the comparison of a warrior class with the Jedi Order and its masters as the guardians of Plato's republic. It represents the concept of virtue ethics— the behavior of a virtuous person. Its major drawback is the amount of trust Plato gives to this class of guardians, and the assumption that their interests would be the same for all members of society. It is an elitist system in which those with the inherent ability to rule should rule, a system that has perpetuated the aristocracy of any number of civilizations. One aspect of Plato's thesis is strikingly similar to that of the midi-chlorians, which gave the Jedi the genetic right to help rule the galaxy. In the Plato's *Republic*, individuals with souls of gold should rule; those with souls of silver would be a warrior class; those with souls of brass or iron would be everyone else (*Republic* 3.415a–e). Writers have criticized the elitist nature of such a thesis[44]; Christian philosophers have characterized the notion of metals within the soul as idol worship. While Lucas has never made a direct connection to Plato's *Republic*, Barad's essay proves useful in understanding the virtuous behavior of the Jedi Knight.

Social organizations—institutions—generally reflect the individual values of its creators. On a larger level, institutions reflect the values of society at large. So, when one looks at the Jedi Order, one cannot help but be struck by the religious nature of the archetype. They wear the outer habit of a Franciscan monk while their inner garments resemble those of the traditional Japanese kimono. Their headquarters—the Jedi Temple on Coruscant—has the grandeur of the Vatican. The High Council of the Jedi Order has the trappings of the Prussian general staff (High Command) or the British Protectorate under Oliver Cromwell, wherein a limited council held the reins of government. In the case of the general staff, the Jedi Council acted as the coordinators of the military effort during the Clone Wars. As in Prussia where the military government began to pursue its own interests, the Jedi Council pursued its policy according to its own authority. Gordon A. Craig characterizes the High Command as a "silent dictatorship."[45] The rule of the major generals in England had an important impact on the perception of the military to America's founding fathers. U.S. military forces have traditionally been disbanded after major conflicts, and the assurance of civilian authority over the military hierarchy is formally expressed in the military chain of command that places the Joint Chiefs of Staff outside direct operational control of the armed forces. Combatant commanders, in charge of large regions around the globe, report directly to the president of the United States, preventing an institutional military council like the Joint Chiefs of Staff from exerting political influence on the civilian government, or, moreover, preventing it from taking political control through control of the military. Given the fact that the Galactic Republic has no military force, a Jedi coup d'état remains an effective possibility.

As seen in the Prequel Trilogy, the Jedi Council did serve as a consultative body on military issues, as the U.S. General Chiefs of Staff does for the presidency. Drawing the line of distinction between civilian and military control was a glaring problem in the organization of the Republic, however, because the Jedi, while generally known for their open role as occasional ambassadors of the supreme chancellor, could also be seen as an internal state police. *The Ultimate Visual Guide to* Star Wars points out that Count Dooku sees the jedi as "a glorified security service to protect the interests of the Galactic Senate."[46] Though not organized along military lines like a modern para-military force in a country such as France, the comparison to the security apparatus of many countries can be made. The Roman army had the *speculatores* who acted as couriers, special agents, and a secret police. The clearest analogy of the Jedi's relationship to the political establishment, however negative it may appear, is that of the Praetorian Guard, which, in its early days, was a military arm that served as the bodyguard of a commander and later fell into disrepute. The Jedi's destruction can be likened to that of the Guard, whose powers were reduced under Diocletian before they were later disbanded. The defeat of the Praetorian Guard at the battle of Milvian Bridge (Rome, A.D. 306) led to Constantine I's consolidation of power as the first Christian emperor of Rome.

The creation of a military is often characterized by its necessity rather than as a result of a social desire, though governments have always resorted to a legacy of tradition in order to assert the effectiveness of their army. The foundation of Rome was based on the martial capability of its legions, so a spirit of civil militarism has always been perpetuated about Roman soldiery. Again the model for *Star Wars*, the Roman propensity for civil war is not without merit. Machiavelli, in his desire to strengthen Florence's defense against mercenary *condottieri*, sought to create a spirit of local pride. But in many instances, a civilian authority may seek the services of a paid professional army that might serve the interests of the sovereign and not a public that lacked the necessary military skill and/or were prone to insurrection and rebellion.

The Swiss Guard served the French monarchy in such a way. Scythians served Athens in classical times. And today, the French Foreign Legion, made of non–Frenchmen, serve the French government when military action is not supported by the general population. On occasion, foreign advisors may be able to bring a local muster into better military preparedness. The Spartan Gylippus assisted Syracusans against an Athenian invasion. Xanthippus, another Spartan, was employed by the Carthaginians against Rome.[47] And in the early 1800s, Ottoman Selim III employed Russian and Austrian prisoners to develop a clandestine force called the *Nizam-i Cedid* to supercede the traditionally organized Janissary Corps.[48] During its presence in Iraq after the U.S. invasion in 2003, the U.S. military employed more than 100,000 privately paid soldiers to take care of security issues. Many brand these paid armed soldiers as mercenary. Established historian Philippe Contamine (*War in the Middle Ages*) described a mercenary as "being a specialist, stateless and paid."[49] Probably the most famous mercenary army is the Vatican Swiss Guard, which protects the pope in Vatican City. Paid, employed troops are distinguished from United Nations peacekeeping forces, which are recruited from member states and generally have governmental permission to occupy the countries in which they serve their duty.

With the infrastructure needed to maintain the headquarters of the Jedi Order, it would be useful to know the source of their funding, which might include the Senate, general donations, or religious benefactors. It is also possible the Jedi Order received special tax exemptions as is common in many places in the world. As explained by Contamine, "The military system of a state is explained by its resources, principally financial, the structure of its government and administration, the level of its technology, the organization of its society and the nature of its economy, but one must also take into account its objectives and strictly military imperatives. Every state in effect seeks to raise armed forces adapted to its ambitions and to its own fears."[50] In *Star Wars*, financing fear is expensive, but history also provides many examples of how certain trades have traditionally been exploited by the clergy: education (schools and universities), medicine (hospitals and hospices), poverty (bread making), agriculture (farming, cultivation, viticulture), religion (iconography, publishing, religious paraphernalia), pilgrimage (shrines, hostels, food). In Asia, mendicant monks are supported by the lay community, which provides food and clothing as a form of religious obligation. Banking has also been an avenue of fund-raising for Church functions and charities. There was no indication that the Jedi Order had control of significant land holdings, whether on Coruscant or elsewhere in the galaxy, but the management and care of historical Church properties and even regions has been a source of economic income, revenue, and taxation. Indulgences were a questionable practice that helped contribute to the Protestant movement, which saw the growing wealth in Rome financed from their own pockets. With travel expenses, the maintenance of basic living and communication logistics, capital costs of maintaining a Jedi space fleet, the Jedi Temple's physical plant, and observances and practices (such as lightsaber training), the economic burden, despite the free service of its religious and the volunteered time by laypersons, would have to have been staggering.

Probably the closest approximation to the Jedi Temple is the Vatican city-state in Rome, Italy. While it is presumed that the Jedi Temple did not have the independent sovereignty of the Vatican, it is easy to see how a self-sufficient religious organization could be run along the lines of a pseudo-military administration. The Vatican is remarkable in its ability to draw upon and communicate with the billion Catholics around the world. Its hierarchical organization, modeled on that of ancient Rome, reaches from its titular head down through Vatican bureaus out into the world through its episcopacy of bishops who control dioceses that promulgate and administer guiding directives from Rome. From the St. Peter's throne in the Vatican, a religious doctrine or decree can be disseminated to Catholics through a network of parochial parishes. It is not known if the Jedi had this vast a network, but details from the *Star Wars* saga permitted the possibility.

As the most successful religious and military organization in the Republic, the Jedi Order must have had an ancient reputation for its military competence. They were well known for their ability to employ the Force in their combative skills. But it has to be assumed that the Jedi Order, since the inception of the early years of the Republic, acted as repositories for culture, economic, and military skills, like monasteries in the dark ages of Europe. In a galactic universe that has not had a standing military, it seems the Knights of the Jedi Order are the closest tie between the present needs of the Republic and its ancient past, a preserve of ancient learning, a syllabus of best practices, a container of wisdom and knowledge that might be considered a baseline for future development.

The Jedi Order was not a military academy in the modern sense, but early film production designers contemplated a military uniform for the Jedi before they realized Lucas wanted to retain the religious costumes of Obi-Wan. The educational and training curricula in the Jedi Temple reflected a monastic system in which both classes and direct one-on-one instruction took place. Indoctrination ideally began at 6 months, after Jedi "recruiters" had discovered a child with a significant midi-chlorian count. Though accused of being "baby snatchers" by some critics, there is some precedent in the real world for early indoctrination of children into a military corps like the Jannisaries and the Mamelukes (see chapter four); in Burma, Theravada Buddhists encourage preadolescents to become disciples. With its pedagogy of early development and an emphasis on monastic group life, Buddhist practices sometimes resembled the eugenic policies of the Nazis, who collectively raised children on behalf of the state. Teaching a child during the early, impressionable years may be effective, but the ideal age for instruction and indoctrination is a physiological as well as an academic question; the development of the neural networks of the brain may have different peaks than the traditions that are typically imposed in the education of children in a public school setting.

The master-apprentice system (chapter four) is clearly evident in the saga. Giving direct contact with a young student raised without traditional parents is a clear substitute for the maternal upbringing common in most cultures. Though pairs of Jedi would be considered typical, the degree and influence of the master on the student would most likely be a function of the individual personality and training style of the instructor. Given the monolithic nature of an organization a thousand generations old, the limits and manner of such personal instruction would probably have been established long ago. And yet certainly a master would not have been a master in all topics and subjects. Would there not be room for the traditional academic classroom in which an expert or experienced practitioner was the instructor? Especially where a large body of knowledge is required — diplomacy, history, astromechanics, alien psychology, astronomy, physics, theology, economics, banking, medicine, etc. — there is a benefit to group instruction. Indeed, Yoda gives this very kind of example when he is training the Bear Clan in the basics of lightsaber fighting in Episode II. Practical skills associated with the Force required both a general fitness as well as group and individual instruction. Jedi martial arts, as well as other practical training such as meditation, lightsaber construction, and sensitivity to cultural standards and customs could require instruction in unusual settings—

a meditation chamber, a dedicated foundry, and "field trips" to worlds outside the Jedi Temple and Coruscant.

One potentially problematic area was instruction that was arcane and, perhaps, illicit. Apart from a skill like underwater breathing, the Jedi seemed quite capable of pursuing clandestine operations such as that which befell Qui-Gon and Obi-Wan at the beginning of Episode I. Qui-Gon was able to exploit his situation on Tatooine in order to achieve his objective of returning to Coruscant without calling undo attention to himself. Anakin and Obi-Wan, as they pursued leads regarding the attempted assassination of Senator Amidala, showed the analytical and forensic skills of a police detective. In Iga, Japan (modern Mie Prefecture), it is reputed that espionage and stealth skills—*ninjitsu* skills—were developed by the area's inhabitants. Enclosed in a relatively remote location and kept hidden by reclusive traditions, practitioners of shinobi skills were recruited for the Tokugawa shogunate. Not only were night operations of infiltration and espionage part of their repertoire, but knowledge and social skills that allowed them to remain "undercover" while still participating openly in society (as a musician, farmer, etc.) were considered essential skills along with their fighting abilities. The practitioners of the Yagyu Shinkage Ryu were the open instructors to the shogun Tokugawa Ieyesu; they were also known as the shogun's secret police.[51] The open social customs and mores of the daimyo and his samurai retainers played a vital role in the maintenance of the general society. Resort to untraditional and furtive arts such as assassination, sabotage, and infiltration required a secrecy and training that was not part of the ordinary samurai's preparation.

Lightsaber and the Force

The last moments when Luke gives up his lightsaber illustrate the fleeting nature of a sword for the swordsman. A swordsman was defined by his ability to use the sword, but it was not the lightsaber that made Luke, Obi-Wan, and Qui-Gon Jedi no more than a painter is defined by his ability to use a brush. Both the Jedi and the painter are artists who simply use their tools to express their creative energies. Where Jedi in their heyday served the Jedi Order by assisting the Galactic Senate on missions of peace, arbitration, and negotiation, the painter, as well as all other artists, including Lucas the filmmaker, serves humanity by helping men and women understand something about themselves.

A major difference between the art of the swordsman and that of the painter is that only one has the potential to physically destroy society and all its creativity. This is the swordsman's paradox. He is both an instrument of creativity and destruction.

The samurai and the knight were the key influences on the *Star Wars* saga. It was a time when romantic ideas surrounded the swordsman because it was possible for a single person to fight and defeat multiple attackers. Both the knightly and samurai culture relied heavily on their weapon of choice — the sword. It was a weapon that suited all cultures because it was martially effective, elegant in design, and a simple symbolic representation that suited aristocratic fashion. The cumbersome halberd or bow had little social functionality; a small knife simply did not present the grandeur of a sword. A Jedi's lightsaber represented not only his honor and authority; it was also his life, as Obi-Wan instructed Anakin. Lucas had made very few statements on the origins of the lightsaber, referring to it as a lasersword as often as he does a lightsaber. His space-age sword was to be a weapon of futuristic quality, but with the typical swashbuckling swagger of an ancient weapon. It had a physical quality, but it also had a spiritual one as well, which has led many to speculate on the lightsaber's connection to the Force.

The difficulty for modern audiences is their failure to understand the huge gap between the romanticism of the sword and its harsh realities. The fantasy takes over, perpetuating a purely escapist perspective of the lightsaber, which is reinforced by the creative industry of the *Star Wars* production process. There is always something fascinating about the power of weapons, but there must also be a realism present in the understanding of the utility of the weapon. From a moral point of view, the weapon is a tool that, in and of itself, is not evil. It is the person who carries it who should be characterized by any moral attribute.

Within the *Star Wars* universe, an interesting conundrum was the extent to which lightsaber technology was used in general society. No one gave Obi-Wan a second glance when he brandished his lightsaber in the Cantina or in the Coruscant bar when he cut off a patron's arm or hand, so it is curious that perhaps the lightsaber was not as technologically unique as it is perceived to be. Like many things taken for granted today, the technology of the lightsaber ought to be considered as ordinary as a kitchen knife or the combustion engine instead of some mystical object deified in Expanded Universe novels.

A very influential article for *Star Wars* fans was written by David West Reynolds entitled "Fight Saber: Jedi Lightsaber Combat." Reynolds, an anthropologist, parsed the first five movies and created a hierarchy of lightsaber moves and categorized them into seven "styles" called Forms. The only problem in Reynolds' fictional combat is that it is informed not from knowledge of actual sword fighting, but from an archeological construct. Instead of taking information from swordsmen who have trained in either competitive or combative fencing, he romanticizes actual techniques into a silly fantasy of foreign-sounding techniques ("arturo," "sai cha," etc.) and unrealistic styles. Basic techniques are called Form I (Shii-Cho), while the most dangerous techniques verging on dark side Sith styles are Form VII (Vaapad). Reynolds created a hierarchy of techniques in which disarming (sun djem) is the most peaceful technique in the Jedi arsenal and the cutting of a person in half (sai tock) is the most insulting way of killing an opponent.

The problem with Reynolds' hierarchy is that sword fighting techniques are movements that do not have any moral quality. And in a pure sense, all sword fighting attacks are equally reprehensible. Were it not for the fact that swords (like all weapons) were also used to enforce justice or a punishment, society would ban them as it has certain toxic gases like agent orange. Another problem with Reynolds' article is that there is no hierarchy of techniques in any combat. One employs whatever methods will work to either incapacitate, kill, or defeat the opponent. The cut to the wrists that permanently disable the sword hand is as equally effective as cleaving into the head if it prevents the opponent from continuing to attack. And lastly, the sword must be understood within the social context of its use. A lightsaber is presumed to be a deadly instrument and must be used only in proper, legal circumstances. To make a modern comparison, a police officer is trained to use his gun only in situations in which physical danger to his life is present. If he chooses to use the weapon, it is presumed that he can and may kill the opponent. One can imagine the legal problems involved if a police officer were required to wield his weapon to simply injure an assailant by shooting him in the leg, but accidentally kills the person. A deadly weapon presumes its deadly use according to reasonable circumstances.

As a writer, Reynolds also has a tendency to make statements that make little sense to the swordsman. For example, Form II required "the precision of blade manipulation to its finest possible degree and producing the greatest dueling masters in the galaxy." Every technique requires precision of the blade, while the hyperbole of the greatest dueling masters includes no clarification. For example, Gillard states that Yoda is a 10 on his scale of fighting (10 is best, 1 is worst) while Mace was a 9. It is clear that Yoda is better than Mace, but what does that actually mean in a practical sense? Are there techniques that Yoda can do but Mace can't? Is Mace lacking some Force control ability? In another description, Reynolds implies that only gifted Jedi would use "seemingly unconnected staccato sequences." The truth is that *all* fencers use staccato sequences. It is a fundamental skill taught at the earliest levels. Early fencers are taught to vary tempo (i.e., differ the timing of movement) because even tempo allows the opponent to predict what a person will do.

Swordsmanship has always been imbued with a mystical element without having to resort to fantasy. Part of the mystique of swordsmanship is that good technique is virtually invisible. This is part of the reason why sword competitions are not popular. An audience without training cannot observe the subtleties of swordsmanship. As will be discussed in chapter seven, sword fight choreography was created in order to be seen.

In the West, the mystique of sword fighting was expressed in its secretive nature. Knowledge of technique was a commodity that was assiduously learned from training or combat. To know how to use the sword effectively was a skill sought after by individuals willing to submit themselves to the art. There is an element of pure bravado and physical stature akin to the pugilism of boxing, but sword fighting was also a very subtle art whose techniques required a certain frame of thinking and training. For the Jedi, basic drilling would be the starting point in their lightsaber studies, but more sophisticated techniques required direct instruction. In Japan, these secret techniques of a particular school were called *okuden*. Western schools referred to them as *bottes secretes* (secret attacks), which were supposedly so effective that there was no defense against them.

Philosophical and religious language was also appropriated into the instruction of swordsmanship. In Spain, the circle and chords presented on the floor for training presented an almost enigmatic element to training, especially when esoteric symbology was included in the swordsman's training. In Japan, Buddhist terms were also included in instruction. Zen concepts of no-mind (*munen*),[52] energetic emanation (*kehai*),[53] or immovable mind (*fudô-shin*)[54] were incorporated into study of the sword because a free but focused study or intensity is believed to lead to enlightenment (*satori*). The emphasis on ki training also has had a profound effect on many martial arts.[55]

Physical training created a kind of mystical element among non-swordsmen. The fabled Coup de Jarnac has achieved literary notoriety as a secret, despicable attack Jarnac used to disable his opponent François de Vivonne, seigneur de La Châtaigneraie. The attack was a cut to the hamstrings that disabled and caused Vivonne to bleed to death during an open duel. In the Kashima-Shinryu styles of Japanese swordsmanship, there is a technique called *Sokui-tachi*[56] in which the defender strikes an opponent's blade and connects to it so that a subsequent counter strike can be made. To an outside observer, the technique is unfathomable because it appears that the defender actually caused the attack to deflect his own strike away from the intended target. Even the simple contact of one blade against another has a mystical quality in it because fencers can tell so much about intention through the small variances in the contact between the blades. This ability to "read" an opponent's intentions is simply termed *sentiment de fer* (feeling of the steel). All fencers develop and hone this ability, which is a skill that can be taught and learned.

Many unusual movements in swordsmanship may also appear to outsiders as if there is some mysterious philosophical or religious underpinning to them.

The salute has its origins from the knightly kissing of one's sword before battle. In Japan, a movement called *chiburi* is a quick flick of the blade to remove blood from the blade after it has been used. Other esoterica have hidden meanings. In Japan, the martial emphasis of a dojo can be judged by the way weapons are placed on holders. Swords that are placed horizontally with the blade to the left indicate a martial emphasis in their practice because the weapons can be grasped quickly off the rack. An extra step is required in deploying the weapon if it is placed in the other direction. The concept of *zanshin* (remaining mind), a stillness after using the sword, has a kind of religious aspect. In reality, zanshin is a pause used to prompt a swordsman to become aware of his surroundings during combat.

There should be a healthy balance between respect for the weapon as an instrument of destruction and a fanaticism for it. The samurai lived and died by the sword, but that was only one aspect of the unique role they had in society. Samurai, Jedi, and all swordsmen are also humans endowed with gifts to do good and the potential to do evil. The sword may represent ideals, but swords are not in and of themselves those very ideals. For the swordsman, the blade is simply a particularly shaped piece of metal. In this sense, the sword is simply a tool. For the Jedi Knight or the swordsman, the greatest tool is not his weapon, but his mind.

The lure of power has the potential to transform the brotherhood of the sword into a cult of the sword. The method of training a swordsman, similarly, must contain a mode of questioning the master without exalting him to the status of a god. History gives many examples of citizens following charismatic individuals for the wrong reasons. When such leaders can co-opt the general feeling of the population, the whole society can be made into a veritable military camp in which freedom and creativity are stifled when opposed to the regime in authority. And when individuals take so myopic a view of the world that everyone else's views and lifestyles are considered wrong, this fanaticism goes underground. It is no different from what past megalomaniacs and dictators have wanted — absolute and complete security in their position gained by the means of authoritarian rule. Steps in that direction include political bullying, blackmail, and the threat of retribution, whether political or physical.

Certainly, the lightsaber aspect of the *Star Wars* universe is one area in which its romanticism can be emphasized at the expense of swordsmanship's realism, but this superficial view must also be understood within the context of a larger picture. *Star Wars* is entertainment, but Lucas also implies that "all of *Star Wars* is reasonably political."[57]

Interpreting *Star Wars* lightsaber fighting as an artifact dug up from an excavation site is a false assignment of values to an activity with its own logic and theory. One cannot simply watch what people do and fully understand the emotion or reason behind it. Many daily acts can be explained by basic needs and wants; the chopping of meat, the lighting of a fire, the creation of a blanket or a cap or a rag doll. Other acts border on the inscrutable, like the way a woman combs her hair or the way a man kicks the dirt from his boots. These things appeal to no reason in and of itself but one can find logical answers if the question is posed. Sometimes these acts are creative moments that border on the mysterious or the sublime: the moment of contemplation, prayer to one's god, or the tears shed at a moment of joy. It is in this way that the observation of acts with the sword sometimes provides the observer a misleading impression.

The Jedi Order and the Sith provide an easy example of the danger of ascribing too much mystery to straightforward practices. Where an open society of knights like the Jedi must maintain a dialog with the public in order to justify their continued service to the Senate, the Sith do everything to obfuscate facts, realities, and truth for their own ends. One of the political lessons from *Star Wars* is underscored by the manner in which the Jedi handled their lightsabers at a time when the Sith plotted their return to power. The Jedi did not travel secretly around the universe until the Sith were able to manipulate the universe to their end. As the prophecy foretold, however, there is a way for even the Jedi to return balance to the Force.

Sith Versus Jedi

The enemy of the Jedi Order has always been conceived of as a rival order of Force-wielding knights. The power of the Force was originally so important that its secret was limited to the Skywalker family. From the concept of Sith pirates who eventually fight against the Force-gifted Starkiller family to a two-man order of a master and his apprentice, the Sith are noted by their drive and quest for power and their willingness to do anything to achieve their goal of destroying the Jedi Knights, for which they prepare with infinite patience. The ultimate utilitarians of the galaxy, the Sith lords shun any law, ethic, or rule that would prevent them from exterminating their enemies and expanding their wealth and influence.

At its head was the Emperor who Lucas envisioned to be Darth Vader's master, a phantom force making his appearance in the final episode of the *Star Wars* saga. The Emperor was created to embody "pure evil." He was conceived of as the "devil"[58] incarnate as well as the nefarious political figure at the head of a galactic political apparatus. At his side were various henchmen — Darths Maul, Tyrannus, and Vader — who helped him start an interstellar war and destroy the guardians of the Republic. The dark side also spawned a pantheon of evil characters outside the six episodes, including Sith lords like Darth Plagueis, Darth Bane, and the equally evil Durge and Asajj Ventress of the *Clone Wars* cartoon.

The Sith were the antithesis of the Jedi. Instead of an open organization with the duty of protecting the Republic, the Sith are a conspiracy of two. Instead of the symbiotic relationship of Jedi Knights, the Sith act like a cancer, feasting upon and then eventually killing its host. Instead of nourishing the universe and goodness of the Force, the Sith exploit it. The Sith make their choices, just like the Jedi, choosing the freedom to do anything to accomplish their goals without any reference to justice or paternalism, engulfing the entire universe in a galactic war to install themselves at the head of the political order. The Sith freely chose actions that had negative consequences on the general public: the presumably millions of lives that were lost in the Clone Wars; the cost of displacing civilians caught in the fight; and the economic and production lost to the disruption of a universe. The Jedi, by contrast, sought to mitigate Sith intrigue by waging war against Separatist forces.

Both the Jedi and the Sith believe in the Force, which is the source of their extraordinary powers. The Sith saw the Force differently, however. The Force was not love and compassion, as it was for the Jedi. The dark side was not an expression of the Force's opposite, but a denial of it. While the light side of the Force attempted to maximize benefits for all people in the universe, the Sith desired to maximize the benefits of the world for themselves. Lucas draws from Buddhist teaching in that obtaining power is an attachment — a desire which leads to suffering. In the case of the Sith, their attachment was the desire to obtain power, whether through physical wealth or control even if it required them to present an outward face of morality and peace. For the Sith, the lightsaber taught that politics was the sheer force of power, the determination of an individual to exploit and maximize the cost-benefits of opportunity in a competition that saw no reason not to fool, trick, or kill in order to achieve their ends. The Sith saw no reason to hold back in their passions, as this world, not the afterlife of a Netherworld, was the reality of the universe. Order allowed the Sith to impose their will on the universe. It provided a stability that maximized the potential to overcome any challenge that attempted to subvert their control over the system. Life was not fair; the universe was not supposed to provide equally for each person. For the Sith, the respect for an individual was a function of those individuals who know how to employ force with the greatest efficiency.

The Order of the Jedi Knights, having maintained their power for thousands of years, were the Sith's primary obstacle. Having time on their side, the Sith worked assiduously to prepare for the moment of their attack. Training for the Sith was best accomplished through a severe regime of punishing calculation. As a student of Darth Plagueis, Sidious would have been taught the rigors of punishing discipline. Endurance of pain led to an increased willingness to inflict pain upon others when difficult decisions would eventually have to be made. Complete obedience to instruction was required. Obedience was the most efficient instructor. It demanded perfection. It required commitment and loyalty that went beyond following rules and laws. The laws of the universe were those physical laws that determined the extent of the power a person was capable of wielding. If a person was strong enough to determine their reality through the focus of their power, then they would benefit the most from its fruits. Slavery was the yoke of those who could not or were not willing to undo the reigns of their masters.

So, too, in lightsaber training, domination was to be achieved through intimidation backed by the ability and willingness to hurt, maim, or kill. The universe is a battlefield in which the individual with the lightsaber is able to control those who lack the strength to resist. Sidious's apprenticeship under Darth Plagueis was complete when he had learned everything that was necessary for his own ascension to power. Had he lived, Plagueis would have probably praised his apprentice for the manner of attacking him. Plagueis would have had to have been a fool to think that his own student would not have learned the importance of striking at a moment of maximum opportunity. Plagueis would have praised Sidious for his ability to accomplish what he and every Sith lord had aspired to do for the thousands of years of their exile. Their greatest tool for creating the upheaval that will destroy the Jedi Knights is war.

For the Sith, the greatest means of achieving their end is through the deliberate and hostile environment of the battlefield. War creates a state of affairs that destroys the laws and rules of society and returns the world to its violent state of war in which power is the greatest necessity. Under their control is the power of the Force — it bends minds, it gives them the physical edge in warfare, and it allows them the creativity to use the universe to meet their needs. The goodness of the light side of the Force was considered a contemptible weakness. As power, the dark side allows the Sith to manipulate the physicality of the universe for a purpose. It is aggression that gives the Sith master his power with the lightsaber. The bravado and the display of strength associated with effective lightsaber mastery permits the Sith to win, to dominate, to exploit his position. Their goal is victory, so the niceties of the rules must ultimately be dispensed with during training and during actual combat.

It was not until Episode III that the world realized that Lord Sidious was not simply the universe's greatest manipulator. He was a lightsaber expert as well, capable of personally instructing Darth Maul, Count Dooku, and Darth Vader. Each had their own unique abilities: Maul his exceptional martial skills, Dooku his elegant training and knowledge of Jedi ways, and Vader, up until his defeat against Obi-Wan, his raw potential of becoming the ultimate expression of the power of the dark side. Key to the Sith's rise to power was not only political maneuvering, but also their skills as lightsaber fighters.

It is possible that the Sith also learned from the Jedi and their lightsaber training. As the Shaolin monks do today, the Jedi may have demonstrated their skills before the public. If there were something beneficial in mastering the Force in their lightsaber techniques, then the Jedi might have decided that it would be worth sharing that gift with the world. It would be another way to promote the understanding that leads to the compassion of the light side of the Force. The Sith would have quickly taken advantage of the Jedi's willingness to demonstrate their powers, but they would have found it more beneficial to hide those techniques in order to prevent others from using their skills against them. It was also possible that the Jedi could have written manuals or tracts elucidating their martial skills and prowess with the lightsaber. Again, it would have been difficult for those who see goodness in the universe to hide it from the rest of society. Additionally, the Sith might have learned other sword fighting traditions not associated with the Jedi and continued their training on an off-world planet far from the prying eyes of the public.

Droids, too, would have been easily used to complement the dark lord's direct training. Artoo-Detoo and See-Threepio were examples of the independence mechanical robots had in the *Star Wars* universe. They would have proved efficient in conducting repetitive drills with emotionless speed and unrelenting ferocity. Droids may have been expensive, but they were also dispensable, permitting the Sith trainee to employ the live blade without concern that an accident might "kill" his training droid. If a Sith were injured, it would have been a learning experience; the Sith trainee benefitted from the actual use of his blade.

Ultimately, however, mastery of the dark side of the Force was demonstrated in the Sith's ability to channel the energy of the universe into Force lightning, which leaped from the tips of one's fingers. This was the power of the dark side that the Jedi, in their weakness, have chosen never to explore; and because of it, the Jedi were deprived of a useful ability that would have helped them to maintain their influence in the Republic. Imagine what the Jedi would have been able to achieve had they been ruthless enough to go after the Sith with the same unrelenting attitude the Sith gave to the destruction of the Jedi.

On the whole, the Force in lightsaber combat is simply a visual convention that does not contribute to enhanced swordplay. Nowhere in the saga is the Force's causal mechanism logically explained. For example, when Vader chokes Admiral Motti on the Death Star, is the Force actually moving the muscles on the neck, which in turn squeezes the trachea? If the Force can move particles without touching it in the manner that a magnet can move metal, then it would be possible to say that the Force could move and excite electron particles which create the Sith lightning used to great effect against the Jedi. From this premise, one could then assert that the Jedi could accelerate the force of a lightsaber cut by "pushing" on the molecules that make up the lightsaber blade. Other Force powers, like the ability to see into the future (prescience), have caused *Star Wars* fans to create their own circumstantial (and logically flawed) explanations. An example is the assertion that the Jedi's ability to see into the future permits him to know where a Jedi will attack with his lightsaber. This line of reasoning, however, leads to an infinite regression of which Jedi can "out-see the future?"[59] Others who identify blaster bolts with lasers have asserted that the ability to deflect blaster bolts is a Force "skill" stemming from the ability to see into the future. In this case, the visual reality of actual film footage shows that the blaster bolt moves more with the speed of an arrow than at the speed of light.[60]

For Lucas, the metaphysical underpinning of the Force is not as important as the effects which can be shown before a camera. While this superficial underpinning works to explain powers on the screen, it undermines a deeper, more substantive philosophical purpose for the Force. It gives the Jedi "cool" powers, but it does not give philosophers or theologians any good epistemological assumptions. One cannot create an ethical system for the Jedi. In fact, the simplest ethical exhortation that can be gleaned from *Star Wars* is "be good," which does not lead one to greater conclusions such as whether rolling through a stop sign is ethically bad (and therefore punishable) or whether Spartan infanticide is evil. This is compounded by the fact that some uses of the Force are considered unethical by present-day standards— influencing a "weak mind," for example.

What we do know is that the Sith exploit others for their own ends, while the Jedi supposedly help others for their own ends, and perhaps in spite of them. So, to enhance the prestige of the Jedi (and the Sith), Lucas gave his fabled warriors "powers," which, according to David Brin, equated the Jedi with the demi-gods found in Greek myths.[61] Overall, though, the Force powers in the *Star Wars* saga, as an energy field between all living creatures in the universe, do not amount to particularly powerful abilities. Presumably the Jedi praying in the Temple cannot physically call a star into being, much less destroy a planet as the Death Star can. Nor is the prescient ability to see into the future — if Yoda is any example — a very reliable predictor of events to come. Jedi Force powers, then, actually amount to parlor tricks that have very limited and temporary effect. In fact, all of the Jedi's and Sith's powers can be replaced with technological achievements— Sith lightning equates with real lightning, a Force push equates with the magnetic repulsion of metal, etc. Lightsaber fighting, as well, cannot even be said to have been enhanced artificially because none of the footage in any of the lightsaber fighting in the saga was sped up as is typical of most martial arts films. Even the Force push used by Anakin and Obi-Wan on Mustafar only amounted to outstretched hands and digital animation. The Force, therefore, does not affect the Jedi's (or the actor's) skills with the lightsaber, and has a minor, if not a negligible, effect on actual combat in the saga.

Apply this same idea to the machinations of the Sith in the *Star Wars* universe. Would the Sith have been able to pull off the same conspiracy without the use of the Force? Sith morality did not have the civilizing outlook of historical political bodies that sought to create a philosophy that legitimized their authority. The Sith government was not a Confucian state where concord reigned when leadership was in accordance with harmonious virtues. Theirs was not the world of Clausewitz's trinity of war, which portrayed warfare as a balance of a violent world, the creative energies of a commander, and the logical extension of the state's political apparatus. To the Sith, there is no internal largess in accommodating the weakness of a giving and virtuous society. Outwardly, however, they maintained the veneer of democratic legitimacy in order to placate the psychological needs of the general population.

The universe was a ferociously feral place and taming it through control and mastery was what distinguished the civilizing universe from the unkempt wildness of the natural world. Coruscant, the capital of the universe, was the greatest example of civilization subduing the earth for occupation and exploitation. To the Sith, corruption would have been a failure only if it did not achieve the purposeful ends of a desired society. Corruption in the Galactic Republic was the natural state of a political society because it employed the efficiencies of a society's willingness to achieve a beneficial outcome. That is why black markets exist in every economic system. They provide a lubrication for the goods and services the general public is unwilling to openly tolerate. Such vice and decadence is always derided by the society above ground, but it would be naïve to deny that all vibrant surface economies depend on an underground black market.

If one were to look at the actual events of the *Star Wars* as if they had occurred through the holonet (the *Star Wars* version of the newspaper), one has to ask the question about the likelihood of such events coming to pass. On one hand, the personal agenda of particular individuals is an easy one to speak to, though on a more basic level such broad assertions are easily and often dismissed as conspiracy theory. If one were to look at the election of Senator Palpatine as supreme chancellor, there was a credibility in the manner of his ascendancy. According to the background histories created by a host of Expanded Universe writers, the rise of Palpatine came on the heels of Supreme Chancellor Finis Vallorum, who was removed from office by a vote of the

Senate when Amidala, acting on advice from the then Senator Palpatine, called for his resignation because he refused to react immediately to the invasion of Naboo. Ostensibly, this created sympathy in the Senate for Palpatine, whose planet had been invaded, and his later election to the office of supreme chancellor. In the original Alan Dean Foster novelization of Episode IV, Palpatine was termed "President of the Republic."[62] The new title of chancellor was a clear reference to Germany and the unification of the many German-speaking states in central Europe. Otto von Bismarck was the first chancellor of a unified German empire (1871–1890). Similarly, Paul von Hindenberg, who was the 1925 president of the Republic, appointed Adolf Hitler chancellor of the Reichstag (the democratically elected parliament) in January 1932.

Palpatine's election was the result of a minor trade incident to raise funds for the Republic's growing financial debt.[63] After eight years of service in the Senate,[64] Palpatine was legally required to finish his term as chancellor, but with increasing security concerns, he moved on to push the approval of the Military Creation Act, which would create an army to be used against the Separatist movement led by a former Jedi, Count Dooku. Senator Amidala was opposed to the act but the assassination actually underscored the need for a military. She became a tool to be manipulated by Darth Sidious. Jedi investigation revealed the existence of a clone army on Kamino. And with the help of Jar Jar Binks who was then an Associate Planetary Representative in the Senate, Lucas (as a bow to the near-universal derision of Jar Jar in Episode I) had him go to the Senate to propose that emergency powers be given to Chancellor Palpatine. Palpatine then created the Grand Army of the Republic (GAR) by decree. An interesting twist absent in the actual movie was the novelization's indication that not only were Yoda and Mace Windu present at the proposal of emergency powers, but Mace actually supported Jar Jar by encouraging him to "stay strong" when his initial statement was met with laughter and boos from senators.[65] It was clear that the Jedi had made a political decision to support the chancellor; they were actually complicit in acquiescing to his assumption of dictatorial powers.

Again going back to the early moments of Hitler's rise to power, the Emergency Decree in Article 48 was created in response to the burning down of the Reichstag. Specifically enacted to combat Communist anti-government activity, the decree suspended a broad range of civil liberties, including habeas corpus, freedom of the press and assembly, and the privacy of postal notes and telegraphic and telephonic communications. Soon after the passage of Article 48, the Enabling Act permitted Chancellor Hitler to create laws without receiving approval from the parliament. A similar declaration, which was deleted from the final cut of Episode III, was made by Chancellor Palpatine when he personally appointed the governors of regional star systems. The representative authority of the Senators was being undermined, if not replaced, by Palpatine's personal men. This scene would have added additional information about the loyalist Committee of Two Thousand, senators opposed to the increasing and unbridled powers of the chancellor.

To the Sith, the real power of the universe rested in the hands of those who could manipulate others. The Sith represented an extreme version of realpolitik — the unsentimental view that events in the universe were a result of actions and inactions, and that military power was an expression of the real and actual state of the universe. Those that denied the reality of the world were subject to being carried away by history instead of being the driving force at its epicenter. Sidious had to use the very laws that were meant to protect democracy to his own advantage until he could achieve complete control. He orchestrated the Naboo incident and then used it as a pretext to gain his election. Then, successive crises were used to create a public sense of impending military threat, enabling Sidious to maintain the legality of his position. Once his power was consolidated, Palpatine would have been in complete control to exercise his policies with little fear of challenge. Palpatine participated in the public charade of working to protect the Republic, maintain the judiciary to legitimize his regime, restore order, unify the galaxy, and punish successionists.

As long as his secret dealings remained hidden, Sidious had succeeded in framing the Jedi Order. It was Count Dooku, a Jedi, who tricked Sifo-Dyas into clandestinely ordering a clone army on behalf of the Jedi before murdering him. Dooku then joined Sidious and organized an intergalactic movement to separate from the Republic in much the same way southerners tried to succeed from the Union during the American civil war. Suddenly, the Separatists had organized and created a droid army that threatened to overwhelm the Jedi. Conveniently, the clone army was timed perfectly to be ready when the Separatist army became a threat. The Jedi were on both sides of the conflict. The common galactic citizen would have little difficulty in recognizing that the Jedi Order's internal feud had become the source of a greater galactic war. The Jedi had increased their influence on politics by becoming the generals of the clone army until they had reached a point when they had the opportunity to take over the Republic, which actually happened when members of the Jedi Council attempted to assassinate the chancellor. A state of emergency was subsequently declared and the Jedi were systematically exterminated by the clone army to prevent a larger civil war.

In one sense, the Jedi had fallen into a trap of their own making. Though not so clearly explained in the actual movies, there was a conspiracy within the Jedi Council to arrest the supreme chancellor before he had become so politically and militarily powerful that they would have been helpless to act. The truth is that they waited too long. Their reluctance to act, based on concepts of democracy and freedom, would have been proof to the Sith of Jedi weakness. Members of the Council, which included Yoda, Mace Windu, and Ki-Adi-Mundi, openly discussed the growing threat Palpatine posed to the freedoms enshrined in the galactic constitution, the presumed charter of the Galactic Senate. They were not alone in their growing suspicion that Palpatine was the mastermind behind a legalistic power grab. Members of the Senate also recognized the threat to civil rights. The truest sadness was that Palpatine's rise was not simply a fiction but a reflection of actual events in the world in which democracy became the mechanism for authoritarian rule. In ancient Greece, it was the democracy of the state that sentenced to death Plato, the enlightened philosopher.

But one might ask whether the Jedi Order deserved their downfall. The Jedi Order failed to adapt to the coming changes in the universe. Yoda, himself, spoke of the arrogance of the Jedi. They acted neither swiftly enough to adapt to the coming war nor with enough vigor to prevent Palpatine's accumulation of power. It was the battle of Geonosis that demonstrated the military weakness of the Jedi as a fighting force. Like the battle of Sphacteria in 425 B.C. when 120 Spartiates surrendered to Athenians for the first time in known history, the Jedi warriors were saved by the new army of clone troops, who would prove their invaluable worth in the fight against Separatist forces.

Or were the Jedi a victim of the times, a casualty of the greater sickness that infected the universe? Lucas has always compared the Republic to a massive tree that has rotted from corruption. It stood firm on the outside, but at some precarious moment, the entire structure would collapse on itself. And what part did Anakin play in the destruction of the Jedi Order? Did the Council have some blame in the way they treated Anakin throughout the period of their association with the boy? It was no wonder that Anakin became an easy mark for Palpatine to exploit. Anakin, too, became a tool in Palpatine's conspiracy to take over the universe.

The first *Star Wars* movie — Episode IV — was the epitome of the classic adventure film. It had action, adventure, romance, and a predictable moral ending. Each subsequent film surprised us in that they had a broader story arc, culminating with Luke helping his father achieve redemption. In the prequel movies — Episodes I, II, and III — Lucas had to go back and create a compelling story that meshed clearly with the 1977 film. Everyone already knows the ending, so in many ways the audience's focus is much more on detail than it is in the general substance of his new movies. This was no small trick, and in many aspects Lucas both succeeds and fails in his telling of the story.

In many respects, the Prequel Trilogy is much more a commentary about human activity. It is not an allegory in which specific people and events in the movie reflect events in reality. Rather, *Star Wars* events are approximations of history and serve, in another sense, as a warning. The Prequel Trilogy described an imperfect universe in which a Sith conspiracy sought to destroy the Jedi Order, corruption undermined government authority, and the energy and trade companies placed the desire for money over the well-being of the citizens. Authoritarian government was on the rise and democratic institutions ceded their own powers to the dictator in the name of safety and security.

It is not too far off the mark to look at certain events in the world, but art has its own way of asserting itself in the universe. Lucas's intention may have been to critique the corruption of the Republican Nixon administration and the Vietnam war, but in the 1980s, Republicans were able to co-opt *Star Wars* by interpreting President Reagan as a Jedi Knight fighting the evil empire called the Soviet Union.[66] Lucas himself also admitted that while he had always aspired to remain a filmmaker independent of the Hollywood establishment, his Lucas-related companies have themselves become a kind of monolithic empire. Criticism has centered around the economic frenzy of the unrelenting merchandising associated with *Star Wars*. Lucas counters that the public wants the goods and that Lucasfilm is also at the forefront of technology development, which costs a lot of money. In the end, Lucas says that everyone will benefit.

What remains at the heart of *Star Wars* is the story, which is both tragic and heroic. It is tragedy that the Jedi Order was destroyed by the actions of Darth Sidious, but the saga is still testament that the goodness that is the Force will triumph over the dark side, which is a negation of all the Jedi Order stands for. It is important in this world, as it is in *Star Wars*, that political leaders be imbued with a sense of honor, justice, and compassion for all people. The saga serves as a general warning that citizens must be vigilant of governments and powerful conglomerates who desire social order over freedom, monopoly over free enterprise, and conformity over individual expression.

Not only do general themes bear this out, but details do as well. Darth Maul's "cool" butterfly flip is tactically useless. The Sith don't simply use their lightsaber in combat, they also have the savagery to use other objects (debris, cave ceiling, senate platforms) in their fight, very much like a cheater throwing sand in an opponent's eyes. But it was Yoda who demonstrated that he could master Sith lightning by collecting and dissipating the energy thrown at him by Sidious. Palpatine, the supposed master of evil (and a lightsaber fighter as well), could not even defeat Mace Windu without the help of Anakin's betrayal. Even during the Jedi Order's moment of absolute destruction, the Jedi at Geonosis refused to be taken hostage as pawns of the Separatist army. History bears out that even with the extermination of the Templar Knights, the most successful militant order, the essence and spirit of the Christian message would not suffer.

Even one of the fiercest attacks on *Star Wars* by David Brin is refuted when one looks at the Force as it was meant to be — a spirit of energy common to all living creatures of the universe. His accusation that the destruction of the second Death Star was accomplished by Lando Calrissian and other non–Force-sensitive individuals falls flat when one understands that the goodness of the Force depends on not only the Sith Lord and a redeemed Jedi Knight, but on all individuals. In fact, a democratic theme to the *Star Wars* saga can be argued when an elitist organization like the Jedi Knights decapitates an Empire's evil master so that the common person might bring about the destruction of the Death Star.

Sidious pointed out that those with power want to keep their power — "Even the Jedi," he said. It is true that everyone is self-interested. It *is* natural and desirable. Individuals are defined by their character. They are judged by their actions, as well as their intentions. Is not Anakin's intention to help Padme? Does he not want to bring an end to the war? Does not a company CEO wish to help people, its clients, its shareholders, its employees? At what point does concern for others turn into exploitation and personal greed? And when one has come to realize that his life was predicated on a lie, when one discovers that he has been more machine than man, what hope does one have?

Lucas made it clear that in the *Star Wars* saga there is hope for everyone. He does not make excuses for the evil that Vader has done in the world. Justice would have meant Vader and Sidious being tried for their crimes, but in another sense, there is some justice that they paid for their deeds with their own deaths. Sidious was returned to the bowels of the earth suffering eternal damnation, while Vader made a final choice in his life that finally led him away from the dark side, one final opportunity to repent for his sins. Deep in his heart he realized with regret what he had accomplished with his life — turning away from the kindness of his master Obi-Wan, squandering the opportunities provided by the Jedi Order, betraying the hope and the faith others may have had in him as the chosen one. In this last instant, Anakin found the heart to undo the worst decision of his life — he rids the universe of the Emperor and pays for that choice with his life.

No one would dare absolve Vader for his past, but for Anakin, like the rest of humanity, there was hope of redemption even at the very last moment. There will be those who cynically list the evils Vader has wrought and then insist that Vader, like Hitler, was beyond redemption for the evil he has caused in his life. Lucas made his own choice when he created his saga, and it was clear that the basic tenets of the Force have evolved with each successive movie. Lucas had the choice of being a romantic or a vigilante. His choice was to be ever hopeful in the human spirit. It must always be remembered that the *Star Wars* saga does not end with *Revenge of the Sith*, but with *Return of the Jedi*.

Three

Master, Padawan, Apprentice

From the very beginning in Episode IV, education has been a commanding theme in Lucas's six-part epic. Luke, the unschooled adopted son of a moisture farmer on a desert planet, desired to escape his repetitive and uninteresting life by going to the Academy. Like his father Anakin did as a boy, Luke looked up into the heavens with a burning desire to see the stars firsthand with his own eyes. Neither, however, expected to receive their education from the likes of Jedi Masters, space warriors charged with the very protection of the galaxy itself. As in many great tales, protagonists did not choose their destiny. It was thrust upon them in a unique master-apprentice relationship that has been the model of education for swordsmen of countless societies. In theory, their obligations are simple — the apprentice follows the master's instructions.

The Nature of Education

The duty of a master teacher is to get someone to think well. The duty of a master swordsman is to teach honor. In Episode V, Yoda captured the heart of what it means to educate a swordsman: "Only a fully trained Jedi Knight with the Force as his ally will conquer Vader and his Emperor. If you end your training now, if you choose the quick and easy path, as Vader did, you will become an agent of evil." Luke then asked if staying was worth sacrificing Han and Leia. Yoda replied, "If you honor what they fight for ... yes!"

In societies in which armed fighters walked the street with impunity, their code of honor separated them from thugs, ruffians, and bullies. Though much maligned in history as a reasoned excuse for bloody excess, the concept of honor still resonates deeply within the human psyche. Honor requires no written contract, a person's public reputation being held as collateral for any transgression. The gentleman's agreement was sealed with a handshake, though words alone sealed the commitment until death. In that same conversation, Luke said he will finish the training that he has begun: "You have my word."

In order to best cultivate honor, the apprentice swordsman first had to learn the knowledge of not only skills and technique, but also the world in which the swordsman lived. It was therefore critical for the teacher to be wise and experienced and to teach for the duration of the apprenticeship. This master taught the novice how to *think* and *act*, all in an attempt to impart the obligations of those given the right to wear a sword of power. The swordsman, because of his ability to coerce, had to learn how to rein in his passions. He had to be trained properly so that the temptation to abuse and exploit that power was circumvented. Sometimes, as in the case of Anakin, a master's instruction failed.

The master-apprentice relationship was a traditional form of instruction that dated back to ancient times. Through trust, affection, and submission, it was hoped that the student's dedication might one day lead to his eventual affection and love for his teacher's instruction. The apprentice system was an intimate relationship quite different from the distant learning found in modern classrooms. Direct instruction was seen as the best method of imparting not only knowledge, but also values. It allowed a master to carefully monitor a student's progress and it permitted the student the rare opportunity to benefit from the formal guidance of an expert.

Martial arts training speaks loudly to the training that occurs in *Star Wars*, but mentoring also occurs in a variety of other fields: carpenters, brick and tile layers, painters, sculpture, religious disciples and leaders, teachers, attorneys, and writers and editors. Within fencing, there was no more hallowed individual than the *maître d'armes* (Master of Arms) and the sensei (Japanese for teacher). Masters of Arms in European societies taught the king's men the art of the fence, but they also served as important advisors to the military and the court. Through their skill of arms, they became professionals who demonstrated their knowledge and skill in instructing a new generation of soldiers. They were often arbiters on courts of honor and their role, above all else, was to safeguard the sanctity of a gentleman's word. The modern equivalent — the sports coach — draws little from this tradition, but his role is no less important than that of the master fencer.

In Japan, as in most of Asia, teachers were held in the highest esteem. They were wise men and women worthy of society's respect. Without them society would cease to exist and their culture would lack the glue needed for its preservation. A person's vocation in Japan was not simply a function of money or influence. Even today, the sensei, whether a grade school teacher or a college professor, is still highly esteemed and equally revered. Teachers are not simply instructors, but conveyors of society's culture and history.

The relationship between the martial arts instructor and his student was always one of a higher and lower. There was nothing, short of intimate friendship, that could break this bond because the nature of the martial art required a clear distinction between instructor and learner. The relationship between the two was an ethical one, not simply of roles. One might come to his instructor in the capacity as a practiced soldier with the rank of general, but the relationship with the instructor was still one of respect, if not obedience and service. This relationship even continues when a student has outperformed the master in his technical mastery. Musashi, renowned for his mastery of the sword and the formalization of a two-sword curriculum, was still expected to bow to his sensei. While this may seem foreign to Western students who equate influence with position and wealth, the same ethical relationship still exists. Takuan Soho, a Zen monk and samurai, instructed that a lord and his retainers should act as if their opposite were an ideal form. A servant would therefore serve not a particular lord with a particular name, but a lord to whom a faithful retainer would serve. The lord, too, should treat his retainers as the abstract servant who deserves "love and sympathy." In this way, the obvious power relationship commanded both respect and obligation from the higher and lower.[1]

When Yoda took Luke as a student, an explicit relationship defined by the instructor came into force. Luke had to pass Yoda's initial test to determine whether he possessed intensity. Luke then had to prove commitment and perseverance as his master looked blithely and indifferently at Luke's struggles. Through time and space, Yoda had kept an eye on Luke's progress on Tatooine — presumably through the use of the Force. Dave Lowry (*Autumn Lightning*) was turned away at the door countless times until the reclusive swordmaster saw that he was deeply committed to learning the sword and enduring its hardships.[2]

Yoda, similarly, did not submit to Luke's initial entreaty for instruction. Luke did not even know how to ask for a master swordsman's help. And against his own instincts and experience with Luke's father, Yoda accepted Luke into his tutelage. Yoda hesitated because the skills and abilities he would teach could not be taken lightly and had to be used properly. He also knew how Anakin's well-intentioned training led down the path of the dark side. Most importantly, Yoda had to ask himself whether his student was ready to learn, whether he had the necessary maturity, and whether he had the potential for wisdom. Yoda saw a lack of focus in Luke who yearned for adventure, not discipline. Yoda was fearful of a repeat of Anakin's fall, and fearful of Luke's lack of preparation, especially of his age. While Master Yoda himself is not all-knowing or perfect, it is still up to Luke to prove to his master that he could survive the training, develop the necessary discipline, and ultimately break the cycle of evil found in his father. Indeed, it is at this point that both Yoda and Obi-Wan saw the death of Vader as the only way of saving the universe; an assumption which Luke rejected from the moment Yoda confirmed Vader was indeed his father.

Luke's experience, while not normal to a school of fencing, was that of a fairy tale. Yoda, originally meant to be a frog-like creature, was supposed to be an insignificant animal whom Luke would happen upon as he passed through the forest in his quest for his master. Luke would have to suppress his human pride and listen to the subtle ramblings of a speaking beast. He would have to see the power of nature as a teacher in its smallest forms. The powerful youth would have to submit to what looked to his eyes a weak and silly old creature. Luke would have to humble himself, prove he was ready to learn, and show that he would have the open mind necessary for severe training. Above all else, he had to obey.

In the real world, the problem in finding a teacher was separating the charlatans from the true masters who were talented, experienced, and professional in their standards. Today, the student looking for a martial art must carefully examine the credentials of the instructor. What is his (or her) emphasis in teaching—competition, practice, children, adults, self-defense, making money? How many longtime students does he have? By talking to students, watching practice, discovering where he trained, and asking directly about a teacher's goals, the prospective student can discover clues about an instructor's abilities. Finding the right teacher is often a matter of luck, but it is natural that a student truly committed to learning will seek out and find the best instructor. As an ancient saying goes: When a student is ready to learn, a teacher appears.

The closest approximation to the Jedi Temple is not a military academy or university, but that of a dojo, the Japanese training hall, which is easy to enter and, if training is successful, difficult to leave. Entry is simply a matter of filling out a registration form and paying monthly dues. The rest is up to the student, who may never catch the eye of the headmaster. In classes with a mix of senior and beginning students, the hierarchy of the dojo rules. Sensei looks out for the senior students, who are charged with supervising the progress of their juniors. The beginners must prove themselves worthy of the Seniors' attention through hard training. Even the most experienced martial artist may founder like any new student. The person with previous martial arts experience should not expect anyone to take him under his wing. The more someone expects praise, the less likely he will receive it. Pride is more obvious than anyone would care to admit.

In the *Star Wars* universe, Padawans entered the temple as babies. Students were raised alongside senior Knights, who supervised the progress of the children into their teens. Yoda himself taught young children until they reached the age of thirteen, when Jedi Knights would come to observe children's classes to find an apprentice, whom they would groom, hopefully, into full Jedi

Knighthood. Those who were not chosen were destined for the Agricultural Corps, which served the needy and poor on planets around the universe.

The Jedi were similar to the Jesuits of whom only the solemnly professed had the potential to reach the order's highest ranks. The rest remained spiritual co-adjutors and often continued to serve honestly within the order. Whether it was God's will or a novice's ability to apply himself to his studies, aspiration into full service was considered a privilege. To be meek and self-effacing showed commitment to service, and unrealistic aspirations were outward signs of pride undesired at higher levels. Though bitter as it may seem, a co-adjutor had only the highest respect for his colleagues who met the highest academic and moral standards of the order. The same was true of the Jedi. Anakin had much to learn! While modern laypeople may misjudge the inequity of a hierarchical system, they must also remember that the goal of a spiritual life is not personal aggrandizement, but service to a greater good. This has been indoctrinated in every religious preparatory school as it would have been in the Jedi Temple.

Traditional Fencing Instruction

The overarching idea of the martial arts dojo and manner of instruction was one of submission. Because the teacher's obligation was to teach a pupil to his highest potential, the onus of study and willingness to submit to the master's instructions rested solely on the shoulders of the student. In a dojo, this meant giving up your ego and pride to the student who began training even a day before you. In an environment in which a year's training may have meant rudimentary instruction in the art's techniques, it was not unlikely that a talented student may have felt his skills were superior even to the five-year senior. Recognition by the headmaster, however, comes only in relation to a person's commitment to study. Sometimes, it might never come at all.

A student's relationship with his instructor could be a close and informal one in which direct dialog was a regular part of the learning process. The teacher acted as a personal tutor. Under such circumstances, there was often some individual spark that developed into a friendship. Most teachers, however, because of their responsibilities to all their students, remained aloof, though usually kind and caring. To have the direct link like that of a Jedi Knight and a Padawan was an extremely unusual circumstance, especially in modern dojo where attendance is usually a function of filling out an application. While it was common for senior students to circumspectly guide an individual, the formal relationship of a master and student did not occur until a senior student was permitted the privilege of teaching his own classes.

To be recognized by a teacher required a commitment and self-effacement that seemed contrary to the reward system of modern societies. The apprentice system flew in the face of a university's awarding of a higher degree, which simply amounts to the completion of an institution's curriculum. Similarly, the conferrence of a black belt is secondary to the knowledge and skills that a person has mastered. Even in the university system, the greatest learning occurs not from obtaining a degree or multiple degrees, but from studying under the most respected professors in a particular field.

While money was often necessary to care for basic necessities, the idea that a student was paying for one's knowledge was repugnant to the learning process. Fencing masters did need to support themselves, but their goal was the formation of young minds that are the foundation for a future society. It was crass to talk to a headmaster about payment. A student paid a fee for an opportunity, not the right to impose his will on a teacher. In traditional Japanese schools (ryuha), students were required to sign pledges (*kishomon*) not to reveal the secrets of the style.[3]

Swordmasters understood implicitly that their obligation was a far greater commitment than the work exerted by even the most diligent students. Not only have they already gone through the apprenticeship process, they were now responsible for its proper continuation. No matter how hard the student worked to meet their master's expectations, it was far harder to create the curriculum for their students than to follow it. While a minimum standard of knowledge must be met—knowledge of forms (*kata*), the ability to execute technique, and the proper spirit of mind—the master was constantly adjusting to the needs of his student's strengths and abilities. Teaching is not a skill to be learned through book learning or completion of a course but one that takes years of experience. Even those that have become successful know there is always something new to learn and that continued success is not guaranteed.

It was out of selflessness that the greatest teachers answered the call to become masters. He did not desire a cult of sycophants, nor did he advocate a particular agenda other than the proper training of his students. Abuses of this obligation have led to the establishment of private armies by warlords, petty princes, praetorian guards, and outright dictators. Perhaps in the politics of the nation in which a fencing master found himself, he could not avoid the machinations of the political process unfolding in the surrounding land around his school. His commitment to one political side or another would be the greatest test of the master teacher. The survival of his life may have hinged on his decision but so did his school of fencing and its students. They might have become puppets of politicians, who saw their abilities as a means to their political end.[4] The Jedi Council understands this more fully than the casual observer would think. Indeed, it was the allegiance to the Jedi Order that led to its eventual extermination in Episode III.

All teachers, whether the most experienced or the newest to the profession, must create an environment conducive to learning. Often this is determined by the teacher's demeanor, whether a person is rough, vivacious, petty, hard, considerate, or even inconsiderate. The worst teachers are bullies, unworthy of their title. They goad, annoy, and even threaten their students. The best teachers are both hard and resilient, strong and yet supple in their teaching. They command and their orders are carried out not because of fear, but because of trust.

The amygdala in the brain regulates the body's fear mechanism. When a person fears some situation, the amygdala causes an endocrinological response that begins to shut down the cortex and prepares the body for physical danger. If the student is in a continual state of fear or anxiety when a teacher enters the room, the cortex, the heart of the brain in which learning takes place, is not free to function normally. So, from the teacher's first point of contact with a student, confidence and not fear must be the student's initial reaction. This was even more imperative for the swordmaster whose job it was to teach the student to be fearless in the most fearful of circumstances.

Master teachers must teach competence, critical thinking, and creativity. And whether they start with a formal education in fencing such as that obtained from a nationally licensed body or from informal study and experience in bouting, training, and, though rarely these days, from battlefield experience, the teacher must impart a body of knowledge and then get the student to apply himself to that instruction. The onus of a master swordsman then is a delicate task of encouraging without patronizing. His students will recognize meaningless and repeated praise. Baby talk or terse instruction that has the appearance of talking down to the student's intelligence also impedes the process. The master must be both intimate and distant; he must lead and not coerce. He must know the specifics of a student's abilities, but he must not give him attention that might make the student think he is getting special consideration. The instructor must demonstrate techniques that are beyond the reach of his students so that they may aspire to what they are not yet ready to accomplish, but he must not give too many advanced techniques that are still beyond the ken of the student's ability to perform.[5] Like a tantalizing apple, techniques must be within sight but just a little out of reach in order to move the student forward. Perfect execution of technique is always a requirement of the master, though he must also realize that the student is not any more capable of doing a technique the first time than is a baby grasping a mother's finger for the first time. In time, all will be accomplished.

The ability to "make" a student do his best is a difficult feat. Quite often it is a question of being firm, yet sometimes indignant at the hint of a student's slacking attitude. A reassuring voice, however, is often the key to soothing an anxious heart. This is especially so, since failure before the eyes of one's teacher is an ever-present anxiety in the dojo. Even the student with the most bravado harbors an inward fear, else he would not need to perform so obvious a display. And yet the swordmaster must give only the slightest suggestion or word of advice.

Yoda spoke in short aphorisms not dissimilar to Zen koans. Lucas, with Leigh Brackett and Lawrence Kasdan, decided deliberately to have Yoda talk in proverbs and commandments. Irvin Kershner, director of Episode V, was personally interested in Zen Buddhism, distilling some of the slight nuances of Yoda's character from what he knew of Zen.[6]

Often instructors on the mat teach in a similar way. During instruction, which usually lasts between one and two hours, the instructor both demonstrates skills and observes his students. Whatever the format, the martial arts class is a series of supervised drills. Each comment a master gives, whether to an individual or the whole class, is an immediate critique of their performance. He gives immediate feedback on their process. The comment may be a suggestion for improvement or it may be criticism of a technique's execution. The student may understand exactly how to correct the problem. Quite often, he knows exactly what to do but does not have the physical skills to execute the movement and fails. The master gives only a lifeline that keeps the student from drowning. He cannot make the student swim; it is up to the student. An instructor cannot correct every mistake one or every student makes. He must address the most grievous problems, and when spoken by an excellent teacher, a critique meant for a particular individual sounds to every student as if it applies to them.

In aikido, a student finds extreme satisfaction in being chosen to partner with the teacher for a demonstration. And during regular practice when everyone is practicing a demonstrated movement, an instructor may interrupt a pair practicing together. Certainly, the chosen student whom the instructor chooses feels special attention, as the other must sit quietly watching his partner train with the instructor. Often, however, it is the instructor's intention to show the watching student subtleties in a technique. Clever students realize that every moment of direct instruction, if even of a duration of fifteen seconds, is a gift from the instructor to the student.

Anakin received this kind of instruction several times in Episode I. When Ric Olié taught Anakin the ship's cockpit controls, it was up to Anakin to remember and learn. Qui-Gon told Anakin to "be mindful ... always remember, your focus determines your reality." Anakin took Qui-Gon's instructions to heart when he was told to stay in the cockpit of the Naboo fighter, which would inevitably carry him into the dogfight above the planet. In Episode II, it was Obi-Wan who acknowledged that Anakin was already quite independent and capable of saving Obi-Wan's life. Later, in Episode III, Anakin showed a growing arrogance. While both Obi-Wan in Episode I and Anakin in Episode III demonstrated their indebtedness to their master's instruction, a growing self-assuredness had to be tempered by humility.

A teacher's lack of attention, or even indifference, is the greatest source of anxiety for novices. Without a strong feeling of mastery, a student naturally desires a guide. And for every moment a teacher spends with one particular individual, there is a majority of students who feel as if they are not significant enough to be attended to. The student's inclination is to desire praise, which underscores one's desire to have a master who will give him personal attention. Little do they realize that when an instructor is working with someone else, he is demonstrating to everyone, including the student. This is little solace to those who feel neglected, especially those who put out so much effort in trying to do their best. The fact is, however, that not every beginner deserves attention. They must earn attention through humble practice, which formalizes their technique before teachers who are observing students more often than they think.

Students naturally desire to be recognized by their teachers. This desire is in itself an attachment motivated by greed. Feelings of accomplishment are not the ordinary staple of regular practice. Experienced students understand this and no longer base the success of a practice on whether the instructor pays any attention to them. Improvement is obtained not through praise, but through practice.

In kendo, the custom for beginners is to drill endlessly with seniors. It is not uncommon for a student to train for months or even a year before being permitted to don armor. On occasion, a lesser student might be permitted the privilege, but an experienced and patient student knows there must be some reason for this. It is not simply done on a whim. Training must continue diligently even to the point of nausea from exhaustion. A student is expected to turn away from practice, facing a wall for a moment to compose himself, before returning to training. Sometimes drills are so grueling that a person has to muster every ounce of energy to keep from crying. Half expecting pity from sensei, one could hope for even a moment of reprieve in the practice. Instead, a student will be encouraged to practice even harder than before, and always the good student strives to make this possible even if they fail. That is the mark of a good teacher.

Discipline of Apprenticeship

One the fundamental issues students of traditional martial arts must grapple with is the need to exert their independent creativity in a system that demands the subordination of one's ego to the will of another person. The dojo's environment seems to fly in the face of the creativity modern students are raised to expect when they endeavor any artistic expression.

All artists believe creativity is the heart of their artistic expression, but not until an artist finds himself under the strict tutelage of a master does he discover the true meaning of creativity, that source of energy that drives the soul forward and compels the artist to create. Georgia O'Keeffe was once asked if discipline was not a hindrance to her artistic creativity. She responded by saying that it was not creativity in the first place if it could survive the test of discipline.

While a master with strict expectations seems to tell a student to suppress his personal inclinations, the discipline of staying one's natural inclinations, desires, and intuitions pushes the creative soul to stretch its limits. It forces the artist to put himself in a new box in which he can discover something new or assimilate a manner or method that improves the present state of his "suppressed" creativity. To paraphrase O'Keeffe's retort: if discipline destroys your creativity, you were never meant to have it. Creativity is tenacious and defiant. It knows no master, no matter how hard someone tries to suppress it.

The final expression of any martial art was a test in the uncertainty of a real fight. Unpredictability creates a stress on the intellect and pushes the body to meet the cognitive expectations that are needed to defeat the concerted attack of another person. The act of foiling an opponent trying to kill you with his sword is nothing less than a creative enterprise. It is that fact that makes the combative nature of fighting such a tragic event. Throughout history, around the world, men and women of the greatest potential were trained to kill each other when they could have focused all their energies on peaceful purposes.

The modern swordsman, because of the evolved nature of war (and probably because of luck), enjoyed the luxury of learning the martial discipline of swordsmanship and used it as a peaceful means of self-expression and growth. Swordsmanship preserved an honor code that had enriched culture and society because it valued the spoken word over the written contract. If it were not for discipline, no man would have had the will to suppress his natural inclinations to take an easy path, which often entailed the breaking of one's word. Individuals learned to keep their word just as they learned to be courageous on the battlefield. Society, as reflected in its literature, valued the man who subordinated his will to the greater good of others. So, when a gentleman gave his word, he upheld a standard rarely found in modern litigious society.

The suppression of the will, a good working definition of discipline, is a test that separates the dutiful student from the pretender. At the aikido hombu dojo in Tokyo, the student, whether Japanese or foreign, continually battles the disinterest of the teachers. The secretary who registers new students at the front desk gives the simple instruction that the main dojo is on the third floor and the change room is next to it.

The excellent teacher never needs to look for students. If the discipline of his art has not molded his character, which serves as the demonstrative expression of his skill, then he never developed the mastery of his art. A master does not need to demonstrate his mastery; it manifests itself in the very essence of the person: how he carries himself, how he handles the ordinary or stressful situation, how he drinks his tea.

Dave Lowry recounts a story told by his master of a man who came up to the swordmaster seeking instruction in swordsmanship. To test the man, he raised his sword as if he were going to strike him down. Noticing his calm, he told the man that he was already a master. But of what? The man explained that he had no discipline to apply himself to any activity, especially the martial arts. He concluded he would die very quickly and after serious contemplation of his predicament, he came to the realization that he should no longer be afraid to die. The swordmaster looked at the man and said he had nothing to teach him because "to overcome life and death is to know the greatest mastery."[7] This imperturbability manifests itself in the very slightest action. No one can take away the fear one feels before combat, but the true swordmaster is its complete master.

Discipline forces a student to learn on his own without the help or the prodding of an instructor. Ultimately, it is the student who is responsible for his own learning. "A student has to steal from the instructor what he can."[8] The student's discipline eventually transforms technique into an art. If the artist relies on the assistance of outsiders to create his art, it is, in principle, tainted and corrupt. That is not to say that there cannot be any help from others, but that the ultimate responsibility for artistic expression resides within the student. The mastery of art is never easily obtained. All art is the conjoined expression of an individual's toil, dedication, determination, and resolution.

Struggle and hardship in life are the greatest test of one's character. It separates humans from animals and their animal instincts. Man's conscious ability to subordinate his will and sacrifice it for others out of a sense of justice or righteousness is a distinct line separating himself from lesser creatures. If a starving man were to steal a loaf of bread, he can be dismissed for behaving like an animal by following his instincts. The true man of personal honor would rather die than descend to the level of an animal. An even greater man would humble himself, suppress his pride, and employ his intellect to ask for the loaf instead of taking it by force of arms.

Despite the general aversion to hardship, art improves during economic hardship because there is something over which the artist can express himself. Indeed, the imperative is one of life or death. In the most trying of times, a person feels every emotion to its greatest degree: anger, hate, love, compassion.

It is a matter of struggling to raise one's soul without falter or failure and remain above the pettiness that is so common.

In Kurosawa's *The Seven Samurai*, a band of helpless villagers obtain the services of samurai to protect them from thieving bandits demanding their harvest of rice at the end of the planting season. The wise man of the village said that in order to find samurai who would work for the meager subsistence that was their harvest, one would have to find starving samurai. Powerful and prideful are samurai, the villagers said, as they contemplated their search for a samurai. Yet they *did* find a samurai who, through the goodness of his heart, was willing to sacrifice his life for villagers who would subsist on millet in order to pay the samurai with three meals of rice a day for their services.

There is a belief in Japan that the spirit is indomitable and permits the body to accomplish unbelievable, mind-over-matter feats. The force of a person's will, or his passion to accomplish something allows the body to surpass its limits. Since the intellect is the safety mechanism that reins in the physicality of the body, it goes without saying that subordinating the intellect to the will can allow the spirit to attain its full potential.

This appeal to suppress desires of the flesh was considered a healthy expression in the search for enlightenment. The ordinary Japanese engages in ritual acts of purification that seem absurd to citizens of countries in which access to personal and physical pleasure is an inherent right of living within society. Cleaning in Japan is considered an act of personal purification symbolic of the cleaning of the soul. Every year on New Year's Day, Japanese do their spring cleaning as a way to wash away the old year and welcome in the new. This is also why students of the martial arts are expected to ritually clean the floor after practice. It is an act of purification to submit to the humblest of actions after the most empowering of activities.

Ascetics all over the world see perfection of the soul in the perfection of the body. Yoga masters perform incredible feats of their body through extreme belief and practice. The ritual of a repeated mantra and profession of faith helps raise the state of the soul, as does quiet contemplation or prayer. Self-flagellation and the wearing of a sack cloth are Christian expressions of denial of the bodily pleasure of the flesh; meditating in the snow or naked under the frigid flow of a winter waterfall are Asian methods. At the aikido hombu dojo, windows are opened during daily winter practice. There is no heater and the windows remain open in cold wind and even snow. Though there is a hot water heater, it is never turned on. The building itself is simple, frugal, and unimposing, and yet it attracts the best students of the world for training. It is through the denial of pleasure that there is the possibility of touching the ethereal world. Through ascetic denial, one awaits, but cannot expect, inspiration, epiphany, the touch of God.

This is the reason why the Jedi Code would prohibit Anakin from taking Padmé as a wife. And while there is much evidence in the real world that physical pleasures of the flesh are not incompatible with a religious vocation, there was a strong tradition that a Jedi was already married to the Order in the same way that the priest is married to the Church. Celibacy has had a long history among religious, ascetics, and mystics. The physical expression of love and shared companionship are basic needs. It is, therefore, among the most difficult sacrifices a person can make.

Enduring hardship underscores the fact that no focused work is pointless if it develops the person and allows him or her to change and grow. Dedication develops character, attention to detail, and the refinement of the soul. And despite the ordeal of the struggle, there is often a joy that seems to express itself in the demeanor of the best dojo. Students still enjoy themselves and their practice. No command or order is taken as punitive and expressions of laughter and camaraderie cannot be stifled. It is not the simple satisfaction of accomplishment, but the joy of simply existing in the moment.

For swordsmen, training had to be seen as essential, for his life depended on his skills. For the modern swordsman, however, while the imperative of killing is no longer the focus of practice, it does not mean that there should be any less intensity in training. The inner joy of tiny achievements through the honing of skills enables a modern swordsman to survive an encounter with real swordsmen in battle. The Jedi could have just as easily understood this imperative in their daily practice, for it is inherent in the art of the sword.

The joy of students after training certainly reflects the accomplishments of practice, but it is only temporary and brief. Students revel in it momentarily and then continue with practice. As Eugene Herrigal said in *Zen in the Art of Archery*, the archer, after loosing his arrow, "steps quietly into the background."[9] Training begins, finishes, and begins again.

Training

The student's first command is to begin practice with an open mind. This openness leads to trust. He must trust his master without judgment, which truly means a trust in one's self. Trust, in turn, leads to respect, and respect to confidence. Even upon mastering the basics, the student is still charged to develop his own repertoire of techniques. No matter how technically imitative he is of his teacher's technique, the student must master technique in his own fashion. The Japanese refer to this as *shu, ha, ri. Shu* insists on the complete adherence to orthodoxy in the memorization, practice, and display of techniques. *Ha* describes the destruction of those basic forms learned during early training. *Ri* refers to a new acceptance of the basic techniques into the manner of the individual's style and ability. He makes the techniques he has learned his own.[10]

In the traditional dojo, the beginning student starts training by learning how to serve tea. It teaches servitude. It humbles the most physically powerful person. It forces the strongest ego to obey. It is also a way to test the character of a student who manifests his strengths and weaknesses in his manners at the table; in the way he approaches the table, how he picks up the tea kettle, the manner in which he places down the cups before pouring, and how appropriately in the host's conversation he retrieves their empty cups. Every moment around the master is one of a test, and while most of us fail at some point in our daily activity, the master also recognizes this as part of the process. While the student may feel demeaned by the expectation to serve tea, he may not realize that the sensei is also introducing the potential swordsman to a cultured society. And not only does the master learn about the student, the student is also introduced to his guests by his very presence as a tea server.

During practice, especially in the free-flowing practice of aikido, which is essentially swordsmanship without the sword, there is a tendency for Western students to intellectualize their way through verbal practice. While there is an internal dialogue in the routine of regular practice, it is not a conversation. A student learns movement not through talking his way through a kata, but by actually doing it. "In the martial and other traditional Japanese arts, knowledge of the cerebral sort matters less than *understanding*—learning acquired by the heart rather than by the intellect."[11]

There are two methods of learning in the martial arts—behavioral and cognitive. The former teaches through experience and practice, training the body and its systems to react and operate efficiently under the challenging circumstances of a fight. The body is trained to perform particular actions in a certain order without hesitation. Reflexes are matured and the stamina and musculature are developed to carry out the movement needed for the execution of technique. Concurrently, the hormonal system is pumping the body with its natural chemicals, which heighten awareness and permit rapid and instantaneous execution of the mind's will. Instead of continually asking questions, the student needs to simply practice and forgo his tendency to ask if the particular execution of movement was correct. An aspect of behavioral learning includes "muscle memory" from repetitive movement and kinesthetics. Behavioral learning includes a broad set of skills related to the physiology of the human body.

Cognitive learning, the other half of mastering a martial system, refers to the brain's retrieval of information from the person's history of learning. Where behavioral learning deals with the physical movement and control of the body, cognitive brain function determines what moves a person does and in what order to perform them. The mind cognitively examines the situation and determines the best attacks, defenses, and counter actions based on its storehouse of information. A harmony between behavioral and cognitive functions of the body leads to an efficient performance of body movement needed for sword-work or any other martial art.

In the heat of an attack, there is no time for conversation. There is only time for the action of defeating your opponent as efficiently as possible. Once the amygdala has mastered the fight-or-flight mechanism, the mind is calm enough to save the body. As opposed to relying on an anticipatory fear and haphazardly adjusting to the situation ("picking up the pieces," as it were), the mind must allow the body to act according to reference experiences that make the individual fearless in the face of impending death. Relying on emotions leads to the possibility of mistakes instead of a cool examination of the situation. Nick Gillard, sword fight choreographer for the Prequel Trilogy, said this was the essence of why Obi-Wan defeated Anakin on Mustafar in Episode III.

All learning is to be changed by knowledge. And in a situation in which an opponent has a weapon designed to extinguish a person's life, self-defense training must immediately flow from the mind. Disciplined and repetitive training prepares the body for movement. Free training and competition allows the body to use the body's skills to create a strategy that can defeat an opponent who is simultaneously trying to defeat the martial artist. Yoda's chiding of Luke spoke profoundly to the imperative of allowing a resolution to find itself during combat. "There is no try. There is only do. That is why you fail."

There are two ways of encouraging any enterprise. The first is to say that failure is okay: "Let's move on and try again." The second is to say that there is a goal that needs to be met — success is the only answer and we must find it. To achieve the highest caliber of a person, the second must be the mentality for successful combat. You must survive. But in order to reach this point there must be room for the admission of failure up until the fateful moment of a duel. In the real world of a fight, there is only one mentality — do or do not.

Practice is the place for failure, though practice is a continual striving for perfection. In ordinary drilling, it cannot be any more emphasized that technique needs to be practiced as perfectly as can be mastered. To do otherwise would be to perfect imperfect movement. When a student lunges during drill, he or she must do so with the intention of making it the most perfect lunge possible. There must be perfect form, perfect balance, perfect execution of the different parts of the body. If an instructor were to let the student do half-lunges, or lunges with a slightly turned ankle, the likelihood of him doing the same during the uncertainty of a real bout is more probable. In the case of the turned ankle, it is more likely that the high energy of a bout will cause the fencer to twist his ankle.

In a metaphorical sense, fencing is likened to Plato's theory of forms. Fencing, like all other activities, seeks to accomplish a goal. In the case of sword fighting, the goal is to strike your opponent with your weapon. Based on all the factors of where the sword is and what the opponent is doing, there is an ideal attack that, in the mind, can be executed most directly and efficiently for any given point. What the fencer must do is to execute his attack as closely to the ideal attack as possible. To want to do less would be an unnecessary expenditure of energy. The ideal is perfection, the execution is the attempt at perfection, and the strike on target is the intended goal. Of course, the perfect execution of an act may not be possible in this world, but neither is the goal impossible. A person seeks standards with which he can compare himself, and because of the life-and-death nature of swordsmanship, they ought not be anything less than the highest. There may be more than one approach in obtaining a target, but a hit a fraction of an inch away from the intended target is still sufficient to accomplish the fencer's goal. Fencing is the art of the possible but it strives for perfection; and perfection implies the exact control of the weapon, complete grace of movement and action, and the attainment of the goal. This perfection is beauty in the conceptual sense, but also in the physical sense. There is nothing more beautiful than the perfect execution of an attack that even the opponent must appreciate and acknowledge.

In Asian martial arts, instruction is taught through kata, forms of predetermined and precise movement that contain a series of techniques to be mastered. The master provides this model of perfection for a technique, and the student must discern the essence of the movement in his mind and try to imitate it. He is not imitating the exact movement of the teacher because every movement reflects the circumstances of the teacher in relation to the person with whom he is training. The student is imitating the ideas embodied in the demonstration and then applying them to his own movement.

A story is told about a photographer who asked Morihei Ueshiba, founder of aikido, to repeat a move that he liked so he could photograph it. Ueshiba Sensei tried to recreate the movement, but to the consternation of the photographer, he could not do it. Finally, Ueshiba told the photographer that technique is free flowing and amorphous, and that whatever technique he saw was a product of the circumstances of that moment. This is what makes the master indispensable to the student, and the reason it is important that the newest beginners be exposed to the best instruction, that of the headmaster himself. Each student in the end is responsible for his education, but excellent teachers are vital to the development of that student.

During a beginner's training, there is the inevitable desire for the student's body to take the path of least resistance, which is analogous to the repeated warnings from Yoda and Obi-Wan that the path to the dark side is easier and more seductive. The student's body only knows one way of moving. With training, his body is being commanded to move itself in new and more demanding ways. In an attempt to practice this new movement, the body resorts to a previous comfort level, which often runs counter to the proper execution of martial techniques the student is learning. The body rebels against the new movement because the relief of pain is a greater imperative during practice than fulfilling the cognitive ideal the mind is trying to achieve: the production of new musculature and reflexive systems. Compared to a hopelessly reactive defense in the face of danger, the training of a martial system produces efficient and specialized movement.

The ultimate goal is the physical execution of any technique the mind commands the body to perform. The threshold of mastery is to be able to do any technique 100 percent of the time. In a combat situation, time travels in slow motion and the body acts without any thought and yet remains within complete control. The heartbeat races and blood, testosterone, and endorphins race through the body. Training allows an individual to move in ways to protect himself. It allows him to make life and death decisions that save not only one's own life, but also that of the attacker.

While the success of winning a fight can make a person feel powerful, the true test of one's skill, however, is how he faces failure. Fighting is for self-preservation, never to teach someone a lesson. In a scene cut from Episode I, Anakin gets in a fight with Greedo, who was a child at the time, accusing Anakin of cheating during the pod race. Qui-Gon ends up pulling Anakin off Greedo and chides the boy, saying that even if you defeat Greedo once, he's still liable to return to pick another fight. Qui-Gon continues that Anakin cannot use force to make someone come over to his way of thinking. This is a lesson some people never learn in their entire life.

Jedi Training

Unlike the established testing systems of the martial art dojo, the training that has been shown in the *Star Wars* movies to date indicate two methods of training Jedi. These depended, of course, on the circumstances of two time periods: the height of the Republic and the heyday of the Jedi Order, and a post–Jedi period after the extermination and purging of the Jedi Order during the time of the Empire. A rough correlation of the Japanese kyu-dan ranking system can be seen in the Jedi training system: pre–Padawan status represents kyu ranking, while dan (black belt level) corresponds to the Padawan period when a student is attached specifically to a Jedi Knight for the final preparation of his masterly level, that of full knighthood status.

The prequel movies did not actually reveal much about Jedi training methods. A class of children wielding short lightsabers (which are purportedly benign blades that cannot cut flesh) was seen in Episode II. Dooku, Qui-Gon, and Obi-Wan trained under Yoda in this way. With Yoda as their instructor the scene vaguely alluded to the beginner's mind (a child-like mind), which is necessary for enlightenment in Zen Buddhism. But there was no actual training taking place. One did not see the Jedi attending classes; they did not participate in debates or self-defense classes. The "trials" Obi-Wan was supposedly prepared for were never fully explained because Obi-Wan was granted the title of Jedi Master at the end of Episode I.

Luke Skywalker went through a very different and personal manner of training. He did not have the resources of the Jedi Temple and the training he received from Yoda was learned under unconventional and difficult circumstances. Obi-Wan, in the brief time he spent with Luke, worked on some simple training with seeker balls on the *Millennium Falcon*, but the most important contribution the elder Obi-Wan gave to Luke was to convince him to begin Jedi training. Sacrificing his own life so that Luke and his companions might live and his subsequent visitation at the beginning of Episode V convinced Luke to seek out a new instructor; one who trained Obi-Wan when he himself had become a Padawan at the Jedi Temple — Yoda.

Starting with the traditional method of physical conditioning to which any new recruit is familiar, Luke began to feel the pain in his muscles as he strained to physically mold himself into a man who would have to endure unknowable hardships. Raised as a boy in the remote and inhospitable clime of Tatooine, he had already had firsthand knowledge of an unforgiving world. At his very doorstep came imperial troops who summarily killed his aunt and uncle, forcing him to leave his home and answer the call to become a Jedi. As in any tragedy, man is confronted by the hideous circumstances that will either render the protagonist something less than a man or it will test his mettle, allowing him to retain his identity as a human being who can and will face challenges even if it means his own destruction.

Yoda already knew the circumstances of Luke's birth, yet it was not for him to reveal the fact that Luke's own father was responsible for the destruction of the great Jedi Order. Yoda had to prepare Luke for his future encounters not by indoctrinating him into a political mold, but by teaching him respect, courage, justice, and loyalty. When Luke finally learned of his family's secret, it was no longer in Yoda's hands to command Luke to a particular course of action. Yoda may have attempted to convince Luke of one plan or another, but when it comes to training swordsmen, the inherent reality is that they will one day have the power and the will to discover a destiny of their own. The neophyte fencing teacher will soon discover their student's independence. The master's only charge is proper training, not the living out of their apprentice's life. It is hoped, however, that a master's instruction will be enough to allow the apprentice to make the proper decisions based on firm concepts of justice, honor, and a deep trust in peace.

After all of Luke's physical training, Yoda told Luke of a cave powerful in the Force. Luke himself felt drawn to it and approached. He asked what was inside. Yoda replied, "Only what you take with you." Admonishing Luke not to take his weapons, Luke still hooked his utility belt with lightsaber and blaster to his waist as he turned away from his master to enter his first test.

Luke encountered Vader. He struck him down, and then saw his own face in Vader's mask. Though it was Vader's specter who approached Luke with an ignited lightsaber, it was Luke who, out of fear, immediately struck out at Vader. We, the audience, like the master of a young swordsman, knew that the events of the cave were portents of a life that was yet to come. Luke, as he learns the power of Jedi training, may yet become like Vader. Lucas's message, however, was that all swordsmen have the potential to become evil, and more frightening still is that every person, no matter how innocent and caring as a child, also bears a similar possibility.

The cave sequence was not a realistic test, but a cinematographic exposition that allowed the movie-goer to leave the world of reality for that of the mind. In this case, action spoke louder than conversation, the simple premonition of the final confrontation between Luke and Vader. This certainly was not a standard test that the Jedi Temple would be able to recreate in some kind of spiritual holographic room that could read the mind's greatest fears and then test the individual's mettle.

A cave strong in the Force was a literary device easily used in books and film to get the audience to go through the same experience without the possibility of personally failing. For individuals in today's society, as it will be later for Luke, the audience's trials come not from presuppositions and "what if" scenarios. They come from actual tests in life, which in turn become tests of humanity. They manifest themselves in an individual's greatest life decisions and in daily life — from the decision to commit to a marriage, to join the military, or to become a nurse, as well as during a simple stroll down a street when a beggar holds out his cup. These are the true tests that determine who an individual is and who or what he is to become.

Fortunately, the audience can live the swordsman's life through proxy in *Star Wars* without having to bear the burden of real suffering. In Episode V, Luke was still brash and impetuous. He left his training and his masters and then became fearful that he would fall prey to the dark side like his father. The rich symbolism of this film shows Luke's arrogance and his fear, his impending doom, and that of the universe. When he confronted Vader, he lost, as should any swordsman who breaks away from his training before he is ready. But Luke was not without choices. Upon hearing that Vader was really his father, Luke resisted the temptation to join his father and sent himself off the edge of the precipice at the end of the metal gantry during the final acts of their lightsaber fight. Luke's survival was a literary device, an exposition on Luke's shattered ego, his humiliation, and his humbling. Without resorting to tragedy, Lucas, like a Greek god, preserved his actor for another encounter.

Luke had a second chance to face Vader in Episode VI. At the beginning of the movie, Luke entered in the priest-like colors of black. He was reserved, more mature and confronted Jabba fearlessly. He did not leave his execution to extemporaneous action. Luke had already developed a plan, using his intelligence as well as his martial skills to extricate himself and his friends from the clutches of Jabba the Hutt.

His first venture was a success; Han was safe, the notorious gangster dead, and their attention could then turn to the defeat of the Emperor. Luke returned to Yoda to complete his training, but Yoda was at the twilight of his life. Even if Luke could continue to train under Yoda, his ultimate test would not depend on the perfection of technique so much as mindfulness of the learning he had already received. Just like Obi-Wan in Episode IV, Yoda must vanish before Luke faces his ultimate challenge. Luke has to assume the responsibility of his own actions without the help of his mentor. In his confrontation with Vader, Luke reached out to Anakin of the past, not the Vader created by Palpatine. Just as he did in Episode V when Vader offered him a place by his side, Luke rejected the Emperor's offer to take Vader's place.

By shutting down his lightsaber, Luke took the high moral road of the light side and was willing to sacrifice himself. The reality, however, presented a moral dilemma that could have been, in itself, untenable. By sacrificing himself, he would at least deny his use to the evil plans of the Emperor. His sacrifice at the hands of Vader and the Emperor was the greatest good Luke could do, but was it the greatest good he could do for the universe? Not attacking Vader and the Emperor would allow them to continue their reign of terror and evil in the universe. Luke would have failed to achieve the goal of destroying the leadership that commanded the Empire, the very objective of the rebel fleet attacking the second Death Star. This was the moral question that moral individuals must answer.

Vader drew Luke closer to the dark side when he discovered the existence of Luke's sister Leia, which drove Luke into a rage. The possibility of losing Leia to Vader gave Luke a focus. He ignited his lightsaber and attacked Vader in a powerful demonstration of brute force. Vader could not take the onslaught manifested in Luke's love for his sister, and the Dark Lord was beaten down by the young Jedi's raw determination. But at the very moment he could destroy Vader, Luke realized that though he had the power to strike Vader down, wisdom had to stay his hand. Consciously, though with reluctance, Luke gave up the lightsaber, denying the Emperor both his abilities and his weapon. In the tradition of an epic, Luke's faith in his father and his friends allowed him to conquer the Emperor when Vader turned from the dark side. Repeating the cinematic phrase from Episode V when Luke threw himself off the gantry on Bespin, the Emperor was thrown into the pit by Vader, as if Satan had been cast back into Hell.

Unlike the ad-hoc preparation Luke went through in the Original Trilogy, Episode I illustrated a more reflective and prayer-like kind of preparation learned in the more formal training of the Jedi Temple. In the moments before the final battle between Darth Maul and Qui-Gon Jinn, Qui-Gon dropped down to his knees and meditatively prepared for their imminent confrontation. That powerful moment captured the mental and even sacred preparation a swordsman goes through when confronting the possibility of his own destruction. Like soldiers before a battle, mass was said and clerics sought to give solace to human beings confronting the impending moment of their death. The swordsman's momentary reflection was not defeatist — it was preparation for the inevitable reality of combat.

The pursuit of any martial skill requires a deep understanding of an individual's motivation. Is it a lust for power to rule others? Is it to avenge a past wrong? These were the same questions that concerned Yoda and the Jedi Council when they considered the appropriateness of training the gifted Anakin Skywalker. The goal of all martial arts is not the reliance on power but its wise and judicious use. Training is meant to teach humility in the use of skills, and the reining in of one's temptation for power. Wisdom means nothing without the discipline to know when to draw the sword or to stay its use. This is the greatest repayment a student can give to his master.

The danger of the master-apprentice system is the implicit reliance on obedience, which is meant to instill discipline and to prepare the mind for learning. Students are expected to implicitly imitate the technique that is put before them even though their own intellect is telling them that there is probably a better and easier way to accomplish the same act without the punishment of hard and severe training. Though this may seem to go against common sense when one understands the apprentice system, it would be unnatural for a student not to question his instructors. Despite the fact that swordsmen have been training in swordsmanship for hundreds of years, each new novice will exhibit the unwillingness to accept that the instruction they are receiving is already the easiest road to the mastery of technique.

Westerners are well versed in the tradition of doubt. It is the impetus for revolution, creativity, and re-birth. From the earliest days, parents and teachers attempt to imbue in their children and students a sense of identity and individualism while at the same time demanding that they conform to the norms of behavior to which parents and teachers were subjected. But a flippant disregard for a master's instructions is a perversion of the apprentice system. Where the master swordsman may not be competent in arts of chemistry or medicine, he is a master of his own art, and it is not for students to question the master's motivation or his intentions. His intentions are already higher than the beginning student can even imagine.

A master through the voice of his command is really asking for the student to trust in his wisdom. Often, however, in the student's desire for autonomy, independence, and recognition, he prematurely questions the authority of the master and his harsh demands. It is out of kindness that an instructor pushes a student harder than he could ever push himself. If a student were to ask permission to do one drill of head strikes in kendo called *kakari-geiko*, a good sensei would ask, "Why not two?" and then make the student do the drill three times. Karaki-geiko is symbolic of the nature of the master-apprentice system in swordsmanship. In drilling of all sword styles, the master offers up his body to be struck so that his student may learn. The last action in kakari-geiko is the student striking his sensei on the top of the head. It is like the Bodhisattva of Theravada Buddhism who foregoes his enlightenment so that he may help others to enlightenment before him. In Western drills, the master allows his student the practice of hitting the master, who is wearing a thick protective jacket. It is proper etiquette for the student to thank the instructor for a lesson; in Japan they bow solemnly.

Western students are always tempted to give up one teacher in favor of the search for the perfect teacher. The freedom and ease of registering at the front door leaves a modern student with the impression that he is also free to leave as he or she wishes. This is precisely the reason that new students do not receive the attention of the master. The student must demonstrate his dedication, not the master. And yet, this is precisely what happened to Anakin in Episode II. He began on the road to the dark side by questioning the role of his instructors and choosing a way of his own, free of the constraints of a master's training.

Yoda in later years revealed himself to Luke in stages. First, as a quizzical and diminutive creature, then as a host in his own home, and finally, as the great instructor who in fairy tale fashion can literally commune with the dead. The fear of a student's departure was reason for a master's hesitancy in taking on a student. And yet, the instructor must not give in to *his* fear. He must trust the student as the student trusts the master.

The master must in due course diminish the student's ego, a self-effacement that will become a strength when ability begins to match the most advanced techniques of the style. If he learned that raw power only bows to raw power, the swordsman's soul would be put in jeopardy. The tradition of imparting knowledge from a master to an apprentice was the best assurance that the lust for power, for which the Force is a metaphor, does not take hold in the student's education.

The transformation of Anakin into Vader was a device of storytelling to make clear in concise terms what takes years for a student of the sword to learn. *Star Wars* in its brevity taught the greatest lessons a swordsman will ever, or, if fortune wills it, never have to face in his lifetime.

For the Master, the satisfaction that a student had learned the wisdom of swordsmanship is compelling and profound. The learning that teachers give their students lasts for a lifetime. From the simplest act of learning how to tie one's shoes, to matching letters with sounds, to the invention of a new technology that will revolutionize the world, the gift of learning infinitely changes the individual's life. But teachers and masters are but helpers in the process. As someone once put it, teachers are simply students with a longer history of learning. Teachers are only made great by the students who, in their actions, become great people in their own right.

Within the master-apprentice system was the understanding that a good teacher asked the hardest question their students could handle. The great teacher, a master, however, gets students to ask the hardest questions of themselves. It has never been shown that Darth Vader has ever had his own student, but *Star Wars* Unleashed, a video game in which the player takes on the persona of a secret Vader apprentice, demonstrates the allure to the dark side. The temptation to achieve success in life through greed, power, and control remains a constant challenge for every new generation.

In Episode V, Vader tried to make his own son an apprentice, but he failed. Instead, Luke returned to Vader's childhood and adult master for instruction and training. Through discovery on his own and the guidance of his master, Luke broke the cycle of evil that the existence of the Sith implied. The Sith was representative of the breakdown of goodness, of recourse to the easy path of action instead of the difficulty of acting out of justice, goodness, and what is right.

Star Wars is therefore a cautionary tale and warns of the potential in each of us. Whether as modern Jedi or the common man or woman, individuals are defined by their actions, which, in turn, define a person's being, character, and honor. Vigilance is always necessary. Through the apprentice's trust in his master, the wisdom of the sword will be learned, benefitting both the individual and the society in which he lives. A point when the master and apprentice will part will come naturally. Duty will call one or the other away to the responsibilities of a profession or to teach a new set of students. Hopefully, the ability of the student will exceed that of the teacher.

The greatest teachers have the ability to inspire a good person into becoming great. By the same token, the greatest teachers are also those who are most inspired by their students. Teachers, by their very nature, fight the indifference and pessimism of society, and if they simply challenge their student to look to the horizon, they might actually get the student to begin a journey of a lifetime. Swordmasters have the unique charge at their command, but it is up to their students to discover on their own that the power of the sword is not in its use but in its abandonment. The swordsman's journey is complete when he realizes that he or she is a swordsman when a person can toss aside the sword as Luke did his lightsaber. It was at that point that Luke became a Jedi.

FOUR

Historical Precedents of the Jedi

Unlike directors of most modern and futuristic films, George Lucas turns away from the special ops and secret government agent when he looks for heroes to his epic *Star Wars* saga. Part knight, part monk, the Jedi Lucas created are an order of swordsmen that help rule the universe in accordance with law and lofty principles of justice and honor. In his own words, the Jedi are swordsmen, ambassadors, negotiators, and "intergalactic therapists." They are not strictly enforcers, but men of action who are as wise as they are trained swordsmen. The Jedi don't simply sit in the context of *Star Wars* as mere policemen on call to answer emergencies across the galaxy when needed. Instead, they have a more substantive culture to their organization that finds precedence in the life of the religious (that of monks and nuns), military warrior knights, and of enslaved soldier armies. This chapter focuses on influences of historical examples of warrior monks—Jedi of the past.[1]

All societies have had to come to terms with the expression of military values within society. Very often the state owes its existence to the efficiency of a well-oiled military machine. Especially when neighbors pose a threat to a country's borders, the need to keep and maintain that military becomes a self-justifying necessity. Whether or not this fear is warranted, the emotional need to know that the availability of a protective army has become critical to governments who feel threatened by the infiltration of outsiders or outside ideas. At times, governments need a military to maintain order; sometimes that government uses the military not only to enforce order, but also to impose it. The pull between order and freedom was a consideration for countries that had to determine the necessity of the military and to what strength it should operate in the day-to-day running of the nation. The universe of *Star Wars* has been fortunate in that it has not openly needed a military since the early foundational moments of its history. Remnants of that time are the Jedi Knights, who have been able to maintain peace and order in a delicate balance of galactic order and galactic freedoms. Their need has remained constant through millennia, but the threat to their rule appears when economic and military instability menaces the safety and security of the universe.

By drawing not only on the fabled story of King Arthur and his knights, but also on historical examples, Lucas makes the Jedi order even more compelling than if he had simply affixed a noble-sounding name and beast on a multipartite shield. Instead, Lucas drew upon a host of military and religious traditions when he created the Jedi Knights, including the knights of the Templar, Hospitaller, and Teutonic orders, priests and religious of the Christian faith, the fighting monks of Japan called *Sohei*, and the Janissaries and Mamelukes of Islam.

Religious Life

Though the Jedi were not explicitly a religious order professing a specific culture of faith that overtly dictated the belief in a monotheistic God (the concept of midi-chlorians is animistic), the organization of the order resembled the Catholic Church, which predominated Western Europe for two thousand years. While not implying that the Jedi or Sith mimic the Catholic or Protestant faiths, the religious wars of Europe provide a historical example of military warfare fought on the basis of the same faith. For over two hundred years, the European religious struggles led to uncountable atrocities and the deaths of tens of thousands during the Reformation and its subsequent Catholic Counter Reformation.

Religious strife occurs when one faith feels it must compete with rival religions in order to maintain their position in society or to prevent the ascendance of another. The heart of religious life, however, starts with two basic ideas: the worship of God and the purification of the soul. In order to achieve these two goals, three traditions of life were developed for those who wished to leave the secular world and their non-religious societal functions for an existence devoted daily to the worship of God. Within those turbulent times of continual war and strife, it was easy to understand why those seeking a better communication with God would seek isolation from the world. Not only did this give the man or woman the freedom and time to devote to prayer, he or she was also removed from the world of temptation that often led to a life of sin.

The hermitage was the easiest form of obtaining the time and isolation needed for a serious contemplation of God. A hermit's life was to be a constant reflection of his or her relationship with God and a solitude that was a daily reminder of God's omnipotence and an individual's relative powerlessness.[2] Even today, there is no official set of rules for the hermitage; each hermit, who can be a man or woman, submits himself or herself to an austere regimen that allows for spiritual reflection. This isolated life may be wholly self-imposed or it may be officially sanctioned by an outside authority as it still is in the Catholic Church today. Hermits formally submit in writing the purpose of their retreat from the world and the list of rules they will follow in order to fulfill their objective. The Vatican then keeps an official list as a way of recognizing those who dedicate their life to what is probably the most difficult relationship with God.

Part of the hermit's life is a commitment to poverty and a closeness to nature that is often perceived as God in her fullest. While hermits work or cultivate as a means to provide for their sustenance, mendicants wander from place to place, relying on the charity of individuals and the community to provide both shelter and food. For an unspecified time, the monk, perhaps in the company of companion monks, would then work to assist the poor by alleviating spiritual pain, the thirst for drink, and the hunger of the starving who suffered miserable lives in medieval Europe.[3] At appropriate times, though there is no specific prescription, wandering monks might settle down in communities with which they developed a close relationship and bond. Such communities then ceased being mendicant but retained the namesake of their origins by referring to their permanent lodging as friaries.

Capuchin monks, a branch of the Franciscans who based their devotion to God by giving special recognition to Nature — God's creation — were such an order. Monks traveled the European continent and led a life of devotion by example to the secular world. They gave up their possessions and worked to assist the needy. While it might be thought that a mendicant lifestyle was free from politics, very often the time spent in a community caused local feathers to ruffle, either from envy of their charitable acts or because of political differences. Not everyone in the world was willing to have the word of God brought to their doorstep. The life of Bernadino Ochino demonstrated the political dangers in which mendicant monks might find themselves. Ochino was unschooled, but became through personal effort an inspired Capuchin. He came to befriend John Calvin who openly spoke out against problems within the Catholic Church. Because of Ochino's closeness to the heretical priest, the entire Capuchin order was almost disbanded by the pope. Were it not for their history of untarnished service, their actual extinction might have actually come to pass.[4]

The monastic life of men (brothers) and women (nuns) was another alternative for those seeking communication with God. Unlike the often lonely life of the mendicant, communal life, though still austere, was another way to devote one's self to God as well as to the community. Monastic life is distinguished by commitment to a shared common rule recognized by the pope. Like the hermit and the friar, the religious did not usually take priestly vows. The common rules, however, were quite strict and were meant to assist the brother or sister in fulfilling their commitment to God. All orders wore simple clothing called a habit, they usually did menial labor around the monastery (anything from cooking to cleaning to farming), and attended prayer services. Some orders made a vow of silence (except in recognized emergency situations), others gave up shoes for simple sandals, while yet others performed voluntary self-flagellation. The heart of monastic common rule consisted of the vows of poverty, chastity, and obedience. Poverty was direct imitation of the life of Christ. Chastity was meant to deprive both man and woman of sinful carnal lust. Obedience to their abbot or abbotess was essential for discipline in their difficult life.

Monasteries were usually established by devoted individuals who won the support of the community. St. Benedict and St. Augustine established well-known rules that were followed by monasteries around the world. A local community may have donated land, supervised construction, and granted tax exemption or permission to collect tithes, but money may have also come from the head of the order. Many monasteries were often built on high overlooks to symbolize their closeness to God, but they also served to isolate them from secular citizens who had to trek up winding paths to the entrance of the abbey. Monasteries were run by an abbot, and through their dedication some monasteries became quite well-to-do by raising their own funds through either the production of a local craft such as wine or champagne (Dom Perignon champagne was created by monks) or the baking of bread (a service directly related to their care for the poor).

During the Protestant Reformation, monasteries came under increasing criticism for the wealth that they had obtained from their constant diligence. Local rulers, when they canvassed the properties held by monasteries, were often shocked to discover great areas of monastic land that paid no tax to local authorities. Jealous of these fixed exemptions and plagued by the need to raise money or the desire to penalize the Catholic Church, these rulers sometimes confiscated monastic land outright.

Other religious orders did not cloister themselves from the world and devoted their daily lives to the service of humanity. In terms of comparison, the Jesuits[5] stand out as a prime example of a historical precedent for the Jedi Knights. The Society of Jesus' founder, St. Ignatius, was a Spanish nobleman and knight from the Basque region. While convalescencing after a battle, he examined his life and concluded that he could best serve God by leaving the military life for a priestly one. Without training, however, he realized he could not hope to fulfill his duty in service to God, so he decided to attend the prestigious University of Paris to become a priest. He quickly made friends, and he and others who shared Ignatius's vision of service began to act as a team. He and seven companions vowed to dedicate their lives to the service of others by engaging the world, unlike the cloistered life of a monk. Working in Rome for a period before continuing to Palestine, Ignatius and his followers were soon noticed for their unswerving charity. It was not long before Pope Paul III formally recognized their order. Ignatius's Society of Jesus, as the Jesuit order was called, was unlike other priestly orders. In addition to the priestly vows of poverty, chastity, and obedience, all Jesuits had to take a direct vow to serve the General of the Society as well as the pope.

Ignatius held a deep respect for education and he felt it crucial if the Christians were to lead a full, expressive life. Acts of charity in imitation of Christ were esteemed, but knowledge and self-reflection were equally valued. Following a military style of organization, Ignatius established the common rule in his *Constitutions* in which there were several levels of achievement, the highest of which (called "solemnly professed") could achieve full standing in the order. Those who were not deemed both spiritually and academically suitable could still serve the order under the title of "co-adjutor." Ignatius disparaged the Jesuit who self-servingly cloistered himself instead of serving others, and as a way to preserve the dedication of the order to duty, Ignatius prohibited Jesuits from taking high official positions unless so ordered by the pope. He could head a school in order to assure proper Catholic upbringing, but taking a ministerial position or mayorship was forbidden.

At the heart of their formation was the *Spiritual Exercises*, which was a vague written outline of a spiritual journey toward contemplation of God led by an experienced Jesuit. Its purpose was to help a believer reach a higher relationship with God. It may have included meditation, menial duties, and a series of guided instructions. It differed from Jesuit to Jesuit, the one focus being the necessity to emotionally move the person's spirit through the exercise. So fashionable was the desire to partake in the exercises that the European aristocracy came to see their journey through a Jesuit-led exercise as a social badge of distinction.

The Jesuits, being an intellectual order of the highest caliber, trained not to bully converts into believing through guilt or promises of paradise. Instead, Ignatius chose a conversational style to engage the potential Christian (or Protestant) into coming over to the Jesuit's point of view. The Jesuit did not focus on an individual's faults (and sins), but praised and encouraged the virtues of an individual. Conversion was a long and difficult process, but the Jesuit was satisfied a convert was made when the individual's mind and spirit chose independently to embrace Catholic Christianity. This manner of proselyting through intellectual discourse worked extremely well for the educated nobility of Europe. It was equally successful with the Chinese emperors in Asia who admired the Jesuit's ability to learn the language and culture of the court, beating even native Mandarin courtiers in their own arguments.[6]

The Jesuits' role was especially important during the religious wars when the faith of the people of a territory changed with the sovereign. They became the front line in the struggle to deter Roman Catholic leaders who otherwise would have joined the Protestant movement, whether for personal or political reasons. Jesuits were allowed to serve only one "client" at a time, traveling with this count or that prince, serving both as spiritual advisor and confessor to the elite and powerful of Europe. They played a significant role in preventing the whole of Europe from becoming completely Protestant. Their presence in the courts of Europe also served as an important source of information to the Vatican. While not allowed to directly divulge secrets, Jesuits, who were probably the best in documenting their travels and deeds in reports to the General of the Society, could easily share political and social pretensions of their "clients" with the papal bureaus without breaking their vow from divulging confessions.

Seeing Jesuits in regular attendance at noble courts, Protestants undoubtedly saw them as their evil antithesis. The diatribes and invectives slung at the Jesuits goes without great elaboration, being reviled as servants to a devil-pope armed with cursed tongues which could magically ensnare a listener. To Protestant propagandists, the *Spiritual Exercises* were words from the devil himself, and political pressure on the papacy even led to the temporary disbandment of the order in the 18th century. Regardless of one's perspective on the Jesuits, Protestants and Catholics understood the importance they played in stemming growing Protestantism. Today, the moderate Jesuits have fallen out of favor with the reining pope, who has sought allies with more conservative elements of the Catholic Church.

It is certainly clear how the personal search for a connection to the spiritual can take many forms of expression, be it the hermit, the member religious, or a member of a priestly order such as the Jesuits. The Jedi, too, in their religious order similarly bear the trappings of the religious life, one that is admired by secular populations because these individuals willingly give up freedoms that most assume to be their God-given rights.

Military Orders

Contrary to Christian thinking regarding activities of war, the Catholic Church has always held the position that fighting may be necessary for self-defense. The days of Roman martyrdom were over when Constantine, a pagan ruler of the Eastern remnants of the once glorious Roman Empire, converted to Christianity after purportedly seeing a cross in a vision just before his battle with German barbarians. Overnight, Christianity was transformed from the religion of the poor and needy to the official religion of the state. Christianity, however, saw a challenge unlike none in its seven-hundred-year history. Muslim advances in the Holy Land, modern Israel and Palestine were advances for the "Infidel," and for six hundred years, Turkish expansion would remain a continual threat to European Christendom.

News of territorial losses in the Holy Land to the Muslims was seen in Europe as the opening volley in a greater expansion of the Islamic threat to predominantly Christian Europe. So sentimental was the loss of Palestine and Jerusalem that calls were made out by pope and king for worthy nobles to go to the Holy Land on crusades to rid Christ's birthplace of the infidel. Nobles marching off to war was a sincere answer to Christian calls for assistance in the Holy Land. It also helped reigning sovereigns consolidate their control, as rival nobility, who had claims to various sovereign titles in their home country, journeyed to the Middle East.

Among the most grievous of news coming from the Middle East was that of Christian pilgrims falling victim to Muslim attacks. Not only were they being captured and held for ransom until European families could raise and send money in exchange for their loved ones, innocent pilgrims were being attacked and murdered by Muslims who believed in the wrong God.[7] Knights from Europe traveled to the Holy Land, and upon finding comradeship among men of equal rank and religious piety, it only became natural that these European knights organized their service under military forms. Originally, many of these knights sought communal ties for the purpose of assisting and aiding the sick and those wounded from clashes with Muslim raiders. These men formed themselves into bands that imitated the communal codes of monastic orders and the customs of chivalric knighthood. Voluntarily, these men adhered to the customs of religious orders, mostly the Benedictine and Augustinian communal rules. They took vows of poverty, chastity, and obedience, which they gave to a governing head. After a period of service in cities of the Holy Land such as Acre and Jerusalem, they sought recognition of their organization from the pope in Rome. Their lives simple, their piety unswerving, knights that took part in these orders were fulfilling personal dreams that satisfied both a spiritual yearning and fidelity to a faith that was crucial in the mostly illiterate societies of medieval Europe.

While their methods of expressing their faith seem barbaric and violent today, the threat and fear of a violent death by the sword was for many people a real possibility. Unlike modern cities and nations where a police force and army are specifically trained to fight in place of the ordinary citizens, medieval men and women often had to fight tooth and nail for their own protection. Recourse to a court system was rarely an option for the poor, and enforcement from civil officials depended on gaining the favor of important dignitaries of the city who may or may not have had the best interest of the public when they exercised their authority.

Knights were men of action. They lived in a culture that encouraged demonstration of one's military prowess, and as protectors of authority they understood the relationship between the rulers and those who carried out their laws. Knights were the backbone of rulers and it was important to create a culture that supported and justified the preeminent rule of the noble class. In the illiterate society of middle ages, fanfare and open declaration were the method and manner of presenting one's heart and soul to others. Men displayed their social and political prowess, therefore, by attracting the attention of others—either through good speech or through good deeds. Knights excelled in the latter as long as they lived up to the lofty social graces of the aristocratic class.

In an illiterate society, the skill of the educated, which often meant the literate, was of grave importance to the successful administration of any government. Especially in European countries, whose population had grown into the hundreds of thousands, the maintenance of written communication was central to the greatest of governments. But an education was limited to those born into a noble family. Both knights and priests, however, had access to the upper class by the very fact that the nobility needed them. Knights pledged their fealty and died for their lord, while priests advised and disseminated the law of the sovereign while reminding their patron of their obligations to their church. Neither knight nor priest had to be born into his position. Each obtained his privilege and received the deference of the common populace and aristocracy simply on the merit of his actions or ability.

Knights of crusading Europe sought the best of both vocations: that of warrior and monk. Canon law in principle forbade the spilling of blood by a cleric.[8] Knights were laymen, however, which allowed them to use the sword on behalf of their Christian God. In answering a personal call by God, as well as that of pilgrims under siege and attack in the Holy Land, pious knights journeyed to the Middle East and took on the role of protector and assistant of the Christian poor and injured. Without going through the education to become a priest as Ignatius Loyola had done, these knights took a middle ground that served the interests not only of the poor and needy, but also that of the pope, who was quick in sanctioning the establishment of military orders. Though there was some expressed question of whether fighting was compatible with Christian values, no popular outcry opposed the formation of military orders. Quite the contrary, their deeds were celebrated in both oral and written form during the centuries at the height of their power. Nothing was more honorable than to serve society as both knight and pious Christian.

The Knights Templar were the best known and celebrated in Christian chronicles and histories. Like the Jesuits, the available literature on Templars far exceeds those of the other two military orders. Templars took their name from the land they were given, which was supposedly located near the Temple Mount of Jerusalem. They began as knights who were commanded by the Patriarch Warmund of Jerusalem to protect the routes pilgrims used through the Holy Land. Taking the simple color of white, their surcoat was distinguished by its red cross. Members were to exhibit piety and love of God at all times. A single blanket was deemed sufficient for their comfort, they were to sleep in their clothes, and at night, to assure others that they did not take the company of women, they were to keep a lamp lit until morning. Templar knights were required to have a tonsure (the circle of hair trimmed from the top of their heads), and communication, even during meals, was limited to vital or necessary speech. While expected to bring their own horse, armor, and weapons, their possessions were considered communal and could be taken and shared as deemed by the appropriate authority in the order. Among pilgrims and Christian priests in the Holy Land, the sight of Templars was reassuring as they traveled or went about their business in the town and cities in which they lived.

The fame of their success probably led the Templars to their greatest fall from grace. In a political intrigue, French King Philip IV brought charges to Pope Clement V that Templar knights had become corrupt and heretical. Templars all over Christendom were arrested, interrogated, and put on trial. Charges included allegations that they conspired with Muslims, refused to assist pilgrims when asked, and committed homosexual practices. Some charges of heresy alleged that they denied the redemption of humanity of sin, the divinity of Christ, and that they worshiped a false idol. Despite the many testimonies supporting their pious practices, the order was found guilty of many heresies, and Templars wherever they could be found were arrested and burned at the stake as heretics. Regardless, it was clear that the success of their piety led to resentment from many who had reason to personally or politically despise them. The Templars were accused of abusing their position when they refused to submit to local authorities (though they would submit to the pope), became greedy and quarrelsome (they did quarrel with rival military orders), and when they failed to live up to the expressed and spiritual purpose of their order (they did refuse to assist pilgrims when their journeys were ill-conceived). Much scholarly work suggests that a combination of jealousy of their wealth (they had accumulated vast tracts of land from donations) and the political challenges to many local authorities led to dispersal of their land and disbandment of this once respected order. The Chinon parchment, recently discovered after being lost for hundreds of years because of a cataloging mistake, shows papal exoneration of the Templars on many charges.

The second military order to appear in the Holy Land was that of the Hospitallers, which derived its name from the Hospital of St. John of Jerusalem.

They served and cared for injured pilgrims visiting the Holy Sepulcher where Jesus's body had been laid before rising from the dead. In the 1100s, mercenaries were employed to protect the hospital in a city that was the first line of defense against Muslim attacks. Hospitallers, like the Templars alongside whom they sometimes fought, were devoted to assisting Christian pilgrims and their journeys. The Hospital of St. John won great praise for its care of the sick in Outremer (French for the other side of the sea) where many sophisticated medical techniques developed by remarkable Arab doctors were employed.

Early members of the order were French, though membership in the confraternity drew devoted individuals from all over Europe. Early knights were expected to be of the aristocracy and today membership is reserved to those with officially recognized noble titles. Such families would then be able to provide their son with the appropriate mount, armor, and weapons needed for his participation in Hospitaller campaigns. Their ability to fight off the Muslims was generally known (their most famous fortress is the Krak des Chevaliers), though with the loss of Acre in 1291, their headquarters was removed to Malta, and then later to the Island of Rhodes, where the eight-pointed Maltese cross on red became their symbol.

Less about the Hospitallers' actual battles and campaigns is known than of the Templars, but it is clear from contemporary literature that knights of this order were held in the same esteem as the Templars. Ballads and songs about their order did not make the rounds in Europe until much later in the 13th century, almost a hundred years after the order's establishment. Like the Templars, the Hospitallers accumulated wealth and land that was the envy of local political figures. The Hospitallers did not receive the severe political punishment of the Templars, and in the wake of their fall many Templar properties were transferred to the Hospitaller order. Today the order is a network of Catholic, Protestant, and non-denominational orders that still serve to ease the suffering of the world. Their hospital is now a modern building that serves people of all religions.

The third crusading order of renown in the Holy Land was that of the Teutonic order, established by German knights. Like Hospitallers, the Teutonic order began as a medical corps in the service of injured or wounded German pilgrims. Based in the Hospital of St. Mary of the Germans of Jerusalem, the order also had obligations to assist Christians. Supported by the German Emperor Frederick II and the popes, the Teutonic knights gained official recognition and support from the Catholic hierarchy in 1113. They, too, became the object of land and monetary benefices, which allowed them to develop a soldiery that rivaled that of the Templars and the Hospitallers though they were established some eighty years after the other two orders.

Even less is known about their specific battles than the Hospitallers', though the Teutonic knights would become most widely known in Europe for their work administrating pagan areas of the Baltic region. Quelling barbarians became an important function in northern Germany and what is now parts of Poland. After establishing themselves in key cities, they constructed castles that served as headquarters for local chapters of the order. Their battles with pagans were celebrated and their success in bringing prosperity to their region is reflected by the establishment of thousands of towns and villages and its participation in the lucrative Hanseatic League by becoming an important exporter of grain to the rest of Europe. The order did face defeats, and with the Protestant Reformation, the order's military efforts essentially ended with the conversion of its grandmaster to the Protestant faith.

The Teutonic order did propagate itself in many countries around Europe, but with the religious wars of the Reformation much doubt was cast on the order's ability to find a solid purpose. Since the early 16th century, various forms of the Teutonic order have been established with the purpose of assisting others, much of it dedicated to caring for soldiers wounded in the many European wars of the continent. Its present headquarters is in Vienna, Austria.

The legacy of these three orders has made an unmistakable impression on students of European history. Despite criticisms that have plagued the orders, it remains unquestioned that knights of these orders did have the highest regard for both their religion and its commitment to assist others in need. Their network of local houses (called commanderies) and a developed banking system combined with regular revenue streams permitted these knightly orders to maintain their forces permanently. Their original creeds were particularly xenophobic, however, reflecting the orthodox view that their religion could do no wrong. Muslims despised these knights as carriers of a hateful religion, though on the battlefield, commanders of both Muslim and Christian faiths sometimes learned to respect a common code of warfare that could today be described as chivalrous. Without downplaying the atrocities committed by both Christian and Muslim at times between the 11th and 14th centuries, let it be said that within the context of exploring precursors to the Jedi knights, the three orders—Templar, Hospitaller, and Teutonic—are instances of a manner of living that is not dissimilar to that of the Jedi in *Star Wars*.

Sohei of Japan

The samurai of Japanese film that influenced Lucas were not only those who served the feudal lords of Nippon, but also the much romanticized and revered warrior-monks of the mountains. Similar to the Jedi who live in their pinnacle temple on a man-made pyramid in the heart of the capital, the Japanese monastic warriors, called *sohei*, lived in elevated Buddhist temples constructed in the mountains surrounding the former capitals of Nara and Kyoto. Among the sohei were powerful swordsmen who retired to the cloister of the temple serving their abbot as well as the imperial court to whom various priests acted as advisors to the emperor. Like the Jedi, these men of faith were trusted because they openly gave up the self-interested lives of normal citizens for the benefit of their spiritual well-being.

The influence of monasteries on the history of Japan focused not on doctrine and belief as had been the case in 17th- and 18th-century Europe, but on influence and power because they depended on secular contact for monetary support. At times, the sohei were also territorial, becoming jealous of rival monasteries who threatened the prestige and influence of a branch serving as direct advisors to the imperial person. Sometimes these warrior-monks might even turn against the emperor when they had been slighted or insulted. Ex-Emperor Go Shirakawa–In lamented that there were three things outside his control: "the rapids of the Mano river, the dice at gambling, and the monks of the mountain."[9]

Buddhism was first imported from China and was quickly adapted to the temperament and needs of the Japanese imperial court. It viewed life as an existence of perpetual suffering. The founder of Buddhism, Siddhartha Guatama of south Nepal, was raised in the joyous world of the prince's court. It was not until he dared to venture outside the palace gates that he discovered the difficult lives of the common people. Forsaking his birthright, Siddhartha traveled the land and devoted his life as an ascetic and quickly gained a following of disciples. Through meditation and the practice of a good, moral life, Buddhism teaches that Nirvana can be achieved. With thought and reflection, those who devoted their lives to the search for enlightenment came to be trusted by both courtier and commoner alike.

While the general doctrines of Buddhism remain consistent across different branches, some philosophical interpretations have led to the evolution of divergent sects, which was especially true of its Japanese expression. These sects usually maintained cooperative relations, though if threatened by the rise of another sect, rival sects were not above taking up arms against the other.

Priests and monks in Japan did not have the Christian monastic proscription against spilling blood, and, therefore, did not need lay knight-protectors like the Templar. Japanese Buddhist monks protected themselves when they could not secure or rely on the patronage of a nearby samurai *daimyo*. Itinerant monks might have had to defend themselves when traveling, while the need of permanent protection of the temples ultimately rested on the clergy who lived in or near the temples in which they served. In extreme circumstances, entire armies of monks could be used for political ends. And so successful did they sometimes become, that both the imperial court and their appointed guardian samurai clans sometimes found the existence of sohei untenable to the point that they were militarily suppressed.

During the Kamakura period, Zen Buddhism came to be practiced by samurai of the court. An anti-intellectual and non-doctrinaire sect, adherents of Zen Buddhism believed that enlightenment could be achieved by the severe focus of some practice or art, such as the tea ceremony, flower arranging, painting, and, especially among the samurai, swordsmanship. Zen stressed an austere simplicity that appealed to a military class accustomed to the discipline of military life. By trying to understand unfathomable koans (senseless stories with no logical resolution) or through the art of focusing on the wielding of a blade, it was hoped that the samurai could come into his own enlightenment. Precepts like emptying the mind (*munen*) and allowing the blade to act on its own in the hands of a swordsman were concepts that also led to the mastery of the sword. Most of all, Zen taught that life was ultimately meaningless, and that facing death stoically would lead to a liberated and enlightened life. If death were inevitable, the swordsman would not fear his death because he would be prepared for his obliteration.

Because of the attraction Buddhism had to samurai looking for some spiritual meaning to a harsh and difficult life that demanded unswerving loyalty even unto death, it was not unheard of for a samurai to retire to a monastery after a battle-filled life of serving a feudal lord. Retired soldiers could be found among various monasteries and served in times of crisis as instructors in defensive arts for the abbey's monks. In some cases, a retired lord might bring his entire retinue of samurai with him to serve in the monastery. Uesugi Kenshin and Takeda Shingen (both shoguns) were rival warlords who became Buddhist monks late in their lives. Sohei practiced the martial arts, wore armor when available (though with a cowl), employed the sword and bow, and were renowned for the use of the halberd, called the *naginata*. Not all sohei were in fact pledged novitiates, being what might be best described as "monkish warriors" who were employed by the temple but did not directly participate in its religious life.[10]

Abbots and appointed priests had strong ties to the imperial court, serving as spiritual advisors who informed the court of astrological and religious obligations vital to the proper exercise of authority by the Emperor. In an age when astrology and geomancy were considered vital to commanding favor with the gods, the court had a deep interest in maintaining strong relations with Buddhist priests.[11]

On occasion, disputes between an abbey and the court would arise. Often, these conflicts revolved around taxation and funding of the monasteries, which relied heavily on patronage from visitors, gifts from aristocrats, and the legacies of those who served in the monastery itself. An imperial decree could profoundly affect the monetary base on which temples survived and prospered. In other instances, the appointment of an abbot might cause political consternation among the members of a particular temple or its rivals.

When claims against the imperial officials could not be settled through negotiation, monasteries might send their armies of monks, literally an armed contingent of religious, down from the mountain to clamor in the streets, engage the populace to their cause, and even physically approach the divine Emperor himself. The sight of masses of monks chanting in the streets was an impressive sight to behold. In one protest, seven thousand sohei entered Kyoto demanding the government hand a samurai-protector named Kiyomori to the emperor after he had defiled a moveable shrine called an *omikoshi* by shooting an arrow at it. Because Kiyomori and the Taira family were considered vital to the existence of the imperial court, he made amends for his act of sacrilege by paying a nominal fine. Kiyomori would later attack a Buddhist temple in which three thousand five hundred civilians and monks died. Not only was the temple burned down, but the heads of a thousand monks were carried away as trophies.[12]

Sometimes the appeals from the monks to the commoners met with great success, threatening to foment civil violence through peasant riots. Afraid of the curses monks were able to make on citizens, the city inhabitants feared the uncertainty of a temple or shrine in open conflict with the secular authorities.

One manner of rallying public outrage against the government was to bring down an omikoshi from the temple. Usually used during festivals, the omikoshi was considered a harbinger of bad times when removed from the sanctity of the temple. Citizens disturbed by an omikoshi found sitting in the streets unprotected would quickly appeal to secular authorities to appease the monks. This practice of open blackmail was similar to the Catholic Church's imposition of the interdict, which suspended the carrying out of sacraments on either an individual or an area or region. Local populations fearful for their souls would similarly pressure officials to appease the Church. When under the interdict, the Eucharist could not be celebrated, last rites could not be given, and if someone died, burial in holy ground was not permitted. The interdict also absolved vassals of their obligations of fealty to their lords, thus allowing them to rightfully overthrow their lords.

In the Japanese court, such deference was given to Buddhist priests and monks that the emperor might be cowed into capitulating to the monks' demands. If not, the sohei might even attack the imperial palace or its associative administrative buildings. In one instance, when a contingent of sohei accompanied by an omikoshi approached a gate leading to the high court,

Yorimasa, the commander of the palace guard, leapt down from his mount, took off his helmet, and washed out his mouth with water out of respect for the monks. Impressed with his deference, the monks continued to another gate where they were duly attacked by the commander. Several monks were killed and others wounded before they returned to their temple.[13]

Competition between sects, too, was a reason for monks taking up arms. When the capital moved from Nara to Heian (modern Kyoto) in 894, the Nara temple lost power, prestige, influence, and wealth at the expense of the Tendai sect who developed a complex of eight thousand religious buildings. Mount Hiei, because of its geophysical position, served as a ward against evil that might affect the imperial court. In another example, a new sect, the Lotus sect of Nichiren, openly challenged and denounced the priests of Mt. Hiei. The abbot sought allies with samurai lords who, out of their own self-interest, openly attacked temples of the new populist sect. Monks were killed and sometimes buildings, even the principal temple itself, were burned to the ground.

Government rivalry continued intermittently through Japanese history, but none as fierce and lasting as Shogun Oda Nobunaga's eleven-year struggle against the religious-populist Ikko-ikki group. Its leader Rennyo organized a revolt in 1488 in which Kaga Province came to be ruled by the religious order. Mikawa Province seemed on the road to follow a similar fate. Supplied with muskets, the Ikko-ikki proved a fierce challenge to samurai authorities. Over the years, Nobunaga attempted to thwart the influence of the movement, and in 1571, relations had become so poor that he ordered an attack on Mt. Hiei's monastic complex. Encircling the mountain, his troops killed every man, woman, child, priest, and monk that had taken refuge at the mountain's heights. Twenty thousand people were killed and the complex was burned to the ground. Later, in Nagashi, Nobunaga again attacked a temple and burned it, killing another twenty thousand. And in his final campaign against the Ikko-ikki, he surrounded the Ishiyama Hongan Temple after thwarting the Mori clan's attempt to break the naval blockage Nobunaga had imposed. The fate of the temple had been sealed, however, when relief forces did not respond to the temple's plight. A messenger from the emperor then arrived advising a peaceful surrender of the temple. Pressured by Nobunaga, the garrison did surrender, though the temple itself was burned down.[14]

When determined samurai were resolute in stopping monastic orders and their troops, the eventuality of the outcome could only mean victory for the samurai. Despite their influence on both the imperial court and the commoners, the samurai were so well positioned to fight the sometimes violent influence of the warrior monks that eventually the sohei would cease to field armies of their own. Samurai troops were too numerous and well trained to let a small number of monks, fanatical though they were, to defeat the wealth and experience of Japan's vassal armies. So, too, would the Jedi meet its extinction at the hands of troops that far outnumbered the ten thousand Jedi of its order.

Muslim Warriors

The scene in which Qui-Gon Jinn and Shmi discuss Anakin reveals the fact that Jedi were identified in the Republic when then were very young. "He [Anakin] has the way," Qui-Gon said in the Episode I script. And in the Jedi Council, Yoda revealed that even a boy like Anakin at the age of nine was already too told to begin training. Especially for a boy gifted with powers of the Force, it was important to begin training as early as possible. Practitioners of go and chess (both strategy board games) agree that the best players require training from the youngest age in order to properly develop the brain connections that will make the child into a master.

History had its own version of the child trained warrior. Taking children in their youth as the Jedi do was something Muslim commanders did after the initial Islamic conquests of North Africa and the Middle East. Mamelukes and Janissaries took slave children and trained them to become the powerful fighting forces of Islam. Slavery, while typically thought of as a complete deprivation of freedom and rights, held an important economic and social role in Muslim societies, as it does in *Star Wars*.

It has only been in the last three hundred years that modern concepts of total emancipation of the human population came to be accepted by church, the state, and the general populace. The concept of human rights did not exist in the form it does today. Freedom and freedmen, however, were constructs that did exist in ancient societies in which slavery was commonplace. Our modern prejudices against permanent servitude and ownership of humans contrast starkly with attitudes of all the civilized cultures of the world, in which slavery was a fact of life. In the high cultures of Greece, Rome, Persia, and Egypt, slavery could just as easily mean an improved and even privileged position as it might have meant total subservience to a master.[15]

Slave soldiers eventually became the principal military force that propped up many Muslim-controlled territories. It seems contradictory that armed slaves did not forcibly overthrow their masters. In fact, the culture of the military slave became the backbone of military forces for many Islamic leaders. Most slaves were non–Muslims, often Christian, who were brought as young children to Muslim countries and trained as soldiers of Islam.

The need for non–Muslim military forces came from the desire of Muslim leaders to consolidate their authority after successful campaigns against other Muslims. War against the infidel was unhesitatingly permitted, but war between Muslims was abhorrent to the Koran, which told of a single kind of war; that of jihad against non–Muslims. The struggle for authority came when caliphs—leaders linked directly to Mohammed's supporters—and secular rulers tried to justify their authority and control of governing institutions.

This difference played itself out in the two main branches of the Muslim religion between Sunnis and Shi'ites. Sunni and Shi'ite both hold the Koran as spiritual doctrine, but each interprets other cultural facets of Islam in different ways. Sunnis, the more numerous branch, accept the first four caliphs as successors to Mohammed and admit the importance of the Umma, or the collective of Muslim people. Shi'ites have a stricter outlook, rejecting the first three caliphs and regarding Ali as the legitimate successor to Mohammed. Links to Mohammed are held at the highest level by imams, or religious leaders. The Shi'ite branch, because of its more conservative interpretation, tends to be the more militant and fundamentalist of the two Muslim branches.

Since warring against a brother Muslim was blasphemous in the eyes of God, foreign troops were established as a way to circumvent Muslim fratricide. Their practice was not without precedent: Athens had its own Scythian troops, numbering around three hundred, who were directly owned by the state. Numerous European monarchies kept paid Swiss Guards as palace troops. The use of foreign troops was meant to assure loyalty from a military force that would not be swayed by the factionalism that populist movements brought to Muslim countries. Umayyad Caliph al-Hamim of Cordova and Abbasid Caliph al-Mu'tasim of Iraq had their own slave palace guards. In time, a soldiery of free Arab soldiers would become an anachronism among Muslim leaders.

The creation of slave armies depended completely on the indoctrination process that re-educated children for an Islamic society and established a code of behavior that would assure loyalty to the aristocratic leaders to whom these troops had been garrisoned. Discipline was strict, and members were expected to follow orders exactly without regard for their own interests. In return, their numbers would become a privileged and elite class who were the protectors of the state and of Islam. Muslim leaders had a soldiery that did not follow popular whims, though there would be moments when the slaves did wrest power for themselves. Such takeovers were uncommon, and in the end, resulted in the total elimination of the slave soldiery altogether.

The Mamelukes of the Abbasid Caliphate of Egypt came to power after the Mongols conquered the Baghdad caliphate that ruled Cairo at the battle of Ain Jalut in 1260. Many of the Mongol horsemen were of the same Turkish and Circassian ethnic stock that would make up the Mameluke troops that served the Egyptian sultanate.

Mamelukes started our their military lives first as slaves from the steppe areas of the Black Sea and were then brought to Cairo where they followed a military lifestyle. They developed into an elite corps that served both as slaves and as protectors to the sultan. The nomadic Steppe horsemen lived on basic staples of milk and meat. It was said that Steppe nomads were conceived and birthed on horseback. These Turkish and Circassian children were taught the basics of Islamic culture and were trained in the *furusiyya*, the sword and archery skills of the mounted Steppe warrior. So convinced were the Mamelukes of their military prowess that they held an open contempt for the firearm when it began to appear in the armies that marched out against them. Portuguese from the east and Ottomans from the north, both armed with muskets, became significant threats to the sultanate, which quickly engaged black African troops and instructed them in the ways of the firearm. In response, the Mamelukes renewed their study of the *furusiyya*, giving them a false sense of confidence in their military ability. While the Mamelukes shared a similar loathing for the gun as did the samurai, the latter quickly recognized when Commodore Perry's ships arrived in Japan that superior weapons were at the heart of a new army. The Mamelukes would eventually be defeated by the new weapon.[16]

In the battles of Marj Dabiq and Raydaniya, Ottoman armies with their rifles would defeat the Mameluke pride. At Darj Dabiq, troops were deployed in typical crescent formation. Mamelukes fought fiercely but Ottoman firepower drove the Mamelukes back to Cairo. Seven thousand of their number died in the battle, and the Ottoman army advanced on Cairo and routed the Mamelukes. The Mameluke leader Kurbay, in lamenting their fall, said that three Mamelukes could defeat an army of 200,000, if only the Ottomans dared to put down their treacherous weapon, the musket.

The Mameluke institution did survive the Ottoman conquest, but they still refused to take up the musket. Napoleon and his modern army had relatively little difficulty defeating them at the Battle of the Pyramids. Chafing under Christian domination, they maintained their disdain for Western weapons and training. Though under new rulers, the Mamelukes kept their elite superiority but eventually their institution would become anachronistic in an age of cannon and continually improving firearms.

The Ottomans were not as intransigent in their acceptance of the new weapon as the Mamelukes. Indeed, their army of Janissaries would become one of the strongest in Europe. Not only did the Janissary form the bulk of the Ottoman military, but soldiers were drawn from their ranks to serve in important administrative positions at the highest levels of government. Their fate, while heroic, would end as tragically as that of the sohei monks at Mt. Hiei.

The Janissaries were first established by Osman, who took power in the early 14th century. Lack of manpower led to his open welcome of immigrants fleeing Mongol incursions. Regardless of race, religion, or ethnicity, Osman accepted any who would learn about and accept Turkish customs. This openness also led to a state-sponsored military, which was entirely paid for by the state to maintain the power of his sultanate.

The creation of the Janissary forces came from the system of *divsirme*—a customary tribute of Christian children, usually of Slavic or Albanian origin, who were sent to serve in the Sultan's military. The *divsirme* was originally prohibited by sharia (Islamic law), but military needs and tribal customs won out against the arguments of Muslim scholars. According to the practice, every four years, boys between eight and ten (though sometimes as old as twenty) were taken by a Janissary commander. In total, 10 percent to 14 percent of the male youth population was taken during the quadrennial tribute.

Recruits would be divided between a regular group, which lived in Anatolia (modern Turkey) for acculturation with a Turkish family for three to five years, and an elite group, which was sent directly to the sultan's palace. The elite group trained in the palace for up to fourteen years working in the palace garden or in the shipyards. Recruits, called *kul*, were not allowed to leave the palace or see the outside world, and they engaged in a rigorous education that involved learning Arabic script, literature, and the languages of Turkish, Persian, and Arabic, while still pursuing military and physical training. As difficult as it was, service in the Janissaries was considered a desirable alternative to rural peasant life. Some Muslims saw Janissary service as quite honorable, and there are many accounts of Muslims bribing Christians to take their sons during the *divsirme*.

At around twenty, the young man was released from the palace for service in a Janissary corps. They did not get complete freedom, being still required to serve the sultan. Freedom to a Janissary only meant that they could no longer be bought or sold as a slave. At this point, they were given a chance to join the cavalry, in which there was the possibility of becoming a respected general. If chosen for palace service, the Janissary had the opportunity to serve as a governor, vizier, and even grand vizier who administrated the thirty-one provinces of the empire. Under Mehmed II, all governors were products of *divsirme*. Because all were still technically slaves, the Sultan could still easily punish or even execute them without hesitation should they fail in their assigned duties, or even at the slightest hint of disloyalty.

Originally celibate, eventually Janissaries were allowed to have children, many of whom were later permitted to enlist in their father's unit. They were renowned for their orderly use of the musket and were a threat to all potential invaders. Janissaries wore pantaloons and a distinctive white turban. Never was a Janissary allowed to grow a beard, which was a sign of a freed man.

Threats of disloyalty and politicking began to surface in the 17th century when many coups d'état were organized by the Janissary. Growing from twenty thousand in 1574 to one hundred thirty-five thousand in 1826, sultans and their court came to understand the threat the Janissaries posed to their own authority. Janissaries lived under their own rules and culture, forming corporations and even making alliances with outsiders.

It was during the Auspicious Incident in 1826 when secular leaders, with the approval of the religious community, began a campaign to break the power of the Janissaries. Sultan Mahmud II began making plans for a Westernized army.[17] Despite their mastery of musket tactics, the Janissary elite was still reluctant to reform their own institution. When the Janissaries heard of the creation of a new, more modern army, they began an open revolt against the sultan. Mahmud ordered the arrest of the rebels. When the Janissaries retreated into their barracks and refused to surrender, he ordered his cannon to fire directly into their buildings. Those that did survive were either executed or banished, leading to a most inauspicious end to their elite corps.

The Jedi of Star Wars

It is now clear how the Jedi drew from a long and eclectic history of warriors from various times and cultures. Whether from the monastic and military rule of Western knights, the sohei tradition of Japan, or the indoctrinated children of Muslim serfdom, it is clear how the unusual upbringing of Jedi novitiates from a tender age was not unknown to actual history. The institution of war had its equal in religious life, and it was not accidental that the two came together in a seemingly unthinkable convergence. Religious life, however, mimics a military life because it easily submits to a hierarchy for the order of its institution.

In an organization requiring orthodoxy and control of its members, a military style of governance is quite natural. Religious zealotry easily transforms itself into militancy. And where there is some natural tendency for the faithful to desire military life, it has been a predictable reaction on the part of the religious to exercise some control over military forces. The Knights of Columbus of the United States were created in response to the desire of Americans to join a Catholic military–style organization rather than a masonic lodge. The creation of scouts also had its origins in secular governments seeking to establish civic formations of youth to support nationalistic agendas.

The Jedi Order follows the established patterns of many historical religio-military institutions. The details of the Jedi Order are unique to *Star Wars*, but the spirit of uniting religion and militancy has long been established in history. Much of that history is informed by desires to harness natural tendencies in order to obtain higher goals. Often, the business of bellicosity becomes mired in a litany of unspeakable acts. Atrocities of genocide, enslavement, crusade, and jihad result in human suffering. Rather than blame a church or a religion, however, it is important to look at the details of conflicts that have employed religion and its army in battle. Senator Amidala argues in Episode II that the creation of an army was tantamount to a declaration of war. In some cases that may actually be true. In many others, the case against refraining from war was equally compelling.

FIVE

Nature of the Sword: How the Sword Works

Three characteristics distinguish the manner in which the sword can be used as an effective weapon: (1) the sword must hit its target either as a slash or a thrust, (2) the blade must penetrate to do physical damage, and (3) the swordsman needs enough physical space in which to wield his weapon. Similarly, the lightsaber, owing its unquestionable inspiration from the sword, can be better understood and appreciated when seen in the context of real fighting experience, which goes much further than a simple slash, thrust, and draw.

Indeed, the simplicity of the sword belies a complexity that even the general historian often fails to understand. Instead of focusing on the sword's interaction with defensive armor and the military culture that trained soldiers in the art of swordsmanship, curators and hoplologists alike endlessly emphasize the evolution of the hilt and the blade or the sword's role in courtly fashion as parade and dress accessories. What is needed, however, is a discussion on how the physical properties of the sword affected combat and the battlefield experience.

In duels and on the battlefield, the sword was the weapon par excellence employed by pre-explosive societies. No matter the person's height, weight, and age, the sword served as an equalizer without rival. Strength mattered less than skill, and experience easily outperformed the vim and vigor of the young man or woman who joined the ranks of the sword-armed soldiery. And while individual and natural talent seemed to receive the lion's share of attention, common drilling and regular practice created better swordsmen than natural talent or ability alone. In the hands of an exceptional swordsman, honed skill could be manipulated in any number of ways to inflict a slight graze of the skin, a non-lethal penetration of a limb, the deadly pierce of the torso, or the sanguinary chopping of a limb. Though most literary portrayals of the sword emphasized the individual hero's use of the sword, the true heroic skill of the swordsman was its basic and coordinated use at the front of the battle line.

Physical Properties of the Sword

Function Defines Form

The sword's shape, length, size, weight, and edge allowed and limited the sword's utility. Recognizing the need for a cutting instrument — the basic shape of a blade with a handle — people developed the knife tens of thousands of years ago. Extending the knife by tying it to a long shaft — a spear — gave the additional distance between the hunter and its prey. It also gave the blade an added grip, allowing even greater reach when thrown. When a simple hand-to-hand weapon to be used against other humans was needed in war, the extension of the knife blade into a sword was a natural development. Not only could it inflict considerable damage to flesh, but the severe trauma of a laceration had a more potent psychological advantage than clubbing with a blunt weapon. And unlike the spear or bow, the sword could be used without limit until it broke.

The invention of the sword was no feat of cleverness, but elements of its design and construction were often extremely sophisticated examples of creativity, if not outright genius. The search for unbreakability, rigidity, and cutting power in a blade led to a variety of forging techniques that attempted to blend the best balance of these three universal qualities. A good sword should not snap when used against flesh and bone, and it should hold together when striking hard surfaces— an enemy blade, metal armor, a metal or wooden shield. It also needed both rigidity to hold its shape and the ability to flex or bend with the pressure of thrusts and slashes. Finally, the sword's cutting power depended on the blade's ability to hold its edge while the cut or strike cleaved into its target, which included toughened leather, the fabric of metal rings, and plate armor.

As armor evolved, so too did the sword, developing into more specialized shapes that allowed more effective penetration. Specialization, however, tended to weaken the overall strength of the sword, leaving it less capable against certain types of armor or fencing styles. The estoc (Italian: *stocco*, English: *tuck*) was an example of how a two-handed sword completely lost its cutting edge so that the point could be used to penetrate weak points in plate armor. Because the swordsman relied so heavily on the sword, a stronger all-purpose sword was more desirable than a specialized weapon. This explained the relatively long history of the simple double-edged sword and the sabre. Its basic shape dominated swordsmanship until the development of courtly fashion and thrusting styles of sword play led to the lighter, faster-moving small swords.

The development and evolution of a weapon like the sword did not occur in logical steps, however, and was influenced by external factors such as available materials, group organization, and a tribe or village's cultural and scientific development. A severe climate and threat of incursions from hostile neighbors propelled successful tribes into a more disciplined, belligerent, and/or military existence. Survival depended on securing food, sheltering against the weather, and defending one's territory, even if it only amounted to space of one's encampment or the distance illuminated by a central camp fire. Not all cultures developed and used the sword, but like the wheel, its universal simplicity made it an invention that transcended cultures around the globe.

The typical medieval footman of Europe carried a small falchion that was suitable for hand-to-hand combat. Knights carried the long sword with a strong point that could be employed only by the best of swordsmen, as did the typical Chinese warrior. Many nomadic tribes of Asia employed the curved sabre because of its crescent shape, and the Japanese, of course, preferred the curved shape of the tachi and katana. There are examples of cultures that used the straight blade, but a general argument could be made that mounted warriors often chose the sabre as their principal weapon because it was easier to use as a slash-and-draw weapon. Mongols, Huns, and Persians preferred the curved sabre, as did many European cavalry troops like the Cossacks and Hussars whose curved swords would be later adopted by French, British, and even American cavalry. This was not always true, as sword designs were a function of available raw materials, the influence of neighboring cultures, and the creativity of sword makers. The straight sabre of French and Russian cuirassiers from the Napoleonic era was a break from the curved cavalry sabre.[1]

In the case of the lightsaber, the development of a focused energy source capable of deflecting blaster fire, the principal weapon of the *Star Wars* universe, was a technological feat that has remained unchanged apparently for millennia. It was inevitable that a sword of this kind would become relegated to the hands of a few elites, because hand-to-hand combat was supplanted by the efficiency and ease of mastery of long-range projectile weapons. Weapons such as the English longbow, the Italian crossbow, and early firearms like the arquebus became weapons of the masses because they required only basic instruction. Mastery of these weapons still required the actual practice and training in organizational drill patterns to be used on the battlefield. The intense training in the use of such weapons can be illustrated by English laws that forbade the practice of any weapon on Sunday other than the longbow. Constricted cities like Venice and Genoa reserved open plazas for crossbow practice as well.

A combat weapon like a lightsaber and a sword required the instruction of a multitude of attacks and their variants as well as training in defensive blocking and the opening and closing of effective distance. All weapons required repetitive drilling, but the distance weapon only demanded that its projectile be let loose or be fired. Sword combat necessitated training with an opponent who would attack, feint, or retreat according to perceived aggressions of the opponent. Skills and endurance had to be accompanied by the development of a combative psychology. Swordsmen had to be drilled by experienced swordsmen, because one does not simply pick up the sword and instinctively know how to use it effectively. The fighting quality of Roman legions, who were drawn from a general citizenry, ebbed and flowed with the experience of its formations.

The gladiatorial uprising led by Spartacus in 73 B.C. illustrated how the honed skills of gladiators could be used to defeat even "battle-hardened" troops.[2] The initial revolt started with thirty to seventy men (most of them gladiators) who quickly began to instruct ordinary slaves in actual combat and tactical maneuvers. Their success against Gaius Cassius Longinus, governor of Cisalpine Gaul south of the Alps, demonstrated how a rabble of ex-slaves could be soundly trained and organized to defeat established frontier legions. When hand-to-hand combat was required, a successful engagement depended on spirit, quality, and the effective use of force-multiplication through battlefield organization. The moral fiber and cohesion of a unit could displace and master the technological advantage of superior weaponry. At the empire's periphery, the élan of barbarian tribes easily defeated and overwhelmed newly formed Roman units, shattering the general conception that the Roman war machine was invincible. The maintenance of well-trained and experienced soldiers required the empire to maintain a high standard of training and battle readiness. Apart from gladiatorial life, which was considered one of the lowest social positions in society, no civilian job provided the skills or training for battle.

In a universe where even the least technologically sophisticated societies could get their hands on the blaster, only the specialized and disciplined training of a group of warriors like the Jedi could develop the skills to effectively wield their light sword against blaster fire. Were the steel sword able to deflect the slug of a bullet, there is no doubt that the sword would have remained an essential weapon today as the lightsaber does in the *Star Wars* universe.

Construction

The construction of a metal sword (called bladesmithing) consisted of combining metals and then forming the blade into its shape. Early techniques consisted of simply hammering metals together to shape them into a blade. In the stock-removal technique, metals were combined in a molten process and then poured into a metal cast. The final step was the grinding down of the flat edge into a sharp one. Smiths using this casting technique could manufacture weapons more quickly than by the hammering process and achieve a high degree of consistency in the quality of their products. Cast metal, however, because of its high degree of homogeneous content, did not fully meet the needs of the exceptional blade.

A rigid blade gave strength to the sword, but it also left it susceptible to shattering or chipping when pushed to its integral limits. Too soft a blade allowed the blade to bend under stress, but it quickly dulled. The answer to these seemingly mutually exclusive qualities was to combine soft metals with harder metals. Bronze, a combination of copper and tin, was formed and shaped by either cold or hot pounding, a process called deforming. Iron is a tough material, but when shaped into a sword it had a propensity to bend. Steel, a combination of iron and carbon, is too brittle and prone to snapping when stressed. The logical step, then, was to combine the steel and iron in a forging technique called pattern welding, which produced a strong and durable weapon.

An alternative to pattern welding, which was a physically demanding process of hammering and folding, was the development of wootz steel, most commonly referred to as Damascus steel. The process was developed in India, though its use was quickly spread by nomadic conquests throughout Asia and westward into the Middle East and North Africa. Because Damascus was one of the centers of Islamic culture that depended heavily on the production of bladed weapons, the city became synonymous with weapons of exceptional quality. While still requiring hammering, wootz steel gets its strength during the solidification process of the steel, which created a patterned effect that is characteristic of Damascus blades. It does not have the toughness of pattern-welded blades, but does keep a very sharp edge.[3]

Blades from Japan provided one of the best examples in weapon forging techniques. Not only did they have exceptional durability and utility on the battlefield, but the sword's status among Japanese crafts was regarded equally as art. A complex nomenclature and plethora of foundry histories in Japan speak to the quality of sword making in that country. Blade making in Japan is a ritualized activity that takes on the trappings of an outward religious expression. Purification rituals from Shinto origin are part of the sword-making process, as are the traditional garbs of the most illustrious blade-making families.

Japanese blade makers responded to the necessity of both a rigidity and resilience by creating a blade with a soft core (which allowed the blade to flex) surrounded by an outer skin that held an edge of exceptional sharpness. The secret to its strength was the process of manufacture, which consisted of hammering down the steel and folding it back over itself, creating an exponential number of microscopic steel layers that gave the steel extreme resilience. Folding a billet of steel ten times resulted in over a thousand laminations, giving the blade an interwoven and layered pattern that strengthened the blade.[4] Since weapons of such quality demanded such intense labor, it became the custom of families to hand down their weapons to succeeding generations as venerated family treasures. Even today, there is an etiquette in the appreciation of a samurai blade when a family heirloom is shown to a visitor.

It was not at all defined how the lightsaber as a technological discovery occurred in the Republic, though much has been said and made up about its inner mechanisms. Arguments abound: Does the "light" of the blade have the physical properties of light? Does the blade radiate heat? Is the "light" of the blade really plasma? What inner mechanisms power the lightsaber? All these questions (and others) have an impact on the definitive properties of the blade, but such scientific minutia affect the understanding of the lightsaber in only a minor way for the purposes of this book. Instead of going into the science of the lightsaber, it is sufficient to examine the weapon's outward properties as found in the actual *Star Wars* movies.[5]

Because of limited experience with actual sword fighting drill and combat, there is a tendency among fantasy writers to mystify the creation of the lightsaber by a Force-powerful Jedi in the *Star Wars* Expanded Universe. Instead of a more logical and scientific explanation, writers have been drawn to Vader's statement in Episode VI ("I see you have constructed a new lightsaber. Your skills are complete."), interpreting it to mean that a required skill of a Jedi Knight was the ability to create a lightsaber.[6] Numerous (and more plausible) explanations could exist. The technology of a lightsaber could have been developed serendipitously during the invention of some other "light-dependent" experimentation. Perhaps in the search for a new kind of laser to quarry stone or cut metal the lightsaber "blade" was discovered. Another posits that scientists early in Jedi history sought the invention of a laser-deflecting substance to replace their metal swords. Writings in the Expanded Universe reject these theses, arguing that the lightsaber owes its invention to the ancient Jedi and Sith from the Dark Horse graphic novels, which shows early lightsabers as attached by a cable to an energy pack carried on the torso. The scientific leap of a power-pack lightsaber without the prior development of a mundane sword constructed of metals seems utterly preposterous.

The one conundrum in lightsaber technology rests with its ability to deflect Sith lightning. Is its deflection a result of the physical properties of the sword (much like fire is used to extinguish fire) or is it a result of the Jedi Knight's ability to utilize the Force in conjunction with his lightsaber? It has never been explained, but it might be possible to press the assertion that manipulation of the Force involves manipulation of the physical atoms of the universe. If one were to consider Force lightning as a substance with gravitational mass, then manipulation of Force lightning would be akin to the ability of a black hole to bend energy molecules toward itself. There is no convenient answer; nor does the story necessitate one.

In Episode V, circumstances necessitated Luke's need to create his own lightsaber. Luke could have created his weapon alone without the help of others or, more likely, he sought outside assistance. The former would imply that his basic skills with mechanical objects (especially with as complicated a transport like his skyhopper) permitted Luke to invent or "discover" the mechanisms for creating a new lightsaber. This would also imply that the technology of the lightsaber was rather common and available throughout the universe. The other possibility involves Luke seeking out Jedi documents or individuals who might have been able to explain to him the physical mechanisms of a lightsaber. Yet for lack of a better explanation, magical events and mystical experiences were used to explain the presumably antiquated technology of a weapon that has been around for centuries if not millennia. *Jedi Quest: Path to Truth*[7] sidesteps the question altogether when author Jude Watson has Anakin "unconsciously" construct his lightsaber during a meditative state that leads to a threatening vision about Darth Maul.

Without contradicting Vader's canon statement from Episode VI, Luke could still have been responsible for the construction of his own lightsaber, if even by supervising the making of its component pieces and then putting them together on his own. Rather than a clandestine quest for crystals (as shown in the *Clone Wars* cartoon), hard-to-find metallic fuses, and/or rare electrical wiring, why not take advantage of the greatest minds and resources available to the Rebel Alliance and its network of sympathizers to create the best possible lightsaber since the extinction of the Jedi Order a decade earlier?

In the time of the Jedi, it is hard to believe that every Jedi had to scrounge up pieces and parts in order to construct his or her own lightsaber. Did every Jedi have to reinvent the wheel when it came to the construction of the lightsaber? Did the Jedi temple not have dedicated lightsaber workshops? And were apprentices barred from Knighthood if they could not show the aptitude to construct one? The simple calculation of procuring materials for thousands of Jedi and prepubescent students not yet even at the Padawan level requires deliberate thought and inventory. With a weapon as dangerous as the lightsaber where even the slightest miscalculation or absentmindedness could mean the loss of a finger or even a limb, it would seem that the construction of a lightsaber is best left to specialists.

It would seem that the general dis-use of the lightsaber could be easily explained by the preponderance of a more pragmatic blaster, though the continued use of a weapon like a lightsaber might have nostalgic value to some in the galaxy. The Episode IV novelization includes a statement by Obi-Wan about the general accessibility of the lightsaber: "At one time they [lightsabers] were widely used. Still are, in certain galactic quarters."[8] The opulent and extravagant times of Anakin's youth (the prequel era) expressed a period of designed and crafted regalia. Likewise, in our own contemporary history, the collection and admiration of fine blades is still appreciated as it might have been in an earlier age. While latter sword blades may have been stamped out in presses for mass consumption, hand-crafted aristocratic swords would still have been considered a necessary accessory to the gentleman's ensemble. His weapons had to have an aesthetic design that impressed one's friends *and* adversaries of the culture and richness of the sword wearer.

In light of the lightsaber's general utility (it was as relevant in a firefight with blasters as a bootstrap knife would be in the hands of a commando during a hand-to-hand combat situation), the Jedi's weapon was also easily understood as a court and parade weapon on the Jedi's regular visits to the courts and governments of the Galactic Republic. It was a clever feat that Lucas captured both the romantic and utilitarian aspects of the cinematic sword fight when he created the lightsaber.

Function Follows Form

Shape Relates to the Cut, Laceration, and Thrust

Apart from the construction of the blade, a great deal of sophistication was devoted to shaping the blade and adorning it with decoration. On a practical level, the shape of the blade had an impact on the cutting, slicing, and chopping power of the blade, as did the point, which allowed the tip of the weapon to become a useful part of the sword.

Swords are generally divided into curved and straight-edged blades. Straight edges are of simplest manufacture and are found throughout the world from Asia (especially China), Europe, and Africa. Curved swords are common in many cultures, including India, Persia, and the Islamic lands of North Africa and the Middle East. On a cultural note, the religions of Christianity and Islam have had a deep effect on the shapes of their swords. Christians preferred the cruciform weapon, which echoed the shape of the cross on which Jesus died, while the scimitar imitated the crescent shape that is sacred to Muslim iconography. Even today, competitive Western fencing begins with a salute that imitates the Christian kissing his blade before battle.

The shape of the sword has a subtle impact on the cutting power of the weapon. And depending on the skill of the sword wielder, its cutting effectiveness could be used to greater efficiency. If a sword is balanced properly, the proper striking edge of the sword, called the center of percussion, is found a little above the center of the blade toward the sword tip. When a blade strikes a target at this point, there is no jar during collision, effectively permitting an efficient cut that uses the weight of the sword, added momentum from the swing of the arm, and the slicing action of the blade.

Properly speaking, there are two kinds of cuts that are impacted by the shape of the blade — the cut and the laceration. The cut is the contusion of a blade directly perpendicular to the target, usually made by a straight blade. The blade touches the outer skin, pushing it downward until it braces against bone. Because of its elastic nature, the skin spreads until the epidermis breaks along the line of the sword's edge which then pushes through the flesh. If there is enough force, the edge smashes through bone (and possibly through to the other side of the appendage) or lodges itself into the flesh or bone. The laceration (slice) can be achieved by both the straight and the curved blade, though it is more easily achieved by the latter because of a more acute angle at impact. A laceration is made when an edged blade tears into the skin at an angle, pulling or pushing at the flesh and ripping into the epidermis. The pull of the flesh in the downward slope is enhanced by a curved blade, but most straight blades, because of the angle created from a dropping arm, pull naturally toward the swordsman's body, slicing into flesh, though not as easily as with a curved blade.

Generally, a blade edge is straight (i.e., it is not serrated) and follows the curve of the sword so that the width of the sword remains constant along the length before tapering off at the tip in either a point or a flat, though often rounded end. Most swords are distinguished by the shape of the flat of the blade. A straight edge cuts with greater facility, though, as has already been mentioned, the cut is really the microscopic tearing of the skin. Serrated edges have also been used, very often for aesthetic effects of an undulating or wavy appearance. Blades of this kind are not generally as effective as a straight edge because the ridges tend to impede the slice because of added friction. The flamberge, which takes its name from the French root for fire, is a huge two-handed sword with a wavy edge, some five to six feet in height, and is carried upright without a scabbard like a rifle on the shoulder. When used in battle the rounded notches prevent the blade from digging into the wooden hafts of pikes, slightly preventing them from sliding down the length of the blade toward the wielder. This type of wavy edge has a very pleasing aspect and can be seen on many dirks and daggers, which relied less on serration than on thrusts. The Filipino kris is an excellent example of a serrated stabbing knife.

The second use of the sword in attacking is the thrust, which works through incision and then separation. The point penetrates the epidermis and then separates as the blade pushes into the flesh. The point is deflected or stopped entirely when it strikes bone. While modern styles of fencing seem to emphasize the thrust in its extreme, the use of the point has always been an effective way of attacking an opponent. When facing a single opponent, the use of the point is a very effective tactical approach. Against multiple attackers, a blade edge is more easily employed against aggressors approaching at varying distances and speed. Armor has always been the primary means of thwarting a slash, but no armor short of a sealed box is immune from penetration. The thrust into the joints of an opponent's armor has, therefore, become a secondary method of attack. Attacks to the arms or legs will immobilize the appendage (the muscles, ligaments, or tendons will render the muscles too weak to carry on the battle) while attacks to the torso will result in a soft kill (a slow death) if it does not hit a vital organ.

The lightsaber had particular qualities that seemed to depend more on the technical requirements of film that reflect a "commonsense" approach to lightsaber characteristics than on any scientific properties of the physical world.

In the Original Trilogy, the lightsaber was used against two living beings (the Walrus Man and Luke) and a host of metal objects, including Darth Vader's armor and his mechanical right hand. In the first case, there was no cauterization as evident from the blood spread around the arm's socket joint. In Episode V, Luke's hand is burned cleanly, sealing body fluids behind a cauterized stump. In the case of objects, the lightsaber seems to burn into metal with a blinding flash and a burning cut. In all instances, the lightsaber, while it is said in the *Star Wars* databank to cut through "almost anything,"[9] depends on inertia to penetrate into harder substances. Following a commonsense expectation, slicing through biological material would be far easier than cutting through metal, which hinders the lightsaber blade with visible resistance. Vader's shoulder plate also demonstrated a resistance to the lightsaber blade, which would have otherwise cut to Vader's neck.

Lightsaber fights in the Prequel Trilogy provided a new set of circumstances under which lightsaber scenes were filmed. The lightsaber was used against living beings, as well as a host of metal objects (battle droids, blast doors, bulkheads, and MagnaGuard electrostaffs) that were penetrated without any resistance. It was as if the lightsaber sliced through thin air, which was how many fight scenes were actually filmed. The lightsaber scenes were in reality a blue-screen fight in which actors wielded lightsaber props with short fluorescent stumps that served as guides to Industrial Light and Magic (ILM) animators who digitally created a host of characters, droids, and background creatures. In the case of lightsaber attacks against digital objects or creatures such as battle droids or Geonosian drones, there is no resistance whatsoever. Strikes against clone troopers do superficial damage cutting through armor, but unlike Obi-Wan's injuries against Dooku on Geonosis, Episode III lightsaber cuts were deadly.

When used against Qui-Gon at the end of Episode I, Darth Maul's double-bladed lightsaber pierced through Qui-Gon's chest cavity without any visible resistance. In addition, there was no visible flesh pushed out against Qui-Gon's back, which implies that his flesh was "burned up" when the lightsaber rammed through his chest. Were this the real world, Qui-Gon probably would have died instantly because his spinal cord would have been too severely traumatized to allow the body to continue functioning. The fight on Geonosis between Dooku and Obi-Wan/Anakin illustrates the Jedi's ability to make shallow, non–life-threatening cuts. Dooku's eventual beheading reflects the ease of cutting through the neck while the climactic battle between Anakin and Obi-Wan demonstrates the ability of the lightsaber to effortlessly and quickly cut through three of Anakin's appendages. How that cut is accomplished is quite curious (it is never actually shown on film), but Lucas has always been known to take as much creative license as he wishes in order to carry out his story.

Sword Length and Weight

There is, at least in principle, an ideal sword length for each individual. But since swords are not generally constructed with a particular individual in mind, it has always been difficult to find the "perfect" sword for an individual. Construction standardization also meant a universal design to which the individual had to adapt himself, especially in the case of the "mass produced" stock-removal bladesmithing technique. When warriors were expected to provide their own weapons, the quality and variability in length, size, and weight differed considerably from one weapon to the next.

The ideal sword was also affected by the purpose and use of the weapon in question. While swords could be quite short — the Roman *gladius* measuring twenty inches typically — there was no true measure that technically separated a sword from a dirk, dagger, or knife. Standards that do exist, such as those surrounding the categorization of Japanese blades and the Oakeshott typology, were an arbitrarily established by custom and personal preference. Shorter bladed weapons usually derived their name from the style of design generally associated with its use. The knife was therefore meant for short-range cutting, mostly as a utility tool. Daggers and dirks were meant for stabbing at close distance, the latter being more streamlined and lighter. Shorter weapons like the medieval falchion were good basic weapons for close infighting. One can easily imagine the difficulty trying to swing a weapon at the initial clash of the line. The short sword clearly had an advantage. While it did not have the same slashing power of a longer weapon, the clashing lineman's weapon was best used for quick thrusts at weak points in his opponent's armor. The Roman gladius worked extremely well in the battle line because its size allowed legionaries to use their swords in close quarters.

Longer swords, unless they reached too absurd a length, were generally classified in the same category. Variants were more easily set apart by their manner of grip than by blade length. The hand-and-a-half sword, more commonly known as the bastard sword, was therefore distinguished from the full-length two-handed sword, of which, the claymore was probably the prime example.

The success of an attack depended essentially on the ability to reach the target. Added length accorded the swordsman a slight advantage over the inferior sword. A simple rule follows that no matter the distance — whether a millimeter or a mile — if the sword is out of range, it can inflict no damage. Short swords therefore had a slight disadvantage against long swordsmen while suffering a notable disadvantage against mounted horsemen. On the other side, there was a gain in lightness, maneuverability, better balance, and a certain advantage in phalanx warfare with a short sword.

The weight of a sword, because of the pull of gravity, contributed substantially to the cutting power of the sword; but with added weight also came the possibility of increased fatigue. The weight of a sword, especially that of the two-handed type, had acquired a certain reputation for being so heavy that medieval sword fighting was clumsy and slow. Evidence has shown that both single and double-handed swords were of a weight that permitted ease of use.[10] A little over three pounds was typical for a single-handed sword; four and a half pounds for a two-handed sword. Certainly, the size of the person in relation to the size of the sword, as well as his manner of gripping the weapon — whether one or two handed — affected the relative power to a blow. Unequal men did not employ equal swords in equal manner.

The length and weight of the sword was usually designed according to personal preference, but limits on resources, availability of iron ore in particular, affected the manufacture of swords. Simple math shows that for every inch in added length to a series of equal swords there is a decrease in the number of total swords if supplies are limited. An interesting example was Darth Maul's double-bladed lightsaber, which has no historical precedent. Were double-bladed swords to be manufactured in vast quantities, it would presuppose a greater fighting distance between swordsmen because the two ends are equally dangerous to friendly forces and foes. Similarly, the gain in creating double-bladed swords would necessitate half as many traditional, single-bladed swords. On top of this, a completely different training regime would have been necessary to learn the double-bladed sword. Of course, it was because of these characteristics that the double-bladed lightsaber was ideally suited to the solitary Sith lord.

Weight, as well as the size of the hilt, also had a tangible bearing on whether a sword was held with one or two hands. If a larger sword was to be employed, increased strength and more specialized technique were required of the person of a smaller stature. A weapon's weight could also be mitigated by the manner in which it was gripped. The balance of the simple cruciform sword could be changed drastically by a grip called fingering in which the pointer finger was wrapped over the cross-guard. It was easier to maintain the balance of a sword if the grip were closer to the cross-guard as possible, but a technique called slipping was a grip with the fist at the pommel end of the grip.[11]

Grip and weight also had bearing on a sword's manner of use. Two-handed swords could not be effectively used while riding horses for a practical reason; one hand was used to control the mount, or, with advanced horse riding skills, the extra hand was used to hold a shield, to brace oneself against the horse for added reach, or to simply act as a counterbalance to the stroke of the one-handed slash.

The use of centrifugal force was also paramount to the sophisticated technical use of the sword. Again dependent on the weight of the sword, cutting power could be further enhanced by the controlled "throwing" of the sword toward the target. The sword, if held strongly enough to keep in the grip of the hand and lightly enough to allow for the subtle downward swing of the wrist at the end of a slash, could greatly magnify the speed of the sword. Combined with a quick squeeze just before impact, the slash received a substantial increase in the velocity. The principle was the same as launching a stone from a sling. By swinging the sling around the head until a comfortable speed was attained, the slinger released one of the two ends, sending the missile in a straight but descending line toward its target. Timing and the proper technical release of the first string was of utmost importance, else the stone would completely miss or fall harmlessly to the ground short of its target. Where the consequences of improper technique were evident in the sling, the proper strike of the sword with maximum potential force was equally difficult. If the sword hit too early, an increase in percussion (a jarring) of the cut would hamper the smooth execution of the cut. A late strike also decreases the power of the cut.

Another important consideration was the psychological importance of a substantive weight to the sword, which gave the wielder important feedback as he drew his weapon back for another strike. If a slash felt too light, the wielder was less likely to feel capable of inflicting the maximum potential damage; too heavy a feel would cause him to feel slow and sluggish in the execution of the attack. This posed an interesting problem for the lightsaber wielder.

By all commonsense standards, the lightsaber had neither the weight of a steel sword, nor the balance of one. It would then follow that there was less cutting power and a stilted point of percussion in a light energy blade. Since we cannot measure the scientific nature of the lightsaber, observers are forced to make assumptions that may or may not fit with the "reality" of the *Star Wars* universe.

From a swordsman's perspective, the reality of the lightsaber is simply that a prop sword is used. The lightsabers were made out of light metal or perhaps fiberglass, which meant that all movement was substantially faster than if a person had used a real sword. The weight of an attack with a prop was therefore much lighter than that of a solid metal sword. Since there is no reference for lightsaber sword fighting, the stunt coordinator/swordmaster was generally given free rein to create a fencing style that met Lucas's expectations for Jedi swordsmanship. His first swordmaster was Peter Diamond, a trained Western fencer. The swordmaster of the Prequel Trilogy was Nick Gillard, who admitted that his experience with the sword is self-learned and not directly influenced by personal training in any particular sword style. Assisting each swordmaster were a number of stuntmen with differing levels of sword and fencing experience who helped train principal actors and even acted as stunt doubles. Probably Lucas's best decision in creating a realistic lightsaber fight was the hiring of martial artist Ray Park. He took the choreography and gave it the appearance of believable lightsaber fighting. By knowing the technicalities of real sword fighting, Park was able to teach Neeson and McGregor a true feeling of the sword fight. His absence in Episodes II and III, as will be shown in chapter seven, has had an impact on the quality of lightsaber fighting.

Guarding

While the task of protecting the body was generally left to armor and shield, the sword could be used to parry a slash or thrust, serving as effectively as if wearing armor. Indeed, the name given to modern swordplay—fencing—conveyed the defensive purpose to which the sword was often used. The guard might also be called a block, a parry, or a stance. While all refer to the defense against an attack, the emphasis of each differs slightly but accomplishes the same objective—preventing an attack. A guard and a stance had a more general emphasis on the static position of the swordsman, while the block referred simply to the act of denying an attack its target. The parry included the idea of a block in motion.

A Japanese swordsman referred to the middle stance (called *chudan*) in which the sword was thrust forward with the point at the height of the opponent's head. Chudan referred to a static defensive position designed to thwart an attack; it was also an end point of movement as a swordsman moves his weapon to other offensive and defensive positions. For Henry de Sainct Didier (1573), the guard was the equivalent of an invitation or parry, emphasizing a static position that served to invite an attack to a particular part of the defender's body.[12] Francesco Antonio Marcelli (1696) emphasized the guard's defensive ability as "nothing other than that natural and composed position of the body."[13]

When the sword blade was used as a guard, the blow of an enemy strike had to be absorbed with either the flat of the blade, or, in the case of a sabre, with the back side of the blade.[14] Some sabres had a cutting edge up half of the back side of the blade, while the traditional long or broad sword had a sharp blade running along both sides of the weapon. The Japanese katana was a good example of a single-edged blade with a strong blunted backside, while many European sabres had a sharp edge along only half of the backside. The styles and variations were numerous and reflected mostly traditional (and often arbitrary) customs of the troops that used the weapon. In all cases, a clash of edge on edge had to be avoided in order to prevent chipping of the blade. While a slightly flattened edge could be sharpened with ease, there was little that could be done to fix the jagged teeth of a severely chipped edge. With a sabre, the blunted edge could be used to "catch" the slash of an enemy strike. The only option with a two-edged sword was to use the flat of the blade.[15]

Giving additional protection to the hand was a cross-guard. Simple at first, many hand guards later developed into a sophisticated and ornate form of hand protection. Rapiers (a cutting and slashing sword) and broad swords (a straight sabre) were increasingly affixed with more protective sword guards, giving protection against the thin-bladed point of a small sword. Others were characterized by the simple extension of prongs that wrapped around the fingers. Cup-hilt rapiers and basket-hilt sabres were the best examples of the sword guards that completely protected the hand. The Turkish yataghan and Russian shashqa dispensed with the guard altogether, giving particular emphasis to the offensive nature of the sword.

Especially from watching the clean cuts, parries, and counter-attack (technically called a riposte) in movies and theater, the general audience is apt to think that the reliance on the sword blade as a guard is an essential and preferred manner of using the sword. Reinforcing this was the Jedi use of the lightsaber as a shield against blaster fire, demonstrating an exceptional degree of control, especially when turning laser bolts back on its shooter. Too much reliance on defense, however, was a misguided strategy. The ideal and perfect attack was one that hit the opponent during an opening at the beginning of their own attack. The target area and the timing assured that the opponent had no physical possibility of moving out of distance, blocking, or completing his own attack. Any competitive fencer knows the perfect attack is not very rare and can be recognized when an attacker scores an attack so well that both he and his opponent know. Luigi Barbasetti (1859) in *Das Säbelfechten* said the parry "is really nothing more than a simple corrective measure, which, no matter how efficient it may be, remains only a passive factor." He continued that the "best parry is the blow."[16]

If a swordsman never attacks, he can never win the encounter. By allowing the opponent to keep the initiative, it becomes increasingly likely that the attacker will find an opening in his opponent's defensive blocks. A swordsman can only block one part of the body, which gives the attacker several open areas to strike. Mathematically, the probability that the defending fencer can choose the correct block diminishes with each attack because defense requires more energy and physical strength than an attack. A series of consistently threatening attacks will eventually overwhelm the defender because each parry must be made successfully to prevent the next attack.

If a parry or a block is to be made, it must be followed by an immediate attack called a riposte. It may be an immediate attack involving speed, or it may be slightly delayed, which causes the attacker-turned-defender to move prematurely into his own counter defense. When pressed by a strong attacker, the fencer has no choice but to begin a slow retreat in order to maintain proper fencing distance. Stepping back out of distance in response to a specific attack is called voiding. When there is no room for a deliberate retreat out of distance, the initiative moves completely to the attacker who can attack or feint at the moment of his own choosing.

In Episode VI, Luke demonstrated the necessity to attack during the fight scene over the Sarlacc pit. When faced against a host of attackers from every direction, Luke followed a basic rule of engagement that there is a better chance of survival by attacking than by waiting defensively for opponents to attack. By bringing the fight to his attackers, Luke prevented Jabba's henchmen from mounting a concerted effort against the young Jedi. The battle on Geonosis also showed how the defensive strategy of blocking blaster fire eventually overwhelmed the Jedi. One by one the Jedi were picked off because they were no longer able to maintain the complete deflection of every successive blaster bolt.

Qui-Gon and Obi-Wan in the opening scenes of Episode I demonstrated the need to cut their losses and avoid defeat by retreating from advancing droidekas. Darth Maul, just after he was forced into the power generator area, made a strategic retreat in order to get into better position against his two adversaries. Retreat for the sake of retreat and defense for the sake of defense, without the strategic purpose of gaining better offensive position, is a doomed enterprise. Even Yoda in Episode III must beat a final retreat from the Senate chambers because each passing moment meant the impending approach of clone troopers to defend the Palpatine.

Aspiring swordsmen quickly fall into the trap of trying to find the sword that provides maximum cutting or slicing power. Such a quest is a useless exercise, for no single blade achieves any specialization without admitting some area of weakness.[17] The situation and use of a sword best determine the ideal weapon. Experience is often instructive, as are many customs and traditions. The tendency for mounted warriors was to use a curved blade because it was functional as an edged weapon against both footmen and other cavalry. As the charge with points forward became a principal tactic used by 19th-century horsemen, the straight backsword (a sabre with a straight blade) became the favored weapon. During the Peninsular War (1808–1814), the French used their straight-bladed sabres in charges against the British, who used a curved sabre.[18] A two-handed sword would be more effective against an armored opponent, but the advantage of this weapon evaporates when confronting a nimbler opponent with a lighter rapier. Eventually, plate mail rendered even the heavy two-handed sword a less desirable weapon than the poleax, which had both a powerful smashing hammerhead and cutting snub-nosed ax.

What served the swordsman better than any particular blade and its specialization was his skill to adapt to the strengths and weakness of the sword in hand, the protective armor of his opponent, and the tactical weaknesses of his enemy. In a one-on-one fight, a Goth warrior might push a Roman's shield up with his left hand to cover his opponent's vision for a moment while slipping in around the Roman's left to attack behind the shield for a strike under his helmet to neck below the left ear. Even if one were to find the perfectly balanced weapon with exactly the correct weight and center of percussion, one must never exclude the possibility that the sword might be broken or lost during the melee. More than in any other situation, attachment to one's own specially crafted weapon was an invitation to its loss at the most opportune moment. This was true of the warrior on the battlefield, the fencer in a competition, and the student in a training hall. A deleted scene in Episode I showed Qui-Gon scolding Obi-Wan for losing his lightsaber. What could not be replaced was the swordsman's personal training and his commitment to the values of the profession, which, for the Jedi, were respect for the law and desire for justice. Respect shown for a weapon was respect for what the lightsaber stood for, not a cult of its worship. Attachment to a weapon reflected one's greedy desire to stand out among others for the simple pleasure of being admired. Both Obi-Wan's admonishment to Anakin that "this weapon is your life" and the cliché that the sword is the soul of the samurai are hyperbole. Respect for one's weapon should not be confused with idolatry. In combat it was not the sword that won. It was the swordsman who had to win.

Battle

While swordsmen in a duel fought on roughly equal terms, soldiers of the battlefield confronted (and expected) gross inequalities. Unless a ruler had the power and resources to fully arm his troops, the weapons, armor, and training of melee combatants varied as much within one army as it did between armies.

In the duel, the spirit of a level playing field between gentlemen assured the use of the same weapon for both men; if one used armor, so, too, did his opposite. On the battlefield, however, troops very often armed themselves as well as they could afford or as well as inventories lasted.[19]

When armies opposed each other on the battlefield before the general use of the arquebus or musket, the victor was not necessarily the commander with numerical superiority or superior weapons. Apart from demoralizing enemy troops with a show of superior troops, victory would go to the commander who could mate superior troops against weaker troops while minimizing or maintaining the strength, position, and moral of the weakest units. A common custom among Western armies was to place the best troops (*primatus pugnae*) on the far right, considered to be the place of honor for elite and specialized troops. This also permitted the most ablest troops to control the rightward drift of lines, which unconsciously moved to protect their unshielded side.[20]

The battle line was designed to be fought on uneven terms, the commander sacrificing one advantage for a weakness in hope that his combination of tactical lines would be strong enough to break and sever the lines of his opponent. Opening volleys of arrow, crossbow, or spear were meant to loosen up the lines, while advancing troops— spearmen, swordsmen, or cavalry—would deliberately advance until the final moments when troops from each side would meet. Sometimes the advance would be filled with yells and taunts; more disciplined troops would advance in silence. Roman sources provide an evolution of the final close of troops. During the time of Polybius (3rd to 2nd centuries B.C.), Roman soldiers would bang on their shields and yell war cries. In later years under Caesar (1st century B.C.), lines would march forward silently so orders could be heard, then throw their javelins, called *pili* (singular: *pilus*), before charging with a loud scream just before impact. The period during the late Roman army (3rd century A.D.) was characterized by the *barritus*— rising war cry just before the charge.[21] Footmen would continue the push against their enemies, while elite troops, usually mounted knights or cavalry, would be advanced to critical points of weakness in the enemy line. When one side's morale broke, soldiers would begin to think more of their own lives than their comrades. Battles, being the culmination of strategic movement and position, may have lasted the better part of a morning or afternoon; perhaps even the better part of a day as soldiers retreated in order to reassemble for another charge. Once the general rout had begun (often characterized by the retreat or fall of the commander in the rear), there was little that could stop the victor other than his own exhaustion. The victorious commander would then have to decide whether a full pursuit or a regrouping of his troops was necessary. Pursuing troops were prey to ambushes or even the surprise of reserve troops.

The greatest fear of any warrior was the open wound from a piercing weapon. With weapons in hand, one of the greatest obstacles in hand-to-hand combat was the fear of exposing one's flesh to an opponent's weapon while at the same time trying to inflict similar damage on an opponent. Especially for soldiers with little or no experience or practice with a weapon, sword combat was a competition of firsts in which one had to dispatch the enemy before he could receive an injury. Preparation ahead of battle by donning the passive protection of armor was reassurance against the solid blow. But no armor gave maximum protection. Rather, armor's purpose was to give the warrior the chance to deal a decisive blow to one's opponent without being first incapacitated.

Unlike ranged weapons, which prevented a face-to-face exchange of arms, the use of armor in battle has never been considered a dishonorable practice. The development of armor and its evolution reflected a realistic assessment of the conditions of the battlefield. If one were to engage in a conflict without being able to engage in combat, as would be the case if archery or gunfire would dispatch the most experienced and trained soldier, then soldiers would have to adapt to the new threat. And where improvements in weapons, such as the superiority of the longbow against chain mail and the crossbow against plate mail, have generally been acknowledged as technological advances that gave victory to one side, the effects of superior armor were rarely acknowledged because documentation of the effectiveness of armor was generally reflected in the dead bodies in which armor failed. One hundred twenty-five soldiers at the battle of Wisby died of arrow or crossbow bolts through the mailed head.[22] This does not indicate how many survived strikes to the head, nor how many arrows were deflected because of angles in the chain mail or additional covering like a solid helmet. Indeed, some of the historian's difficulty is being able to pick through historical accounts and observations to distinguish between heroic and literary "description" and accurate reporting.

The effectiveness of armor can be examined in part by looking at the evolution of weapons as countermeasures to armor. Only in the rare battle did armor so completely fail that victory was lost because of it. Even in the famed battles of Crecy (1346) and Agincourt (1415) in which French knights were decimated by English longbow arrow, there were conflicting accounts of the importance of the bow on armed knights. Some asserted that it was the courage and tactics of the commoners that led to the defeat of the French knights at Crecy,[23] while others said it was more a result of footmen attacking as darkness fell upon the battlefield.[24] At Agincourt, it was not the longbow that doomed the French knights, but a combination of missile fire tightly packed knights, and muddy terrain, followed by a close-quarter melee of ax and sword.

More often than not, victory or defeat was generally given to troops with the stronger force of will or superior tactics. Swiss soldiers began their century of dominance when their simplistic tactics (a mass of pikes) and stubbornness held the cavalry charge of Burgundian knights. Swiss soldiers equally proved themselves against Imperial landsknecht who adopted the same strategy of pike formations. Critical to Swiss superiority over the Germans were iron will and determination. So contemptuous were the Swiss and Germans of each other that each refused to accept surrender from the other. The results were massive casualties from the initial clash and the determined slaughter of the losing troops. So devastating were such clashes between the Swiss and German landsknecht, that commanders on both sides hesitated to commit their troops to such ill-ending exchanges unless absolutely necessary.

For elite troops, reputation has an unerring positive effect on morale. Such troops were not unbeatable, but they fought with such audacity that they were perceived as invincible. Due to their zealous and fanatical nature, the mere mention of their advance has been known to have a chilling effect on troops preparing to meet them in battle. The Spartan reputation caused fear in the ranks of Greeks during ancient times; many accounts mention the devastating effect the appearance of the Spartans' scarlet capes had on the morale of troops just about ready to meet them in battle. Even in modern times, stories were told that many Argentinean troops in the Falkland War (1982) were want to flee upon hearing that Gurkha units were advancing.

Examples of superior tactics abound and need little illustration here, but it becomes clear that apart from the morale and experience of one's troops, battlefield success is generally considered a function of strategic planning and execution — the proper composition of soldiers placed in the proper formation followed by the proper execution of attacks.

Every line of men was generally imbued with certain distinctions that were used to exploit the weakness of an opponent army. Spear and pike men held lines against cavalry. Longbows threatened mailed knights at a distance. Crossbows could penetrate plate mail, while cavalry decimated lightly armed bowmen and crossbowmen at close range. Expert generals could arrange these formations to best exploit the weakness of enemy troops.

As in a game of chess, certain formations may have been used to hold the main force, or even be sacrificed, in order to allow troops elsewhere to penetrate a weakness in the enemy line. Cavalry was a highly mobile shock force, while range weapons of spear, arrow, and bolt could inflict heavy losses on advancing troops. Later, when the use of the cannon was more fully developed, shot and cannon balls were used to break up highly organized formations. It became imperative that cannon be neutralized, if not taken out completely, before the main lines advanced into their range.

Because battle was a creative enterprise, the successful general was he who made the best use of his strengths, while denying exposure of his weaknesses.

The ideal was to command a force far superior in numbers to the enemies, but other considerations also affected the quality of his troops, including how well armed they were, their experience, their esprit de corps, and, of course, their armor.

Armor

The availability of armor depended on monetary and material resources, manufacturing capabilities, and quality of craftsmen. And while the bulk of most armies were made of men with relatively limited training, armor did make a difference in units trying to resist better armed troops. Greek soldiers purchased their own armor or took it as a trophy from earlier battles. In medieval Europe, knights were obligated to provide for their own arms and armor, while in the 17th century, European monarchies, in particular the Swede King Gustavus Adolphus, created one of the first European professional armies that had both standard uniforms and equipment as well as training.

Among the principal benefits of armor was the ability to take an attack without complete incapacity. The helmet was basic to every army the world over. Some were complete metal masks while others were simply wagging feather. The composition of body armor ranged from the most rudimentary materials (cloth, wood, studs, leather) to heavier and protective metal (mail, plate).

Helmet

The helmet was a simple form of protection for any kind of soldier. Helmets came in a variety of shapes and sizes, from basic metal caps to elaborate helms, and afforded reasonable security at a very inexpensive price. The psychological necessity of protecting the face and head cannot be overemphasized. Whether from thin strips of hammered bronze or forged from thick plates of heavy iron, the helmet was essential protection to the head from either minor lacerations that allowed blood to drip down into one's eyes or from powerful cuts that clove through the skull, which meant near instantaneous death.

In the ritualized practice of Japanese sword *kata* (precisely determined practice movement), the strike to the head requires the greatest amount of training. Kata with wooden swords called bokken revolves around basic strikes to the head that stop inches from the forehead. In actual training, these attacks are not pulled strikes, but ones with the force necessary to split the skull open. A real cut could, therefore, be made if the threshold of the target were simply lowered a mere 3–5 inches. A swordsman is not unrealistically trained to expect complete penetration of the target. He has to control the depth of the strike according to the circumstance. He might therefore give more force to the cutting of an arm with the intent to cleave it off, while limiting the strike and power to penetrate the armor of a leather glove to cut wrist tendons. To use massive power to cleave the entire body from a head cut was a stupid and wasteful expense of energy. The head cut had to penetrate the skull, but the blade then had to be dislodged in order to continue combat.

Without the helmet, soldiers would feel exceptionally vulnerable to sword cuts that were quite simply designed to traumatize or impede the vital control functions of the brain, including seeing and hearing. Consequently, there was always an exchange of protection for the ability to use one's sight and hearing. Flat top helmets protected faces from the sun and allowed clear vision and hearing. Conical helmets were superior to the flat type because they allowed blows to glance off the head, and where they covered the ears, diminished hearing was an unintended consequence of better protection.

Helmets could be worn under or over chain mail. Roman legionary helmets had a pivoting side plate that allowed both protection and unobstructed hearing. Larger helms provided greater protection, especially those with a neck skirt of chainmail called an aventail. Unfortunately, they isolated the ears completely and only permitted forward vision through thin slits. Helms that covered the face entirely had to have ventilation holes for breathing, resulting in the last minute lowering of the helm or visor. Other derivations of the helmet included the sallet, which covered the head below the ears and was accompanied by a thick metal throat plate called a bevor.

Headgear is to this day a distinguished feature of every military force. Whether for parade or for combat, any type of head protection, whether a foxskin cap, a wrapped turban, or a metal or kevlar helmet is therefore the second most important object to the soldier after an offensive weapon. And even the pageant-like ostrich or eagle feather, horsehair crest, or tricorn hat served as a practical impediment that made the visible outline of the head less obvious. So if a helmet, like a quilted jacket or leather suit, can stay the clash to the head for just a second, it acts like armor by giving the defender those extra seconds in which to strike back at his opponent decisively.

The helmet is the easiest way to distinguish warriors on the battlefield. The same was true of *Star Wars*. Among Naboo forces, distinctive head gear could be used to identify security officers, guards, and palace guards. The simple cap or a leather helmet often shows rank. The evolution of clone trooper helmets can even distinguish between generations or eras in their development. Bounty hunters like Jango and Boba Fett or Zam Wessel use the helmet for both identification and protection. And unlike any other *Star Wars* military unit, the blue Senate guards with their democratically Greek appearance contrasts with the sleek and modern headgear of Palpatine's Imperial Guard.

Shield

The shield was critically important in the development of warfare. Even in early design concepts, Ralph McQuarrie envisioned the stormtroopers carrying a shield and lasersword. Like the sword itself, the shield was considered a basic form of defense because it protected against distance weapons like arrows and thrown spears, the *ango* (dart), as well as a sword. In addition to armor, the shield acted as both a defensive barrier and an offensive weapon. Its weight, edge, or a boss in the middle of the shield could be thrust forward either to thwart an onrushing opponent or to bash into his opponent's shield, possibly knocking him off balance. The shield could also be manipulated as a cutting weapon by forcing a corner or edge into a face, thigh, or arm. Mostly a shield was used to absorb the blows of an attacker.[25] A shield could also be used in conjunction with those of other warriors by interlocking them to provide a static wall against charging attackers or incoming missiles.

The shield's size played an important part in the manner in which the soldier would fight. The larger the shield, the more effective it would be against missiles. Italian crossbowmen carried a large shield called a pavise, which stood upright on its own so the crossbowman could retreat behind it in order to reload his weapon. A medium-size shield provided enough protection for the upper body. It was considerably lighter than a full-size shield and could be easily manipulated into a high and low position as needed. Larger shields like those of the Romans and the Normans protected much of the body, reflecting a personal preference in combat. Roman drills permitted strict discipline within the ranks, which made a shield very effective. Romans were even able to create a shield wall on all sides called a testudo. Even smaller shields were used by very mobile troops. The Greek peltast carried a small moon-shaped shield in addition to his javelins. During the middle ages, a buckler, a small shield a little bit larger than the hand, was an extremely mobile defense used in the same manner a small dagger would be employed with a rapier.

The shield was constructed out of many materials, including wicker, leather, wood, and metal. Like the breastplate, size and weight counteracted mobility and encumbrance. The larger the shield, the more difficult it was to move it quickly. It fatigued the warrior as well. A thicker shield provided more of a defense against arrows but it also weighed more. To combat the shield bearer, a kick was very effective. The Romans invented a bendable spiked spear that was meant to stick into a shield if it did not hit exposed flesh. The barbed hook and the weight of the spear would weigh the shield down, perhaps even forcing the opponent to dispose of it altogether. They even created a dart called an ango, which was a short spear connected to a rope. Once the spear penetrated a shield, men holding the ropes would then pull to either wrest the shield out of the opponent's hands or tug on it intermittently to distract him during combat.[26]

In *Star Wars*, the shield McQuarrie conceived for a shield-bearing stormtrooper was discarded when the lightsaber was reserved for the Jedi knight. At that point, the Imperial trooper, as well as his clone trooper precursor, came to reflect the modern soldier with a medieval warrior-monk as his leader or arch-nemesis. Gungans in Episode I employed a shield that actually reflected blaster fire. Their effectiveness seemed to be an effective countermeasure to battle droid weapons, but it was clear that the sheer number of battle droids would prove too much of a match against the Gungan army.

Leather Armor

The earliest and most basic form of armor was developed by layering thick fabrics. Slightly better were those made from hides of leather. By layering leather, this relatively cheap form of protection was ideal for northern climates. Such "hide smiths" required neither exceptional ability nor exceptional tools, and could be found anywhere leather workers could be found.

In the case of sword blows that did not squarely strike a target, leather could prevent deadly lacerations and allow a counterattack. Rings, studs, or metal bars sewn to the outside of the leather could further absorb the force of the sword edge by distributing the force of blow to a wider area. But leather could not fully prevent penetrations caused by direct hits from sword points. Accomplishing a penetrating thrust could be a rather difficult task, however, requiring a strong thrust on the target. Such a penetration had to be quick (and painful) to prevent an opponent from possibly mustering several slashes. Such thrusts could only be made with sharp points, using the force of body weight to prevent the opponents leather armor from pushing into the soft fat of the skin and absorbing the thrust without being penetrated. Daggers or dirks certainly prove their usefulness in this kind of situation.

When large numbers of individuals were poorly armored (individual peasants often had to find their own armor), the protection of the group suffered greatly. Without the benefits a possible second or third chance to slash at his opponent, the unprotected man in the front line. was more easily dispatched by the enemy. The loss of an additional sword strike was significant when the sight of one man falling had a psychological impact on the three to five men standing around him.

An interesting development regarding leather armor occurred at a time when the gun was beginning to render the full suit of armor obsolete. Because handguns and muskets had the penetrative power to pierce even the thickest suits of plate armor, the cost of acquiring and maintaining such specialized and heavy gear increased. The answer to the decline of plate armor was the development of the buff coat, which was essentially a new version of leather armor that protected against most sword cuts and still gave the swordsman excellent mobility both on and off a horse.

Combined with high leather boots, the buff coat was a good form of protection to the swordsman at a time when armies were becoming increasingly manned by commoners. National movements such as those during the English Civil War and the French Revolution made the clothing of vast armies a top priority. The blacksmith and the increasingly rarer armorer had neither the supplies nor the expertise to produce metal armor in the numbers required by newly formed national armies comprising virtually every male citizen. These armies maximized the remnants of armor such as the epaulet, which could be made of strong metal to thwart a sword blade. A heavy material or leather adornments would also defend against a sword cut.

Asian armies, and to a lesser extent Middle Eastern armies, also made extensive use of leather armor. Nomadic tribes, especially, made use of the hides when they culled their herds. And early in Japanese history, the leather coat was worn as a uniform and easily produced. Indian armies made extensive use of an overcoat very similar to the aketon. While covering the shoulders down to just below the knees, it provided good protection and extensive mobility. In Episode I, Gungan troops seem to be wearing light armor, which had limited resistance to battle droid blaster fire. Naboo security forces also took advantage of leather's aesthetic and protective qualities.

Scale Mail

A common improvement in leather armor was to attach strips of metal to the exterior much like roof shingles, with upper layers overlapping the studs used to attach individual plates of metal to the leather coat. Such armor was called scale mail. It created an impressive and often beautiful outer skin that dissipated the cutting power of a sword by distributing the force over the entire plate, small as it was. The basic design of scale mail centered around a protected torso held over the body by shoulder pieces. Eventually, the design gave over to the cuirass, which was a chest protector fitted more closely to the upper body. So universal was this bell-shaped design that the Greek *linothorax* looks like a carbon copy of modern kendo body armor—both even have a layer of overlapping pads over the groin area, called a *tare* in Japanese and *pteruges* (feathers) in Greek.

A reversed form of scale mail was the coat of plates, which had iron or steel plates riveted to the inside of a tunic or coat. In such instances, rich and expensive fabrics could be used for a nicer, more fashionable appearance. Coats of plates were usually identified by the series of studs that were obvious on the outside of the jacket.

Roman scale mail, often referred to in contemporary Latin as *lorica segmentata*, was the most recognizable expression of scale mail. In earlier times, the Romans widely used chain mail, but scale mail became common because of its relative ease in construction and maintenance on campaign. Assyrians and later medieval Europeans also made use of scale mail, though it fell into disuse when more protective forms of armor were developed.

Tradition Japanese armor can be generally categorized as scale mail. Early designs were barrel-shaped skirts. Later, torso protection was supplemented by elaborate shoulder, arm, and leg protection held together with tough fabrics, stiff stitching, and lamellar plating. As in Europe, the strength of the trunk protection was fortified by multiple layers of metal plates, lacquering, or thicker metal. Japanese armorers also used crossbows and firearms to test the reliability of the metal.

Hauberk of Chain Mail

The introduction of chain mail, also called a hauberk, added even greater protection against the sword cut. Made of interlocking iron or steel ringlets, an "overgarment" of sorts could be fashioned to cover the head, shoulders, torso, and if length allowed, the groin and upper leg. Mail stockings, called chausses, were also developed in 13th-century Europe to protect the legs, allowing the entire body except for the face to be covered.

Individual armorers fashioned a variety of patterns and shapes for the rings, but always the end result was a coat of metal that provided excellent protection against sword blades and points. It provided relatively good protection against arrowheads at great distances, though at closer range its strength diminished. Since chain mail did not allow arrows to glance off as did full body armor, large shields were still widely used with mail during the 11th and 12th centuries among soldiers in Europe and in the Middle East.

Mail armor's biggest drawback was the uneven distribution of the weight on the shoulders. Its weight depended on the construction and length of the armor and typically varied from 25 pounds to 35 pounds, including the weight of padded undergarments to cushion blows against the skin. Mail worn under a padded tunic called an aketon was somewhat cumbersome (it could weigh upwards of 60–70 pounds) and taxed the swordsman's stamina. Still, it was a weight to which the swordsman could easily adapt himself.

While a new set of freshly made chain mail was excellent protection for the swordsman, it did take considerable punishment in combat. Slashes from swords that cut squarely into the mail chipped away at the metal links, allowing subsequent slashes the ability to cut through the corselet of rings. Weather and heat had detrimental effects on the wearer as well as on the armor. The sun would heat metal, making it untouchable to the bare hand. An outer garment, called a surcoat, became a common sight in the 13th century. The surcoat was still little protection against the rust from humidity, rain, poor storage, and even perspiration in the armpit area. Bathing chain mail in a solvent of water and vinegar was one manner of removing the outer layer of rust, but at some point major repairs or the purchase of a new set of mail after a long campaign was essential.

Mail did afford the wearer sufficient protection. Combined with a tall shield and movement of the body to reduce the most vulnerable areas, mail was an effective defense that could easily save the wearer's life. As a result, sword cuts had to be made to the unprotected area of the body, which included in early hauberks of mail the wrist, calves, elbows, and face. Sword cuts, when made directly on the mail, had to be targeted at areas that rested solidly against the body, including the shoulders, upper arm and the thighs. Blows to hanging mail around the neck and at the sides would catch a series of links before the pressure of the sword edge could dig into individual links when it pushed against the body.

If opportunity allowed, thrusts instead of cuts could be made to the face and armpits. Great axes, those used as two-handed weapons (like those of the Vikings and the Saxons at the battle of Hastings), because of the greater force at the impact of the cutting edge, were even more effective at cutting through mail than a sword. War hammers, with either the small head on one side or the sharp pick on the other, also did considerable damage piercing mail. Bow and arrow, with its 60- to 80-pound pull, did considerable damage at close range, while crossbow bolts could easily penetrate mail.

Mail was so simple to design and construct that warriors from Europe to as far east as India and China made regular employ of chain mail according to their own customs and tactics. Saracens employed coats of mail when it was available, as did Turkish and Indian warriors. Mail would not only go out of fashion but would be replaced by more protective cover pieces that would eventually make up the full-body plate mail. Perhaps because of its expense or its historical association with the medieval period, chain mail was not used in the construction of armor in the *Star Wars* saga.

Plate Armor

Plate armor evolved over a period of hundreds of years, due to developments in technology and the need for increasing protection against superior weapons and battle field tactics. The "invention" of individual parts of what would eventually become a full suit of plate mail (also referred to as a harness) can never be dated precisely.

The individual looking for regularity and consistency in the development of armor will be sorely disappointed. Not only was the use of armor haphazard among national or regional armed forces, personal armor differed greatly within armies as well. Similarly, the development of more sophisticated types of armor did not necessarily indicate its use, though it does help to examine arms and armor of European troops in relation to the passing of significant battles in European history.

During the 11th century, around the time of the Norman invasion of England in 1066, the mail hauberk was the general form of armor worn by the nobles at the battle of Hastings. Later, during the Crusades in the 12th century, mail was beginning to see threats from the crossbow, which could penetrate mail with greater efficiency. In centuries following, Christians, upon their earliest ventures into the Holy Land, brutally defeated lightly armored and armed Saracen troops. In response, the Muslims learned to avoid direct confrontations, choosing instead to fire arrows into the crusader lines until they were sufficiently softened for a direct attack.

Early in the 13th century, additional body protection was developed to be worn over chain mail. Greaves were used to protect the leg; first as padding, then metal plates on the front attached over mail or as studded leather coverings, and finally, a complete metal-covered leg. Surcoats and gambetons (metal plated overcoats) provided additional protection, as well as a fashionable medium for heraldry. It was at this time that elbow protection called couters were strapped over the mail on the elbows. Espaulers (shoulder defenses) also came into use. Because of the addition of metallic components to armor, the sword, too, began to evolve into a heavier and more pointed weapon than the shorter and lighter swords of the earlier century.

The 14th century led to the development of full sets of armor. The battle of Crécy, which marked the fall of the French nobility to an army of English composed of mostly longbowmen, was made up of mostly armored knights wearing coats of plate. Other knights wore older armor, which amounted to plate attachments to hauberk, chausses (leg mail), and metal forearm guards, while the richest wore complete sets of plate that exposed only the under arm, and insides of the elbow and knees, which were still protected by layers of mail. Fifteenth-century armor in Europe was characterized by a northern German style that was textured and attenuated, while the Italian design was smooth and round. Later, the two styles would begin to converge into a style best represented by German Maximilian armor.

It was not long after, in the 16th century, that plate armor began to give way to lighter armor because of the threat from guns. The first reaction was to make armor, especially the chest plates, thicker. Eventually, guns made plate armor completely obsolete. Despite noble desires to preserve their monopoly on sword fighting skills, the expense and weight of plate armor became an unnecessary burden to bear during typical combat. Like commoners, noblemen began to arm themselves with handguns and muskets while still preserving their skills with the sword for close combat. Eventually, the sword would be replaced by the bayonet, which served as a makeshift pole arm and piercing blade.

As the sword began its decline, only aristocrats and officers kept the tradition of wearing a sword. It became fashionable to wear the sword either as part of civilian dress or as part of the uniformed soldier who walked the streets of many capital cities. In Japan, the use of the sword was an essential part of daily dress until the Meiji Restoration in 1868 when the sword and the samurai topknot were banned during the country's new love affair with Western culture.

In the *Star Wars* universe, the use of armor was quite evident in the uniform of republican clone troopers and Imperial stormtroopers, as well as in Vader's black costume. Not unlike Japanese helmets and face masks (*mempo*), the stormtroopers' and Vader's masks serve to take advantage of the power to shock enemies with their menacing appearances.

In early drafts of the original script, stormtroopers were described as fascist white troops, whose pristine and shiny body armor reflected the precision and discipline of modern armies such as those of the Third Reich. Hitler's SS divisions even had a skeleton patch as a sinister symbol of their position and potency. The stormtrooper's mask not only resembles the skull, but his entire body was that of the body's skeleton. Lucas conceived the stormtroopers as specialized shock troops who only knew how to move forward. In Episode VI, Lucas created the scout troopers to be like race horses with blinders at the sides of their heads. The tighter fitting helmet denoted their importance while distinguishing them from the elite stormtroopers.[27]

Black uniforms, like those of the Imperial gantry officers in Episode IV, had a sinister allure. German Panzer division troops spoke fondly of their black uniforms, which gave them a sense of superiority over the common civilian as well as among other German troops. Even today, the use of the black beret, now common to all American army troops, was once a coveted symbol of its elite rangers. It was no mistake that Darth Vader towers over his own troops in a uniform of formidable and impressive black. The Emperor, in his transformation of Anakin to Vader, understood that the spectral use of a fearsome appearance had a psychological affect on those under his command. While modern, democratic soldiers of today's armies scoff at a "leader" who uses fear as a tool to get his men to fall into line, the fear of an officer's appearance and the punishments he could impose were common practices in most armies. The humiliation of flogging, running a gauntlet, or public and humiliating decommissioning of an officer were cruel and often effective forms of disciplining an army made up of unchivalrous and uneducated commoners. One of the most notorious forms of military capital punishment was the Roman practice of decimation wherein 10 percent of the offending unit was put to death.

Armor such as those worn by clone troopers, stormtroopers, snow troopers, and Jango and Boba Fett served as effective forms of deflection against blaster fire. Not only might laser beams be deflected, it was possible that they might also be specially treated with energy-absorbing layers of plastic or paint. The Clone Wars also saw the development of more refined and specialized troops than those found in the Original Trilogy — advanced recon commandos (ARCs), marines, shock troops— who came equipped with a host of specialized equipment: macrobinoculars, camouflaged armor, specialized visors, jetpacks, and the kama (a blast resistant skirt).[28]

Despite Obi-Wan's claim in Episode IV that Imperial troops were precise marksmen, the Original Trilogy was characterized by the cinematic convention that only heroes could hit their target. Historically, the appearance of shock troops had the advantage of surprise and the ability to inflict critical damage on an unsuspecting adversary. Complete surprise, a tactic used by American troops against the German Hessians after crossing the Delaware River, was employed to obtain complete surrender with relatively little resistance. Clone troopers on Geonosis and Utapau had the benefit of complete surprise, which was a clear advantage when enemy troops were more numerous. Trade Federation troops on Naboo demonstrated the same kind of fearsome élan as Soviet troops during the 1979 invasion of Afghanistan. Soviets disembarked from massive transport planes at the Kabul airport like battle droids did from their MTT transports in Episode I.

An interesting enigma is the uniform of the Jedi in Episode I. Keeping with the simple robes Ben Kenobi wore when he lived in Tatooine, Lucas decided to keep Jedi of the Republic in a similar costume. Early conceptual drawings entertained the notion of a more modern militaristic appearance in keeping with the idea that republican Jedi were more of a United Nations–style para-military force. They had a contemporary appearance, which would have suited troops in a capital city more than an old hermit hiding in the Dune Sea on Tatooine. While one would think that a man hiding from the Empire like Kenobi would wear clothes other than those that would immediately identify him to Imperial troops as a Jedi, Lucas opted instead to preserve the image of the Jedi as a meditative and sacred order so that the audience would immediately associate them with Yoda and Obi-Wan from the Original Trilogy.

Anakin's new uniform in Episode II showed a more urban and flared appearance. Made of leather, the pointy shoulders and the shiny curves of his jacket seem more akin to the Germanic tunic jacket called an ulanka. Luke's black Jedi uniform had a similar, more modern appearance, though his color is more reflective of the vicar's black than of a gestapo uniform. In the *Clone Wars* cartoon, Obi-Wan was shown wearing clone trooper armor, which made perfect sense as a combatant fighting alongside clone troopers. Like modern armies who dispensed with swords because they identified commanders to marksmen on the battlefield, it would seem ridiculous that the Jedi would not appropriate the kind of armor that would help protect them in a modern fight. Certainly, the ease of identifying a Jedi was important on screen, but their general disdain for armor might also convey the Jedi Order's refusal to evolve with the changing times of the universe.

Battle Formations and Combat

The earliest combat situations were probably little different from haphazard encounters between rival tribes. But just as quickly there must have been a rapid transformation as bands settled land and became more aggressive in protecting their territory. Tribes may have had direct dealings with nearby tribes or they may have come into conflict as stubborn hardheadedness made them decide to fight for their territory rather than giving it up without a fight.

Even the many "primitive" tribes that have existed in the last half century — pygmies, Easter Islanders, Zulu, etc. — demonstrated sophisticated military cultures despite the basic weapons of sword, spear, and blow darts. As culture and societal organization evolved, so, too, did military forms of organization. When a tribe became large enough to manage troops that numbered into the hundreds, the effectiveness of an organized and disciplined military became apparent. Quite often the entire male population was expected to perform warrior functions. Empires like those of the Aztecs, the Babylonians, and the Chinese were firmly maintained by the ability to manage large armies that could march out to quell a neighbor or to extend their borders. Battles were no longer mere skirmishes, but sophisticated forms of warfare.

The most basic type of formation was that of lines of men looking across a battlefield toward their enemies. Since the amassing of armies worked poorly in the confines of woods, marshes, or mountains, most battles took place on the foothills or plains where warriors had ample room to exercise movement of men. This also permitted them the ability to take advantage of subtle differences in terrain such as muddy flats; a dry, flat plain; or a defendable hillock.

"Citizen" warriors (i.e., unprofessional soldiers) were more likely to form themselves into ranks alongside family or neighbors. Athenians fought next to family, Scots with their kinsmen, and Perugians with friends from their neighborhood. Professional elites, often aristocrats, fought with not only an esprit de corps, but also using superior weapons and armor. Very often they were mounted; they were the only members of society able to raise enough money to pay for their expensive mounts. For obvious reasons, citizen soldiers or commoners were generally footmen, while the cream of the army were mounted aristocrats.

Unless warriors trained together specifically as a fighting class of soldiers, the tendency for foot soldiers was to mass up in a line and begin an approach toward their enemy. The clash of troops would then determine the victor by sheer stamina and determination. It would not be too soon after this kind of battle that survivors, especially commanders, would learn that organization and discipline would permit a more efficient use of the troops.

Once weapons (and armor) were accounted for, it then became clear that more disciplined units had a better chance of surviving than those that were simply allowed to march out and then sprint toward their opponents. The march was a common and daily event for all troops on campaign. It taught men to rely on each other and served as an impetus to those in a unit who might have straggled behind. It was in numbers that safety was best assured. Even today, the outdated skill of marching is a training tool used to instill a military attitude in new recruits. It teaches discipline, trains them in the ability to follow orders, and gives them a sense of belonging.

Troops may also have been organized into groups of similar weapons, or into squares or phalanxes (rectangular formation). Troops, like German 16th-century cavalry, were organized into wedges, with greater numbers massed in strict lines more on one side than the other. It was hoped that cohesion could be maintained by a mathematical arrangement and the psychological reassurance of organized comrades. Civilized combatants who benefitted from the organization of large cities and economies naturally felt organization was more decisive than the disorderly approach of a barbarian.

Despite the order, once battle was engaged, the neat lines were thrown completely into disarray. While lines were important at the onset, it then became more important to maintain a sense of movement toward the opponent. With men surging forward and back under the muted conditions of men under helmet and the din of battle, it was important for warriors to know that for every man their side lost, more of the enemy were being killed.

For the swordsman, this clash was the ideal situation for their weapon. Even after long spears had crashed into the first ranks, swords were drawn to continue the battle on an intimate and personal level. It was here that the three rules from the beginning of the chapter that characterize sword fighting come into play. The sword had to hit its target. The blade had to penetrate to do physical damage. And the swordsman needed enough physical space in which to wield his weapon effectively.

Within all battles was the fear of being attacked from some unknown direction. In the front line, there was no fear of attack from behind or the flank. Of more concern was the blade edge or point coming from a direction that didn't allow the swordsman to effectively wield his sword for either a parry or a counter thrust. It was the push of men forward or the shove to the side that impeded the swordsman and prevented him from employing his weapon in the way he was trained. And when shields were used at the front lines, it became even more difficult to effectively wield the sword. The swordsman could not senselessly strike or thrust out with the sword. He had to push and shove until a crack in the enemy wall of shields was opened enough for him to thrust his sword.

As troops dropped from the initial clash, weaknesses in the line began to open up. Here the largest men were best suited to pushing into breaks in the line. With a large warrior's momentum, even the smallest and most timid of men are willing to walk in his wake. It was at this point that there was enough space to begin wielding the sword by slashing with its edge. Slashes were answered by parries or counter slashes or the firmness of a shield. The best attacks were those that met no enemy blade at all and struck the enemy directly. Ideally, the opponent's armor would be insufficient to resist the thrust or slash. In the next best of situations, a second thrust or slash would penetrate enemy armor.

It was this chaos that reigned on the battlefield, defining whether a man was a coward or not. In the heat of the battle, all fear was put to the test. Would a warrior die valiantly as a hero? Or would he flee at the sight of the enemy? This kind of natural selection became a human form of survival of the fittest. Collectively, over tens of thousands of years, war has acted as a method of rooting out the weakest in a tribe or nation. And in the spirit of even the ancient, honor and glory become synonymous with survival on the battlefield, the place where the swordsman learned that power was the ultimate decisive characteristic of human societies.

The clash, however, did not have to be the only way of conducting combat on the field of honor. In the same way that the citizens of Greek city-states resolved to settle their differences on the battlefield in lines that would run headlong into the enemy, the Japanese of the Heian period sustained their combat by individually engaging an opponent in a one-on-one contest for victory. Soldier aristocrats would march out to the battlefield and call out their lineage and history to challenge an opponent with equal rank and valor to a duel. Couched in niceties of noble insults, the two swordsmen, once they had finished their discourses on their pedigree, then fought in combat. When one survived, he might mark his fallen adversary by sticking a pin into his ankle to lay stake to his claim. After the Mongol invasions of the thirteen hundreds, battle would evolve into pitched warfare similar to the other parts of the great continents.

The 15th century led to more organized military systems. The wars of the Roses in England led to a neo-feudal system of livery and maintenance, a patronage system in which a soldier took service with great landowners. In France, soldiers were called up as an administrative tool to obtain certain numbers of particular kinds of troops. A 1536 ordinance called for 603 spearmen, 80 halberdsmen, and 300 arquebusiers in addition to commanding officers for every 1,000 men.[29] In France, Charles VII tried to engage aristocrats into royal service and to maintain an army of permanent cavalry by reorganizing his forces into 15 *compagnies d'ordonnance*, each of which was made up of 100 units of *bande d'ordonnance*, called a lance in English.

The lance was a basic unit that described an individual knight and his retainers. Often this differed slightly from country to country. In Germany, a lance referred to the nobleman and his retainers: a squire, two bowmen, and a pikeman. In France, it typically included the nobleman in heavy armor (a *gendarme*), a mounted page called a *coustillier*[30] (an armed servant), three mounted archers, a crossbowman, culverineer (handgunner), and pikeman. Spanish lances omitted the *coustillier* and page, while Burgundian lances in 1473 included a knight, a mounted page, a mounted light spearman, three mounted archers, and on foot a crossbowman, handgunner, and pikeman.[31]

At first, the burden of arming oneself and his retainers was left to individual nobles. Not only did the knight have to have some royal pedigree, but he also had to be able to afford the ostentatiousness of his position. He had to purchase his own armor, which may have cost the equivalent of three months' wages, as well as those of his retainers. Obviously, few could afford to purchase a full harness for his military servants. Instead, each was armored as befitted their participation on the battlefield: coats of mail for mounted horsemen and light cavalry, brigandines for pike, arquebus, and landed archers. The cost of war mounts was also a heavy burden. A good destrier cost twice the price of a harness of armor and availability was dependent on the proximity of qualified stables.

At the same time, monarchs and great lords also recruited soldiers from the lower ranks of society to fill the lines of infantry that supported cavalry action. Increasingly, despite their organization into lances, the knight saw threats from the ranks of commoner armies, like pikemen, billmen, archers, and handgunners, who developed into semi-professionals. For the nobleman, the lofty ideal of chivalry still ruled their purpose. Commoners, often from the lowest strata of that class, fought for their lives and dispensed with rules of chivalry when necessary. They had no problem cutting the horse from under a knight, pulling the *gendarme* from his saddle, or tearing to pieces the shiny nobleman with their arrows, quarrels, and shot. Survival was foremost in their minds, and taking down a noble who looked down on them with disgust made the knight's demise even more palatable in their eyes.[32]

Despite new methods of military organization, the ingenious construct of the lance remained an effective manner of organizing field armies, which still relied heavily on the massive power of cavalry charges. The lance clearly specified a noble's obligations, and as a matter of practicality, preserved the feudal system of continental nobility. The page served as a fetch boy and herald, while the other armed retainers traveled essentially as support and infantry to protect the knight. The lance was in essence a Renaissance "tank" with support horsemen and footmen for protection. A knight might charge an enemy accompanied by his servants in support. When he tired or needed a new weapon, he could retreat behind his men who would act as protection with their bows ready to shoot footmen who approached.[33]

Retainers were also called upon to help bring troops to proportional strengths. And on the battlefield, troops could be massed with soldiers of a similar type: knights with knights, pikemen with pikemen, archers with archers. Such units became very disciplined groups and were deployed on the battlefield according to the strategy of their commanders. French and Spanish knights formed lines in single ranks, called *en haie*, in front of archers or *coustilliers*, while Germans formed deep wedges designed to push into enemy lines and maintain the momentum by pouring through the broken ranks.

The evolution to full plate harnesses was complete in the 15th century. Referred to as "white armor," plate over aketon or arming doublet, which had chain mail at articulated areas of the body called gussets and heavy sheets of metal, provided such complete protection that the shield was dispensed with altogether except during the joust. Lines were sometimes carved into the armor, called fluting, which guided arrows and quarrels off the armor. While missiles were most effective when striking armor at a 90° angle, fluting now made the 90° angle a virtual requirement for penetration to occur.

Swords, too, evolved with the times. Because horses were particularly vulnerable to missiles and pole arms, knights sometimes dismounted before engaging the enemy. With both hands free, the hand-and-a-half sword came into use. This sword could be used either with one hand or with two hands for close-quarters fighting. The poleaxe, a spear with a hammer, beak, or blade, also became popular with knights fighting on foot. Taking various forms, they had names such as *ravensbill*, *bec de corbin*, *guisarme*, and *voulge*. Their long shaft and piercing edges could be wielded with great strength, shattering or breaking apart plate armor. The butt end was often encased in steel so that it could be used to crush feet, armored or not. Such polaxes were very popular in the lists (the tournament battlefield) in which knights would compete for pride and glory in friendly combat. Such tourneys sometimes resulted in severe injuries when participants got carried away in the heat of the exchange. Other popular weapons included the mace and war hammer, which were very effective in smashing through armor and causing trauma in the form of bruising and concussions. Supplementing the sword were thrusting daggers such as the cinqueda, supposedly five fingers wide. These finishing daggers were used to dispatch opponents with thrusts to vital areas in plate armor — neck, arm pits, elbows, and knee joints.

The coup de grâce of the mailed knight was the increasing sophistication of the gun. The crossbow was earlier supplanted by the effectiveness of the longbow, which in turn, was supplanted by the gun. A gunner could take down a knight with a single shot without the eight years and more of training that was needed to develop an English archer. The knight's charge would continue well into the 16th century, but despite having better armed and armored footmen, the knight faced an even greater threat on the battlefield.

The 16th century served as a watershed period that led into the modern era both militarily and culturally. This was the era that dealt a blow to the plate armored knight. The defeat of the French and Swiss halberdiers at Bicocca, Switzerland, at the hands of firearms was the beginning of the dominance of gunpowder as a personal weapon. Three years later, at the battle of Pavia in 1525 between imperial and French forces, the knight, when cornered by pike and arquebus, died in an easy slaughter of nobility. The power of cannon had been demonstrated thirty years earlier when Charles VII invaded Italy virtually unimpeded as he shot down curtain wall after curtain wall in his furious campaign through the peninsula. A revolution in military construction would soon follow.

Warfare during this century would be marked by advances in tactics that required less armor. Swiss hedgehog tactics, followed by phalanx pike warfare, were recent models for the Spanish men, and contributed to their rise on the continent. The Spanish tercio was organized into squares of 1,500 to 3,000 mixed pike and arquebusiers. At the threat of cavalry charge, the pikes, measuring in excess of 15 feet, were lowered. Mixed within their ranks were lines of arquebusiers who fired their shots in a steady stream. Once a line fired, another line would move up and allow the first rank to withdraw into the protection of the pikemen to reload. Spanish soldiery were more lightly armored, with either steel plated brigandines or breast plates, and a steel cap. Their added mobility would prove advantageous, allowing the tercio formation to move at a pace that preserved their formation but cross the battlefield in short order.

The armor for armies composed more of commoners was relatively light, but effective. Infantry armor consisted mainly of the cuirass (also termed corselet), which included the gorget, breastplate (and sometimes a backplate) and armplates. When available and permitted by the regiment, leg armor, mail, and various helmets would be worn. Knights still wore full harness, though the armor became increasingly decorative and was used as parade armor. Two styles evolved at this time: the German style (called Maximilian), which is recognized by its fluting or the imitative puffed and slashed style, and the Italian style, which was more plain and rounded, better to deflect sword blows.

The medieval sword did not evolve much further during this time period other than adding more protection for the hand in the form of crossing guards and a knucklebow to cover the fingers. Societal influences also had their effect as the sword became a fashion accessory for the civilian gentleman. Not only were swords to be used on the battlefield, but also in cities between lightly or completely unarmored opponents. Invariably, this led to the evolution of the sword from a cut and thrust weapon to a more exclusively point-oriented weapon.

The *Star Wars* saga has finally borne out the evolution of clone troops into stormtroopers as well as the downfall of the Jedi Order. In many respects, the evolution of war in the galactic universe parallels many events in history. The Jedi Knights correspond to what the Muslims saw as a primitivist era of lost perfection, an idealized state in which everything was better. European *chansons de geste* also equated the past with a perfect state to be emulated. The Grand Army of the Republic corresponds to republican Rome and France when a large militia fought on behalf of the state. The Confederacy of Independent Systems fits neatly with the two sides in the American civil war: the Union and the Confederacy. And Palpatine's Empire mimics the ascendance of any number of authoritarian regimes: the Delian League, the Roman empire, the first and second French empires, and the British and American empires.

As in *Star Wars*, the rise of any military force did not come without great forethought and foreknowledge of impending threat. The price of neglect could mean the utter destruction of a society. In more developed societies, there has been an increasing tendency to normalize war in the events of human history. Talk of rising nationalism, of military-industrial complexes, and of real and perceived threats all raise the specter of invasion and the need to heighten the readiness of national defense. In ancient Sparta, the Spartiates declared war on the helot slaves each year so that they could attack and punish them without violating the Greek practice of openly declaring war. The Romans, too, celebrated festivals to auger good fortune on the military campaigns that would be fought that year. And in southwest Japan, the Choshu clan held ceremonies and rituals that celebrated their hate for the Tokugawa regime.[34]

It would be naïve to explain the existence of war as the result of one particular factor. The world is more complicated than that. And while the details of conflicts—those particular moments that set large-scale wars into full motion—are insignificant except in their timing, it is important to remember that all events take place within a context.

In the *Star Wars* saga, it is important to look at a critical element that distinguishes Lucas's universe from our own—the lightsaber. Like the sword in history, its use as an individual weapon affected the way men and women looked at life and death, peace and war. On one level, the value of life was set at a different threshold because life as a matter of daily existence was more precarious. Disease, hunger, greed, and pestilence were factors difficult to control. And because the sword was so ubiquitous, it was easy to fall back on the crude ability to bully or threaten others. In one sense the sword limited the amount of damage that could be done—killing with the sword took much more effort than a shooting rampage—but in another sense the use of the sword demanded that its wielder learn and accept certain forms of behavior. Brigands, ruffians, and thieves did not value the aristocratic idea of honor, but at least there was a symbolic reference to the sword as justice.

How does this play out in today's society, especially in a world where nuclear weapons have a consequence unlike that of any other weapon in human civilization? If you look at *Star Wars* with the understanding that the Death Star is a parallel for the nuclear bomb (but on a larger scale), it is possible to understand that the values of the Jedi Order represented by their lightsaber was a standard for the galactic universe. It was through their example that the lightsaber represented something other than the sheer exercise of power. Lucas also puts a pacifist twist on the lightsaber, asking whether it is necessary to carry a sword. Each generation will decide which path they will follow.

SIX

Sword Style: Movement for Victory

Style defines the human condition. It defines an individual; and given enough time and discipline, style develops into an art. Give someone a tool and that person will develop a repetitive and consistent manner in which to use it. Expose the same person to others with the same tool, and quickly each individual will begin to conform and an orthodox style will develop. Because sword fighting is combat, initial orthodoxy will be defined by a limited number of limited movements that have proved themselves successful. In time, the most talented will begin to dominate the instruction of others, and in the hands of the most talented, the style will be refined. Movement will become more subtle until mastery is so complete that the style can be called an art.

The previous chapter focused on the physicality of the sword — on its cutting power, its shape, and its weight. This chapter focuses on the manner in which a swordsman uses his weapon; whether with one or two hands, with a wide or narrow stance, with rapid successive strikes or with a single heavy blow. While it is obvious to the non-fencer that different cultures and different time periods had their own styles of fighting, the fencer of any time or place had to be able to distinguish not only between different schools of swordsmanship in order to defeat an opponent, but he had to be able to discern the individual's particular style. Swordsmanship is a combination of mastery of technique and strategy, as well as sheer determination of mind and spirit. For the swordsman and the Jedi alike, it was not enough to have mere possession of a sword or lightsaber. The swordsman had to have the ability to use his weapon efficiently and without delay, while simultaneously recognizing the limits of his skills and his weapon.

Star Wars provided ample evidence of a swordsman's need to adapt himself to the changing situations of a fight. Without this the swordsman could not survive. While battle droids were limited in their ability to deploy and shoot their blasters, Jedi had to quickly change their lightsaber tactics and strategy according to the circumstances in which they found themselves. On the Neimoidian Control Ship at the beginning of Episode I, Obi-Wan and Qui-Gon retreated from attacking destroyer droids when they recognized that their lightsabers were no match for repeating blaster fire and the droids' defensive shielding. Far from being defeated, Obi-Wan and Qui-Gon made a strategic move that assured their survival and allowed them to regroup for another attack. In a similar move, Darth Maul retreated from the Theed Hangar bay to get better positioning against Qui-Gon and Obi-Wan. By isolating Qui-Gon from his apprentice, Maul was able to defeat his adversaries one at a time.

A swordsman's style of fighting was primarily dependent on the training he received, but more immediately, it was affected by the fighting style of the attacker and the kind of armor he wore. This continual evolution prevented historians from reconstructing a sword fighting style. Unlike the sword, which can be physically dug up in archeological sites, the manner in which the sword was historically employed disappeared with the swordsman who perished in combat or died from old age. Most of history's sword fighting styles have been lost to history, and what we know of swordsmanship, especially Western swordsmanship, is at best supposition distilled from contemporary expressions and explorations of fencing manuals. Asian styles, in particular those of Japan and China, are closer expressions of true battlefield swordsmanship because of the strictness in which technique was taught and conveyed from generation to generation, but these arts, too, lost many effective battlefield techniques during times of peace when many fighting styles evolved into sport. Moreover, a lack of new students (or their death on the battlefield) could obliterate a style of sword fighting forever.

While it can be generally said that every culture that has used the sword had their own particular style of sword fighting, it can be reasonably argued that invaders fought with greater ferocity than a more insular and non-aggressive society. This, in turn, makes the modern historian confident that Romans fought differently from the Visigoths, who in their own right fought differently from the Celts. Similarly, it is true within a particular culture that different styles existed at different times of its history. Therefore, it can be reasonably argued that a samurai from the age of Tokugawa rule fought differently than those who anticipated Mongol invasions centuries earlier. And lastly, while it is difficult to qualitatively compare the effectiveness of one fencing style with another because of the many factors involved in encounters between swordsmen, it is possible to say that there were cultures that, because of their experience and war-like tendencies, produced inherently better swordsmen than others. Pastoral villagers in the heart of the Italian peninsula lived a reasonably secure life quite different from those of Celtic tribesmen in central Gaul.

Some sources (both in written and iconographic form) help the modern historian understand sword fighting. Whether from direct accounts of battle or from images in a woodcut or amphora, it is possible to gain some insight in the evolution of swordsmanship through the dynamics of battlefield tactics and strategies, as well as by the changes of the shape of the sword itself. While examination of major fencing styles would encompass a lifetime of research and writing, it suffices to explore the two principal influences on *Star Wars* lightsaber fighting — Western fencing and samurai swordsmanship.

While it is easy to classify sword fighting into European and Japanese styles, the true authenticity of a combative art can only truly be expressed in the details of a particular style. It may be convenient to speak of a samurai style because the Japanese were generally isolated as an island empire, but within the Nippon islands, there was also a host of regional sword fighting traditions that could be thought of as unique and distinct martial arts. Because Europe did not have the geographic isolation of an island culture like Japan, the evolution of swordsmanship varied widely in technique and mastery. Sword fighting styles developed along tribal, regional, and eventually national styles, but because there was never one predominant culture like that of the Yamato in Japan, sword fighting skills were comparatively eclectic and impermanent. As one culture grew or disappeared, so too did their particular fighting style. One could speak of a Roman style distinct from that of the Carthaginians as much as one can say that neither style survives because neither culture exists. Subsequent cultures would later gain ascendance, which eventually propagated their sword style.

There was always a cross-pollination of techniques when armies clashed; but the transference of a style only occurred if there were survivors to learn from their conquerors. Attila was a Hun, but because he was raised as a hostage in a Roman culture, his early sword fighting influences were predominantly Roman. Later, as he returned to his people, his techniques were subsequently influenced by the battle experience of Hunnish warriors who had a reputation for tactical mobility. In Asia, as well, a degree of cultural transference occurred as martial arts traveled and established themselves in a new land. Bodhidharma, who, according to legend, taught the Shaolin monks in China, originally came from India. Many Japanese techniques were also learned from immigrating Chinese martial artists. In Roman armies, a distinctive local fighting style would permeate an army if they were recruited from a particular area as in the case of units created by Hannibal in Spain.

Centralization of a culture also had an impact on the development of sword fighting styles. While a battle could perhaps wipe out an entire army and its particular sword fighting style, a style could also face extinction from disuse, especially when a school failed to maintain a cadre of talented instructors and aspiring students. In Japan, as the shogunate gave way to a new government under the Restoration, Choshu samurai were invited to form the base of a new military force. Quite rapidly, their techniques, even their dialect, came to have the strongest influence on swordsmanship taught in the Tokyo police academy. In Europe, a Roman legion raised in southern Italy might be influenced by instructors who learned to fight in Ilyria. And even within a strong national culture like 19th-century Italy, a northern and southern school of sabre fencing challenged each other for dominance in national fencing academies.

It was both the uniqueness of a particular style as well as a melding of those styles that led to a blurring of techniques. Because orthodox fencing styles were continually challenged, the disposal of older techniques or adoption of newer techniques led to newer styles. And very often these changes occurred within great shifts in culture. There was no evolutionary transformation of sword fighting style, but a haphazard invention, refinement, and extinction of technique. Particularly in the West where dominance of the firearm relegated sword fighting to civilian duels, it was not until only in the last fifty years that individuals have tried to methodically recover ancient and medieval sword fighting techniques.

In many ways, the approach of the Japanese swordsman was fundamentally different from that of the Westerner. This must be kept within the context that all sword fighting was limited by the human physiology of the human body, which wielded a sword with either one or both hands. On the conceptional level, however, it is helpful to consider the terminology of John A. Lynn in *Battle: A History of Combat and Culture*. Lynn uses the terms "military enlightenment" and "military romanticism" to describe the development of military strategy and technology in the 17th and 18th centuries. Characterized by the spirit of logic and reason, the military of the Enlightenment reflected a regimented and ordered organization, according to Lynn. As a reaction, the successive century emphasized the romantic period of emotion and sentiment. For this chapter, however, it is helpful to adapt Lynn's terms and apply them in a different context to the broader generalities of Western and Japanese sword fighting.

The principal remnant of Western sword fighting is competitive fencing, which was derived from the evolved point work used during the Renaissance in southern Europe. Because of the increasing effectiveness of the firearm, the sword began to play a less significant role on the European battlefield. It was still vital for close-quarter fighting, but armies more and more began to meet in lines with muskets and rifles in their hands. The carriage of the sword continued as a basic article of the European uniform, but the sword found more of its use in the one-on-one civilian duel than in the battlefield melee. During the Enlightenment, logic dictated to swordsmen that the point was closer to the target than the swinging sword edge. Western fencing curricula were marked by practical drilling and had to meet the pragmatic challenges of the encounter primarily in the form of a duel. Within armies, point work was encouraged as a refinement over sword edge techniques. In cavalry as well, the mounted charge was made with the point instead of an edge. With the point aimed directly at the enemy's face and torso, there was not enough time to parry the blade and effectively mount a counterattack. Cavalry charges effectively became the medieval joust with extended sabres instead of couched lances. The edge of a sword could be used when cavalry closed after the initial clash, but the favor of the point reflected an acceptance of the principle that a point was better able to decisively kill the opponent than an exchange of blade edges. Eventually, swords evolved into the rapier and then lighter court weapons before eventually finding their most common forms in modern competitive fencing.

The Oriental perspective, however, was quite different. Following Confucian patterns of society, the Japanese style of sword fighting was basically an ethical system that adhered almost dogmatically to precedent. The Japanese not only honor their ancestors like their Western counterparts, but they also revered them. For Asian swordsmanship, a proper frame of mind and discipline was needed to extol and preserve the correct technique of their ancestors. Perseverance, discipline, and the heart must lead to the proper art of the sword. In many ways, this perspective was the opposite of European ideas of logic and order. Instead of using a rational system of fencing techniques, the Japanese looked toward emotion and spirit to inform their swordsmanship. Instead of clear rationality, the heart guided Japanese swordsmanship. In the Yagyu style of swordsmanship, ancient techniques were purportedly learned from forest spirits called Tengu. While few believe the veracity of such a history, it shows the emotional, rather than the intellectual, level to which the Japanese sought to define their art.

On a very basic level, the Western swordsman found solace in the intellect, the Japanese in passion. Returning to the theme of *Metropolis* in chapter two, George Lucas's Jedi developed a style in the middle. Jedi sword fighting was a half-way point between the sword fighting of an edged weapon and the sword fighting of the fencer.[1]

The Evolution of Western and Japanese Swordsmanship

Western Fencing

For thousands of years, swordsmanship had been dominated by the double-edged sword, commonly known as a long or broad sword, but during the

Renaissance, the European sword underwent a rapid transformation as culture and the means of warfare evolved on the continent. With the technological improvement of firearms, including arquebus, musket, rifle, and cannon, the nature of warfare was at a watershed in history. While its immediate impact was recognized by the nobility, the gun did not take hold until its use became predominant between armies on the battlefield. Earlier changes in distance weaponry occurred with the bow and crossbow, but because they still required extensive training and lacked the firepower of an explosive, they did not change the course of warfare as gunpowder and nuclear technology would.

Though the speed of the demise of the armored knight differed from country to country, the rise of democratic ideas combined with the easy-to-operate matchlock would eventually make the position and station of the knight and the aristocracy he protected obsolete. Training commoners in the competent use of the musket was achieved with relative rapidity, and with a huge population base to replenish the lines of musketry, the educated and trained knights of the realm had neither the numbers nor the cadres of squires to compete with newer democratic militias. Dominance on the field was no longer a question of amassing experienced and well-armored swordsmen as it had been during Roman times, nor of mounting charges by aristocratic knights. The protection of a complete harness became a liability, and the heaviness of arm and leg plating were quickly discarded to allow greater mobility. A breastplate, a metal cap, and perhaps greaves if they were available became the new standard of protection for the new units of commoners that would make up the body of national armies. When the metal breastplate was not available, a gambeson or jack (a thick quilted jacket), a brigadine (a studded leather garment), or a buff coat (a thick leather jacket) were used to thwart sword cuts.

But the rise of the commoner occurred hundreds of years earlier with the increasing importance of the mercantile class. It was not unheard of that nobles faced the possibility of losing land through the simple mismanagement of their properties combined with an over-extravagant lifestyle. Merchants, with their coffers full of gold and florins, made natural conjugal allies of the nobility. It would not be too long before ordinary folk began to see themselves more in terms of a citizenry of a nation and not simply the serfs of a landed class. Nobles continued to hold rank in their society, but the commoner pushed upward into higher social strata by their ability to earn money. This competition expressed itself in civilian life as the noble guarded his right and privilege to continue carrying the sword at his side when he walked the streets while commoners still carried a knife for both eating and self-defense.

The sword's development also followed trends from the battlefield. A response to heavy plate armor were swords with stronger blades and points. Later, as armor got lighter because heavier plate was more easily pierced by a bullet, so too did the swordsman's weapon. Swords with finer and more delicate blades were made, and an increased emphasis on the use of the point became a standard among the aristocracy. Refined civilian styles in dress, which consisted of a fancy shirt and light jacket, now permitted effective use of the point, and the nobleman could protect himself against both offending men of his own rank as well as those of commoners, ruffians, and highwaymen.[2]

The rapier was a weapon without equal for both slashing and piercing.[3] With its two edges and sharp point, the choice weapon of the French musketeers was a valuable offensive and defensive weapon when bullets and powder were exhausted. It was the Italians, however, who led Europe in the delicate civil and cultural arts of the Renaissance. Italian masters developed a subtle form of point combat; this had the advantage of a quick thrust over the heavy-handed slashes of the broad sword, which had to travel as much as five times the distance the point took to reach its target. Not only did they systematize their art according to the spirit of the military Enlightenment, they published books and traveled to teach foreigners outside the peninsula. Marozzo, Agrippa, and di Grassi were well-represented because of the manuals they published. Others hid their art by taking on students and obliging them to hide their fencing style and refrain from teaching it to others. A kind of mystical reputation developed among fencing masters, who were said to have learned secret moves and attacks that could defeat any fencer.

The fencing *salle*, which amounted to nothing more than a civic club akin to a modern country club, arose from the increasing urbanization of the capitals of rising European nation-states. A master's reputation depended on his ability and skill, which was subsequently nourished and eventually advanced by the quality and breeding of his students. Not long after, the state took on the responsibility of authenticating the mastery of the individual club by establishing a national curriculum and requiring instructors to prove their skills by passing a battery of tests in order to officially earn the title of *master, maître, fechtsmeister*, or *maestro*.

Another change occurred when the rapier gave way to the lighter small sword carried by courtiers of the greatest kings and queens of Europe. The nobility still held political power, and as part of their courtly clothes, more extravagant and lighter blades became the fashion. The heavy and simple robes of the Middle Ages gave way to the decadence of the 17th and 18th centuries. Small swords were still practical arms used for friendly play and combative duels, but the small sword became more of a jewel and ornament among the many accessories of a lace covered courtier.

Eventually, the cruciform hilt of the medieval long sword was no longer a standard for public occasions. As heavy and light cavalry units such as the Hussars, Grenadiers, the Imperial Guard, and the Life Guards replaced the knight, the sabre reappeared and came to dominate the military costume. With the development of muskets, soldiers relied on banks of men who fired en masse at their opponents in a large barrage. Bayonets made the pikeman obsolete, and with musket in hand and the sabre at his side, the soldier was no longer the warrior of the past.

The demise of the nobility was far from complete, but Adolphus Gustavus, the most famous modern military commander, and his military reforms made professionals out of what used to be the armed flower of a nation's nobility. The disappearance of the caracole, in which armored cavalry paced just outside the pike's point, executed a half-turn, and then fired their pistols at the line, ended the noble's prerogative of shooting at the enemy army at will. It would become the privilege of highly trained sabre-carrying cavaliers (drawn mostly from humble origins) who would be used as an elite unit to threaten and tear asunder slow-moving lines of footmen.

Another sword that caught fashion was the hanger, which was essentially a straighter version of the cavalry sabre. Used initially as a hunting weapon for dealing a death blow to wild pig, buck, or bear, the hanger came to be widely carried by gentlemen and ordinary citizens who needed a practical weapon within easy reach. The gentleman may have carried it as a daily accessory or as a weapon when journeying from his estate to the capital.

The sabre also became the favored weapon of naval troops who needed a short-bladed edge to fight on the limited space of their decks. Used for cutting a thick line, hacking down at boarders at the edge of the deck rail, or parrying a wild cut to the head, the cutlass, as the naval sabre was called, was adopted by marines, pirates, privateers, and buccaneers. The musket, the deck cannon, and the light cannon were easily supplemented by the cutlass.

Just as the sword was essential to the generals and officers of early 20th-century armies, so too does the lightsaber play a significant and symbolic role as guardian of the Galactic Republic. The sword was the embodiment of power and today it reflects many of the values that are no different from those in the past: justice, honor, virtue. Though the sword is no longer standard issue for modern soldiers, probably the greatest testament to its enduring importance is that it still remains an important accessory to the honor guards of most nations.

Japanese Fencing

Unlike in Europe where gunpowder and the change in armor had a direct impact on the physical form of the sword, the evolution of the sword in Japan was focused more on its *role* in battle and in civilian life than on its shape. Since the style of fencing was always affected by the cultural experience of its practitioners, the relatively constant state of war in Japan assured a predominant role for the samurai feudal lord vying for the coveted position of de facto ruler, or shogun. As had occurred in the West, the gun would alter the course of history in Japan as well, but where the European aristocracy failed, the samurai successfully imposed a retrograde policy that banned the gun.

Though it might seem hard to believe, early Japanese swords were not the curved kind with which most Westerners are accustomed to seeing in Japanese samurai films. The *tsurugi* was a straight sword, probably of Chinese origin, that looked very similar to the European broadsword and was common during the Dolmen Period, which ended approximately A.D. 700.[4]

Early governments of the Yamato peoples established themselves on the main island of Honshu. An imperial court evolved, and culture radiated from its center. Assisting the court were military retainers, many from northern frontiers, who assured the position of the emperor and the court that served it. Through the early periods of the Jomon, Yayoi, Yamato, Nara, and Heian periods, the relative stability of an imperial government was maintained with the assistance of armed forces that guarded and expanded frontiers, while quelling rebellions that threatened the emperor. In the Heian court, the nobles (*kuge*) ruled in the opulent splendor of the capital city. Early soldiers to the imperial court were considered rough, vulgar, and untamed armed servants. Contingents supporting one noble might clash with those of a challenging noble, but most retainers refrained from openly taking power for themselves.

Military warfare before the Mongol invasion reflected an insular competition between nobles of one house against another. On the battlefield, cavalry would first charge toward their enemy, launching arrows from their bows at a full gallop. Lines would then re-form several more times before the horsemen would dismount for hand-to-hand combat. After declaring their background, worthy opponents would approach each other and then personal combat would take place.[5]

During the Heian period, Japanese society was dominated by the Fujiwara family, which built a dynastic relationship with the imperial family. In exchange for protecting the heir to the throne during a 7th-century revolt, the Fujiwara were accorded the privilege of ruling in the name of the emperor. With rare exception, the empress was drawn from members of the Fujiwara clan, solidifying the de jure preeminence of the exalted family.

In the 12th century, pretenders to the throne, however, challenged the emperor who, according to a long tradition, had retired at an early age from political life to monasteries while the Fujiwara administrated the country. Intrigue at the court and the later weakness of the Fujiwara convinced samurai of both the Minamoto and the Taira clans to wrest control of the country from the Fujiwara through the use of the powerful armies they had developed after years of cultivating their provincial and military resources. The Taira was temporarily successful in repelling the Minamoto clan, but in answer to the emperor's request for help, Yoritomo Minamoto, a leader from the defeated clan, raised an army and eventually destroyed the Taira's power forever.

Yoritomo's victory led to the establishment of a seven-hundred-year period in which real power in Japan lay with the shogun. While beholden to the emperor for naming him shogun, Yoritomo quickly removed himself from the imperial court and ran his government from a new court in Kamakura. To the detriment of the dynasty, Yoritomo's children were never successful in controlling the country. Instead, his widow entered the political scene and installed her family, the Hojo, as regents ruling on behalf of the emperor. They arranged for the appointment of a shogun, but they, like the emperor at the hands of the shogun, were manipulated as puppets of the Hojo regents.

In 1274, Japan faced its first outside threat from Kublai Khan, grandson of the Mongol conqueror Ghengis Khan, who set his sights on Japan to further increase his prestige and rid the Chinese coast of notorious Japanese pirates. Envoys were sent demanding Japanese submission as vassals to the Mongols. Rebuffed by the Japanese, Khan sent an invasion of fifteen thousand men. Unsuccessful in making a beachhead in Hakata Bay, forces retreated to the safety of their boats. That night a storm destroyed the greater part of the fleet. Remnants hobbled back to China to tell of their defeat. Five years later, after conquering the Chinese Sung emperor, Khan returned with a fleet of over 150,000 men divided into two forces. As before, his forces could not make a beachhead and troops retreated to their ships. Again, as had happened in the first invasion, a massive storm struck the Mongol and Korean fleet, which returned for a second time defeated at the hands of the Japanese.

From these two invasion attempts, the Japanese quickly learned that their traditional methods of fighting would not be effective against foreign troops. The Mongols did not respect the challenge, and while victorious, they knew the ultimate defeat of the Mongols was not achieved entirely out of their own efforts. During the limited battles that did occur, the samurai discovered that their swords were vulnerable to breakage and that their armor, while properly suited to cavalry movement, was too heavy for ground fighting. Tactics as well were adjusted to reflect the new state of warfare. Instead of issuing challenges after bow-and-arrow cavalry charges, troops were organized into lines according to weapon type and deployment was determined by strategic considerations. Polearms were used against cavalry, while archers fired at their enemy from behind large, moveable shields.

The succeeding Muromachi period (1338–1573) led to the development of the *katana* (also called an *uchigatana*), with which most Westerners most closely associate the Japanese samurai. Instead of hanging their sword in a scabbard at their side as had been done earlier, it became fashionable and practical to place it within the folds of the samurai's belt with the sword edge upward. Along with the katana, a shorter sword was worn called a *wakizashi*. Together the swords were known as the *daisho*, literally the large and small sword. Eventually national law would restrict the daisho to the samurai class, which acted as both the police and militia of regional fiefdoms.[6]

The use of the katana led to the development of a new style of fencing that relied on the immediate slicing cut of the sword when drawn. Given the nature of Japanese society in which assassination was as close as any passing samurai in the street, the instantaneous use of the sword was vital. Practice in a simultaneous draw/attack was required. Because attacks could come at any moment in the day, daily paraphernalia were used as adjuncts to the sword. A cup or chopsticks may have been thrown at the assassin if attacked while at tea or a meal. A samurai learned to roll across the tatami mat floors while still wearing his short sword in order to escape the initial attack of an intruder. Clothing too, especially the long sleeves that were popular, could be used to a samurai's advantage by pulling his opponent slightly off balance. The samurai's ability to defend himself from attack was the only assurance he had of surviving the tumultuous times of his society.

The Mongol invasions accelerated the squabbling between Japanese rulers and the lower nobility. Some feudal lords, called *daimyo*, and their retainers went unrewarded for their efforts in maintaining an expensive military presence to fight against possible future Chinese attacks. Outlying fiefs rebelled against the Hojo regents and through open warfare two rival courts were established: one in the north and another in the south. In 1467, the Onin rebellion led to a hundred-year period of endless warfare that came to be known as the *Sengoku Jidai*,[7] the Age of Warring Provinces. Peasants, unable to protect themselves from wandering soldiers called *ronin* or from armies traveling through their territories, organized themselves into military coalitions that challenged the military class. These groups attacked the capital, waylaid government troops, and even defeated a professional samurai army.

Daimyo, as leaders of the military class, organized against these rebellions and even co-opted men from the peasant ranks who served as foot soldiers called *ashigaru*. While recognized as essential to society (farmers ranked higher than merchants), the samurai class asserted their prerogatives over what in their eyes was a subservient class. As history would have it, another foreign intervention to the Honshu islands would mean political and military upheaval in Japan.

In the 1540s, Portuguese ships began arriving off the western coast of Japan in search of possible trade ventures. Feudal lords in those provinces soon recognized the potential of purchasing muskets from the Europeans. As was being discovered in Europe, the firearm would become as important a weapon on the Japanese battlefield as it was in Europe. It also proved to be the biggest threat to the samurai, who were easily killed by trained peasant musketeers. Warfare now depended on the musket. Renowned leaders Oda Nobunaga, Toyotomi Hideyoshi, and Tokugawa Ieyasu would use the musket to successfully take power and hold it for themselves.

All recognized the usefulness of the new weapons, but the very state of armed insurgency by both rival lords and the peasantry created a countryside ready to move against any centralizing authority. Under Hideyoshi, a policy of decommissioning weapons was pursued. Called the Taika Sword Hunt, Hideyoshi, under the pretense of collecting steel for the building of a great Buddha statue, promulgated a law that allowed only the samurai class to carry weapons. Government officials proceeded to disarm peasants and merchants both near the capital and in outward regions. Not only did this hamstring rebellion against the government, it allowed officials to collect taxes from the peasantry who no longer had the means to resist the samurai class.

Under a later shogun, Tokugawa Ieyasu, a set of sweeping governmental reforms instituted a period of relative peace unheard of in Japanese history, preserving his dynasty for over two hundred fifty years. Upon establishing his government in Edo, he instituted laws that locked his country into a rigid societal structure in which the shogun exerted influence over every aspect of daily life. He quelled rival lords by requiring them to maintain expensive entourages and to spend substantial time in a household in the capital. When the daimyo was away visiting his feudal holdings, his family was required to stay in the capital as hostages. The country was divided into administrative regions that maintained border checks throughout the country so movement of important officials and troops could be kept under surveillance. To prevent peasants from acquiring weapons or organizing against the samurai class, traditional expectations were imposed. And in an unexpected reversal of previous foreign policy, Western Christians were expelled from the country because of the influence they had gained in making converts and in engaging in musket trade, which threatened to re-arm the outlying daimyo. Tokugawa declared that foreigners would be allowed limited access to the country in the port cities of Nagasaki and Yokohama. And to suppress non–Japanese influences, Japanese citizens were forbidden to travel outside the country.

Under Tokugawa rule, war, while not completely eliminated, became infrequent and of limited locality during the Edo period. The vast armies now without purpose presented a challenge to Ieyasu's government, so samurai were now required to directly administer and maintain their land or that of their lord, while martial experience had to be maintained in case of state emergencies, but in a tempered way. Religion, too, was used to Ieyasu's advantage as

Confucian ethical principles of strict hierarchy were exalted, respect and observance of Shinto practices were imposed, and Shintoism became the state religion. Samurai, in addition to keeping up their skills as swordsmen, were encouraged to cultivate the arts of poetry, calligraphy, and literature.

It was during this time that *kenjutsu*, the killing art of swordsmanship, began to evolve into *kendo*. The skill of the sword was maintained, but pacified into a non-violent exercise by the use of a bamboo sword instead of sharp blades. Kendo armor, based on real armor, was adapted for the new sword fighting style, and etiquette and a set of customary rules were established for this new form of friendly competition.[8]

Zen Buddhism, which extolled a stoic, disciplined, and simple life, also had a large impact on modern swordsmanship. Not only did the rigidity of religious life appeal to the austere life of former soldiers, it gave samurai a religious culture in which to express themselves. Zen did not have an overt creed, so when esoteric religious practices were combined with swordsmanship, the Zen sword came to be accepted by samurai of all sorts. Zen swordsmanship was not, however, a religion. Rather, it was a simple and direct process of mastering swordsmanship that allowed an individual to achieve a higher level of existence, often referred to as enlightenment, when individual purpose and a simple satisfaction with daily life met in a harmonious convergence.[9]

In 1853, the arrival of the American Commodore Perry in his four men-of-war black ships at the harbor of Uraga marked a watershed in Japanese history. America was looking for a base of operation, and in order to secure "proper" relations with representatives of the Japanese government, impressive sailing ships were dispatched to negotiate trade agreements with them. The colorful meeting was a polite exchange, but from that moment onward, the isolationist Japanese knew they could not permanently shut out nations that carried the impressive array of cannon that protected the American black ships. Even if these four were taken by force, Japan was not in any military or political situation to defend herself against a determined musket- and cannon-armed invader.

The arrival of the Americans demanding the right to trade with Japan unleashed a cultural mania for all things Western. In its wake would be a traditional backlash of conservatives clamoring to "expel the barbarians." The emperor would soon be restored to power and the samurai, once allowed to carry his *daisho* proudly, was abolished in favor of Western modes of dress, thought, and education. Japan hurried to catch up with the West in an unprecedented industrialization that led well into the mid-twentieth century. At the conclusion of World War II, Japanese militarism gave way to a peaceful idealism that manifests itself in a constitution prohibiting the creation of a military that may one day be used for expansive purposes. While the samurai became a soldiery of commoners, study of the sword still remained an important expression of Japanese culture.

Star Wars draws from cultures worldwide, but the influence of Japanese swordsmanship stands out to fencers who have had even a cursory introduction to the sword fighting arts of the world. Lucas, like the Japanese of the Meiji period fascinated with Western culture, was infatuated with Japanese samurai films. Although Lucas did not imitate samurai traditions explicitly, it is evident that there is much to learn about *Star Wars* by examining Japanese swordsmanship.

Swordsmanship and the Brain

When a fencing student picks up a sword—a foil, epee, long sword, bokken, shinai, iaito, or katana—for the first time, he or she begins an activity more dependent on the brain than on the body. Certainly, the initial focus on physical conditioning further emphasizes the physiological aspect of the art of fencing, but disciplining the body is far less important to a fencer in the long run than the physiological changes that will be made in the brain.

As was discussed in chapter one, the human being is driven by the primal and necessary instinct of self-preservation. Because of the nature of their art, swordsmen, as is any other practitioner of a combative art, are exposed to the most challenging of situations—combat with another person. There was nothing like the sheer terror of facing another human being willing to kill you, especially one armed with a long blade. This fear of another person, combined with the fear of not being able to defend oneself, made the impending struggle a fearful and terrifying affair. Swordsmanship, in its very essence, sought to tame these fears so that there could be only one outcome—the swordsman's survival.

Through disciplined training, swordsmanship sought to alter the physical body and arm it with the executive control of the brain, which would lead to optimum functioning during the chaotic struggle of a life-and-death situation. The interplay between the body and mind had to be developed, distinguishing the swordsman from the non-fencer or the inexperienced fencer. Experience teaches the master swordsman that the fencing encounter is more psychological (and cerebral) than it is physical or skill-related. Whether fencing is 90 percent brains and 10 percent brawn or 60 percent brains and 40 percent brawn is debatable, and will probably never be known. The importance of the intellect over the body, however, is evident to the good fencer.

While most manuals on fencing elucidated the subtleties of posture, control of the weapon, and basic skills, there was little discussion of the physiological factors that had a major impact on the human brain during the stressful situation of a sword fight. Now, however, there exists a body of thought that states that genetics, the body's endocrine system, the structure of the brain, and culture have a profound impact on swordsmen.

In keeping with Darwin's theories on natural selection, scientists have argued that over the course of thousands of years, the human being has evolved into a particular kind of being with particular instincts for survival. One would go so far as to assert that certain tribes or groups may have a natural predisposition to war-like behavior, while others do not. Though it is doubtful that scientists of the future could ever identify whether Vikings and their blood-related Norman descendants were more predisposed to pillage and plunder than a Polynesian culture, there is compelling evidence that because of our sexual genetic makeup, men and not women tend to be the warriors.

Behaviorists argue that for thousands of years, *Homo sapiens* (who are said to have been around 35,000–150,000 years ago) have been imbued with certain physiological differences that make men the warriors and women the home raisers. Much of this evidence suggests that much of the gender difference is related to the amount of testosterone in a body and how it controls or influences an individual's reaction to outside or emotional stimulus. The old saying, "Men are from Mars, women are from Venus," if taken along general terms and not as a specific criteria with which to judge individuals, leads many to conclude that men and women use their brains in different ways, according to the strengths that were needed of women that lived in strong role-driven societies thousands of years ago.

Because of natural selection, males, who had better musculature and spatial skills for hunting and fighting, and women, who had childbearing ability and better perceptual skills for foraging, survived to procreate. These gender differences also affect both an individual's education, as well as how the brain functions during a life-threatening sword fight.

Genetic makeup also influences how the brain is able to learn. Males are on average more capable of right-brain functions like spacial, visual, gross motor, and gestalt skills. Women, on the other hand, start out with more advanced left-brain skills such as auditory, language, fine motor, and detailed-sequential thinking. This can be one factor in explaining why boys gravitate toward aggressive and competitive sports, while girls tend to be quieter, more attentive, and disciplined students in the classroom.

While such assertions may seem sexist and inappropriate in today's modern societies that advocate the equal abilities of men and women to perform similar jobs, predispositions do not in and of themselves explain the development of individuals as we encounter them. While this thesis posits that certain predispositions in men and women start out at birth, the growth and development of individuals do not necessarily predetermine that all men will be neanderthal sports lovers or all women soft, feminine homemakers. Biological predispositions can be enhanced or diminished through training and acculturation, which had tremendous implications for fencers.

In the early pre-adolescent years, the brain is still in the stages of developing the network of connections that allow the flow of electricity through the brain in what is typically called "thinking." Different parts of the brain control different functions. Brain mass is made up of neurons, which are connected to each other by dendrites. One key to improving a person's thinking skills is to build up the mass of dendrites connecting the neurons of the brain. This is accomplished by performing activities that stimulate particular parts of the brain associated with specific skills. For example, if a girl participates in activities that rely on gross motor skills such as throwing a ball, corresponding parts of the brain begin creating more dendrites. Not only is the girl developing the musculature for throwing a ball, her brain is developing the ability to coordinate the thinking skills that allow her to more easily accomplish the task. She is learning.

The inherent problem with the educational system today is that it tends to work for the benefit of the boys. If one looks at the boys' tendencies, they generally gravitate toward their stronger abilities: they like to explore, enjoy the visual stimulus of comics, relish sports, and look less at detail than overall purpose, which helps them in math and science. Girls start out deficient in these areas and are greatly suited to traditional classroom learning, which emphasizes listening skills and the use of language as a way to express themselves; the physical act of fine motor skills associated with writing is natural to them, and they pay attention more than their male classmates. Girls and young women get better at these skills as well, but they don't get as much stimulus in right-brained activities. Boys, however, get the benefit of right-brain activities because they have a tendency to follow their natural talents, while they get the left-brain activities in school.

The implications for fencing from an educational point of view is that it develops both left- and right-brain skills in a manner that puts neither a male nor a female at a physical or intellectual disadvantage. Fencing, primarily because it is combative, requires a constant readjustment to threats from an opponent. Whereas most weaponless martial arts tend to favor the physical strength of a man, fencing uses a weapon that compensates for the physiological advantages that favor men. With a minimum expense of energy, the woman can mortally wound a man endowed with greater physical strength. The same can also be said for physically weaker opponents, whether male or female, in that the person with better brains can be a serious threat to the physical brute. Soft martial arts, like aikido and tai chi, also start out from the premise that minimum energy can be used to defeat physically stronger opponents.

Modern Western fencing, by its very nature, already favors the female who has better balance and fine motor skills than his male counterpart. Because of fencing's aggressive nature, a male does have the advantage of being more suited to attacking, which is the primary way of hitting an opponent. Fencing teaches confidence, risk taking, and gives immediate feedback for learning. It also focuses on the right-brain functions that require spacial and visual acuity—one has to physically see an attack and judge proper distance—as well as the gross motor skills and a larger focus on the overall situation of the strategy of the bout. For males, fencing de-emphasizes brute force and requires an attention to subtlety of movement to control the point of the weapon. Sequential thinking and the use of language—fencing has its own vocabulary—are the typical methods of teaching fencing, while the reliance on sound is an aspect too often neglected by fencers.

Fencing is a series of trained responses to a fight-or-flight situation, employing the sword to attack or defend against an aggressor. Where physiology tends to produce a fight response in men by sending adrenalin[10] through the body and flight in a woman, training hopes to develop reactionary responses to the stimulus of a threat. Without thought, the body reacts to the unexpected by following the training that has been drilled into a person.

Our instincts are not always the best or most efficient means of dealing with threats. Hopefully, it is skill as a swordsman, not a response to chemical functions, that will be used to defeat the opponent. Skill is developed by practicing movements with a sword that will allow the fencer to win in combat. It therefore becomes critical that practice be done with the intention of practicing perfect movement. During a fencing bout, the fencer typically falls back on the instincts that have to be learned through training. If the fencer continually practices an advance with a slightly turned front foot, it is very likely he will tend to do the same during a real bout, which, in this case, could lead to a twisted foot during a lunge. This search for attainable perfection translates into efficient and instinctual reaction to the stimulus of an attacking aggressor.

Once trained, a man or woman who is ambushed by a highwayman counters with new instinctual reactions to draw the sword and fight. Similarly, when confronted with an attack from arrows or gunfire, the swordsman, knowing his limits against missile attacks, instinctually runs and seeks cover. The development of specialized skills will protect the life of the swordsman.

The fencing match is a combative situation in which the winner is determined by better cranial capacity. If one relies on fight-or-flight instincts when a sword is drawn, the match turns into a slugfest in which one attack (a stimulus) is met with a reactionary counterattack (a reaction) from the defender. When a fencer does not have a technique in his repertoire to counter a particular attack, he tends to ad lib a reaction, often accompanied with the addition of sheer strength to "make the attack work." On the other hand, the skillful execution of a proper technique requires but a fraction of the exertion made in a wholly improvised attack.

When one has the ability to outperform the opponent, choosing attacks and parries is relatively easy. For the undertrained fencer, it seems like the adversary is capable of predicting his movements and counter his moves even before he has begun an attack. The building frustration continues to play into the advanced fencer's advantage as the novice continues to add unnecessary strength to his attacks, which tends to slow down the execution of an attack. This is one reason why young fencers in their late teens or early twenties who rely on their youthful reactions and strength are easily bested by men and women in their late fifties and early sixties. Until the body loses its ability to respond to brain stimulus, the more experienced fencer will always defeat the less experienced one.

Fencing Wisdom

The superior fencer does not depend on physical ability when technique and skill can be used. Not only is the reliance on skill more effective, it also tends to be the more efficient movement, which, in turn, leads to less energy being spent. Because the experienced fencer has learned how to react, he can remain poised and calm enough to handle the fencing match. Instead of reacting to an attack, a fencer has learned how to best, most efficiently, and quickly exploit his opponent's weaknesses. This is the reason why fencers do not race head-on toward the enemy without first knowing what kind of attack will be successful.

Apart from practicing certain movements in drills and forms, experience from free practice is often considered the next best way of improving one's skills other than engaging in an actual duel or battle. But how does a fencer decide what movements should be used to defeat an opponent? Common sense would seem to indicate that simply reacting in the proper, prescribed manner will defend against an opponent's attack. Speed, strength, and endurance all seem to be qualities that would determine a victor. Wisdom (knowledge and insight), however, is what really makes one fencer better than another. Wisdom in fencing is an understanding of four fundamental concepts: (1) timing defeats speed, (2) leverage defeats strength, (3) technique defeats instincts, and (4) distance defeats the sword.

While knowledge is helpful in trying to solve a problem of defeating an enemy swordsman, it is only a single competence of a great fencer. Knowing what attack an opponent will use can clearly lead to the proper defensive response, but fencing is too fluid and quick for there to be time to think about the attack and then cognitively plan a defense. It may seem counter-intuitive, but fencers engage in the battle *not* with a host of information, but rather with a *lack* of information because it takes too long for the body to react to stimuli from the brain. Instead, the body must act on perceived and actual threats, while both anticipating an attack, discerning between feints and real attacks, and simultaneously preparing a defense. When attacking, the fencer must make his moves with the ability to anticipate possible counterattacks and prepare a proper response. Such a complex activity does not employ cognitive thinking, but more a kind of intuition that is heavily influenced by experience and an understanding of the art of fencing.

Cognitive thinking (the execution of executive brain activity) is used to solve intellectual problems. Involving more senses increases the brain's ability to learn, which is why the educational field has begun to emphasize holistic activities in lower grades to engage as many or all of the students' senses as possible. Designing and constructing three-dimensional projects or reading out loud supplements what most have assumed to be the internal process of thinking and learning. The Chinese adage, "I hear and I forget. I see and I remember. I do and I understand," has new meaning. Cognitive learning, as it becomes more difficult, requires more energy from the brain and body. Concentration focuses the mind's attention and senses are used more keenly for a specific, rather than general purpose.

The mind is also capable of associative functions: multi-tasking, to use a modern word. Doing two or more things at the same time, like driving and talking, is an associative function. Outside factors, however, can make associative functions more cognitive. If, for example, it begins to rain heavily while driving an old car with balding tires, almost instantly the brain understands that it is in a hazardous situation. It must focus on controlling the car, which, a few minutes earlier, was done without concentration. Chemically, the body's senses become heightened and the brain examines the stimulus with increased attentiveness. Extraneous stimulus, such as casual talking, stops, the driver sits up, turns down the radio, and looks more attentively at his mirrors. Every datum from the five senses is examined for relevance to controlling the car. The driver is learning to handle the situation.

Conversely, the inattentive driver finds himself in a situation in which an accident is more likely to occur. A common experience for urban drivers is that of a driver talking on his cell phone. It is not that a person can't talk, hold the phone, and drive at the same time (which will improve with practice), but that drivers don't adjust their driving to the complexity of their associative activities. Without realizing it, drivers who talk on the phone often dangerously slow down below the speed of traffic, make over-cautious turns, and do not hear ambient noises, such as ambulance sirens or the honking car behind them. Worst of all is the act of dialing, which requires complete cognitive ability to recall a phone number and then locate and push the correct buttons.

Cognitive and associative functions are a matter of life and death to the swordsman. Not only must he remain focused on the task of fencing (attacking or defending), but he has to also be aware of everything that is going on around him. Glands begin secreting hormones that heighten senses, and the body and mind fall back on the training that has prepared the soldier for this moment. Viking berserkers gave all their energy to emotional rage so that they might begin attacking anyone around them, friend or foe. The one-on-one swordsman, especially the duelist, must have a greater balance, maintaining sufficient adrenaline and testosterone to fight fiercely. Too much of either would impede the body's cognitive functions during the fight. This heightened state of battle preparedness on a simple endocrine level is extremely difficult to maintain. Olympic athletes must not only maintain their physical peak, but the ups and downs of their psychological training tax the body even more than most people realize or understand.

Maintaining this intensity also had its inevitable side-effects: the emotional drain, the physical exhaustion, and increased paranoia. The body can only take that heightened alertness for a limited time. Constantly looking over one's shoulder to evaluate every stimulus for its potential danger is not unlike small birds and animals, which live in a constant state of fear, fidgeting, constantly looking for predators, and overreacting to even the slightest sound. This state of mind is necessary for a creature in the wild, but not for a typical citizen living in his peaceful urban or suburban world. Security and a diminished, if not nonexistent, fear from attack have thus become prerequisites for inhabitants of modern societies.

Western and Japanese Styles

The traditional history book on warfare often paints warfare in broad strokes as a way to contrast the military culture and tactics of the opposing sides. Examinations of a commander's experiences, reliance on battlefield disposition, and a brief vignette of the typical soldier are the usual fare in the discourse of such treatises whose purposes lay in placing the battle in the larger perspective of a war. And when discussion of battlefield technique is found, it focuses on the tactical movements of bodies of troops in relation to enemy units on the other side of the battlefield. What one does not find is a description of the specific techniques of the weapons used. This dearth stems from the fact that most historians are not or were not soldiers themselves, or there is no historical source recounting such details. And even when such documentation does exist in the form of a treatise, guide, or manual, the historian must read it with the understanding that (1) treatises did not necessarily describe the general manner of fighting within a particular body of troops, (2) it was propaganda for one particular style of fighting, and (3) the subtleties of pictographic and textual explanation do not substitute for direct training or practice. So, while traditional histories of warfare lack discussion of manual techniques in sword fencing, this section hopes to give the reader a better sense of the swordsman's actual fight by comparing Western and Japanese fencing.

As has already been seen, styles of Western fencing evolved with the physical transformation of the sword from a slashing weapon to a point weapon, while Japanese fencing is best described as an adaptation to the conditions of the battlefield and civilian life. In most cases, Western fencing styles were forgotten as instruction in new methods of warfare were developed. Unlike Japan, where strict observance of precise movement led to the complete transmission of the style to later, contemporary generations, Europeans focused on new methods of organizing firepower rather than devoting nostalgic attention to the art of swordsmanship, which was quickly in decline.

Japan's isolation prevented open warfare, and while new styles of fighting did not develop, established schools (*ryu*) of fighting systematized their style for an increasingly peaceful period. Head instructors of kenjutsu quickly realized that an era of peace meant less patronage from the ruling government, which would inevitably lead to the demise of a style. Fencing *ryu* faced the scrutiny of the government because they were sources of education that might train the future armies that would challenge the government. Conversely, samurai disaffected by the changed in the shogunate would return to their home province and train a new generation of samurai to eventually overthrow the shogun.[11]

In both Europe and Japan, students would be first found among the nobility. Because their numbers would always remain limited, there was a natural impetus for commanders to begin to look to the commoners for recruits. Knighthood and the priesthood were traditionally the two ways of entering higher levels of society, but commoners who demonstrated fighting ability and the sensibilities to adjust to the upper class were accepted out of military necessity. In Japan, fencing halls trained a new generation of samurai through the patronage of noble families, while in Europe swordplay was a skill expected of all officers during their postings at a garrison.

The fencing hall was the haven of a military culture, so initial training included basic etiquette toward their superiors. A soldier would often begin with physical training to toughen the body and prepare the mind for instruction. Often, instruction was harsh and punishing. Officers or lead instructors, like the modern drill sergeant, gave their charges difficult and physically demanding jobs, believing that difficult tasks would break new recruits of the laziness of civilian life and prepare them for the battlefield.

In Japan, since the samurai was the servant of a lord, learning the humbling skills of serving tea was another task that emphasized attention to detail needed during exercise. Because subtle movements were required in fencing, the small and precise manner of holding a utensil or pouring water had the unintended effect of teaching fine motor skills. Since tea, as in the West, involved polite conversation, it also became a way of introducing the student to honored and respected instructors and individuals. For noble children, it taught them not to expect instant privilege, and for commoners, it served as a way to learn the refined social etiquette of the upper class.

In the training halls, called *dojo* in Japan and *salle d'escrime* in Europe, instruction began by teaching stances that are the starting and stopping points for any martial art. Mastery of footwork was essential to the proper execution of any movement. Once the feet are in place, the upper body is then free to perform the thrusting or slashing required of the fencer. So distinctive are stances that it is easy to recognize the type of training a person has received. Sometimes it is possible to identify not only a particular style within a school of fencing or martial art, but the individual instructor as well.

In competition, the stance indicates to judges when participants are ready to begin. In the street, when threatened by muggers, a stance will indicate the potential "victim's" knowledge of self-defense. A martial artist, caught in such a situation, has the choice of hiding his ability in order to surprise the assailant or he can take recognizable stance to scare off the aggressor. Between competing martial arts, as well as styles within a particular art, the stance serves as a distinctive declaration of their fighting style.

In swordsmanship, the stance not only serves as a starting point, it predefines the movement of the art. Kendo stances are characterized by parallel feet meant to allow the kendo fencer (called a *kendoka*) to maintain a forward position opposite his opponent. Traditional kenjustu, which anticipates an attack from any direction, places his feet in a V-shape. This allows the swordsman to turn in any direction instantly. Western fencing has the feet at a 90° angle, which best permits the fencer to move up and down along a thin strip that designates the bouting area.

Placement of the hands also has an impact on the way the sword is held. The extended forearm and opposite arm hanging out behind the head are characteristic of Western fencers. Japanese swordsmen can be recognized by the two-handed grip with their weapon's point aimed at the opponent. Not only does the stance allow the swordsman to initiate an attack quickly, it permits him to block enemy attacks with little or no movement.

Contrary to what most would assume, there is no single perfect stance. Basic stances do, however, act as an initial defensive posture that allows a person to quickly attack or defend according to the circumstances of the situation. Each stance has both advantages and disadvantages. For example, the foil and epee held in a guard that defends only one side of the body better protects the swordsman than if the weapon were placed squarely in the middle of the body. If the foil or epee is placed along the center line of the body, the entire torso is partially open to attack. In the reality of a fencing duel, there is no single stance, but a series of stances appropriate to the opponent's attack.

The manner of holding the sword is probably the most obvious difference between Western and Japanese fencing. Again, each style reflects the culture of the swordsman as well as the manner in which he would initiate an attack or parry. The Western foil and epee emphasize subtle movement of the point toward the opponent, which is appropriate for the civilian dress fencers wore — clothing that allowed penetrations to the torso and the body's appendages. Japanese stances, being still more closely linked to the attack of an armored opponent, relied on the penetrating strength of two hands. In both Japan and the West, the single-handed use of a sabre or its Japanese equivalent, the Heian *tachi,* reflected the necessity of using the non-fencing arm to control the horse or to act as a counterbalance to the outward sweep of the sword. Earlier European knights actually carried a shield that served both as a counterbalance and protective shielding.

Attack and Defense

Fencing, whether Western, Japanese, or any other, depends on the swordsman's ability to both defend and attack. Victory, however, is almost entirely dependent on the ability to attack.

In Western fencing, the body is customarily divided into four basic target areas that protect the most vital part of a human's anatomy — the torso. The body is divided across a vertical line through the middle of the torso; the side closest to the fencing arm being called the "inside line," while the other is the "outside line." Another line, this one horizontal, bisects the torso into upper and lower halves, creating, in effect, four squares that need to be protected.

The defensive parries in foil and epee are divided into four basic parries that protect each of the four torso areas. These parries are further divided into two grips called supination, in which the palm faces up, and pronation, in which the palm faces down. Together there are a total of eight parries, two for each part of the torso. While all parries move upward or laterally, supinated parries are inherently stronger in that the downward force of the arm acts as a stronger brace and allows for an easier push through the opponent's blade. The supinated hand allows the muscles of the arm to extend more quickly for attacks. Additionally, supinated parries allow the blade to lift an opponent's blade upward and away from the larger torso area.

Because of the blade's thin profile, it is only possible to defend a single line at a time. This is accomplished by holding a guard that deflects attacks past the body on the inside line, while twisting the torso to reduce the openness of the outside line. When threats or attacks are made to the outside line, a simple shift in the wrist allows the fencer to take a parry on the opposite, outside line.

Kendo takes a different approach to defensive postures. Because the grip of the shinai (a bamboo practice sword) is with two hands, the body forms a frontward stance toward the opponent. This stance is much like that of a golfer who lifts the head of his club upward to eye-level with the top of the club aimed at his naval. Instead of dividing the body into four parts, the kendoka uses the tip of the sword as the forward end of a triangular shield. Any attack, whether a thrust or a cut, must pass on either side of the blade. As the attack moves toward the kendoka, he pulls his shinai slightly toward the side of the attacking blade, forcing the opponent's point away from the center line. A slash is caught in mid-cut before it has a chance to reach the kendoka's body. Low parries are made in the same way except that the point is lowered. More traditional Japanese fencing styles pull one shoulder back behind the other, in much the same manner as the Western fencer turns his torso to limit body exposure.

Swordsmanship, however, is learning to properly attack, whether it is from a direct attack, which strikes unopposed at an undefended area, or pushes through a defensive parry. An attack may also be done immediately after a defensive parry (a riposte) has been made to block an attack, though the psychological training of swordsmen must continually focus on the advance and attack, deemphasizing defensive tactics that will never emerge victorious.

While the strategy of biding time may be necessary to catch one's breath or to wear down the opponent, it must always be done with the strategic goal of preparing for an attack. Giving more time to the enemy to prepare their own attack during the short encounter with an armed opponent in hand-to-hand combat allows the enemy to take and use the initiative for his own. The press of a concerted attack allows the fencer to expend minimal energy while imposing a disproportionate expense of energy on the opponent. Consequently, it is always to the fencer's advantage to maintain an attacking posture, especially on the battlefield where opponents may attack from any direction. This is true even during a regulated duel in which there is no fear of surprise attack. The better fencer who "toys" with a less skilled fencer, thus lowering his guard in an arrogant and misguided sense of confidence, allows the opponent to plan an attack. The most expert swordsmen understands that *he* has more to lose against desperate fencers, who have nothing to lose and everything to gain.

Apart from the gentleman's duel in which the goal is to be the first to draw blood, the ultimate goal of the swordsman is to incapacitate the enemy to prevent him from temporarily or permanently returning an attack. While the former involves disarming, knocking the opponent unconscious, or causing him to flee, the battlefield encounter requires the efficient killing of the enemy. The brutal truth is that sword fighting that merely injures the opponent gives the injured another opportunity to kill the attacker.

There are two ways of killing with a sword: the first uses the edge of the blade (a hard kill), the second uses the point (a soft kill). The hard kill relies on the cutting of the limbs, trunk, or head, resulting in instantaneous death (in the case of decapitation) or the eventual loss of blood that quickly leads to death if left untreated. The soft kill uses the point to kill by piercing vital organs like the brain and heart. Penetrations to any non-vital organ may, in time, kill the opponent either through the eventual failure of vital body systems or from possible infection. Ideally, a slow kill will at least prevent the opponent from continuing his attack. Superficial cuts, if allowed to heal free of infection, do little permanent damage to the injured, apart from obvious scarring.

Without question, the most important area of the body is the head. Injury to the executive controls of the body — the brain — impacts not only the five senses, but the body's autonomic and reflexive controls. Every moment leading up to the encounter is the psychological building of fear —fear of pain and fear of death. When the first hit strikes at the head, a swordsman's vulnerability becomes evident in the quality of the attack. Did the sword cut penetrate the helmet or bounce off? If it penetrated, did it damage the scalp? And to what degree?

An attack on the head has two purposes: to disorient the opponent so another, more fatal attack may be made, or to penetrate the skull decisively and kill the opponent instantly. An attack on a bare head has even greater implications; cleaving into the skull is more likely to kill and if even a graze is made on the scalp, the subsequent blood dripping down to the face and into the eyes has a demoralizing impact on the opponent. Not only does blood impede a swordsman's visual perception, it makes him conscious that he has been hit when, because his sense of touch has been dulled by adrenaline pumping through the body, he might not have even noticed his injury.

Making the sword "sing" is one way of testing the angle of attack. The swish heard from a perfectly aligned swing of a metal sword can also be heard with a wooden bokken. When combined with the precision of an attack that stops inches from one's eyes and ears, the most experienced and toughest fencer receiving such a strike cannot but express an uneasy nervousness that the strike might actually hit. The control needed to stop a wooden sword, much less a live blade, so quickly without losing cutting power is an incredible combination of the natural use of gravity and a very focused coordination of the arms' and hands' muscles. At such intensity, practice evolves into sheer acts of faith that an attack will stop short of the head each and every time.

With a real sword, the potential for permanent damage is even more evident. In kendo, the strike with the two-handed katana is made with a frightening quickness. The sword can be raised above the head and then thrust forward at the enemy in just under a second. Once the attack has made its forward motion, there is not enough time to consciously perceive the destination of attack and then cognitively raise the arm for a block. The tell-tale signs of tensing hands or arm muscles, or the intuition that a head strike will be made allows the recipient of a head attack to raise his sword for a block, but determining the target is simply a guess. A close approximation of the block is certainly a possibility but other factors may allow the defender to determine the target. The opponent might favor a particular target, for example. Or he might have unconscious patterns of movement that betray a particular attack.

Attacking with the point is also an effective, though more difficult, method of hitting the head. Many European treatises have imagery in which blades penetrate the brain through the eyes, nose, or mouth. Because of their location and the anatomically round shape of the head, eyes are rarely pierced by a sword. But points that succeed in striking the head have a fair chance of penetrating the eyes, which have no cartilage or bone that could deflect a point away from the sunken orbits of the eye. The side of the head is an easy target for a sabre cut. Penetrating the skull has immediate and devastating consequences. In one instance during an Olympic fencing tournament, a foil broke during a rough exchange and penetrated a fencer's mask, lodging into one man's skull. Though he did not die instantly, the penetration was so severe that he expired soon after.

Below the head is another area that is particularly vulnerable to attack — the neck. While it is the softest and most exposed area of the body, because of its size and location near the head, it is probably one of the most difficult areas of the body to hit. Blocking attacks to the throat must be extremely swift and precise in its timing because the body's natural instincts is to raise the arms to protect the throat and head.[12] Not only is the carotid artery located in the neck, but a crushed trachea or blood from a punctured artery could literally drown an opponent in his own blood.

Aiming for the throat with a rapier or court sword is extremely difficult and rarely worth the effort. Not only must the point lodge exactly on either side of the Adam's apple, but it must puncture deeply enough to pass through the neck to either slice through the trachea or cut through the neck's artery.

Turning the blade so that it cuts horizontally or twisting it as it passes into the flesh is also necessary to properly penetrate the throat. Only a hard and direct hit into the spine can sever the backbone, which is a very difficult task.

The target areas of Western competitive fencing do not lend themselves to attacks on the throat. The foil (a descendant of the court sword) targets the torso. The epee, because the whole body is target, targets the wrist and arm, while sabre practice emphasizes cuts to the top and side of the head. Kendo teaches a powerful and direct thrust to the throat, but it must be used very rarely in order to preserve its effectiveness as a surprise attack.

Severing the head, made famous by the *Highlander* movies, is a strike that can only effectively be made when the opponent does not wear armor. The success of such an attack depends on critical mistakes by the opponent. His own attack has to miss the attacker, opening the neck to an attack. Then the attacker has to make a horizontal cut to the neck before the opponent can recover his balance and weapon. The defender only needs to raise his sword or contort the body to deny his neck to the attacker. The only other way of cutting to the neck is if the opponent doubles over, presenting the neck as a target. But this is a near impossibility. Combat depends on face-to-face contact, so competent fighters will never willingly offer up their back or neck to an opponent.

This kind of coup de grace is rare and is only accomplished by the complete domination of the opponent. On a battlefield, a person might be held to the ground by retainers. Or on the executioner's block the convicted might willingly submit to the inevitable. Beheading serves as an effective propaganda tool to terrorize a local population. A severed head might also have served as a victory trophy, as was the case in feudal Japan. The tale of the forty-seven Ronin illustrated the cultural etiquette of bringing the enemy's head to the samurai's master. In this case, the head was brought to the grave of their dead master. The presentation of heads as proof of killing an enemy was a common custom of many cultures. Herodias asked for John the Baptist's head on a silver platter. The head of the Wampanoag, King Philip, was cut off by the Pilgrims, placed on top of a spear, and then planted in the center of Plymouth, following a cruel tradition common to many European cities. Even the scalping of native Americans in exchange for a bounty at government offices perpetuated the same barbaric act. Tamerlane supposedly left ten-foot-high mounds of severed heads. In some instances, he used them to build towers as a legacy of terror to make unconquered enemies cower before his army.

The Japanese saw beheading as the last step in ritual suicide called seppuku.[13] Under particular social circumstances, suicide was the culturally respectable manner of proving an individual's inner mettle by dying in dignity at one's own hands. Even in the West, there are many instances of Roman citizens committing suicide to preserve the honor of the state, their family, or a social standard.[14] The ritual was a carefully prescribed affair that resulted with the samurai piercing his abdomen with his sword and then pulling it across his belly in two distinct cuts. Recognizing the difficulty of the act (an act one never gets to practice), a swordsman trusted by the samurai committing suicide struck down at his friend's neck at the very moment the victim was about to lose control of his motor functions. Proper technique requires the swordsman giving the coup de grace to slice off the head in a single cut, leaving a thin piece of skin at the throat to prevent the head from rolling away from the body, though this was not always the fashion. Not only did the samurai preserve his own personal dignity by taking his own life, but the suicide served as a final test of his strength as he fought the grueling pain and maintained the iron discipline needed to complete his task.

Slicing through the spine was a skill in which Japanese swordsman formally trained. Called *tameshi giri*, the swordsman would practice cutting through a bamboo pole surrounded by thick straw that had been tied together and soaked in water. The bamboo simulated the spine or bone, while the heavy, water-logged straw represented the flesh. An alternate method involves taking old tatami mats and rolling them up to the thickness of the neck. The rolls would then be put on a vertical stick to be chopped down with a live blade. A more difficult practice would be to go out into a bamboo grove and cut down the shafts in clean strokes. In both kinds of practice, the swordsman quickly learns that it is not the strength of the muscles that makes the cut, but the edge of the blade that slices through the "flesh." The hardest cuts are the horizontal slash and the upward cut, which require the blade to move in a perfect plane to avoid lodging the blade in the flesh. An improper cut can damage the blade by bending it; a blade bouncing off the target might even hit the attacker's leg.

Apart from the upper body, the body's appendages are more easily hit. Striking at the limbs is ideally done by shattering the cartilage of the kneecaps, ankles, and elbows. Not only is it easier to cut through, but even minor penetrations will have a greater effect on a limb by severing ligaments and tendons than if cut between the joints. Muscles, because of their fibrous nature, are more difficult to cut. A cut through the tendon allows the muscles to move, but prevents execution of body movement. If the tendons in the forearm can be cut, an attack that requires swiftness and only a minimum of force, the fencer will be completely prevented from controlling his wrist. Superficial damage to muscle will heal over time, but tendons or ligaments, unless reattached, will permanently disable or damage fine motor skills.

In striking at the torso, the fencer must consider the anatomy of the opponent. The ribs and sternum will stop a sword cut, so thrusts to the mid-section must be made between ribs by twisting a flat-bladed sword into a horizontal position just before piercing the opponent's trunk. A blade that penetrates the chest can hit any number of vital organs, some of which when hit may cause instant death — a hit to the heart, for example. Soft hits to other organs, while not immediately fatal, may eventually cause the body to go into shock. A hit to the stomach is a nasty penetration that releases acids that begin to eat away at the linings of the internal organs. If not stopped, the damage to other internal organs will become permanent. Puncturing the lungs similarly releases fluids that will internally drown the injured swordsman.

Because of the rudimentary state of internal medicine or the lack of medical attention on the battlefield, the damage inflicted on a soldier was often quick and swift. Whether from shock of massive hemorrhage or exposure to the elements, severe lacerations or internal puncturing of the organs meant eventual death. While some armies supported either a small unit of surgeons or other medical personal, their knowledge was limited, their equipment basic, and their skill too undeveloped to save all but the least wounded. It was often the responsibility of the light infantry, or even noncombatants who assisted in moving the army's baggage train, to follow in the wake of the front line's offensive to finish off the wounded that still lingered. In other instances, armed servants dealt the death blow after his horse-bound master dealt the initial attack.

The traditions following the end of a battle varied from culture to culture. The Greeks ceased further operations when it was apparent the enemy had retreated and then made obsequies before taking armor from the dead as part of their trophy panoply. Others buried troops in mass graves with their full arms and armor, at other times without. Whatever the custom, the aftermath was a gruesome scene even for the victor as friends and comrades were counted for national registers. Battlefield warfare in its minutest detail was a senseless event of brutality, but when faced with the alternative of invasion and possible annihilation, war on these terms justifies the necessity of the swordsman's art.

Comparing Styles

Once one learns some of the subtleties that distinguish Western fencing from samurai fencing, the most immediate question that springs to mind is who would win if a European and a samurai were to engage in a fight. While it is difficult to chose a victor, it is possible to share some generalities. Theoretical encounters like this would be influenced by many factors, including the armor each wears, the swords used, and the time period from which they come.

Certainly, the swordsman who is used to fighting opponents of varying cultures has the advantage over the swordsman who is only used to fighting similarly armed and armored opponents. Likewise, the swordsman who is not dependent on armor will have an advantage over the man who is used to compensating for technique with the help of armor. The discrepancy in ability and skill, however, is impossible to quantify in an activity like swordsmanship except by actual combat. Swordsmen did have a way of measuring their skill, though it rarely crossed cultural lines and was limited to combat with swordsmen in neighboring regions.

The traditional method of seeing who was better was to send out a representative of the school and challenge a member of the opposition. A swordsman of a Barcelona fencing school might travel to France and challenge a swordsman in Paris, for example. In Japan, students of one dojo would sometimes travel to other dojo in search of challengers. If the challenged school accepted, it would send its best student to meet the visitor. Rules would be decided and then the "friendly" duel took place. If the school's representative won, he preserved the honor of the school. If the visitor won, he would take the placard on which the name of the dojo was written as a trophy. Challenges could be made to the death, but such serious encounters were unheard of except in the case of a personal feud. Challenges served both the challenger and the challenged by providing fresh sparring partners against whom they could test their fighting skills. On occasion, the feuds did get personal, especially between nearby rival schools.

But still the question remains as to which is better: Western or Japanese fencing? Or, in broader terms, what swordsmen were technically superior to others?

One cannot respond without first saying (as has been done in the previous chapter) that armor played a crucial role in combat. For all the emphasis on fencing style, not even the best technique amounted to anything if it could not penetrate an opponent's defensive armor. Next, given the divergent evolution of Western fencing and kendo, there is a clear difference in the martial applications of each competitive sport. The foil and epee were developed for courtly encounters, while kendo came out of a more recent and practical history in which the katana was actively used by the samurai class late into the 19th century. And while a comparison might be made between the modern sabre and the katana, technique in the light sabre of Olympic-style fencing does not have the same martial application as kendo, much less kenjutsu.

History does provide circumstances in which European sailors encountered Japanese pirates. Yet these examples do not decisively favor of one style over the other. Chance encounters did exist but explanations of one culture's victory over swordsmen of another is not definitively explained in terms of better swordsmanship. Samurai boarders may have been successful swordsmen who could have easily been cut down by Western pistols and muskets, but even novice samurai could have been bested by Western sailors and nobles experienced in boarding enemy ships, though this feat was rather a rare occurrence.

While anecdotes are rare, there is one historical report of the quality of

Japanese hosts who personally drew their own swords and dispatched several renegade samurai attempting to assassinate several European diplomats. But given the fact that Europeans had already gone past the sword and employed the musket and pistol, it was increasingly rare that Europeans would allow themselves to fall into a situation where a talented samurai might draw his sword. While one-sided in terms of fairness, survival in combat eventually depended more on technology than it did on fencing skills. It is this very reason that Europeans were able to extend their empires across the globe.

On a practical level, there have been many informal exchanges in the past century between Western fencers and Japanese kendoka. On a purely anecdotal level, kendo strikes beat out the refined forms of international fencing. While the Western foil fencer practices to depress a point with only 500 grams, the kendoka practices the slicing cut, which can easily be transferred to a live blade. Put a katana in the hands of a kendoka and a rapier in the hands of the foilist, and the physical nature of kendo easily smashes through the Westerner who is not used to the infighting the katana favors with its blade length edge. Even when a live blade sabre is placed in the hands of a Western sabre fencer, the strength in his arm for one-handed parries cannot sustain itself against the heavy and rapid attacks of the two-handed kendoka.

That is not to say that there are not advantages to fencers of the Western style. The lighter sabre also has a speed that allows for a rapid counterattack if the two-handed samurai misses with his first attack. The Western fencer is also quick and agile in advancing and retreating when compared to the sure-footed and deliberate samurai warrior. Subtle movements of the point also allow the rapier to plunge into an on-rushing samurai who might fail to catch the Western blade. A rapier point in the eye, throat, or chest was as deadly as any slicing motion of the katana.

So the answer to the initial question does not really apply to which style is better than the other. The answer, however, ultimately depends on a more important question: Who is the better swordsman? For it is the swordsman who best adapts to the situation, making the best of his offensive capabilities and denying access to his obvious weaknesses, that will win any sword fight encounter.

In terms of comparing modern fencers to their historical predecessors, quality of swordsmanship is heavily dependent on experience. It can probably be argued that modern fencers are more physically capable than swordsmen of earlier generations. Similarly, the modern swordsman, if he trained in order to fight with a real sword, could, in time, readily adapt to its use in this fashion.

There is also the tendency to ascribe more weight and credibility to sword fighting styles of earlier periods. The age of a style, however, does not necessarily indicate a superior style, rather that the style successfully attracted talented students who transmitted of the style from one generation to the next. And were moderns somehow required to use the sword in hand-to-hand combative situations, there is no doubt that with modern attitudes and training methods, the modern would be able to acquire skills and abilities equal to or surpassing those of historical swordsmen under similar circumstances. It is by luck and fortune that contemporary men and women will never need to learn the art of swordsmanship, and that its activity is best appreciated by the fencing afficionado as well as the *Star Wars* fan interested in learning about lightsaber fighting.[15]

SEVEN

Star Wars Choreography

When George Lucas released *Star Wars* in 1977, he had no idea that the Jedi Knight would have such a profound impact on the lives of millions of people around the world. Because so many identified with the virtues of the Jedi fighting for justice and peace in the universe, it was inconceivable that years later thousands of citizens in Commonwealth countries like Great Britain and Australia would list Jedi Knight as their official religious creed. It goes without saying that the Jedi would not have made such an impact on our collective psyches were it not for the fact that the sword fight is the perfect visual medium to portray humanity's struggle between good and evil, a story with which every person in the world can identify. The struggle of the Jedi, as it is for the swordsman, however, is one not only of having the ability to use a lightsaber or a sword, but knowing when and where to use it. As Obi-Wan Kenobi says to Luke in Episode IV, "You must do what you feel is right, of course." Understanding what is right, however, is a long and difficult journey for the swordsman, *Star Wars* being the ultimate swordsman's adventure tale.

Audiences have a familiarity with popular concepts of sword fighting from the movies that have influenced George Lucas—*Zorro, Robin Hood, Prince Valiant,* and *The Three Musketeers.* It is the world of gentlemen, soldiers, and warriors, though Lucas outdid them all in his creation of the Jedi. He took the swashbuckling choreography and stunt work of his predecessors to create a universe of swordsmen unlike any other. Most influential on Jedi lightsaber fighting was the samurai of Akira Kurosawa and the tales of Japanese warriors torn between their commitment to duty and the obligations of society and the world around them. Unlike the real world of the fencer, however, the silver screen is not about technique; it is entertainment. Cinematic "sword fighting" is an imitation and illusion designed to excite the moviegoer. Every move is contrived around dialogue to create a deliberate cadence and tempo and achieve an emotional effect.

Years of sword fighting cinematic experiences inspired Lucas's final concepts of the Jedi. He wanted a tribute to the sword flicks of his childhood, but he also wanted something even more epic and grand. The key to the success of Lucas's story was not swordsmen, but actors who had to appear as if they were the best swordsmen in the universe. Especially with a masked character like Darth Vader, the emotion of anger and rage and sentimentality had to be conveyed in both subtle and dramatic movements of the body. Every step, line of dialogue, and close-up on Vader's mask had to convey the intensity of the sword fighter.

With Episode IV, Lucas established the rules of his universe. He made only minor changes during the many steps in the creation of his saga, but on the whole, Lucas remains consistent with his own universe and that of the real universe, which makes his fictitious sword fighting even more realistic. The two major deviations concerning the lightsaber involve the blood shown on the floor in the Cantina scene in Episode IV and in the cave with the wampa, as well as with the blood splatter when Darth Maul was cut in half (the lightsaber cauterizes flesh in other instances). In the Prequel Trilogy, Lucas confirms that the lightsaber does in fact cut through virtually any substance except the blade of another lightsaber. Energy, though, as in the case of MagnaGuard staves, can challenge the Jedi's weapon. They also prove useful against Sith lightning.

Creating the conceptional background for the lightsaber and realistically portraying that weapon in front of cameras presented a plethora of practical problems. Because the weight of a steel sword has a tremendous impact on the use of a historical sword, there was a problem of how a lightsaber fight would appear. Mostly because of technical factors, the lightsaber fight of Episode IV was straightforward. Holding the lightsabers with two hands, the swordsmen exchanged slashes and thrusts. The shimmering effect of the lightsaber was created not with special effects but through the use of metal-coated dowels turned by a rotating motor hidden in the lightsaber casing. The movement of the two actors was restricted so that the delicate spinning blade would not be damaged during the fight.

In theory, the real power of a light energy blade depended on its ability to "push" the light edge of the lightsaber into a target. Whereas an actual sword relies on a combination of gravity and the physics of a slicing blade, the lightsaber is made up of weightless energy. Certainly, the balance of a lightsaber would be different from that of a steel sword. To add to the realism, there had to be degrees of penetration such that the lightsaber would more easily cut through living tissue than it would wood, plastic, or steel. It would take little effort to cut through flesh. However, as shown in Luke's strike to Vader's shoulder in Episode VI, there is real resistance to the lightsaber's blade, which, more or less, proves that the blade's "grabbing" into a substance gives the Jedi kinesthetic feedback from the penetration of an object or a "feel" for the way another

Jedi handles his own lightsaber. It proves that armor does affect the cutting power of the lightsaber blade. Even though Yoda and Obi-Wan demonstrate with devastating effect the power of the lightsaber when they enter the temple after Anakin's attack, the bodies of dead Jedi are testament that clone trooper armor can be an effective deterrent against the Jedi blade. The viewer can imagine that the stronger and tougher the target, the slower the lightsaber will be to penetrate. Without this realism, the audience would be less likely to believe in the power of the blade.

In addition to the traditional method of fighting with a lightsaber prop, which had a long metallic blade, Episode I introduced a slightly different kind of lightsaber fighting that utilized a lightsaber prop with a short fluorescent blade extension that protruded about a foot and a half from the lightsaber hilt. From this, computer graphic animators could digitally insert the full length of the blade and artificially create the cutting penetration of slicing into metal robot warriors. Actors were literally cutting through air as they imagined the enemies that they were fighting. The lighter weight and shorter length of the prop also increased the speed and manipulation of the lightsaber. This increased propensity for spectacle in the lightsaber fight was an improvement in the breadth of lightsaber combat found in the Original Trilogy, but it also had a negative impression on many purists who felt the increased acrobatics of the Prequel Trilogy reflected the growing cinematic trend in Western action films to imitate the wu shu of Beijing comic opera.

What makes lightsaber fighting so vastly different from any other type of fighting is speed and rapid succession of one sword position (or attack) into another. Any metal sword (or even a resin or plastic prop) has a particular weight and balance that affects the manner in which the sword prop is used. The light blades of many swashbuckling movies allowed a style of fencing that did not correspond to actual sword fighting with real sabres. The use of metal props (especially of the Chinese broad sword genre) creates a style that is much heavier than one would hope for an action film. Their answer, as in the case of most martial arts films, is to increase the speed of the film so that movement appears faster than it actually was during live filming.

The Prequel Trilogy did not have to speed up the film in order to make the duel between Qui-Gon/Obi-Wan and Darth Maul look any faster. Most of the speed comes from the physical weight of the lightsaber props, which were balanced aluminum rods painted in fluorescent colors. Earlier versions of fiberglass were tried, but when the blades shattered from heavy practice, shards of dangerously sharp shrapnel exploded from breaks in the blade. Even the final aluminum lightsabers that were used had to be coated with plastic to prevent bits of metal shrapnel from showing up on film.

The other factor contributing to the speed of the lightsaber fighting was the physical abilities of the actors and their stunt doubles. Ewan McGregor has demonstrated himself to be quite adept in wielding his lightsaber. Many still photographs show his hands in the proper position for holding his lightsaber (wrists twisted in with fingers aligned one on top of the other). Some stills show McGregor in unbalanced position, either up on his toes (which no fencer in any style does) or with his lightsaber directly in front of his eyes, obscuring his vision. Liam Neeson has a basic simple stance, characteristically holding his lightsaber in baseball fashion. Ray Park is most impressive in both his footwork as well as his manipulation in both the single and double-bladed lightsaber. From his years of training and competition, it is evident that experience and practical necessities of wielding the staff and broad sword have informed his Sith style of fighting. Hayden Christiansen complements Ewan McGregor's enthusiasm for the sword fight. While they both emphasize speed over precision, the energy they give to their choreography contributes to the passion of their climactic duel.

Apart from the telekinetic ability of tossing objects with their mind, there is very little emphasis on the Force in the sword fighting until Episode III. While dialogue portrays the Force as the source of the Jedi's lightsaber abilities, the practical fact is that all the lightsaber fighting and stunts were the result of technical sword fighting skill or acrobatics. And contrary to what many think, Han's use of the lightsaber to open the belly of the tauntaun in Episode V speaks definitively that someone without control of the Force can easily ignite and use a lightsaber.

In the real world, the concept of ki (qi or chi in Chinese, prana in Sanskrit) is fundamental to many Asian martial arts. Ki is the energy that flows through the body, giving vital energy to a human's physiological function. While Western scientists have not been able to prove the existence of ki, they do admit, in their complete reliance on the tangible and reproducible qualities of scientific knowledge, that there are currents of energy that transmit signals through the body's nervous system. Chinese medicine and even Western homeopathic and holistic doctors believe in the ki energy of the human body and study its curative effects. Without ki, there could be no life. Many Westerners have tried to explain the mechanisms of ki according to human physiology and physics, but the practitioners of Chinese medicine base their practice on the deliberate and demonstrative effects of ki therapies rather than on theoretical belief.[1]

The Force in *Star Wars* is simply a convention, however. It is visually "created" on the silver screen through the physical wave of a hand, the digitally enhanced speed of a run, the effect of an invisible pulse that throws people and objects across distances. The Force is the illusion of a reality influenced and penetrated by some "mystical energy field" that controls one's destiny. Despite the sweeping theological statements, the Force is really a very limited power.

No one action in the saga indicates that the Force is actually used to control the lightsaber. Even Qui-Gon's statement that Anakin can control his podracer because he has the Jedi trait to see into the future is no direct indication that the Force gives the Jedi the ability to *know* where an opponent's attack will come. The act of knowing where an attack will come is not a function of seeing it in the milliseconds before the attack strikes its target. It comes from the intuition any combatant has for the movement of his art. The act of seeing where in space and time a speeder will be a few seconds hence is quite different from the combined purpose and will of a swordsman to deceitfully mislead and plant the seeds of false intent in the mind of one's opponent in order to exploit that person to achieve their total obliteration.

In Western fencing there is a move called disengagement. It is accomplished by extending one's arm perfectly straight with the point of the weapon menacing the opponent's body. The attacker has what is called a point-in-line. If the opponent attacks, he will impale himself. The only way to attack is by removing the point by beating the extended point and then attacking and striking the opponent before a counterattack (called a remise) can hit. In order to defeat the opponent's attack, the defender needs only to disengage by displacing his blade so subtly that the defender's attack will completely miss hitting the offending point. If timed perfectly, the attacker will disengage his point and the defender will miss beating the point-in-line and carry himself into the point. J. Christoph Amberger (*The Secret History of the Sword*) refers to a successful disengagement as one of the most intellectually satisfying moments a person can have. The disengagement is not blind luck. It is a skill that can be repeated over and over according to proper preparation of the ideal circumstances.

The success to combat is not *knowing* what will happen, but intellectually creating the moment when to execute an attack, a defense, or a pause. This is the emptying of the mind, called *munen*, which Zen swordsmen use to enable them to provide instantaneous movement without thought or will.[2] Much like the moment when the spectral Obi-Wan exhorts Luke to "use the Force," the swordsman releases the intellectual control of his body in order to act in an offensive or defense manner based not on what he knows will happen, but what must happen according to the circumstances. This ability comes not through anger, which only clouds the mind, but from the wealth of experience that allows the swordsman to intuit what needs to be done.

In this sense, the expert swordsman is already capable of doing what the Jedi with the Force is able to do. The only difference is that the real swordsman is better and more capable in skill than the Jedi shown on film. Jedi lightsaber movement is but mere choreography; scripted movement in which a physical dialog is created by the movement of lightsabers. Choreography's goal is to *show* movement, while the swordsman's goal is to hide movement even though it is "displayed" for everyone to see. The Force as seen in the *Star Wars* saga simply creates the illusion of a power that helps the Jedi. Most of a Jedi's skills, especially those with his lightsaber, come from practice and discipline. As has already been stated, it is not the lightsaber that makes the Jedi, but the way he uses it.

Star Wars *Swordmasters*

Swordmasters are responsible for making the director's vision of the sword fight into reality. Starting out in a typical and mundane fashion, the swordmaster goes through an interview process like any actor or technician. Their résumés are submitted and their experiences are examined to glean whether a person can handle the job for which they are interviewing. Sword fights in past movies are examined to see if the technical requirements can be met by the swordmaster. Once that is done, early in production a sample fight is created and filmed to show what the sword fight scene might look like as it would appear within the context of the episode at hand. If approved, the swordmaster could then begin training the actors for their roles to make their performances look believable and realistic. For Episode III, a dedicated camera crew was used to document choreography in order to visually judge its merits and to submit working ideas to Lucas for his approval.

During the very early days of *Star Wars*, Lucas expressed the desire in Episode IV for a sword fighting that was reminiscent of the samurai style. It would be exotic to Western audiences, which were accustomed to the sabre fight from swashbuckling movies, and it captured the essence of Japanese samurai films. For the Prequel Trilogy, a time during what Lucas calls the Prime of the Jedi, Lucas looked for a fencing style that was more dynamic and energetic. Lucas described the sword fighting in the Original Trilogy as combat between an old man (Obi-Wan), a cyborg half-human (Darth Vader), and a young boy (Luke). Lucas revised his own estimate of the quality of the lightsaber fighting in the Original Trilogy, and gave in to the general expectation that prequel era lightsaber fighting had to rival more recent films like *Crouching Tiger, Hidden Dragon*, *The Matrix*, and *The Musketeer*.

Peter Diamond, who did the choreography for the Original Trilogy, expressed his regret that Lucas chose a new stunt coordinator to create the lightsaber fights for the newer films, but it is not surprising, given the volatile world of movie-making, that Lucas sought a new direction. Nick Gillard, who did the choreography for the prequel movies, was associated with the Indiana Jones TV series, which was considered a test run for many of the digital techniques that would be used for the new *Star Wars* movies. His success and affiliation with Rick McCallum, who produced the series, led to his successful bid to have Lucas take him on.

The decision to go with a new fight choreographer was a major statement in the decision Lucas made to diverge from the sword fighting style in the Original Trilogy. Emotional expectations are often high in these kinds of situations and the pressure to meet the expectations of an audience raised on *Star Wars* was certainly a key part in Lucas's and Gillard's motivation to make the new sword fights an artistic and technical improvement over the Original Trilogy.

In order to create these lightsaber scenes, the support of many professionals is needed. The production stage has a natural pecking order focused primarily around the actors and then around the director and people hired to carry out his orders. Each person, from lead costumer to the prop manager, has a specific role in the production. The chain of command goes out to those who can provide solutions to the needs of the talent (the actors) and the crew. A director's wishes are duly carried out by underlings, while attention to actors is given with the anticipation of staving off emotional problems. Extras are typically instructed to refrain from approaching principal actors, while technicians move about their business with a focus that tends to disregard the actors. One does not cross the actors, but without the crew, the actor will not appear before the cameras in a favorable light.

The swordmaster on any set commands a similar kind of attention because he is in charge of one of the most exciting parts of a film. There is a kind of awe given to the swordmaster because there is both an unconscious desire to see some instruction, as well as a healthy respect for the person who will train the actors in their swashbuckling role. Deference is given to the swordmaster because he knows something the typical crew member does not. It is a respect for the danger of the art, the fun associated with it, and the possibility of show. Like any swordsman in history, bystanders move around those individuals who carry weapons. A stunt coordinator draws on the technical skills involving the drops, falls, fighting, cushion placement and mechanical issues during a shoot. A fight director might concentrate on sword fighting as well as other common and esoteric weapons including knives, nunchakus, or sais. Certainly, the use of stuntmen and martial artists provides a modicum of general competence for the choreographer to work with.

Looking like a swordsman rather than an actor trying to be a swordsman is an imperative for most actors who are usually very sensitive to the possibility that they won't make a convincing performance. With the swordsman, there is the possibility of seeing some action. Extras want a glimpse of the sword fight because it is one of the more exciting opportunities on a set. Crew members, too, especially want to see the choreography, since their opportunities are sometimes limited while they hide behind a prop or have their eye to a viewpiece. The moment an actor picks up his prop weapon, heads begin to turn, conversations stop, and anticipation pervades the set. Actors don't want to make any mistake, so the tendency to overcome making mistakes is a significant one. Only the routine of rather boring sets of drills or a fine-tuning of choreography tires the audience from looking on. No one wants to miss the fight, even if it is practice.

Action movies these days require at a minimum the skills of a stunt coordinator who is in charge of any scene that requires the doubling of an actor because of safety concerns. Whether it is jumping from a wall, scaling a dangerous height, or taking a fall, it is up to the stunt coordinator to solve the problems necessary or to substitute a double for the actor. Even minor injuries like a broken arm can delay shooting for weeks. In a movie like the *Star Wars* films, the stunt coordinator is also required to be a swordmaster and action sequence choreographer. One of Mark Hamill's injuries caused a week's delay in the filming during the Original Trilogy. Often it is the swordmaster who has to rein in the enthusiasm of the actors who tend to speed up their movement, take shortcuts in the choreography, and get carried away in the heat of the moment. Stunt doubles, trainers, and prop masters also have a responsibility to make sure practices remain safe.

Choreographers need to have knowledge of sword fights, whether real or fiction. They often have to develop a notation system so that actions can be demonstrated with a certain level of fidelity to the original choreography. Helping him are assistants who help test choreography, run errands, and even provide camaraderie. They can act as a liaison between the choreography team and the crew. They have to know the choreography intimately and have to be able to change sequences, mix up phrases of movement, or create new choreography on the spur of the moment according to the needs of the filmmakers. The scene in which Mace Windu attempts to arrest Palpatine was a difficult day on the set when Lucas decided he wanted to forgo much of the stunt double sequences because he thought face replacement of McDiarmid's body would not be credible on-screen. At the spur of the moment, all of Gillard's choreography had to be dispensed with and new choreography created for Jackson and McDiarmid—choreography complicated in appearance but simple enough for both Jackson and McDiarmid to learn and "perfect" in the space of a few lessons on the set.

When the actor feels he or she can do a stunt or sword work him- or herself, the stunt coordinator/swordmaster must teach choreography of the fight scene to the actors and/or their doubles. Actors do not learn a style of fighting, which takes years, even a lifetime to accomplish, but a series of moves that will have, if executed properly, the appearance of being real. In Peter Diamond's words, he teaches his actors in "parrot fashion."[3] Hayden Christiansen said, "If you ask me to pick up a lightsaber and do some tricks, I can. But put someone in front of me and say, 'Fight'? Unless I've been told where to step and swing, I can't."[4]

The stunt coordinator/swordmaster of the Original Trilogy, Peter Diamond, has an illustrious career in the film industry. A graduate of the Royal Academy of Dramatic Arts, Diamond had extensive training at the foremost acting school in the world. Knowing the requirements of the performing arts in both the acting and technical aspects of film has served him immeasurably in films that include *Raiders of the Lost Ark*, *Highlander*, *The Master of Ballantrae*, and *The Princess Bride*.

Diamond's talents as a trained actor and a technician allow him to communicate directly in the language of actors as well as that of directors. He personally directed second camera footage and entire episodes of the TV version of *Highlander*, and in the Original Trilogy, he played the roles of the Tusken Raider who attacked Luke, the stormtrooper who fell to his death in the Luke/Leia cable swing scene, a scout trooper thrown off one of the speeder bikes, and a detention center guard.

An extremely amiable personality who treats actors, directors, technicians, and extras in the same respectful way, Peter Diamond has made a profound impact on the sword fight in *Star Wars*. Concerned about continuity in the saga, he hoped he would have been asked to choreograph the fight scenes in the Prequel Trilogy, but without bitterness or a bad word about Lucas and the entire crew with whom he worked, he continued on in his personal projects with an eye to maintaining the highest level of professionalism. When asked about the sword fighting in Episode I, he admits that he was surprised by the change in sword fighting style, but adds that it is Lucas's vision that has to prevail.

The prequel fight choreography was created by Nick Gillard, who helped create some of the most memorable scenes in the entire movie. Gillard left military school at the age of sixteen and began working for the Moscow State Circus. Eventually, he became a world-class horse-trick rider before making the jump into film. Known for world records in power boat jumping and full fire burning (holding one's breath while on fire), Gillard is a jovial just-one-of-the-guys kind of fellow. Prior to Episode I, Gillard worked on *The Thief of Bagdad*, his first movie, *Indiana Jones and the Last Crusade*, *Aliens*, *Interview with the Vampire*, and *The Three Musketeers*, to name just a few. He even worked on the original *Star Wars* and expressed his desire to improve on the sword fight scenes in the earlier films.

Gillard is a gregarious, self-assured character who both acts as the head of a choreography team and personal support for the actors involved in the fight. He likes to laugh and was even caught on film engaging George Lucas in friendly mock fisticuffs. He takes his responsibility seriously and from the limited interviews he has given it is clear that there is a no-nonsense part of his personality that insists that it is his choreography that needs to be done. In one interview, Gillard was asked if the actors were given the freedom to creatively express themselves on the set. He insisted that they must follow *his* choreography. It is also clear that there is a discipline in the hierarchy among Gillard and his stunt double assistants, which is important at a corporate level (a production company's effectiveness is reduced when there is more than one chief), set level (safety and responsibility are delegated to individuals not teams), and professional level (his assistants are martial artists who are already used to submitting to authority). This control is important on many levels, but for the master swordsman, it is imperative because the responsibility for success depends on his ability to provide the needed action for the director and the safety and ability to the actors.

Because of the increasing demands on the actors for the later sword fight scenes, both Diamond and Gillard engaged the help of expert swordsmen. In Episode V, Diamond had the help of Bob Anderson, with whom he had done extensive work on past projects. As Anderson and Diamond say about each other, "The sword fight is only as good as the swordsmen." And to have a good fight, you have to have a good partner.[5] Anderson, an Olympic competitor and national fencing coach in Britain and Canada, brought a wealth of experience to the role of Vader in the scenes with Mark Hamill. Reassured by Anderson's expertise, Hamill was able to qualitatively improve his performance as a sword fighter in Episodes V and VI.

Gillard brought in Ray Park with his experience in wu shu, a general term for Chinese martial arts. Hailing from Wales, Ray Park competed in national and international competitions and broke into the movie business in *Mortal Kombat: Annihilation*. In addition to his impeccable handling of weapons, Park brings his background as a gymnast to his work in Episode II. Without his professional expertise, Ewan McGregor and Liam Neeson would never have looked as good as they did.

Several other stuntmen helped Gillard in his choreography. Michael Byrne, who did Palpatine's lightsaber fighting, came from the Sydney Stage Combat School where he and Kyle Rowling worked together. His martial arts training includes goju and kyuokoshin ryu karate. Nash Edgerton, from New South Wales, doubled for Ewan McGregor in several scenes in Episodes II and III. He also happens to be the brother of Joel Edgerton, who played the younger Uncle Owen in Episodes I, II, and III. With a history as an actor and stuntman, Ben Cooke, who was Hayden Christiansen's stunt double in Episode III, worked on *Xena*, the *Lord of the Rings* trilogy, and *Power Rangers*. Bob Bowles doubled for

Palpatine in scenes in Episode III, while Sebastian Dickens played Palpatine twirling through the air as he attacked the Jedi posse.

Professionals

The actors remain, however, the most important aspect of the sword fighting characters in the *Star Wars* films. Where a stuntman or double must act to imitate the actor and his movements in order to help tell the story, the gift of truly telling the story rests with the professional actors who breath life into the dialogue found in the script.

The most respected of all *Star Wars* actors, more so than even Peter Cushing, was Alec Guinness, who passed away in 2000. Not only did his appearance fit the part of the wise, elderly master, but his mere presence on-screen was enough to convince everyone that there were such a thing as Jedi Knights. Exaggerated gossip and stories portray Guinness as bitter about his role repeating incomprehensible "mumbo-jumbo," but he admitted in an interview soon after the release of the first movie that he was attracted to his role as the Master Jedi by the competence of George Lucas and his vision for the film. While members of both the cast and crew were rolling their eyes at what everyone expected to be another sci-fi bomb like *Silent Running*, Guinness stood steadfastly beside Lucas, telling others that he had complete trust in Lucas' abilities.[6]

For sword fight enthusiasts and martial artists of the Asian tradition, Guinness uttered some of the most profound dialogue in the entire saga. With the pauses and the tempo of "It is an energy field created by all living things. It surrounds us and penetrates us. It binds the galaxy together," Guinness gave life to the mystical words that seem to succinctly express the Asian concept of ki. That the Force gave the Jedi power was confirmation to Eastern ears what Asians had felt about the body's life-giving energy.

In the same way that Guinness was able to convince the audience of the mysteriousness of the Force, he was also able to demonstrate the power of the Jedi Knights. Swordplay was considered a skill for actors of his generation, and as a two-handed swordsman, he pays homage to the samurai that Lucas so admired. It was Guinness who was able to set the example for Mark Hamill. Not only was Luke able to convince us of the naïveté of a farm boy on Tatooine, he was able to create a character with whom children, men, and women alike could identify. As Luke looked out over the desert toward the twin suns setting at the horizon, it is hard for the audience not to feel a sense of longing in Luke's desire to find adventure somewhere beyond the Tatooine home he has known. Not only does his performance in Episode V convince us of his burning desire to be treated with respect equal to his worth as an individual, but also of the fear of confronting the terror of growing up in a hostile world. This coming-of-age film set the stage for Hamill to return in the subsequent film as a Jedi who enters into the full rites of the Jedi Order. Not only does he reinvent himself, but he also reinvents the order of the universe in which good triumphs over evil. Though many cynically point to Hamill's failure to achieve the cinematic accomplishments of Harrison Ford, the impact his role has had on the lives of youngsters all over the world is hardly insignificant. Hamill, in his role as Luke Skywalker, inspired generations to reach out for the stars. And unlike the world of the difficult times of the sixties and seventies, the message was positive and good.

Considering the fact that Dave Prowse played one of the most memorable villains in film, it is unfortunate that he has received more derision for his contribution than any other actor associated with *Star Wars*. Early stories have Prowse grumbling about being denied full recognition for his role.[7] In Lucas's initial reluctance to unveil the magic of the movie, the actors behind the masks were kept out of the media eye for fear of dispelling the illusion of alien creatures from the *Star Wars* universe.

Eventually, all the characters were unmasked for the public, but bad blood continued to hound Prowse's relationship with Lucasfilm, starting with the fact that he was not allowed to wear the Darth Vader costume in public and then unmask himself. Another controversy involved the fact that Prowse's voice was replaced by that of another actor, James Earl Jones, because of concern that there were no black actors in the film. The biggest problems, however, occurred when a reporter revealed spoiler information in an interview with Prowse that Vader was going to die in Episode VI. Filming was not yet complete, and Prowse was ostracized during the rest of the shoot.

In the final tally, Prowse played all of Vader in Episode IV, and most of Episode V, and some of Episode VI. The sword fighting in Episodes V and VI was done by Bob Anderson. Memorable scenes in which Prowse played Vader include him in the meditation chamber in Episode V and throwing the Emperor, a double for Ian McDiarmid, into the tower shaft. Prowse never did get to meet Richard Marquand, the director of Episode VI, and his experience on the set remains one of the most difficult of his life.

The role of Darth Vader as a foil for the rebel heroes played well in Episode IV, but no one was ready for the importance of Vader in the continuing saga. Contrary to what might have been expected, Anakin did not start out as the incorrigible problem child. Instead, he was an ordinary kid, albeit with an amazing pedigree, who was both kind and innocent. He did not terrorize kids in his neighborhood, but was a nice, carefree child who was tempted by the lure of power. In an Episode III documentary, Lucas said that it was not his intention that Vader should be seen as the evil character audiences made him out to be in the Original Trilogy.[8] Indeed, Lucas insisted that Vader was a victim.

Much of the success of Episode I was due to the introduction of the new Jedi, Qui-Gon Jinn and a younger Obi-Wan Kenobi, and their nemesis Darth Maul. Senior among them was Liam Neeson, a Scot and veteran actor in such films as *Rob Roy* and *Schindler's List*. Known more for his roles as a romantic lead, Neeson brings a new dimension to the master-apprentice relationship. Soon after the announcement of the new cast, Neeson expressed his love for his simple association with *Star Wars*. Mark Hamill had a similar experience on Episode IV, being infatuated with an adventure story that took place out in space. Harrison Ford in his many interviews associated with the *Indiana Jones* films expressed that same boyish desire to play the iconographic movie hero. Admired in particular for his work in Spielberg's black and white masterpiece *Schindler's List*, Neeson played a savior to Jewish laborers, a role that provided hard-earned experience for his role as Jedi Master. Neeson loves having a lightsaber in hand, and when asked why he decided to take the role, Neeson admits that he's always had a spot in his heart for the *Star Wars* saga.

His experience of sword fighting in *Rob Roy* also provided additional preparation for his role in Episode I. Playing the heroic Scotsman, Neeson wielded the broad sword with believable skill and alacrity. While the steel is vastly different from the shell of a prop that is the lightsaber in Episode I, simply knowing the expectations of a sword fight and how to take direction from Lucas and Gillard proved beneficial to later movies. Apart from his baseball grip of the lightsaber as he takes a stance opposite Darth Maul, Neeson's demeanor is a good example of the cool and experienced swordmaster.

Neeson is at the perfect age for the real swordsman at his peak. Well beyond the energetic and often reckless drive of a young swordsman, Neeson captures a moment in life when wisdom and the body's health and fullness are at their peak. While not those at the physical peak of male development, the acquired and practiced skills of a swordsman reach an apex at a much later age than in most modern sports. The philosopher Socrates participated in battlefield combat into his early forties.

At Qui-Gon's side was Ewan McGregor. Known for his rambunctiousness in *Train Spotting*, McGregor and his vivacious personality brought youthful excitement to the cast. Though quite demure in his interpretation of Obi-Wan in Episode I ("You were right about one thing. The negotiations were short."), McGregor was adopted by the paparazzi as bad boy fanboy.

As a swordsman, McGregor quickly garnered a reputation for having a knack with the mock lightsabers used in training. Footage from DVD documentaries certainly convey the vigor of his fencing style. With no holds barred, McGregor revels in the excitement of the sword fight. Speed and energy describe his ability to learn the lightsaber choreography. Like Neeson, McGregor fell in love with *Star Wars* as a kid, and tells the story of the day the prop department came up to him with a wooden box filled with lightsaber handles. He weighed each one in his hand and waved them around to find the one with the best feel. In January 2002, McGregor was quoted as having said handling a lightsaber is "a more gentlemanly way to fight a war."

With the same youthfulness, actor Ray Park brings his expertise as a wu shu martial artist to the screen. Though early training in wu shu involves unarmed fighting, advanced techniques involve the extended use of bladed weapons, including the Chinese broad sword and spear. From work with these weapons and his experience in gymnastics, Park raises the quality of Jedi sword fight to the level more commonly found in Chinese martial arts films. From his experience with the long staff in *Mortal Kombat: Annihilation*, Park mesmerizes with the twirling skill of Darth Maul's double-bladed lightsaber. Episode I benefits from the infusion of Chinese martial arts, which are more fluid and acrobatic than the grounded-feet style of Japanese martial arts. Even in karate, which stresses high kicks, Japanese martial arts by comparison to Chinese, Korean, and Indian martial arts have broad stances that lower the center of the body for a solid foundation. Most would be familiar with Ray Park's wu shu from the fighting style found in *Crouching Tiger, Hidden Dragon*, minus the fantastic flying through the air.

Where Ray Park's physical stature is diminished by the towering frame of Liam Neeson, he makes up for sheer size by enthralling the audience with an energy that surpasses previous *Star Wars* episodes. Starting with the devilish makeup, the horned Maul immediately evokes fear in the viewer. Park with his quiet and soft-spoken personality mentions the revulsion cast and crew gave him when he looked up during breaks in filming. He would be sitting in a chair letting the time pass away when an aide might come up to ask him a question. When Park looked up to answer, the person would usually turn their head to avoid looking into his red contact-covered eyes. The designs of the shapes and colors combined with his ten horns gave Maul the feral quality that evokes fear in civilized beings.

Despite the meager list of Darth Maul lines in the movie, Park enhances the evil of his character with a body language that epitomizes the dangerous nature of Darth Maul — his jagged teeth, threatening scowls, and the pacing back and forth behind the energy screen and above the pit staring down at Qui-Gon and Obi-Wan. Maul is evil incarnate, a minion of hell sent by his master to execute the first stage in a plan that will finally rid the universe of the Sith's archrivals, the Jedi. Maul's appearance was created to evoke primal urges of repulsion — blackened eyes and mouth, horns, and blood red skin. Maul is a creature from our worse nightmare, transcending culture and language as a minion of evil.

The sword fights would not have come to their full fruition without the help of the crew and designers who created the world in which the Jedi fought. Of course, Lucas is ultimately responsible for the sword fighting, but credit also goes to the stunt and sword fight doubles that make the Jedi into something more than the traditional sword master. Bob Anderson filled the shoes of Darth Vader, Andreas Petrides and Rob Inch doubled as Obi-Wan and Qui-Gon, respectively. One cannot forget the artistry of Ralph McQuarrie, who first designed the initial images of Darth Vader and Luke Skywalker, and design director Doug Chiang, who took the first steps in creating the new images for the Jedi in their prime, as well as the Sith lords. Story-board artist Benton Jew committed the action sequences to life by visualizing the dynamic motion of the sword fight on a still, nonmoving sheet of paper. And lastly, the prop makers created the balanced weapons from the creative designs of the art department. In Episode I, over three hundred lightsabers were made, and as many as twenty were destroyed during daily practice.

One of the most exciting aspects of the action film is the result of a host of professionals who support and frame the actors in their roles. Without the skills and efforts of the many people associated with the fight scenes, *Star Wars* would have been less the richer. One of the difficulties in obtaining detailed information about the sword fight choreography involves two things: the distance time has made on the memories of the actors in the Original Trilogy, and the contractual non-disclosure clauses in the contracts of those involved with the *Star Wars* production. Actors such as Mark Hamill and Dave Prowse no longer remember the choreography, and the details of the set environment have faded in their minds. Death has also taken some of the principals involved in the lightsaber fighting in the Original Trilogy. Peter Diamond passed away in March 2004. Interviews from the public media also fail to provide relevant information on choreography. Interviewers did not care about choreography or they did not have the knowledge to ask proper questions.

Regarding the Prequel Trilogy, individuals associated with the choreography are required not to divulge information to the general public without Lucasfilm approval. It is not that individuals such as Nick Gillard and Kyle Rowling would not like to talk about their experiences, but Lucasfilm considers their choreographic creations as made-for-hire work. There was even an Internet petition asking for 10,000 signatures to urge Lucasfilm to let Gillard publicly teach the choreography he taught to the principals in the prequel movies. And even during official events such as an authorized web chat or an appearance at an officially sanctioned *Star Wars* event, Gillard is very hesitant in giving away many interesting details. He says he doesn't want to spoil the movie for fans by talking about it, but there is also a defensiveness to his responses. In general, Gillard does not like giving interviews, and his refusal to commit to specific details preserves his image as a praiseworthy sword fight choreographer. Responding to a question on whether new styles of lightsaber fighting would be included in Episode III, he curtly replied yes. Or, he evades detailing who was seen on one of the webcams broadcast on the Internet. His non-specific answers provide him with legal protection.

In fact, even without a non-disclosure clause, Gillard protects himself from artistic criticism by remaining vague about his choreography. He avoids the problems of choreographers interpreting the art for an audience who make their own judgments about the choreography. Often, the questions asked of him reflect a fantastical, media-based understanding of *Star Wars*, which is quite different from his experiences on the sets with the actors. Gillard has indicated that he has no knowledge of the seven Jedi forms created by David West Reynolds in the *Star Wars Insider* magazine. Similarly, the concept of Vaapad and its bridge to the dark side of the Force, from Matthew Stover's *Shatterpoint*, has nothing to do with the choreography created for the movies. Hidden behind the keyboard, the general public, whose actual choreography is self-taught or nonexistent, is often quite unabashed in their criticism of amateur and professional choreographers.

But critiques of sword fight choreography can be made by those knowledgeable about sword fighting or theatrical choreography. Movement can be critiqued and placed into a perspective that respects both the choreographer's artistic ability and the limitations of a medium such as film. Without a good fight director who is able to instantly answer questions about the fight, everyone loses confidence in the choreography, especially the actors. It is his job to communicate the possibilities that fit the director's needs. Problems from an inexperienced choreographer could include a sub-par performance with repetitive movements, fast but directionless blocking, and little time for the actors to act. The choreographer must be able to lengthen or shorten fights according to directorial needs. He has to be able to change the character's movement (blocking) to fight in a new location. He must also be able to provide solutions to problems that occur during production: an actor or stunt person's sickness, back-up choreography for planned digital enhancements that might not work, or a movement that does not look professional enough for the editor.

In *Star Wars*, there is a range of lightsaber movements that fight choreographers have to choose from. The easiest to understand is the slash, which reflects the physical cutting motion of a traditional sword. The visual effect is enhanced by the attachment of light blurs and auditory humming. The light blur adds realism to the film because it emphasizes the naked eye's inability to see every movement. Film is typically set to display 32 frames per second, which preserves the brain's interpretation that the visual film is a "live" representation of reality. The sounds of the lightsaber confirm the visual presentation of the film. For swordsmen, this aspect of combat is so common that it is rarely emphasized in manuals or instruction. For a fencer, the discernment of a successful parry can only be made by an auditory confirmation of the clash between the swords. Only at this point can the defender move instantly to his own counterattack. The judge watching the exchange also uses the sound of contact to determine who has the attack during a match.

Star Wars choreography, particularly in the prequel movies, relies heavily on the slash. With arms already stretched out, wrist movement can move from a block to an offensive attack in about three or four frames (⅛ of a second). Dooku's attacks against Yoda, from one blocked hit to the next attack, take from 7 to 14 frames. A full recovery from a block (e.g., when Anakin is on his back looking upward from the Mustafar conference table) takes 14 frames (a ½ second). The speeds of these attacks are calculated in real time; none were sped up for effect. In some instances, the slash is used to achieve an almost comedic effect, as in the example of Obi-Wan and Anakin destroying battle droids in the elevator at the beginning of Episode III; Obi-Wan makes seven slashes (Anakin makes six separate slashes) to kill only eight droids. Combined with their intense training and the lightness of their weapons, the principal actors and their opponent stunt doubles were able to give an impressive performance on-screen.

Contrasting with the slash is the thrust, which is most representative of Western fencing. The thrust doesn't occur in any *Star Wars* film except as a stance like that of Mace Windu who points the tip of his lightsaber at Palpatine's throat in Episode III. Jackson's physical stance adds a nice believability to the scene. His arm is completely extended, his hand holds his lightsaber handle in a direct line with the arm, and the point is pressed close to its intended target. It is interesting to note that for a weapon like the lightsaber in which the mere touch can cause damage, the lightsaber would be adapted to fencing's point-and-thrust style of fighting. In *Star Wars*, artistry overrides the practical considerations of the weapon. Count Dooku's curved handle was actually designed for thrusting techniques; its handle is a close representation of the orthopedic grips that characterize modern fencing weapons.

In terms of physical movement, the full body twirl is iconic of Obi-Wan's lightsaber style. His single 360° turn in Episode IV was multiplied into McGregor's distinctive style. In Episode III, his does eight body twirls throughout his duel with Anakin. This is a significant movement for the authentic swordsman when judging *Star Wars* choreography. The body twirl is an effectively prohibitive technique. It is not that it is impossible to do, nor that it is not found within some martial arts (very few), but it makes no tactical sense in almost all circumstances because it allows the opponent a moment to attack when the twirler is in mid-twirl. A good example can be found in Episode III (chapter 39/51:44) when Anakin does a spin after being blocked by Obi-Wan's lightsaber. It takes Anakin 16 frames to complete his spin before he attacks on the opposite side. During that half-second, Obi-Wan moves his blade down across his front line and then twirls his blade back and over his head for the next block, when he simply could have struck Anakin during the twirl in the space of two or three frames. This can be contrasted with Ray Park's performance in Episode I when, with his bulky double-blade lightsaber, he is able to make a half-turn for a block against Qui-Gon on Tatooine in only one frame. By doubling the speed of the movement, Maul, using a single-bladed lightsaber, could have possibly made his block in three or four frames. Again, it is clear that even Park's ability to do a body turn is still limited despite his honed martial experience. In actual combat, the body twirl is a hazard to be avoided, but it does lend itself to the artistic choreography of staged performance.

Another dazzling piece of choreography is the simple and complex flourish. Like the body twirl, the flourish (sword twirl) is useless during actual combat because it intentionally moves a swordsman's offensive and defensive weapon away from the opponent, giving him the opportunity and time to strike effectively. This movement is categorically unnecessary in any *Star Wars* film, but because of the influence of many martial arts films during the 1990s and later, the inclination of fight choreographers has been to imitate the acrobatic style of Beijing comic opera, which is more a form of quick, swirling acrobatics than it is real martial technique. Since Episode I, the sword twirl can be seen in many martial arts/sword fantasy films, as well as in stage combat and Renaissance reenactments. The flourish is not a part of any serious sword art, so martial artists view this move with a head-shaking contempt. The flourish did not exist in the choreography of the Original Trilogy, but it has become a trademark of the flashiness of prequel choreography.

The simple flourish is the flipping of the lightsaber hilt by dropping the point, and flipping it back, and then up and forward by releasing the three lower fingers and pivoting the blade at the hilt where the thumb and pointer finger hold the grip. The easiest visual example of the simple flourish can be seen just before Obi-Wan thrusts his lightsaber down to finish off the Acklay. The move was taught to McGregor by Gillard during Episode I.

The complex flourish is a combination of martially useless sword twirls done in a single phrase of movement. The earliest variant was done by Hayden Christensen, who holds the bottom of the lightsaber blade (called "slipping") and then twirls it around his back before it ends up out in front of his body. The principal problem with his flourish for a swordsman is that Christensen will bring his left hand to the top of the grip for his final stance. There are appropriate moments when slipping one's grip can be useful, but the way Christensen does it shows that he does not have even a basic understanding of actual sword fighting techniques in which the sword would be held in the principal hand (usually the right hand) at the top part of the tang for the surest grip and the best balance.

The complex flourish is a purely visual movement that cannot (and should not) be used in a real fight with swords. It is flashy and has a certain amount of wow factor to it, but it does not threaten an opponent, it permits the sword to be knocked out of the hand, and there is no strength behind the movement. The most striking example can be seen during Episode III when Obi-Wan and Anakin are standing on the conference table when each Jedi does a long flourish that lasts about one second. There is no blade contact between the two lightsabers, causing the audience to question the point of the movement. Although detailed, expert critiques of lightsaber fighting can be dismissed as an academic exercise, choreography that takes the audience out of the movie because it "looks" fake even to the untrained eye does the film a disservice. One can imagine *Hamlet* being performed for a crowd full of swordsmen when the actor bungles basic sword moves. It is worse for a film when the average moviegoer has the same experience. A move that looks "cool" actually takes away from the movie when it interrupts the flow of the film. In one clip shown before the premiere of Episode III, Anakin was seen doing a blade evasion by twirling his head under the swinging blade. Message boards on the Internet severely criticized the movement as pure fantasy. That action did not make it into the final cut. The first complex flourish has been copied by many *Star Wars* reenactors, but the second example demonstrates how a choreographer can become a little too zealous with his expectation of the audience's threshold for what is fake and what looks real.

Pummeling or fisticuffs (unarmed movements) are another possibility for choreography used in *Star Wars*. Empty-handed fighting has a very raw and realistic appeal to the general public. Everyone is capable of it, and because it draws on the physicality of the body, everyone can relate in some way to it. All good fighting is informed by technical mastery, but it is the reaction of the person being punched, kicked, or pummeled that draws a reaction from a viewer. From a swordsman's point of view, the unarmed strike is called into question because he is trained to use his sword slash or thrust to maximize damage. Why use an empty hand when the sword can do it better? Artistically, the choreographer does not face this problem. The only real factor to consider is whether it is appropriate to use a punch or a strike with the sword guard during the choreography. The answer is sometimes a cliché, like the 1970s karate chop, or the hit to the head with the butt of a gun. At other times, there are moments in real combat when this kind of movement is appropriate.

In *Star Wars*, Obi-Wan and Jango Fett engage in a weaponless brawl on Kamino. Careful thought had to go into first the script and then the choreography during the creation of the fight. Especially with a lightsaber wielder like Obi-Wan and a gun-carrying mercenary like Jango Fett, there had to be a logic behind the fight. Gillard had to take away the lightsaber in a believable way as much as he had to take into account the defensive nature of Jango's armor. In both Episodes II and III, Obi-Wan has a comedic moment when he hits both Jango and Grievous with a bare fist. The Episode III fisticuffs with Grievous was a setup for Obi-Wan's comment that blasters are so inelegant, but the perfect moment for such a move took place in Episode I when Maul hits Qui-Gon in the face with his lightsaber hilt, stunning him long enough for Maul to do his infamous body thrust into Qui-Gon's chest.

Lastly, there is the ubiquitous use of the Force during the duels. Because film is a purely visual medium, there is no indication that the Jedi use the Force to help target a blade or give it more force than is possible from a purely physical hit. The Force is simply used as an invisible field that can move objects or "throw" them at an opponent with a wave of the hand. This visual cue is employed when Obi-Wan influences the mind of a stormtrooper on Tatooine or of Boss Nass on Naboo. Moving objects is a simple convention easily achieved by stage hands throwing objects at an actor (Luke during the Bespin fight) and by digital artists creating the object to be thrown (such as the one Maul throws at the Theed hanger controls, which open the doors at the end of the room). The Force is used to bring down the ceiling in Episode II, to toss Obi-Wan across the room in Episode III, and by Yoda against Palpatine on Coruscant.

One of the easiest uses of the Force in combat is the "push," which can be used to dispatch droids with a flick of the wrist. It is a purely cinematic convention meant to enhance the martial appearance of the Jedi. From a practical point of view, there is no reason why the Jedi should not have used the Force push against all the droids they encountered instead of drawing their lightsabers. One could easily imagine using the Force to pull the clothes off an adversary to embarrass him before dispatching him with his lightsaber. Dooku stripped of his clothes would not have had the dramatic effect that beheading him with two sabres did. The emotionally evil version of this Force is the blue lightning emanating from Palpatine's and Dooku's finger tips. It is a stunning visual effect that has a dramatic presentation like no other Force power. It is not worth the effort to explain the effect because the audience already had a clear understanding of the effects of Force lightning from their knowledge and experience with lightning and electricity.

The slash, thrust, twirl, flourish, brawl, and the Force (along with the cable swing, the wire work, and stunning falls) all contribute to the fighting ability of the Jedi. They are all techniques common to most fantasy/sci-fi movies today, and their influence has been accepted by general audiences in current martial arts films that are popular today. If one were to look at the authentic fighting performed in *Enter the Dragon* (which started the popularity of the Asian martial art film in the West), the moves and techniques look staged and unrealistic. Audiences are now so accustomed to the fantasy of wild throws and incredible acrobatic feats that the true punch or the simple kick has no "shock" effect on an audience unless it is accompanied by a ten-foot throw from which the actor stands up uninjured. This experience has also caused many *Star Wars* fans to disparage the choreography in the Original Trilogy as weak or, as Gillard put it during one convention, "awful." From a swordsman's point of view, this is not at all the case. The Original Trilogy, as will be demonstrated, does hold up in its sword fighting even though it does not have the same wow factor as the prequel films.

EIGHT

Prequel Trilogy and Original Trilogy Critique

Episode I — The Phantom Menace — *The Opening Act in the Prime of the Jedi*

The first of the prequel movies provided the new trilogy with an excellent choreographic foundation for the two later episodes. Much of this is a result of Gillard's choreography and the work of the actors and stunt doubles. Ray Park's performance was critical to the success of the prequel in which the lightsaber fighting is considered the best part of Episode I.

Upon his return to the *Star Wars* universe, Lucas was immediately motivated to create a more energetic style of sword fighting that would be a step beyond the fights of the previous three films. As Jedi trained in the full arts of the Jedi Temple, Qui-Gon and his apprentice Obi-Wan were the new benchmarks for the quality of lightsaber fighting in the era of the Jedi Order. If the Original Trilogy could be termed aspirant films in which Luke must go through the training process as an individual, the prequel can be described as a swashbuckling trilogy in which the high skill (and antics) of talented swordsmen is showcased.

For Qui-Gon and Obi-Wan, the first challenge they face is combat with the digital creations of the battle droids. The premise is presented plainly — droids can move and shoot but they are not free-thinking tacticians. They are easily outperformed by the Jedi who destroy them like flies with their lightsabers. The Jedi are also able to use the Force push to destroy the occasional droid. For the sake of a more exciting film, the Jedi spend more time using their lightsabers to take out battle droids even though it is quite apparent the Force push could do the same job effortlessly.

In terms of choreography, Gillard simply had to teach Liam Neeson and Ewan McGregor complicated sword twirling movements so that digital artists could paint in blaster deflections, flairs, and battle droids. Apart from learning the choreography, a good half of the actors' job was to act, making it look like they were battling a multitude of opponents when they were in fact fighting invisible opponents against a green screen. In many scenes, the lightsaber prop that Neeson and McGregor swung around was the lightsaber grip with a short lightsaber stump, which was extended during post-production when the droids were drawn in.

The final cut of Jedi against battle droid is easily achieved through the industry of ILM technical artists who simply keyed in droids to be cut up in the spaces provided by the choreographer. If Neeson made a slash in front of himself, the ILM artist drew a battle droid being sliced up in the space where the slash was made. In the case of many of McGregor's sword flourishes, ILM artists drew in battle droids who were efficiently cut down as if Obi-Wan "magically" knew they were behind him. Battle droids and the super battle droid of Episode II were consistently cut to pieces by the Jedi on an individual basis, though they are somehow successful against the Jedi in the Geonosis arena. Even up until Episode III, combat against battle droids became faster and more efficient with the mechanical soldiers having little possibility of hurting a Jedi. Like the stormtroopers of the Original Trilogy, only the hero had proper fighting skills. The only real threat to the Jedi were the destroyer droids (droidekas) who, because of a technological edge, were able to challenge the Jedi. It was not that the droidekas were significantly superior to the battle droids, but that their shielding prevented the Jedi from deflecting their blaster bolts back at them.

There is a propensity in the Prequel Trilogy to show Jedi lightsaber competence through the effortless and wanton destruction of battle droids. But actual skill can be shown in very simple movement, as Luke demonstrates on the *Millennium Falcon* in Episode IV when he deflects bolts from a flying remote. It also demonstrates Hamill's technical ability with the lightsaber, which is quite believable and realistic. Luke holds his lightsaber with a decent (though not perfect) grip in a fencer's stance. His weight is balanced and his body relaxed. When the remote shoots a bolt, Hamill tenses up and freezes momentarily before fluidly moving on to deflect the next two bolts. Each deflection shows precise movement from one deflection to the next without abrupt or wild action. In fencing parlance, he shows mastery of a tempo in which movements (attacks or parries) are executed without a predictable rhythm. Luke's remote practice may seem like a minor thing, but to a fencer, it speaks to the real possibility of mastering a real lightsaber.

Luke's practice session also contrasts with the Episode II scene in which Younglings are in a class under the instruction of a digital Yoda. While the scene was intended to highlight the freshness of innocence, the actual movement of the children is quite uneven and unremarkable. Probably because of the limited eye-hand coordination of children at that age, appearance and presentation on-screen bore a greater importance in the choice of Youngling disciples.

Developmentally, it is impossible for a pre-pubescent to match the physical movements of an older teenager. While a pre-teen prodigy martial artist may impress adults with his ability to perform kata or to compete in competitive matches, his ability does not compare with the teenager who has quickly developed the hand-eye coordination that compares with that of a practiced adult. High counts of midi-chlorians aside, the Younglings in Episode II do not impress the martial artist of the Jedi's ability with a lightsaber at a young age.

The true credit for the success of lightsaber fighting in Episode I goes to Ray Park and his weapon and acrobatic ability. Before Episode I, most people would never have even heard of the butterfly jump (also called a butterfly kick). It is rare in martial arts that the buildup of a major evil nemesis actually exceeds the expectations of the pre–Episode I hype. About five minutes of footage associated with lightsaber choreography was shown on *60 Minutes* before Episode I's premiere. With the video technology available at the time, the general public was able to critique the choreography unlike any movie before. Positive comments generally greeted the footage and expectations were heightened to a fevered pitch.

The first encounter with Darth Maul was a brief and relatively uninteresting fight. There was the cool body flip as Maul leaped from his speeder and simultaneously engaged Qui-Gon, but the significance of that movement lay in its technological importance, as ILM designers were creating some of the earliest digital humans. It was a major achievement to create the digital character Jar Jar Binks as a virtually interactive character, but the realism of a dinosaur-like creature inspired by *Jurassic Park* was still a step below the perfection of a human character who did not look like a video game character. The somersault attack was so quick that it was hardly noticed. It is difficult to see that Maul is using only one side of his lightsaber and goes into a fast-paced attack; Qui-Gon is barely able to hold his own before retreating into the ship by leaping into the air to the spaceship ramp. Maul's flowing robes add to the aesthetic appearance of the Sith Lord's movement, and the brief encounter with the Jedis ends abruptly with Maul shutting down his sabre.

It is not until the climax of the movie that the first real clash between the Sith and the Jedi occurs. Concurrent with the attack on the palace is a diversionary battle between droids and the Gungan military. It is hard to understand why the Gungans have an army when they seem to have almost no direct interaction with the Naboo, but their organic weaponry against a mechanical army does provide for a somewhat satisfying exchange between armies in the *Star*

Wars universe. The real battle, however, is taking place in the Theed palace where Qui-Gon and Obi-Wan engage Darth Maul while Queen Amidala makes her way to capture the Neimoidian viceroy.

Both Sith and Jedi take off their robes as John Williams's fight march begins. Maul strikes a pose and for the first time the audience sees the second half of the double-bladed lightsaber ignite. Qui-Gon and Obi-Wan take a stance and then engage the Sith. Technically, their sword work is not perfect — Maul ducks for one of Obi-Wan's horizontal lightsaber strikes, which would have missed anyway; they are slashing at lightsabers and not real targets; and Qui-Gon's hand position doesn't indicate his knowledge of a single cutting edge when he attacks— but the intensity of the battle quickly moves the duel along. Maul goes into his famous butterfly twirl and immediately uses the Force to throw some debris into the control box, which opens the hangar doors.

The two Jedi double team Maul in an attempt to surround him. Obi-Wan advances as Maul goes on the offensive by kicking Obi-Wan in the face in response to his useless lightsaber twirl. Obi-Wan was digitally moved over in order to make contact with Park's foot. The kick knocks Obi-Wan to the floor so he can press an attack against Qui-Gon but quickly he is forced to strategically retreat to the edge of a walkway overlooking a deep power shaft to prevent the Jedi from attacking him on two sides. Obi-Wan feints, allowing Qui-Gon to move in for an attack, but Maul is able to jump across the chasm to another walkway until the two Jedi join him. The two Jedi lightsaber strikes are elegantly blocked together with one end of Maul's double-bladed weapon. The duel proceeds with further fighting on the walkways. The Sith and the Jedi get the best of each other by knocking their opponent down a level, but Maul again retreats into a protective area of the generator room in which he can isolate the Jedi in order to take them out one at a time.

Qui-Gon is initially separated from Maul, so he goes into the Japanese formal position called sieza wherein a person drops to his knees. The tension mounts as Qui-Gon reflects quietly while Maul paces back and forth like a feral cat. Once the shield opens, Qui-Gon advances and cuts to Maul's legs while Maul makes an unnecessary jump against a slash that would not have hit him. With a bash of his lightsaber to Qui-Gon's face, Maul does a quick half-turn. While Maul could have just as easily cut the Jedi master in half, he instead turns his blade and drives the point into Qui-Gon's stomach.

Obi-Wan watches helplessly but then rushes to attack the Sith Lord. There is good distance between the two adversaries. Here, both lightsaber fighters are close enough for any attack to hit and only a true block would prevent the hit from connecting. Movement is crisp, precise, fast, and accurate as one move is thwarted by a logical counter-move. There are attacks to the legs and then the head as the choreographic fight phrase ends with the extension of arms and lightsaber at the same time. Obi-Wan's tactics gain him an advantage when he succeeds in cutting Maul's lightsaber in half. But Maul makes several defensive blocks and then defeats Obi-Wan with a powerful Force push, which sends him over the edge of the pit in the center of the room.

The Jedi hangs on to the lip of the pit as Maul makes his fatal mistake. Arrogantly, he savors the moment and instead of finishing off the Jedi quickly and cleanly he paces the edge of the pit in a premature walk of victory. Obi-Wan sees his chance and Force-pulls Qui-Gon's lightsaber while simultaneously flipping himself out of the pit so he can make a powerful cut to Maul's center, slicing him in half.

Speed and technique seem to be the focus of the sword fights in Episode I, but the overall pacing and technical use of movement in the blocking of the fight lead to a fight scene that will always do justice to the ability of the Jedi. Park's influence is seen in the footwork and sword work of Neeson and McGregor, but it was his own footwork that lent a technical edge to the impressive fighting style of Maul. Park is such a good martial artist that neither limited stature nor his lack of lines takes away from the beauty of his movement. The full extension of his hand as he pulls his lightsaber toward his body just before his butterfly leap is an example of the artistry Chinese martial arts have achieved. It is a shame that Maul does not make a reprise in later episodes, but it is equally sad that Lucas did not find some way of engaging Park in another role, as a Jedi, for example, or as a stunt double. Regardless, Park has made a crucial contribution to the *Star Wars* saga. In terms of martial quality, there is no equal. Certainly, Park earns a place in the pantheon of evil characters on par with Darth Vader.

Episode II—Star Wars: Attack of the Clones—*Technical Challenges, Emotional Success*

With the introduction of Hayden Christiansen as the older Anakin Skywalker, Lucas was able to add much more lightsaber fighting to the second prequel episode, including the much anticipated duel between Yoda and Count Dooku. Another attempt to push the envelope on sword fighting with digital animation, this duel scene was a harbinger of the success of the lightsaber fights in this episode. Learning from the near-universal derision of Jar Jar (as well as the lackluster acceptance of Episode I, of which even McGregor publicly expressed his lack of enthusiasm), Lucas placed a lot of the film's credibility on a successful lightsaber fight at the end of the film. Going into production, ILM was not yet even certain they would be able to pull off the non-fighting scenes with Yoda, limited as they were by the quirks of a puppet that had limited movement. The original choreography even included sections in which Dooku would use two lightsabers as a way to extend the Anakin fight in the possible event that ILM would not be able to create a fighting Yoda worthy of a screen performance.

Episode II, having the most lightsaber performances in all of the *Star Wars* films, was supposed to highlight the martial ability of the Jedi Order. Certainly, with the limited strength of 200 Jedi drawn unexpectedly from the Jedi Temple, the guardians of the Republic were certain to face uneven odds (and were even predestined by later events to eventually fall from grace), but their showing in the Geonosis arena presented the Jedi as an unorganized rabble lacking in any common sense tactics or strategy. This was a far cry from the general hope that the Jedi were a league of expert lightsaber warriors who would be betrayed by one of their own members. The Jedi's disorderly attempt in capturing Count Dooku fails visually because of the technical decision to film a variety of independent vignettes of Jedi against a green screen and then later insert them into a larger visual panorama. Though an unfair examination of choreography meant to be seen on a large screen, repeated viewing of the DVD easily reveals performances which look like the Jedi are swinging their lightsabers wildly in the air against digital elements added later as an afterthought. Isolated Jedi amid droids and Geonosians further emphasizes their digital insertion, as did actors in cumbersome alien costumes which limited their lightsaber performances against adversaries who would be drawn in later by ILM. Instead of realistic fights, actors were told by choreographers off-camera to duck, deflect blaster bolts, or to cut down imaginary creatures.

Compounding the chaos was the circular layout of the arena which prevented the audience from fully understanding the progress of the battle. The typical convention shows one side of the screen to be the psychological "camp" the Jedi; the other, the "camp" of the Federation and Geonosians. This locks in a psychological understanding of the turn of events on a visual two-dimensional screen.[1] An advance from the left would indicate the Jedi are winning; its opposite, their loss of ground (and the battle). In an early scene during the Geonosis arena battle, the Jedi advanced from left to right as they attacked Geonosians and Federation droids. At the end of the battle, however, instead of retreating from right to left to show a retreat to their "camp," the Jedi retreat from right to left, creating a visual dissonance in the audience's mind. Combine this with droids advancing first from the left side of the screen, and then later from the right side of the screen, members of the audience do not know where to look because they do not understand the ebb and flow of the battle. Jedi stand on the battlefield mixed incoherently with battle droids, edit cuts move from heroes to bad guys in a random manner, and the accompanying background music and ambient noise drops from near silence to deafening cacophony without any understandable lull or crescendo in the battle narrative. With Lucas's willingness to kill off Jedi council members with cheap shots from Jango Fett, it is a miracle that any Jedi survived the Geonosian counterattack through the exercise of skill or ability against an army of non-thinking automatons.

Little more needs to be said about the Jedi and their ability to dispatch battle droids. Episode II adds Geonosian warriors and a few herd creatures to the list of the heros' prey. Again, because the Geonosians were digital creations, it was possible to show the Jedis slicing Geonosians perfectly down the middle, providing more instances of the Jedi's precision with the lightsaber. As in Episode I, principal actors McGregor and Christiansen were simply given multiple slashing flourishes during their fights with digital characters. They swung their weapons around their body, and it was up to ILM to insert the requisite blaster bold deflections and bisections of droids, hive creatures, and factory equipment.

The necessity to develop so many moments against digital attackers led to the preposterously sounding (but true) assertion that Anakin Skywalker does not know how to wield a lightsaber. Christiansen's behind-the-back lightsaber flourish illustrates how a fancy aesthetic move undermines the principal understanding of sword movement. While the technical problems of continuously holding a lightsaber at the end of the handle is a major flaw, Christiansen's general movement in Episode II suffers little because of the sheer number of movements, his speed, and the variety of attackers. He quickly kills the kouhuns in Amidala's chamber, summarily takes out nearly defenseless Tusken Raiders, and then gives an adequate performance at the end of the film. One interesting move that gets glossed over in the droid factory scene is a reverse grip flourish that Christiansen executes with nimble precision.

Obi-Wan, for his part, was given a set of empty-hand fights against Jango Fett on Kamino. His quick move in the Coruscant sports bar taking off the hand of mercenary Zam Wesell is an interesting move in that it looks good at a fast speed, but is less impressive when seen in slow motion. The downward motion of the cut resembles the cutting technique of the German long sword, but the contortion of the grip limited the mobility of the lightsaber if Obi-Wan had to defend against another attacker. Luckily, there was only one attacker and Anakin was mixed in the crowd ready to come to his aid. It is unfortunate that there was little lightsaber performance when Obi-Wan entered Yoda's Youngling class, as well as limited lightsaber fighting when he fought Jango Fett on Kamino. It is very clear how the lightsaber renders the blaster useless, so it was important to quickly take away Obi-Wan's lightsaber during the Kamino brawl.

When Lucas announced that he was going to make the Prequel Trilogy, fans anticipated a true performance of the Jedi at the height of their power.

Initial hopes were of a grand lightsaber battle between Jedi and Sith, but Lucas's decision to restrict the number of Sith to two individuals dashed any hope of that ever happening. Another challenge in portraying the Jedi as exemplary swordsmen was the difficulty in mastering the integration of living characters and CGI elements, especially during the arena battle on Geonosis.

The early scenes in which the three heroes escape from their chains involved some basic interaction, but in crucial fight scenes with digital creatures, ILM still falls short. A clear example of the close, but not yet full maturity, of CGI and live-action integration was Obi-Wan's fight with the Acklay in which Obi-Wan cut down the creature's legs with baseball-bat slashes before doing a double twirl flourish and downward stab with his lightsaber. Obi-Wan kills the crab-like monster, but Lucas refuses to show the actual plunging of the Jedi's lightsaber into the Acklay's body, opting instead to imply the slaying of the beast. Similarly, Anakin's ride on the bull-like reek during the arena battle was a better, but not fully believable, CGI/live-action integration, though it was a great improvement over Anakin's ride on the gigantic tick-shaped Shaak on Naboo. It still remains that the integration of living and digital creatures is yet an emergent skill requiring a much greater ability than the portrayal of an isolated CGI creature like Watoo in Episode I who does not physically come into contact with a human actor.

Soon after the three have extricated themselves from their immediate predicament, Windu shows up in Dooku's viewing box and threatens Jango Fett with his purple lightsaber. His grip of the lightsaber with fingers facing downward shows his lack of understanding that, while the lightsaber does not have a particular edge with which a swordsman orients his weapon, the position of the hand does indicate the "edge" where the lightsaber will cut. A small 90° twist of his wrist so that his fingers faced Jango's neck would have placed the cutting edge of the lightsaber in line with the mercenary's neck. Unfortunately for the Jedi, the battle goes awry very quickly. Windu is forced to retreat because of Jango's stream of fire. Trebor, a member of the Jedi Council, would later meet his demise so that Jango would have the opportunity to twirl his blaster before returning it to its holster.

The Jedi are shown in pairs or in groups, each taking silly stances that betray the casting requirement that appearance is more important than facility with a lightsaber. It is almost painful for the martial artist to see Jedi make such unorthodox movements and perplexing poses. Jedi lightsaber skills are further undermined in Attack of the Clones *The Visual Dictionary of* Star Wars in which David West Reynolds created a commentary on Jedi and lightsaber combat. The six principal target areas include the four extremities (arms and legs), the head, and the back. Parries match each one of the attacks. While the attack and parry zones look like a 17th-century Francesco Antonio Marcelli diagram illustrating cuts to the body,[2] each parry in the Jedi target is so broad and imprecise that it is difficult to imagine much subtlety in the Jedi art. The stances portrayed in the images look like a photographer simply asked the actors to strike various poses and then sorted the images to approximate lightsaber parries. The horizontal parries are completely flat, permitting the attack to simply smash through the block. A true sword block would have a raised point and an angled blade to "catch" the blade or deflect it away from the head. Another horizontal parry leaves the head completely open to an attack. A few stances perfectly copy the kendo stances, but the absurdity of parry 4, which is a vertical block protecting the back, is the weakest defense one can imagine because there is no weight or angulation that would thwart a direct blow to the back. Any proper defense of the back (given the defender knew it was coming) would include a half turn with the blade tight to the body either above the head or braced against the body with the elbows tucked in. Reynolds gives credit for the principles of Jedi combat to Jack "Tony" Bobo, and thanks Nick Gillard for some personal training on the set. Gillard, however, admitted an unfamiliarity with Reynolds's Jedi combat creation.

The main problem with Jedi combat in the arena stems from Lucas's decision to isolate individual Jedi in order to film their movement so that they would later be "dropped" into the Geonosis arena. Gillard was asked to create individual choreography for the extras who were recruited from Australian kendo and fight clubs.[3] Extras were filmed individually and then shrunk to the appropriate size in order to fight against digital opponents. Often, a flashing lightsaber is the only indication of their presence in a scene. Perhaps it was Lucas's intention to make the Jedi a completely unorganized mob. The purported 200 Jedi are represented by about fifteen extras who did one scene together in which they do a mass charge against battle droids. Geonosian sonic blasters, the overwhelming volleys of droid fire, and the advance of accurate droidekas begin to pick away at the pride of the Republic.

The heroes also do their best to stave off the enemy's advance. Obi-Wan deflects blaster bolts with his baseball swings, but at least he does hold his lightsaber correctly. Windu leaps through the air and dispatches Jango with an iron determination. Both he and Obi-Wan also manage to swing their swords using a reverse grip in which the blade is held upside down. Japanese iaido (sword drawing) has several kata (forms) that use a reverse grip for both cutting and sheathing the sword. Anakin, along with Amidala, swings his lightsaber at the unfortunate few who stray past his Geonosian chariot.

All seems lost when all but seventeen Jedi retreat to the center of the arena in a circle surrounded by the Neimoidian army. Count Dooku offers them their lives, but Windu refuses to be taken as hostages like the Spartiates were taken at Sphacteria in 425 B.C. It was a rout by all accounts, and if it were not for the recently commandeered clone troops, the Jedi Council would have been wiped out. The arrival of the clones permits the Jedi one last opportunity to use their lightsabers to deflect blaster fire. Ki-Adi Mundi swishes his lightsaber with little precision while council members with gloves do their best to step into blue screen platforms for their entry into the gunships. Upon their arrival at the Republic staging area, the remaining Jedi immediately take their place at the head of platoons, leading them forward into battle on the Geonosian surface. Continuity and the need for instant recognition on the battlefield prevent the Jedi from wearing armor, but its utility (especially after the Neimoidian core ship is brought down) on the battlefield is readily apparent. It was a shame the Jedi presented so poorly in combat, but hopefully this was done in order to keep the story in line with their growing redundancy, their lack of preparation, and the inadequacy of their numbers, and not because of a lack of creative ability to better organize or edit a better Jedi resistance. The age of the Jedi has reached a watershed moment in its history. Their ability to protect the Republic is diminished both by their inability to adapt to a new political and military environment, as well as the Sith conspiracy to exterminate them.

Concurrent with the battle on Geonosis, Anakin and Obi-Wan pursue Count Dooku to his hidden starship hangar. Throughout Episodes I and II, the decapitation of the leadership of the Separatist movement has been seen as essential to the unity of the Republic. With Amidala thrown out of the gunship, Anakin has to decide whether to remain faithful to his duty or to pursue the safety of his growing affection. Again, Anakin must make a choice.

Once in Dooku's hangar, the two Jedi approach with lightsabers ignited. Headstrong as always, Anakin decides that he will take Dooku out by himself. Of course, he suffers a quick awakening when Dooku attacks him with Force lightning that throws him against the wall. Without thought for his own safety (or that of his partner), Anakin has denied his compatriot the ability to work in tandem against a talented opponent. But like most talented tacticians, Obi-Wan turns his partner's impulsiveness into his advantage. Obi-Wan knows Dooku's attack and he imposes his lightsaber between him and the Sith lightning. How or why this is possible is never explained, but it does provide the Jedi with a defense against the seemingly all-powerful Sith attack. Dooku realizes that he must now engage the younger Jedi Master.

Count Dooku was played by Christopher Lee, who was 79 during the filming of Episode II. His lightsaber scenes were performed by Kyle Rowling. Despite Lee's repeated boasts that he had done more sword fight scenes in his history than almost any other living actor, Lee was not physically able to do the complicated and taxing sword fight choreography Gillard created. Lucas had to convince Lee to take the role, promising him that they would have fun. Lee was actually on the set for a single day, and to everyone's happiness the shoot went well. He did most of his scenes against a green screen and was filmed with the idea of taking as many close-ups as possible. For the actual fight scenes, Lee stepped aside and was impressed with Rowling's sword fight performance. It is not difficult to distinguish Lee from Rowling on-screen: static close-ups are Lee; dynamic shots are Rowling. The general thinking involved face replacement to guarantee the audience would see Lee's face, because Rowling's makeup, facial structure, and body mass differed significantly enough that even the broad swishing cape does not hide his identity. Face replacement has not been very successful for Lucas, so many tight shots of Lee were essential to the final editing process.

The Obi-Wan–Dooku fight lasts only about a minute in the final cut and begins with Obi-Wan doing a sword twirl with his lightsaber before going into horizontal attacks. He thrusts, is blocked, and then he goes into a body twirl that ends up in another horizontal strike. Obi-Wan is on the offensive making 10 attacks and twirling his body five times; Dooku makes 14 attacks/blocks and does four of his own body twirls. Like the Original Trilogy, there are moments for verbal exchange as the tempo ebbs and flows between static crossed-sword positions and freely moving choreography. Abruptly, Obi-Wan falls to the ground when he is hit on the left arm and left thigh.

Just before he is able to strike down at his opponent, Anakin is able to launch himself across the room to block Dooku's coup de grâce. Anakin, clearly driven by a will to use raw power to his advantage, begins his own attack on the Sith Lord. Falling on the misleading convention that two swords are more powerful than a single sword, Obi-Wan throws his lightsaber to Anakin.[4]

Anakin is able to get in one attack with his two weapons before he is forced to defend against Dooku's subsequent attacks. His 180° pivots provide good aesthetic movement with the flashing blades in the dark cavernous hall of the hangar. But quickly (too quickly) Anakin loses his second lightsaber when it is cut in two by Dooku. Tactically, if Dooku could have cut Anakin's lightsaber, he should have cut to his arm to end the fight more quickly. The duel continues, however, one lightsaber for each man. For the first time in the saga, a Jedi and a Sith take a *jodan* position with their lightsabers held above their heads at a 45° angle.

Jodan is an iconic Japanese stance that has its equivalent in Western long sword techniques. It is the most powerful attacking position even though it seems like the whole front of the body is open for an attack with a thrust or a slash. The sword held above the head has the most potential energy of any other stance because its position is primed for an immediate descent. The weakness of the overhead position is not the sword's position, but the person's hesitation in executing the downward cut. Once the attack is launched, however, it is extremely difficult to predict where the strike will land. The initial downward drop of the blade does not indicate where the final attack will land; the target can be the top or side of the head, the neck, shoulder, upper and lower arms, wrists, or even the opponent's blade itself. The initial attack might simply be a feint so that when the point drops to a middle position, the blade can be used to beat the opponent's blade away, immediately followed by a thrust to the face, chest, or neck, or a slash to any part of the body. With the initial blade displaced, the entire body is exposed for a slash or even a body slam to further unbalance the opponent and even knock him to the ground.

The defender has several ways to counter this stance. The first is to take a different stance to challenge the strength of the threatening sword. Pushing the point forward into middle position (*chudan*) without completely extending the arms is an effective psychological threat to the opponent. The successful thrust can damage the face. Moreover, the point is used as a distraction, permitting an evasion and counter-strike after the opponent begins to swing his sword downward. A position with the vertical blade held to either side of the body (*hasso-no-kamae* or *kami-hasso*), which is a typical Jedi stance (it is also typical for all sword styles), invites the opponent to attack the exposed areas of the body while also permitting the possibility of an evasion, block, or immediate counter-attack. Contrary to logic, another possibility is to drop the point down in front or to actually bring it back behind the person, exposing the entire body for a strike. This position is perplexing to the person in jodan because the opponent is giving him the complete opportunity to attack. He knows that any number of evasions, counter-moves, and counter-attacks are possible. The imposing question for the attacker is the opponent's ability to complete his movement with perfect timing and speed. Once the initial committed attack from jodan is made, the attacker is now exposed to a counter-attack.

The most obvious position against an opponent in jodan is to take the same position as Dooku actually does, which is called *aigamae* in Japanese. Two different stances between opponents limit the possibilities of movement: a low guard can be raised to block a high attack, a feint to a higher position can be changed to a lower target, etc. The person in jodan must hit decisively or risk a counter-attack if the first attack misses, so when the opponent takes the same position, infinite possibilities open up. The target areas on the opponent are the same, blocks and movements are options to both.[5] The attack can be made decisively by one or both. Timing is crucial, commitment is essential, and one's emotional state must be controlled. The easiest defense against the attack is a timed retreat and then a counter-attack. The most dangerous counter-attack is a perfectly timed evasion with a simultaneous attack to the exposed arms or wrists. Displacement of the body (side step or oblique advance) coupled with a counter-attack and the moment of the opponent's attack can be used as an effective tactic. Proximity to the opponent after the attacker misses also permits a wide range of counter-cuts to the exposed body, but it has to always be remembered that an attack from jodan can easily land on the target even before the defender can initiate his own attack or movement. Unlike the attack and counter-attack of cinema, the single strike with devastating effect is the essence of swordsmanship.

At this point, however, Lucas goes into a dark moment of abstraction in which lightsabers flash across the screen as close-ups of Dooku's and Anakin's faces are lighted by the swirling blades. As Lucas put it in a 2002 interview, this scene had a Scott Bartlett–ish feel to it.[6] Any real jodan techniques were given up completely in favor of a stylistic battle. A visual resolution to two jodan-opposing lightsaber individuals would have to wait until Episode III between the Emperor and Windu. Once the perspective returns to a full display of the two opponents in movement, it moves quickly to Anakin's fateful loss of one arm. By this time, repeated slashes and blocks have been made, and Anakin completes his nine body twirls and 20 attacks. Both Anakin and Obi-Wan are piled together in a heap as Dooku prepares for his final attack on the disabled Jedi.

The climax is hardly over, as the audience finally gets to see the greatest Jedi Master to engage in battle. His fragile approach limping with the aid of his cane provided the greatest setup for the audience. Word of Yoda's fight had leaked to the public months before the premiere of the movie, so the anticipation of this fight was the highlight of the film. As had happened three years earlier, the lightsaber battle of Episode II had to be the equal of the Qui-Gon/Obi-Wan versus Maul duel. The extra Dooku choreography was not needed for the final edit, as Lucas had decided that he was able to pull off the Yoda-Dooku duel without it turning into the potentially laughing-stock moment of the entire saga.

Yoda has his verbal exchange with Dooku and the fight proceeds into what Rob Coleman, the director of the ILM digital team, called the "battle of the wizards," which was created because a pause in the action was needed after the defeat of Obi-Wan and Anakin. The audience had to prepare for Yoda's ability to fight with a lightsaber. Until this moment, Sith lightning had always been the evil superweapon against which the Jedi seemed outclassed. Obi-Wan was able to use his lightsaber to defend against Dooku's lightning, but why weren't the Jedi able to throw lightning of their own? From a philosophical perspective, Lucas gives the Sith this exclusivity because it demonstrates their willingness to wreak wanton violence in the pursuit of their agenda. Yoda, however, counters this ability when he demonstrates that while the Sith are able to dish it out, he is even more powerful because he cannot only turn it back on Dooku, but he can capture it and dissipate it completely. Dooku futilely throws objects at Yoda and then drops the ceiling on him, but Dooku realizes that lightsaber battle is the only way to decide the outcome.

Using the martial arts cliché of the extended arm and the hand gesture to "bring it on," Lucas underscores the seriousness of the fight with a comedic moment. Emotion is high, Dooku gives his fencing salute, and immediately the two leap into battle.

The physicality of the fight, however, betrays some of the limitations of digital technology in the *Star Wars* films. For the martial artist, there is little real interest in the fight between the two because the reality of the situation is that Lee's double (Rowling) is performing a choreographed dance in which the digital Yoda was added later. The final cut of the 56-second lightsaber fight had to be edited with dramatic close-ups when blades are locked together. There is little acting during the long shots because it was necessary to hide Rowling's face during the duel under the darkness of the cave.

For the production, the real issue for Lucas was technical. The fear that a fighting Yoda would not work was already reflected in the extra Dooku choreography, and Gillard's choreography already presupposed the moments during the duel when blades would clash. The principal issue was digitally drawing in a Yoda into the spaces and moments that led up to the next clash of blades. In a four-page article on Yoda in *Star Wars Insider*, the author included only two paragraphs on choreography.[7] The digital team seems to be continually focused on the realism of clothing on their digital characters, but they seem to lack the ability to communicate ideas surrounding the choreography of the fight. Without the choreography, there is no fight.

Most of the excitement of this duel is actually generated by the audience's inability to understand what is going on in terms of the fight. To the expert martial artist trained to discern small movement, this fight was particularly perplexing because it did not correspond to anything martial. And quite quickly, the duel was over.

Coleman said that the movement and choreography from Episode I informed Yoda's style greatly. Additionally, he lists 10 movies considered influential on Yoda's performance.[8] The ability to make Yoda's lightsaber realistically fly into his three-fingered hands was achieved, but the larger question was how Yoda was to move during the fight. During web documentaries, Lucas said that he envisioned Yoda's movement to be that of a leaping frog who would jump about during the battle as he wielded his lightsaber. Again, the technical job was to move Yoda in martial moves to moments when lightsabers clashed. In all, Yoda makes 18 physical jumps during the battle, 8 somersaults (a physical forward turning in which feet go over head), and 17 body twirls (the feet remain in a downward position while the body turns 180° around the central axis). Dooku does a total of 31 strikes, while Yoda does 24 strikes, of which, only about 5 are close enough to actually hit Dooku.

The challenge with Yoda during the duel is something that has been seen earlier in the difficulty of live-action/CGI integration. For a film using green screens to integrate living actors with digital actors, the ability of a live actor to synch with an imagined creature is extremely difficult, as is seen in Qui-Gon's interaction with Jar Jar in Episode I. Although the problem is really one in which the digital animator did not correctly animate a reaction to the live actor's performance, it often appears on screen as if the actor did not properly react to the digital creature. Lucas, himself, expressed the difficulty of portraying the simple movements of Episode I clone troopers who lacked not only a natural fluidity and defensive posture but also a visual cognizance of their environment. The performances of Episode II clone troopers were improved by motion-capture techniques in which ex-military soldiers advanced and retreated on a special set which digitally captured their movement. The absence of a reaction by Commander Cody to the huge Boga barreling toward him as Obi-Wan approaches is another difficulty in the realistic portrayal of the interaction between digital creations. The editorial process can also harm integration by attempting to fool the eye of the audience, which often picks up light discrepancies in a completely animated scene no matter how thoroughly one tries to capture actual light conditions on the set. Even an attempt to combine live and digital footage through the editing process, as occurs in the Dooku fight with Yoda, can actually accentuate the failure to properly integrate the live and digital actors.

What can be said of the digital Yoda in a positive light is that ILM was able to give Yoda technically correct martial movement. If one goes through the Yoda choreography in slow motion on their DVD, the classical position and balance of an experienced martial artist can be seen. The difficulty of such movement can only be achieved from years of experience and training. None of the principal actors compare with Ray Park's ability in Episode I. Similarly, Yoda does do service to the Jedi arts in that he is the example of perfect acrobatic movement. Yoda even executes a butterfly twist according to Park's example.

Trying to outdo the success of Episode II was a difficult process for the production crew. Both McGregor and Christiansen were able to give good performances in their lightsaber fighting, but the key to success was the credibility of Yoda's duel with Dooku. Face replacement, keying in background opponents, and matching movements were challenges facing Lucas during Episode I. The second film largely met the expectations in the sword fight choreography. The audience had to take Yoda as a skilled fighting Jedi seriously and in large measure Episode II was able to pay off. In many respects, the art of cinema makes what is imperfect look perfect; makes what is invisible, visible; highlights strengths and diminishes weaknesses. The combat between Dooku and Anakin and Obi-Wan provided good choreographic footage (albeit with a lot of body twirls), while the Dooku-Yoda fight was able to provide an emotional ride for the general audience. That in itself is probably the movie's greatest success, providing at least a hopeful resolution to the sad plight of Jedi as a fighting order of knights. Their final downfall, of course, is the subject of the third chapter of the *Star Wars* saga.

Episode III— Star Wars: Revenge of the Sith— *The Longest Battle*

Ever since 1978, *Star Wars* fans have wondered how and why Obi-Wan would battle Anakin in a duel that ended with the creation of Darth Vader. No one knew, except Lucas, exactly what a Sith Lord was, or that there were only two in existence at any one time. At that time, no one knew that Darth Vader was Luke's father, nor that it was possible to become a Jedi without having to go to the Jedi Temple. There were inklings of a lava scene from the production drawings done by Ralph McQuarrie. The Emperor was supposed to meet Vader on Coruscant in Episode VI but that element of the plot was replaced by the scenes on the second Death Star. The prequel's fight coordinator had years to contemplate the climactic duel between the two Jedi-in-arms, but it was not until the success of the Episode I lightsaber fights that Gillard was certain he would be the person to create the choreography for the ultimate lightsaber battle.

It was confirmed that Ray Park would not be part of the final production of Episode III, but Gillard still had Ewan McGregor and the stunt doubles from Episode II. Gillard had had years to contemplate this final duel, but it was not until Lucas had finished his final script that Gillard could proceed deliberately with text to work from. Artwork, design, and set creation had begun soon after Episode II, but choreography could not actually be created until Gillard knew the exact parameters of the fights in Episode III. Clues as to who was winning a fight at a particular point were gleaned from the script. Gillard also had to create new fighting styles for Dooku's bodyguards, the MagnaGuard droids, and the droid general who had made an appearance in the *Clone Wars Cartoon* the spring before the premiere of Episode III. There was plenty of speculation about the Obi-Wan–Anakin duel. Would Anakin use a red lightsaber? How long would the fight last? Of course, Anakin fought with a blue lightsaber, but Gillard originally choreographed 12 minutes straight of fighting between the two. Thankfully, this never happened. The final scene turned out to be 6 minutes 36 seconds, interspersed with the Yoda duel on Coruscant.

As in Episodes I and II, the Jedi begin their lightsaber combat against droids on the Separatist starship hangar. The heroes pop out of their fighters and attack the hapless droids. Obi-Wan does his sword twirls, Anakin his blade flourishes. Droids die in the elevators, in hallways, and in the command centers of the vast ship.

Without much ado, Lucas takes care of a key element leading to the end of the Separatist movement by capturing or killing Count Dooku, followed by the demise of General Grievous. Once the Separatist leaders were dead, the Jedi would then move on to limit or repeal the dictatorial powers Chancellor Palpatine had acquired during the Clone Wars. The Jedi do not have far to go, as the Separatists had launched a direct attack on the capital planet of the Republic and its supreme chancellor is already held hostage by General Grievous. Obi-Wan and Anakin make their way to the holding room where Palpatine is bound to a chair reminiscent of his future throne on the second Death Star. They free the chancellor, but behind them is Dooku with two super battle droids, which play no significant part in the duel.

Dooku does a somersault to the main deck and then engages the two Jedi in his final duel. The Jedi cooperate this time. They are completely on the offensive, alternating their slashes from one side to the other, and it is not until Dooku takes advantage of his ability to use a Force push that the 2-minute duel comes to a turning point when Obi-Wan is thrown across the room and a walkway topples over him. Dooku shows so little concern that he is not even attacking (he will make only 6 attacks compared to Obi-Wan's 6 and Anakin's 25). Despite Anakin's relentless assault, Dooku is certain of his ability to defeat the young Jedi as he did in Episode II. But Anakin has become twice as powerful, and in a quick and elegant move, Anakin is able to slice off Dooku's hands and then catch Dooku's lightsabers before crossing them at the base of Dooku's neck, a position used directly in Musashi's two-sword style of swordsmanship. Dooku drops to his knees and awaits Anakin's next move. Convinced that he is in a win-win situation, Dooku believes that his duel is a test to see if Anakin would turn on one he has defeated. Even if he had lost to Anakin, Palpatine, the Sith Lord, would not dare permit anything to happen to his prized apprentice. Of course, he is amazed when Palpatine commands Anakin to kill his prey. Christensen is not convincing in his portrayal of Anakin's remorse, but the deed had already been done, the opening third of the film ending with Dooku's death. All that remained was to capture General Grievous.

They do not have to wait long until they are captured in a force field and taken directly to the droid general himself. Grievous is a coughing coward who would make others fight until he was cornered, and it would not be until later in the film that Grievous would engage in his only lightsaber battle with the Jedi Knights. Up until then, throughout the Clone Wars, Grievous had been hunting Jedi and taking their lightsabers as trophies. He was mistaken when he thought he could add Obi-Wan's and Anakin's lightsabers to his collection.

As always, Artoo saves the day with his mechanical apoplexy. The two Jedi dispatch the MagnaGuards who wield an impressive electrostaff. They cannot be cut by lightsabers, but the guards are ineffective in penetrating Jedi lightsaber defenses. With more droids killed, Grievous escapes and the Jedi are forced to turn their attention to landing the breaking cruiser on the surface of Coruscant.

The politics of the Republic are churning away as battle-filled Episode III takes its course. There is no more exposition nor a detective story, but simply a revelation and then revenge. Episode III is about battle and combat.

The next duel takes place on the sinkhole planet of Utapau. Anakin is already a member of the Jedi Council and his anger is stoked in the fire of the political fighting between the Jedi and the chancellor's office. Obi-Wan is sent in place of Anakin to capture Grievous, while Yoda is on Chewbacca's homeworld of Kashyyyk. Obi-Wan learns of the Separatist council and literally drops in on their meeting. With a wave of his hand, he takes out the four MagnaGuards with a ceiling fixture that drops down on them. The fight with Grievous begins in earnest. Grievous is cornered and he draws his lightsabers, telling Obi-Wan that he has been trained in the Jedi lightsaber arts.

General Grievous is a digital character, so technical problems arise in the execution of this fight. Ray Harryhausen had already choreographed a fight with the six-armed Kali in *The Golden Voyage of Sinbad* (1974). Even today, the sword fight is very impressive; especially given the fact that it was made with stop-motion photography. The Harryhausen choreography of Kali only lacks the speed with which it is executed. For ILM, the biggest obstacle was choreographing a fight scene in which Grievous believably used four lightsabers against his Jedi adversary. As in Episode II with Yoda, the use of Grievous's four arms was leaked early to the public. A web documentary on the creation of Grievous by the design team had aired the year before, but it was not clear how the actual fight would be fought.

Grievous was animated by digitizing McGregor and stunt double Kyle Rowling for the droid general. Rowling's arms represented one set of arms against which McGregor fought using his own lightsaber. Here the choreography and timing are in perfect sync, which contrasts with the Yoda fight scenes in which the stunt double had to fight an imaginary opponent.[9] The art of digital animation, however, had not yet been fully mastered. Examination of the editing reveals a need for more close-ups to create the illusion of a complex fighting style. Lucas expressed the need to have the extra hands cut off immediately so that true battle between the stunt doubles would begin. The digital creation was a "hard wired" digital entity in which parts would not bend through any other parts. Like a real object in the universe, his right arm (or his joints and any other attachments) could not pass through another part of the body regardless of the digital instruction it was given. When each of Grievous's two arms splits into two, none of the parts would share the same animated space, preventing digital artists from artificially faking the animation.

After Grievous's four arms were displayed, the top two arms would begin to rotate like an airplane propeller. A buzzing sound and the visual swirls of the lightsaber blades would enhance the threat to Obi-Wan. McGregor still fought against Rowling who wore a blue suit that matched the blue-screen background. The animated Grievous would be keyed in over Rowling, his hands digitally locked to the movement of Grievous's lower arms. Grievous advanced with the swirling lightsabers, pushing the Jedi back several feet. Obi-Wan attacks with a few slashes, which are promptly blocked. It takes him a few seconds to figure out how to attack his four-armed attacker, and quickly he is able to chop off the first arm and then a second arm. The close-up of that scene prevented the audience from seeing the movement Obi-Wan used to hit his mark, but it does not matter any more. The two arms have been destroyed and the short lightsaber duel ends with a few nice blocks. Two horizontal blades blocking Obi-Wan's lightsaber make for a nice visual. The subsequent hold with one blade, followed by a bash with the other represents an authentic technique a two-sword swordsman would use in such a fight.

The problem of achieving more complicated and realistic-looking choreography is easily resolved when Obi-Wan uses a Force push that knocks Grievous some twenty or thirty feet away against a wall. Grievous loses both lightsabers and in spider-fashion, he scrambles to his speeder conveniently sitting just outside the camera's view. The lightsaber battle is over and the fight turns into a futuristic car chase with the electrostaff from one of the MagnaGuards being used as a spear-like prop. After the speeder crashes, the "fist fight" leads up to Grievous's dramatic death blaster fire at the hands of his Jedi adversary. Grievous's death is spectacular, and the audience has been entertained by a few gags, but in the end, the Grievous/Obi-Wan fight was but a short (and mostly insignificant) lightsaber interlude between a feckless lightsaber wannabe and a cheeky braggart.

The story's plot has moved along, and all that is left before the climactic duels at the end of the movie are the attempted arrest of Palpatine, the execution of the Younglings in the Jedi Temple, and Anakin's execution of the Separatist representatives on Mustafar. There is no fighting in these scenes. Christiansen ignites his lightsaber and the assassinations of Jedi children are implied. On Mustafar, camera angles assured that the audience sees Anakin's lightsaber blade cut down the leaders of the anti–Republican army. Thus he eliminates Palpatine's co-conspirators and covers up his trail of association with the enemies of the state.

Grievous's death leads the Jedi council to their final move against the chancellor. Anakin wants to join them, but Windu orders him to stay in the Jedi Temple. It is but a plot element to delay his arrival at the chancellor's chambers. The entry of Windu and his three "deputies" is referred to as the "Mace and his posse" scene by *Star Wars* fans. Like the marshals mentioned in chapter two, Windu under the authority of the Jedi Council arrives with his subordinates to take the chancellor into custody. The Jedi had no foreknowledge of the danger Palpatine as a Sith Lord presented or else they might have found a different way to force Palpatine to step down. There is a question of whether it was illegal to have a political view different from that of the Jedi, but that is but an understated musing underscored by the elaborate back story created by Expanded Universe writers to fill in the details about the time between Episodes II and III. James Luceno's *Labyrinth of Evil* details the investigation to discover and capture the Sith Lord linked to the Separatist forces. A legal mandate among the Jedi and Clone troops already exists for the apprehension and arrest of the Sith Lord.

Windu's plan was simple, but it quickly goes awry when Palpatine draws his own lightsaber and attacks the posse. Palpatine flies through the air at the Jedi with his lightsaber in hand. He lands in front of them and in short order takes out three of Windu's associates. From a martial point of view, the efficiency with which he kills them is realistic and true. A longer, drawn-out battle is characteristic of movie choreography. Despite its undramatic length, the devastating one-cut attack is the ideal attack for any swordsman. Lucas denies the audience any choreography by only including the facial expressions of the three Jedi as they die in the final edit. More elaborate choreography would be used in the exchange between Windu and Sidious.

The Episode I statement that Maul has been trained well now has a clear and specific meaning. Sidious trained Darth Maul in lightsaber fighting. Sidious's prompt defeat of his comrades is a shock. Windu has to retreat and for a while he takes the offensive against Sidious, who is even forced into a bizarre-looking somersault. The exchange between the two is even for a while and is characterized by their momentary stances in jodan mentioned earlier. Here, the two pause briefly trying to figure out the other's immediate intentions. They both step forward together and twist their lightsabers inward for a strike at their opponent. The movement resembles a Japanese sword technique used not as an offensive slash (the lightsaber blade cuts at any angle), but as a defensive block used to stop an attack to the head. In its defensive iteration, the opponent's head attack is blocked, which can then be followed by an immediate counter-attack or a blow to the blocked blade and then a subsequent counter-attack. For the two, the duel continues until Windu kicks Palpatine in the face, which causes his Sith lightsaber to fly out the window.

McDiarmid, 61 at the time Episode III was filmed, like Lee, was not as nimble a person as McGregor or Christiansen. Nor was Samuel L. Jackson, 57, at the filming of this scene. McDiarmid had no idea that his character was a lightsaber fighter, so he spent little time learning any choreography. Jackson, who wanted any role in the saga and ended up being the second most powerful Jedi, knew he wanted to die a dramatic death. Ever since Episode II, Jackson had bragged about the time he spent studying kendo and sword fight moves. It does not really show in the films that he has done any training, and while he does not show the kind of martial presence of an experienced swordsman, his sword movement in Episodes II and III are passable for actors in general. McDiarmid, on the other hand, does not have the physical stature or experience to sustain the difficult training process McGregor and Christiansen went through. To top it off, there was confusion on the set during the several days it took to film this scene. Gillard's original choreography was not going to be used in the final edit, and because of Lucas's desire to get as many close-ups as possible, Jackson and McDiarmid had to be taught basic moves that showed them in motion with a lightsaber but not in full fight. In the end, some of Gillard's choreography did make it into the final edit, most of it performed by fencing double Michael Byrne.

Anakin's eventual appearance in Palpatine's office comes at a point in which Palpatine is on his back with Windu's point at his throat. Anakin chooses to side with Palpatine by cutting off Windu's hand as the Jedi Council member swings to kill Sidious once and for all. Sith lightning throws Windu out the window and he is seen no more. The Sith have survived, a new Sith Lord, Darth Vader, is created, and the Jedi Order is now about to be crushed with the communication of Order 66.

Yoda and Obi-Wan are the only two significant Jedi who have survived the Jedi purge. Shocked by the completeness of the devastation at the Jedi Temple, they learn who was behind the attack. Yoda makes his own way to the chancellor's office after instructing Obi-Wan to kill the new Sith Lord, Darth Vader. A sign of the times, this will not be Yoda's only moment ordering one of his apprentices to kill Lord Vader.

Yoda's appearance at the chancellor's office is perhaps a scene that gets some of the loudest applause from the audience. Fans have already seen Yoda in his duel with Dooku, but his immediate and unexpected slaughter of the two Red Guards standing guard in Palpatine's office is a clear indication of Yoda's power with the Force. The banter between him and Palpatine is curt and unlike Episode II, Yoda is taken aback when he feels the full brunt of the Sith lightning Sidious launches at him. He takes the fall hard but returns the favor with a powerful Force push. The "battle of wizards" is short and is taken up later in their duel, but the lightsaber battle is to commence quickly so as to be in sync with the raging duel between Anakin and Obi-Wan on Mustafar. Yoda's duel this time will not end with the feeble Force pull of his cane at the end of Episode II, nor with a clear defeat over the Sith. Indeed, the dark side has taken hold of the universe.

With Sidious in a jodan position, Yoda stands in a *hasso-no-kamae* stance waiting for an attack. Much has already been said of the Yoda and Grievous duels in which the digital limitations preclude a real fight between the stunt double and the animated character. Yoda leaps around swinging his lightsaber; Sidious blocks or makes attacks of his own. Actual lightsaber fighting, both in the chambers and in the great hall, lasts about a minute and a half. The Force duel itself lasts a little longer. In total, Yoda makes 13 attacks, jumps 12 times, and does 9 somersaults and 7 body twirls. Palpatine does none of the acrobatics he does during Windu's scenes, and Yoda attacks a total of 27 times. The Force battle in which delegate pods are thrown around the great hall allows Yoda to hop and leap toward his adversary, who has somehow gotten a better vantage after they enter the Senate chambers. The distant lightsaber battle between Yoda and Sidious is easily examined with the zoom function on the DVD player, but the real decisive moments of the battle take place when Yoda attempts to defend himself against the flying pods. Yoda attempts to draw his lightsaber on Sidious but loses it to a flash of Sith lightning. The two are empty-handed and each draws on the power of the Force to defeat the other. The end result is a stalemate in which the equal energy generated by both explodes in their faces, throwing them away from the epicenter. Sidious finds a perch on a platform, but with the military now on his side (Mas Ameda escaped when Yoda was momentarily stunned), the likelihood that Yoda would be able to kill or even apprehend Sidious is all but nil. Like Maul in Episode I and Dooku in Episode II, Yoda has failed in his mission and must beat a retreat in order to fight another day.

Did he actually lose his battle with Sidious? His admission to Bail Organa indicates that he lost, but from a purely martial perspective, it cannot be said the either Sidious or Yoda won the duel. The number of attacks is usually a good indicator, but the Force has a way of turning what looks like a clear win into a sudden defeat. That is, in fact, the very nature of the sword fight. Despite the preparation and practice that goes into training, the fight itself is in many ways prone to the incalculable forces at work during a duel. Not only are there physical problems of terrain and weather, but the minutia of other factors such as humidity, the brittleness of a sword, one's rest from the night before, or the tactical comment that raises an emotional response.

Many fans have argued that the Jedi have the ability to see into the future, permitting them to deflect blaster bolts and predict where an opponent will strike with his lightsaber. An "in-house" explanation (i.e., an explanation using the facts and logic of the *Star Wars* universe) points to Yoda's assertion that the future is always in motion. Even though the Emperor in Episode VI has come up with a plan that falls into place at every step, the emotional problems destroy the logic and predictability of a sword fight. This is the very nature of combat. Despite the limited moves of a swordsman with his weapon, a single strike to the head, for example, is mitigated by a host of subtle factors including the speed of the attack, the actual target (a light hit on the back crown on the head can actually blind the opponent because it strikes the part of the brain controlling sight), the covering of the head (oily hair can have a sheathing effect), or the gaze of the opponent who can steal away the attacker's focus at the moment of the attack. The talented director or fight choreographer takes advantage of these subtleties to create his art. It is the very reason why the sword fight has always had a greater presence on stage than a simple bare-knuckled fight. Whereas the brutal nature of a boxing match captures its audience by the sheer rawness of the act of striking, the sophisticated and complex nature of the fencing art, if performed well, never ceases to enthrall an audience. Surprisingly, the sword's subtlety must be made more plain to the audience for them to understand. That is why the *Star Wars* choreography is often a series of sweeping slashes.

After the Yoda-Sidious draw, all is now ready for the most anticipated duel in the saga. The Jedi Temple is a charred ruin and all its inhabitants are dead. The leaders on Mustafar have been killed and Anakin awaits final instruction from Lord Sidious when Padmé arrives with Obi-Wan on board her ship. Padmé barely survives her encounter with Anakin, and Obi-Wan must now confront and kill the apprentice who has been with him for ten years.

Lucas could not have been any less right in a statement he made about Hayden Christiansen's ability to portray the dark side of the Force. Despite the problems Christiansen had trying to effectively carry out the many clumsy lines he was given and the failed chemistry between him and Natalie Portman, Christiansen was able to give a stellar performance embodying the malfeasance of the young, innocent boy who was created spontaneously by the midi-chlorians. When he has no speaking lines and only a lightsaber to express himself, Christiansen is able to give us a fulfilling conclusion to his duel with McGregor.

In spite of fears that the final lightsaber battle would be an endless repetition of left- and right-sided attacks, Gillard was able to create a lengthy choreography that showed the emotion between the two characters. Flourishes are kept to a minimum, kicks and punches are used sparingly, and the acrobatics are limited to a few instances. The duel between the two Jedi is mostly dominated by Anakin's relentless attacks. Throughout the six and a half minutes of screen time given to the duel, Anakin makes 75 attacks compared to Obi-Wan's 42. Obi-Wan only does two sabre twirls, Anakin three. But the tempo and character of the fight is represented in distinct locales during the fight.

At the beginning, Anakin lays into Obi-Wan, forcing him down a path and through a small tunnel into the Separatist conference room. Lucas did not speed up the fight during the editing process, so the speed and intensity of the lightsaber strikes are very impressive on film. Where their sword work lacks crispness and precision, the energy of the exchange, complemented by Williams's soundtrack, makes for a very intense duel. Probably for many, the total time of the duel lasts a bit too long and appeals to the testosterone-laden side of the audience, but the nuances in the choreography impress the martial arts technician.

The general slash-and-block movement of the fight is interspersed with the occasional example of clever choreography. Ironically, the speed and pace of McGregor's and Christiansen's performance sometimes ends up glossing over Gillard's carefully crafted movement. At the beginning of the Anakin–Obi-Wan duel just before they enter the tunnel leading into the conference room, there is an extremely sophisticated and subtle fencing phrase involving two reversals. As Obi-Wan thrusts, Anakin makes a block and grabs Obi-Wan's sword-arm at the wrist with his left hand. Obi-Wan counters by lifting his arm as Anakin tries to spin away. The move brings Anakin's arm into the air, where Obi-Wan grabs Anakin's arm with his free hand and pushes it (and the rest of Anakin's body) to the side, giving Obi-Wan a clear strike to Anakin's head. Only at the last moment does Anakin lift his lightsaber up for a block. To the general audience, it looks like a simple, quick turn. To the martial artist, however, this exchange represents very advanced techniques found in Japanese aikido or Chinese push-hands. This phase of movement lasts two seconds and is partially obscured by the light flares of the two clashing lightsabers. It is an instance in which the creativity of the choreographer is lost when neither the director nor the editor can see the significance of the movement to highlight it for the final film cut.

The conference room scene begins with Obi-Wan being choked by Anakin's mechanical hand. Obi-Wan is able to extricate himself before they both end up on top of the conference table with their lightsabers knocked out of their hands. Obi-Wan kicks Anakin, knocking him over. Anakin charges and hits Obi-Wan with both feet in the chest before coming at him again, only to have the favor returned when Obi-Wan steps to the side and pushes into Anakin's upper body, sending him crashing down on top of the table. Obi-Wan is ready to strike down at Anakin, but at the last second Anakin Force-pulls his own lightsaber for a block.

Their lightsaber fight continues as an even exchange until they go into the worst moment of the choreography. Standing a couple of feet away from each other, both Jedi do a lengthy flourish in which the lightsabers swing around both Jedi without even a single blade touching. It seems convenient that they pull the same trick out of their hat at exactly the same time, and the tempo of the fight suffers for it. The next instant, each uses a Force push against the other. Power builds up, and like the end of the Yoda-Palpatine fight, the ensuing explosion sends them flying across the room. Anakin leaps across the room and their exchange leads to the destruction of the shields protecting the landing site.

The fight then moves out into the open air where the rushing and exploding molten lava is tearing the landing platform apart. They have to avoid cinders raining down upon them, and as a large antenna array breaks off the main building, the Jedi begin a vertical fight on the tower that floats on the lava. The distance shots, like those of Yoda and Palpatine in the Senate, are inconsequential, with a blade slash here and there. Lucas even gets in a gratuitous rope slash between the two Jedi. By the time the two Jedi escape the antenna array, which has fallen over a lava fall, Obi-Wan finds protection on a mining platform and Anakin drops on top of a mining droid. Their Jedi powers must protect them from the unbearable heat that is taxing their physical strength.

Anakin makes one final jump and lands on Obi-Wan's platform and the two engage in a futile exchange of slashes. They engage in one last flourish before they end up with their blades locked at an impasse. Obi-Wan looks over his shoulder and makes a huge leap to the top of the banks holding back the lava river. Anakin waits and watches as Obi-Wan warns him not to try a jump. He has the "high ground," Obi-Wan says. Anakin jumps anyway, and in an instant he is on his face sliding down toward the lava. The editing of the scene prevents the audience from actually seeing how Obi-Wan's single stroke cuts off Anakin's arm and two legs, but the deed is done. Obi-Wan expresses his sadness. He picks up Anakin's lightsaber and makes for Padmé's ship.

At least the lightsaber battle is finished and the audience knows how Anakin becomes Darth Vader. Does it really change the audience's opinion that Vader is no longer the epitome of evil but a tragic figure in a larger tale than the Original Trilogy? Probably not. To many, Anakin is still the whiney kid who got everything he deserved. There are many instances that by themselves do not really make sense (Was he really that dumb to realize killing defenseless Tusken children, Jedi Younglings, and a captured Dooku was wrong?), unless viewed within the context of the two trilogies. Christiansen's lightsaber performance does the saga credit.

Gillard has certainly provided the audience with exciting choreography. Many will think that it was a bit too much, but overall, this installment succeeded in delivering the goods. Against all predictions, critics gave Episode III the best reception of all three prequel movies. There was little to explain, so the attention to action, in the tradition of the original *Star Wars*, was the central focus of the plot. The Jedi Order has been abolished, the Jedi Temple destroyed, and the final question of how Anakin came to don his iconic costume has been answered. For Lucas, as well as his production team, the completion of the most recent *Star Wars* films means the end of a long and difficult process. For many fans, while it was not always a compelling journey, it was time well spent both in anticipation and the satisfaction of seeing the last piece of the puzzle being put in place.

Episode IV — Star Wars: A New Hope — *Testament to Mastery*

The subtitle of Episode IV suggests the fundamental plotline for the first movie of the Original Trilogy, providing the subtext for every line of dialogue and action sequence. It also acts as a starting point of each sword fight. Implicit in the title is a backstory of stellar proportions. Hope — a small, lackluster word — is the answer to the despair a person finds in life. Especially for those in their most desperate need — the impoverished, the oppressed, the neglected, the ostracized, the forgotten — hope is the single pinprick of light in their lives. Their plight is a struggle for mere existence, and yet deep within a person's heart is the yearning for an act of goodness that may alleviate them of the lot to which they have been subject. Like Anakin and his mother on Tatooine, the downtrodden are slaves to their circumstances, unable to escape until something or someone like a Luke Skywalker comes along and releases them.

For audiences seeing *Star Wars* for the first time, the tiny rebel blockade runner being pursued by the massive star destroyer succinctly explains the plight of the forces of freedom and what they are up against. But it is also the opening act of rebellion against a seemingly all-powerful Empire. In the fourth act, Luke is not the chosen one, but a new hope, one who will answer the call of those in the universe who need a chance to escape oppression. Episode IV also shows the chosen redeemer awakening by means of sacrifice of one person for another; this recurring motif was expressed in Obi-Wan's sacrifice for Luke in Episode IV and Qui-Gon's sacrifice for Anakin in Episode I.

Obi-Wan meets Luke for the first time as an adult when he runs across Artoo in the desert. He saves Luke from the Tusken Raiders stripping his land speeder of any valuables. Like Yoda in Episode V, Luke sees Ben Kenobi as an old, reclusive hermit. He does not know that he is a guardian to a universe greater than Luke could ever imagine. A seemingly unimportant person in a large desert of a planet, Luke could not have dreamed that he was the son of one of the most important (and tragic) persons in the universe.

Ben Kenobi introduces Luke to his first experience with the legacy of his father, Anakin's lightsaber. Luke handles it for all of five seconds, but realizes that the more important things in his life involve returning home and explaining where he has been all day. Little does he know that a chain of events has already begun to creep up on his life. He discovers his uncle and aunt have been murdered and he has no alternative except to follow Obi-Wan on his obscure trip to Alderaan. He sees Obi-Wan wield his lightsaber in the cantina. A quick and simple slash of the blade and an arm is resting lifeless on the floor. His lightsaber cannot protect them from the stormtroopers because their objective is to remain hidden and unknown, a charge Obi-Wan has followed for almost two decades.

On the *Millennium Falcon*, Luke gets his first introduction to Jedi instruction. His feet are in a fencer's stance, but his arms are outstretched like that of a samurai. His right hand slightly overlaps his left hand, but for the most part, he holds a samurai stance. Failure is part of training, but success is also a reward Luke enjoys when he blocks the three bolts shot at him by the remote. Hamill seems to have a natural look when he holds his lightsaber. He has a relaxed posture and the proper reflexes that portray him as a natural swordsman. His natural ability will follow him through all three films as Hamill continues to demonstrate to Peter Diamond, the stunt coordinator, that he, unlike Prowse in Episode V, is more than capable of learning his choreography.

In Episode IV, the elder Obi-Wan and Darth Vader meet in a duel after an obvious but unexplained history. One is the former master of the other, and both know that the outcome of their duel must end with the destruction of one or the other. It is a showdown in its classic sense, but because of its pivotal role in a greater context, Obi-Wan knows that his doom is sealed, as Darth Vader has already discerned the threat from Luke and R2-D2, who carries the plans of the Death Star in his memory banks.

Obi-Wan could not have escaped, and had to play the rearguard for an escaping army that is so celebrated in the stories of Roland, Paladins of the French King, or the tale of the Spartans who held back a massive Persian army. These tales never disparage the quality of the main body of the army, but illustrate that even the greatest commanders may find themselves in a defensive withdrawal. The *Song of Roland* is a paean to the greatest knights of the realm who sacrificed themselves for the greater good of the many. So, too, does Obi-Wan figure in a grander and more glorious tale. Obi-Wan, like the Paladins and Spartans, had to act as the rearward defense, which prevented a phalanx of stormtroopers from entering the docking bay in which the *Millennium Falcon* was parked.

Alec Guinness's climactic end remains to all Japanese swordsmen the greatest testament to their culture and style of swordsmanship. This duel certainly follows in the rich Hollywood tradition of the fencing duel interspersed with dialogue, but when both Obi-Wan and Darth Vader grip their lightsabers with two hands, there could be no other style of fencing than that of the Japanese samurai.

In the Obi-Wan/Vader duel there are no flashy tricks. Even Obi-Wan's only body twirl amounts to a very small departure from traditional kenjutsu and kendo. Attacks are made to the head or leg. One will attack first in a series of two or three attacks, alternating between the higher and lower targets. And then the other would respond in a similar way: head-head, head-head-leg, leg-head-head. Vader uses simple thrusts that Obi-Wan must deflect with circular parries. Accompanying Vader's small steps forward, Obi-Wan responds in kind by stepping back an equal number of steps to retain the proper fencing distance. A thrust forward without a step back places one's blade closer to his target while the other's weapon is still being used defensively. It is the perfect opportunity to attack, but also easily foiled by the simple act of maintaining distance.

You can see Diamond's Western fencing influence in the lightsaber fighting between Guinness and Prowse. Like the traditional fencing drill, an attack is met with a clear and obvious parry. The instructor makes an attack and the student responds in a simple, quick, and appropriate manner. A parry responds to an attack, which is followed by a counter-attack and then a counter-riposte in response to the instructor's parry-riposte. When an opening is given by the instructor, the student must extend toward the target and hit if there is no displacement or parry-riposte. This is the style of modern Western fencing, and not the Italian style in which an attack is met with a counter-attack that simultaneously beats away the attack. In Western fencing, the clarity of an attack and a response reflects the logic of the Enlightenment, the conventions governing the execution of proper technique are essential to mastering an art defined by the physics of a metallic blade.

In the last scene just before Obi-Wan raises his lightsaber in a transcendent salute, Vader slashes forward and moves deeply into Obi-Wan's space, forcing him to step to the side and then back in the place where Vader originally stood. This exchange of positions, necessary for Obi-Wan to avoid turning his back to his opponent, is a common tactical move during a traditional kendo competition in which the *kendoka* (a person who does kendo) circles around in the arena of the bout.

The stances of the two men are those of Japanese fencing called *chudan* (the middle stance), its point at eye level. The kendoka must look into the opponent's eyes to see his intention and determination; as the Western saying goes, the eyes are the windows into a person's soul. When the opponent blinks an eye or averts his gaze, that is the moment to attack. Poor and novice fencers unconsciously betray their intentions by moving their eyes to the area they are attacking. The expert need not see where he will attack, he only need know it.

Footwork is the key to proper upper body movement. Without it, the use of the sword will lack balance and the power of the lower body. Though the feet are hidden behind the folds of their robes, the experienced fencer must discern their opponent's footwork from the movements of his upper body, such as a tilt forward, a small step to the side, and the slight displacement in one direction. Though they may have lacked the power and speed of a strong swordsman, both Guinness and Prowse demonstrate a strong centered feeling in their footwork throughout their duel.

Were Obi-Wan and Vader holding real swords, their cuts would have had to have started from positions closer to the head. Obi-Wan would have had to raise his sword completely over his head, while Vader, because of his helmet, would have had to have lifted his sword to the left or right side of his face. More power is given to the cut, the higher the sword is held.

The short movement of the blade during the Episode IV duel is similar to the quick attacks from kendo that come from flicking the wrists. This attack is only to be used against an opponent's wrists where tendons and ligaments are easy to cut. So often are these feeble attacks made to the opponent's head during kendo bouts, that spectators assume this attack is a proper one. During *kakari-geiko* (attacking drills), a proper sensei requires that the student always raise his weapon completely over his or her head before attacking the upper body.

This kendo style of lightsaber fighting, with its short slashing movements is easily justified by the fact that the lightsaber requires less momentum to penetrate the skin and bones of an unarmored opponent. On the other hand, perhaps Luke might have been able to penetrate Vader's armor in Episode V if his cut to Vader's shoulder had more momentum.

On the whole, the sheer simplicity of the sword fight in Episode IV conveys a critical element of the story line — the sword may be the tool of the Jedi, but even in death, Obi-Wan, the symbol of good in the universe, will become more powerful than the agent of darkness. For the swordsman, the lack of dynamic movement illustrates their mastery of swordsmanship. No more energy than that of a single attack needs to be expended. With a single attack, the dispatch of an opponent is accomplished with minimal effort.

Very few people will ever have the opportunity to watch headmasters of separate dojos engage in friendly competition because the reputation and prestige of the instructor might be diminished by the superiority of one master over the other. Rarer still is the meeting between head instructors who were peers as children because senior students historically acted as surrogates for their masters in competitive matches, thus preserving face (of the masters) regardless of the outcome of any competitive match or combat. Headmasters are more likely to have tea than they are to train together. The president of the

All-Japan Kendo Federation makes regular trips to visit instructors around the country. Because of age, a dynamic energy is not evident in the movement of master swordsmen. Rather, only the slightest movement is made before an attack. Unlike junior fencers prodding and experimenting to discover their opponent's weakness, the master needs only find the opportunity to attack. Instead of a badgering movement to test an opponent, there is only the explosion of the attack. No effort is wasted. There is only the simple execution of extraordinary power and precision without distraction. The power and skill are so awesome that only a swordsman will fully appreciate the mastery of a teacher who tames the most limber and lightning speed of a kendoka in the vigor of his youth. It is not the crudeness of the muscles that allows the master to effortlessly trounce the cream of the student cadre, but the timing and simple execution of the most basic of techniques.

If Episode IV is a lesson to any swordsman, it is that the most skillful swordsmen are not they who can execute the most complex series of feints and attacks, but they who can execute the most basic attacks with impeccable timing. Technically, Dave Prowse and Alec Guinness will not be a model for real swordsmanship, but they do serve as exemplars of the ideal fencing style that is effective and dangerous, not ostentatious and effete.

Even Lucas misses the elementary sophistication of the sword fight when he says that we have only seen an old man and a half-human cyborg fighting with lightsabers. Peter Diamond gave Lucas the best example of true swordsmanship, which lacks the display of the sword fight in every other swashbuckling movie. In the life or death struggle of a fight, a victor is determined in minimal, not excessive movement. The greatest swordsman, in effect, need never resort to extravagant fencing because he can accomplish in a couple of simple steps what a lesser swordsman can only do after extreme physical exercise. The expert seems profoundly enigmatic to even the most experienced but naïve fencers because there is never enough opportunity to see the master execute a complicated series of movements. The truly experienced fencer will observe that the most sophisticated technique is the basic technique that was taught to the student on the first day of practice.

When the casual observer looks at the sword fight in Episode IV with the desire to be impressed with complicated action, he will walk away let down for not seeing the spectacle of the match. The mastery in technique is not in what one sees, but in what one does not see, which is the perfection of the most basic of moves. Mastery is so obvious that we are blind to its simplicity. No instructor can simply tell a student that mastery is accomplished by learning fundamentals. The student naturally desires to graduate to the complexity of advanced techniques. Successful swordsmanship, however, is not accomplished in complexity, but in simplicity, which is the very essence of the sword fight in Episode IV.

The duel between Obi-Wan and Vader accomplishes the several goals necessary in the script: establish the two men as Jedi Knights of an as-yet-to-be-explained order of warrior-monks, establish that one is the former master of the other, and pay homage to the ultimate personal sacrifice that assures a greater good can be accomplished. In Obi-Wan's death, the forces of goodness gain the final convert to their side. Luke understands that greatness is not found only in victory, but in disciplined sacrifice as well. From the moment Luke sees the fall of his mentor, he finally makes the commitment to repay the honor Obi-Wan has bestowed upon him when he was accepted by Obi-Wan as a student. There is no greater duty for the apprentice swordsman than to learn the wisdom that will allow him or her to become the great swordsman his master had always seen in his apprentice.

Episode V—Star Wars: The Empire Strikes Back—*Struggle Against the Leviathan*

Without question, the rite of passage of Episode V dominates the thematic tenor of the entire saga. It is a coming-of-age film for an individual whose very development and maturation are critical to the survival of the rebellion and the destruction of the Empire, which has reduced entire galaxies to its control. Dave Prowse calls Episode V a "thinking man's film," while the most devoted fans (and harshest critics) agree it is the most dramatic and poignant of the six episodes of the saga. Not only does the middle act provide the most important development of the story, it provides a chance for the swordsman to learn how the struggle in training is the only road to mastering the art of the fence. He must discover on his own that it is futile to desire mastery in swordsmanship. There is only training.

The movie opens ominously, with the empire amassing its forces just over the horizon. Invasion is imminent and it quickly becomes evident after the invasion has started that the Rebel Alliance is now a fugitive force on the run. By destroying an AT-AT walker with the assistance of his lightsaber, Luke does what he can to minimize the damage the empire can do to the rebellion, but upon his own escape, he knows he must follow Obi-Wan's command to seek out his own teacher Yoda. Departing from the original plan to rendezvous with the remnants of the rebel headquarters, Luke sets his destination for Dagobah.

From the first instant he crashes on the planet, Luke's every move is a test for a Jedi Master who has trained the greatest lightsaber swordsmen of the universe. Lurking in the undergrowth and watching from afar, Yoda observes the angry and impatient aspiring Jedi establish himself on the planet. Whining and endlessly fretting, Luke does not realize that his attitude is the greatest indication of his preparedness to begin his Jedi studies.

Appearing first as an insignificant denizen of the jungle forest, Yoda comically makes his appearance before Luke as a crazed and silly alien of insignificant bearing. "Wars not make one great," Yoda declares to Luke's desire to find a Jedi warrior. It is not too long before Yoda reveals himself to be the master that Luke is looking for. Not only has Luke failed to recognize his new teacher, he demonstrates with every child-like excuse that he is still a babe in the woods. The use of the lightsaber against an AT-AT walker hatch is hardly proof that he knows how to use the Jedi weapon. Nonetheless, Yoda takes Luke as a student and begins his Jedi training through the physical and mental conditioning of a full routine of anaerobic exercises as well as the honing of his telekinetic abilities.

Luke faces his first challenges when he enters the cave where he encounters a spectral Vader. Taking his weapons despite being commanded not to, Luke ignites his lightsaber and prepares to fight the Sith Lord who has killed his first mentor. Taking a classical kendo stance, there are simple attacks to the leg, the head, and then to Luke's side. In a moment of delay, Luke lashes out and decapitates his enemy. Vader's helmet falls to the ground and rolls to his feet. The mask's face explodes and Luke sees his own face, a premonition of things to come: Luke's potential to become the Sith Lord himself, as well as a thematic indication that Luke is of the same bloodline as Darth Vader.

Luke continues his training traipsing through the jungle with Yoda clinging to his back. He learns that the dark side is not more powerful than the light side, but easier, quicker, and more seductive. Early scripts had Luke practicing lightsaber deflection with seeker balls, but control of his telekinetic powers remain the essence of his mental training. Early in the movie in the wampa cave, Luke enjoys his first steps in his mastery of telekinesis by summoning his lightsaber through emptying his mind not by concentration, but by allowing his mind to become calm. On Dagobah, Luke must now use the Force to help him perform incredible acrobatic feats; to levitate objects, Luke unifies his body with his spirit so that the Force becomes more connected to his will. The Force controls the Jedi's actions, but it also obeys his command. The martial artist eventually learns that the best technique is one that is instinctive and in harmony with the mind and body rather than cognitive and therefore slower.

Luke's new heightened abilities in the Force also allow him to see visions of his friends Han and Leia, whose lives seem threatened unless Luke does something to save them. Foolishly, and arrogantly, he leaves his training without regard for himself and the fact that the torture of Han is a trap to bring Luke as a trophy to the Emperor. Though he promises he will return to his training, both Obi-Wan and Yoda fear that all the effort they have expended on Luke will be lost because again Luke demonstrates a defiant restlessness that brings him closer to the brink of oblivion.

Luke soon arrives at Bespin and quickly finds himself in the presence of

Darth Vader, who hopes to easily trap his son frozen in a protective slab of carbonite metal. As in the cave, Luke is the first to ignite his lightsaber and takes a confident stance against the former Jedi who killed his mentor Obi-Wan Kenobi. The lightsaber clash begins and it becomes evident early on that Darth Vader is the master of the two men. Luke attacks violently only to be quickly blocked by Vader wielding his lightsaber with a single hand. Starting out in chudan, Luke's attacks are made in vain against the leviathan Vader.

Vader attempts to end the duel quickly but is thwarted by Luke's ability to propel himself out of the carbonite freezing chamber. Luke regains some momentum and pushes Vader into a defensive posture, eventually knocking him down to a lower level of the smoke-filled room. Carefully, he descends to the next level and is confronted by Vader who lowers his lightsaber point and employs the Force to throw debris at Luke, who is powerless to fend off Vader's debilitating challenges. Luke is pulled out of the room when a metal casing smashes through an observation window. Clinging for dear life, Luke recovers his senses and re-enters the observation room only to be violently attacked by an increasingly enraged Vader. He charges powerfully at Luke with his lightsaber and pushes him out onto a gantry where Luke fights for his life.

With only one unsuccessful strike at Vader's neck, Luke is finally defeated when Vader cuts off Luke's hand at the wrist, sending his lightsaber falling down into the deep abyss of an interior reactor shaft of Cloud City. Vader offers him a place at his side, but Luke responds in the realization that his greatest duty now is to deny the Emperor the possibility of subverting his abilities to evil. Luke plunges himself over the edge in the sacrificing manner of Obi-Wan. Of course, Luke survives the ordeal, alive with the knowledge that his own father is responsible for the destruction of the Jedi Order.

Again, the script of the sword fight serves to carry out the plot of the movie. Luke takes his first steps in training to master his Jedi skills, and because he rushes out to use them before he has truly mastered them, Luke faces his utter defeat at the hands of his own father. Within the context of training in swordsmanship, Luke learns firsthand how knowledge of basic skills without the wisdom to use them well is as effective as not having any skills in the first place. Like the young fencer who sees an old man standing in front of him with a sword, he rushes headlong to his own defeat.

From the opening exchange, Vader uses the extremely difficult technique of catching and holding Luke's lightsaber immobile with his own lightsaber. With superior strength and leverage, Vader is able to quickly throw Luke back to the ground. Unscathed, Vader presses his fight, evening disarming Luke with a circular flourish of his blade. Luke's lightsaber flies from his hand in a turning motion, forcing him to retreat to a position where he can use the Force to summon his lightsaber.

After escaping the freezing chamber, Luke is able to regain the initiative by surprising Vader with the simple gymnastic ability to escape the carbonite freezing process. With smoke in his eyes, Vader's own arrogance is revealed in his contempt for the young boy. While the best swordsmen are technically superior to the less experienced, the uncertainty of swordsmanship lies in the creativity of the novice who is put in a position of recovering or dying. Vader succumbs to his own anger at not being able to more quickly defeat Luke. Uncontrollable emotion swells in Vader. As was the case with Obi-Wan in Episode I, anger allows Vader to once again dominate Luke. With punishing fury, Vader makes Luke retreat to a position where there is no hope. In one last attempt, Luke attacks Vader but is defeated by a simple circular control of the blade called a *prise de fer,* which pushes Luke's blade out of the way so Vader can cut to Luke's wrist.

The sword fight in Episode V best illustrates the spirit of the drama that is the sword fight duel. The sword fight in Episode V is the visual poetry of film. With the mesmerizing reds, blues, and whites of the freezing chamber, Vader and Luke become alluring silhouettes commanding the shimmering blades of their lightsabers. From the flowing twirl of Luke as he engages Vader's red lightsaber with his own green one, the colorful and delightful play of light frames the struggle of an aspiring swordsman against that of a master in his own right.

The self-assured confidence of Luke early in the fight is later replaced by the terror of defeat at Vader's hands. In a visual prelude to the climactic scenes in Episode VI, Vader sees Luke hanging off the edge of the metal gantry, leading to a renewed spirit against the aspirant Jedi. But Vader succumbs to arrogance, thinking that Luke is still a youth engaged in child's play. He gives in to anger, and as the Emperor had shown him since his early days under his tutelage, anger can and does lead to power. Vader's determination, fueled by his embarrassment at being temporarily bested by Luke, leads to his eventual domination of his opponent. It is this emotional struggle within (and between) Luke and Vader which colors each frame of the fight and enriches the choreography, reflecting the unseen struggle between swordsmen in a real fight. While the sword fight seems to last only seconds in the mind of the swordsman, the sword fight in Episode V endures in the minds of audiences through images on the silver screen.

During the filming of Episode VI, Richard Marquand was reported to have criticized the sword fighting in Episode V because it showed Vader fighting with a single hand. Peter Diamond responds, however, that the use of one hand and then the change over to the traditional style of using two hands was deliberate from the very beginning. Diamond brought in a trusted collaborator, Bob Anderson, who had vast knowledge and experience in sabre fighting in competition and in film, to dramatize the subtleties of the one-handed sword. Anderson says that Prowse was not equal to the challenge of the lightsaber fight in Episode V, but it is clear that Anderson does provide a stunning example of balance and control during his duel with Hamill.

Episode V certainly achieves the goals needed to prepare the world for the third and final stage of the Original Trilogy, the very climax of Lucas's *Star Wars* epic. Foreshadowed first by Luke's failure at the cave, Vader demonstrates that he is a more powerful force to be reckoned with than Luke could have ever imagined. Not only is Vader a superior swordsman, but he is also kith and kin, his own father whom he has never known. The mood is set to lure Luke under the sword of Damocles, and we, as an audience, are visually enticed and enthralled by the light play of lightsabers in the swirling world of smoke and the cavernous interior of Cloud City. Luke's rite of passage is his survival, as is that of the rebels who are fleeing the might of the empire.

Luke learns to understand firsthand that Vader is the embodiment of evil of the universe. He is tempted by Vader to embrace the dark side and take the mantle of an easy knighthood at the hands of his father. Luke is a powerful swordsman, but still in need of supervised training. So great is his potential that the Emperor has foreseen Luke's threat to his order. Vader, seeking to increase his own position by taking the Emperor's place, thinks he can corrupt his own son into following the path to the dark side. His hopes are set back when Luke, recognizing right from wrong, good from evil, denies Vader and the Emperor the means to even greater power in the universe. As long as Luke lives, the threat to the Galactic Empire still remains effective, though it hangs delicately by a thread.

The lesson for the swordsman is made clear by the easy fall of inexperience and an inflated view of one's ability to the demonstrable experience of a Sith Lord. No matter one's skill and enthusiasm, without the tools of mastered technique and the wisdom in its use, one's potentiality remains simply that — potentiality. When Luke is ready to return to his master to complete his training, he will again have the opportunity to redeem his first attempt. Until then, the potential Jedi Knight must simply focus on the daily drama of basic training and practice.

Episode VI — Star Wars: Return of the Jedi — *Epic Battle*

Since Lucas announced that he would not be making movies after Episode VI, Episode VI has become the battle royale in which the two-part arc of two trilogies culminates in the lightsaber battle at the end of the movie. The final episode is about the struggle between good and evil, the highest form of human drama. It is a conflict between son and father observed under the maleficent eyes of Satan incarnate. The sword fight is the cinematographer's perfect subject to showcase the fight between good and evil with which the human race must wrestle. Lucas's screenplay becomes a story not of mythology, but of epic that addresses the struggles of man pitted against man. *Star Wars* is not only about his own nature to do violence, but also the struggle of Man against technology, devices of his own creation that may in the end lead to his own destruction.

Luke and Vader confront each other in Episode VI, but the younger is now more mature after the chastening experience on Bespin. At the beginning of the movie, Luke demonstrates the ability to think like a Jedi instead of relying on impulses to dictate his actions. Even before he enters Jabba the Hutt's palace, Luke has already devised a two-part plan that will save himself as well as his closest friends.

Instead of an outright assault, Luke enters the palace in a face-to-face confrontation with Jabba. Leia has fallen into the Hutt's clutches, and by a freak accident he too becomes prisoner of the Tatooine gangster. Not to be caught completely off guard, Luke has hidden his lightsaber within Artoo, who shoots it out to Luke at the critical moment just before his execution.

Armed with his Jedi weapon, Luke begins his assault on the gangster's minions. He attacks them immediately and directly, cutting down attackers with a single stroke of his lightsaber. He thwarts Boba Fett's blaster fire and the extending rope that wraps around him. In accordance with a makeshift plan that seems hopeless until the last moment, Luke rescues Han and frees his friends while ridding the universe of the notorious Jabba the Hutt.

Now free, Luke returns to Yoda to complete the training he promised he would finish. Expecting to continue the physical practice of rigorous exercise and the honing of his Force powers, he meets Yoda, who is on his death bed ready to pass into the next life. He questions Yoda about the true identity of his father. Yoda confirms every fear Luke has contemplated since his encounter with Vader in Cloud City; Luke is indignant that he has been lied to about the identity of his father and bitter about his realization that both Obi-Wan and Yoda had always intended for him to battle and kill his father. In spectral form, Obi-Wan visits Luke and explains the true but simple facts relating to the way each person perceives the world. When Vader turned to the dark side, "He ceased to be Anakin and became Darth Vader."

There is no more training that will prepare Luke more for his meeting with Darth Vader. He has an inkling that there is still good within Vader. Obi-Wan and Yoda do not see the merit in Luke's perception of the reality, and with Luke's refusal to destroy his own father, the two Jedi Masters are resigned to accept that the Emperor has already won. But uncertain is the future, as Yoda so tersely puts it. In Episode V, Yoda alluded to the fact that there was another who could save them from the Emperor. The existence of Luke's sister Leia is finally divulged as Luke and Obi-Wan talk. With the possibility that Luke may perish or be turned to the dark side, there still exists the possibility that Leia may still be able to defeat the Emperor.

In the middle act of the movie, the heroes of the saga descend on Endor to destroy the shield that protects the Death Star II. Vader is on the star destroyer as the rebel lambda-class shuttle passes through the security zone surrounding the planet. Luke then realizes that Vader is aware of his presence and that he has jeopardized their mission. Before Vader can act, Luke hands himself over to Vader (and the Emperor), again in hopes of sacrificing himself for the sake of his friends. He speaks with his father and attempts to draw out the goodness of Vader who, while acknowledging the potential of the boy Jedi, hands Luke over to his master for his summary disposal. Where Vader failed in pulling Luke to the dark side, it is now the Emperor's turn.

The climactic end is a balancing act between the three battles: on Endor, out in space above the planet, and on the new Death Star. In the Emperor's throne room, Vader and Luke first engage in a battle of emotions as each of the dark lords tries to tempt Luke into joining their cause. Luke fights off his desire to strike out at the two Siths, as the rebel cause seems doomed from the very outset. At each step in the rebels' plans, the Emperor had foreseen its planning and had taken countermeasures to bring the rebellion and Luke onto his own doorstep so he could personally crush the Alliance once and for all. At last Luke succumbs and draws his lightsaber, frustrated by his inability to further help his friends. He ignites his lightsaber and slashes out at the Emperor only to be stopped by his father who has ignited his own lightsaber.

As the battles on the surface of Endor and the space above it turn ill for the side of light, Luke is now embroiled in a battle against the very man who had taken his own hand in their last encounter. Luke is a changed swordsman. He is controlled, calm, and in command of his emotions. His motivation to save his friends is clear and his battle, if it is to end with his death, may in the very least give his companions the opportunity to do what he could not do himself—destroy the second Death Star.

Luke fights well and dominates his father who seems helpless to stop his son's advances. "Obi-Wan has taught you well," Vader says after being knocked down by Luke, who, in response, shuts off his own lightsaber when he realizes that his hate for Vader and the Emperor is what is allowing him to defeat Vader. Luke feels the goodness within his father and challenges Vader to search deep inside himself for an answer. Vader responds by attacking, forcing Luke to retreat by leaping up toward a walkway high above them. Throwing his lightsaber, Vader causes Luke to fall into the lower level of the throne room.

Outside the Death Star, the battle goes against the rebellion and Luke is left hanging, hoping yet that his friends will be able to succeed.

Back in the Emperor's high tower chambers, Vader begins his search for Luke in the darkness of the lower level. He reads Luke's mind and finally realizes that Luke has a sister who Vader might yet be able to turn to the dark side. Enraged at the thought of losing his sister to the Emperor, Luke screams out and attacks Vader with a ferocity Vader has never before seen. Driving him back, Luke lashes out in a punishing fury until he cuts Vader's hand from his arm, as had befallen Luke in Episode V. Upon realizing that the tide has turned back in his own favor, Luke now comes to understand that in order to become powerful, he has become what he most despises in his father. In order to defeat his father, he has to become like his father. The symbolism of Luke's prosthetic hand echoes in his mind as an epiphany reveals that the power to do evil is within is own actions.

The drama of the climax has been masterfully played out in Lucas's script and receives its final performance in the editing room. He creates a pinnacle to the trilogy in which light and darkness are pitted against each other in a sword fight to end all sword fights. At last, the final irony of Luke's training reveals itself—you cannot use evil to destroy evil. It only supplants one evil for another.

In the final moments of the lightsaber scene, Luke makes the greatest statement any swordsman can ever make. He tosses aside his lightsaber. Power does not reside in his weapon, but within his heart when the goodness of his being is best expressed in his love for his family—Leia—and his friends, Han and Chewbacca, as well as the entire Rebel Alliance. In his willingness to sacrifice his own life in order to save others as Obi-Wan had done for him, Luke makes a discovery that some swordsmen never learn. At that very moment when he dispenses with his lightsaber, Luke becomes what he has always aspired to achieve. Never would he have guessed that it had nothing to do with his lightsaber, but with what becomes of his heart. Without his lightsaber, Luke becomes a Jedi Master.

Afterword

Long before the world saw the final installments of the *Star Wars* universe, it became clear that the swordsman's tale in a galaxy far, far away ... was one of an epic story of man. While myths explain the pseudo-religious origins of a universe controlled by the externalities of the gods and the omnipresence of unbridled nature, Lucas's story of swordsmen tells of the conflict of humanity as it continually weighs the needs of a peaceful society and the need of protectors capable of violence against those who would subvert the desire for order, personal growth, and spiritual development.

Lucas's epic is the story of our own development in a universe where the human being is the measure of all things. Instead of being the subject of the unpredictable whims of the gods, man raises his quest for inner peace to mythic proportions. *Star Wars* is the story of good versus evil, not of the world around us, but of the greedy and selfish desires within us. The conflict is between the quests for spirituality, self-fulfillment, wholeness, contentment, and the threats of fear, desperation, domination, and extinction.

Society seeks stability and equilibrium for the possibility of growth and development. The chaos of disorder threatening this peace requires that we protect ourselves from inner and outer destruction. Therein is the call of the Jedi in Lucas's fictitious universe — the need for peace and the need for the tools of violence to safeguard the peace. The Jedi must know the desires of the heart, but they also subordinate personal desires for the greater good of others. They also know the risk of using the skills of violence for abuse or oppression. This must never come to pass. Ultimately, the swordsman's reliance on the sword, like the Jedi's reliance on the lightsaber, is a state of being that may be necessary to assure the obtainment of peace and justice.

The swordsman's life in the heat of battle is grievously short, serving as an imperative to live one's life as fully as possible. When called upon to protect and serve others, the swordsman may use his weapon to further that greater end. But when the very evil nature of men and women confronts our very soul, throwing down the sword is the highest example of a what Aristotle called the "good life." If it were possible to defeat evil by resorting to violence, evil would never be truly conquered, but merely supplanted. When Luke throws down his lightsaber, a way of life dependent on the goodness of the heart and a purity of purpose becomes the ultimate goal of the Jedi. The sword, once an outdated and violent tool, becomes a symbol of that good life. Through effort, discipline, and the influence of an experienced master, swordsmanship becomes a means for inner peace, inner spirituality, and represents a positive and hopeful belief in our humanity. This is the goal of the Jedi Knights and their fabled shimmering sword.

Chapter Notes

Chapter 1

1. The concept of honor may seem to apply to those who carry any weapon, but the regulation of present-day, gun-carrying constabularies stems from duties and obligations associated with the performance of their duties as a professional, not from being part of a brotherhood of melee combatants.

2. Max Boot speaks of two types of determinism that impact war: technological determinism ("What can be done, will be done") and psychological determinism ("Where there's a will, there's a way"). The swordsman is not predetermined to use his sword simply because he possesses it or is capable of using it effectively. Nor is he predetermined to rule others simply because he has the ability. Luke Skywalker's decision to throw away his lightsaber is George Lucas's testament to this idea. Max Boot, *War Made New: Technology, Warfare, and the Course of History 1500 to Today* (New York: Gotham, 2006), p. 9.

3. Inazo Nitobe's *Bushido* and Tsunetomo Yamamoto's *Hagakure* made a notable impact on early interpretations of the concept of bushido to Westerners. Nitobe's intellectual comparison of Japanese thought to Western philosophy and history was an attempt to explain (if not justify) many samurai-related concepts like *seppuku* that seemed repugnant to the West. In many ways, he succeeded in elevating bushido to a level equivalent to the West's chivalry. The *Hagakure* is a collection of writings by a samurai who did not fight in any great war. His perspective is one of a samurai seeking to preserve many of the ideals of the past in his peaceful era. A critique of Nitobe's work can be found in Minoru Kiyota, *The Shambhala Guide to Kendo* (Boston & London: Shambhala, 2002), pp. 99–104.

4. It is interesting to note that in Japan Zen Buddhism is less associated with kendo than it is in the West. English translations (writings by Daisetz Suzuki in particular) have reinforced the perception that Japanese sword fighting and Zen are inextricably linked. Most Japanese practice kendo as a sport rather than as a religious activity.

5. Michel de Montaigne, trans. George B. Ives, "That to Think as a Philosopher Is to Learn to Die," *The Essays of Michel de Montaigne* (New York: Heritage, 1925), p. 111.

6. Montaigne 123.

7. Montaigne 123.

Chapter 2

1. J.R. Hale, *War and Society in Renaissance Europe, 1450–1620* (Baltimore: Johns Hopkins University Press, 1985), pp. 22–29.

2. Hale 22.

3. George Lucas on MSNBC's *Time & Again*, May 6, 1999.

4. Paula Parisi, "Grand Illusion," *Wired*, May 1999: 137–39; George Lucas on MSNBC's *Time & Again*, May 6, 1999.

5. Victor Davis Hanson, *Ripples of Battle: How Wars of the Past Still Determine How We Fight, How We Live, and How We Think* (New York: Doubleday, 2003), p. 213.

6. David B. Ralston, *Importing the European Army: The Introduction of European Military Techniques and Institutions into the Extra-European World, 1600–1914* (Chicago: University of Chicago Press, 1990), pp. 108, 125.

7. Philippe Contamine, trans. Michael Jones, *War in the Middle Ages* (New York: B. Blackwell, 1984), pp. 264–65.

8. John A. Lynn, *Battle: A History of Combat and Culture* (Cambridge, MA: Westview, 2003), pp. 359–69.

9. "Maréchal" in the *Dictionnaire d'étymologie française* (Bruxelles: Libraire de la Cour, 1873), pp. 289–90.

10. Onasander in the first century A.D. said that a general "can aid his army far less by fighting than he can harm it if he should be killed, since the knowledge of a general is far more important than his physical strength" (33.1), p. 109. Harry Sidebottom, *Ancient Warfare: A Very Short Introduction* (Oxford: Oxford University Press, 2004), p. 108.

11. Max Boot, *War Made New: Technology, Warfare, and the Course of History, 1500 to Today* (New York: Gotham, 2006), p. 59. Contamine refutes this assertion as a result of the emphasis writers of the day put on individual action. He said, "Simple combatants as well as leaders and governing authorities had a clear idea of the potential dangers of the achievements of one isolated champion.... The custom was not simply to place in the front rank the best soldiers, chosen individually, or young, newly dubbed knights, but also a body of troops whose reputation for communal valour was well established—like the Templars or Hospitallers, for example, during the Crusades, or again, in the wars in the Empire, the Swabians who from the battle of the Unstrut in 1075 claimed for themselves the first place in battle (*primatus pugnae*)," p. 254.

12. Robert D. Kaplan, *Warrior Politics: Why Leadership Demands a Pagan Ethos* (New York: Random House, 2002).

13. Jerome Miller, *The Way of Suffering: A Geography of Crisis* (Washington, DC: Georgetown University Press, 1988), pp. 87–88.

14. The 1997 Air and Space Museum of the Smithsonian Institution exhibit was premised on the concept of *Star Wars* as myth. Mary Henderson, Star Wars*: The Magic of Myth* (New York: Bantam Books, 1997). The making of *Attack of the Clones* book by Jody Duncan was entitled: Star Wars *Mythmaking: Behind the Scenes of* Attack of the Clones (New York: Ballantine, 2002).

15. George Lucas interview by Bill Moyers, "Of Myth and Men," *Time*, April 29, 1999, p. 89. Moyers accepts Campbell's assertions about the universality of myths with as much (i.e., little) critical perspective as he accepts Lucas's assertions. After the two had met some time after 1983, Lucas became directly associated with the Joseph Campbell Foundation, serving as a past member of its board of trustees, which implicitly means Lucas was a financial donor to Campbell's cause. The ties between Campbell, who died in 1987, and Lucas were so strong that the interviews for the PBS series were filmed at Lucas's Skywalker Ranch in 1985 and 1986.

16. George Lucas interviewed by B. Love, "George Lucas: The Well Rounded Interview." Well-rounded.com. 11 May 1999. <http://www.well-rounded.com/movies/lucas_intv.html>.

17. This example may actually defend David Brin's accusation that the simplistic storyline of *Star Wars* has actually dumbed down the science-fiction genre. See "Charge #3: *Star Wars* novels are poor substitutes for real science fiction and are driving real SF off the shelves," pp. 135–82. Simplicity of story in the *Star Wars* franchise can also be captured in a corporate motto regarding the focus of The Force Unleashed video game: "Kicking someone's ass with the Force." Cf. Video: "Unleashing the Force Part 1: The New Beginning" Starwars.com. Released 25 May 2007. <http://www.starwars.com/gaming/videogames/news/tfudoc01.html>.

18. Michael Kaminski, *The Secret History of* Star Wars, Version 2.0 (www.thesecrethistoryofstarwars.com, 2007), pp. 201-05.

19. Marching workers look like clone troopers in Episode II; the subterranean and surface city look like the interiors of the the Death Star and Coruscant.

20. *THX: 1138*, with its mechanistically controlled and monitored population, draws heavily from *Metropolis*.

21. The implication is that the cathedral, from which the inventor Rotwang is thrown, is meant to make the masses docile, while the

underground church in which Maria compares Metropolis to Babel—constructions in which their conceivers exploit their workers and live a life of decadent luxury — is the true way to save Man from his oppression.

22. Contamine 269–70.

23. Contamine 42.

24. Contamine 269.

25. Interestingly, a pacifist subtext was added to the role of the Jedi in the movie. In various comic storylines, there were Jedi who felt ill-prepared to handle the responsibility of fighting in the Clone Wars and either refused to fight, left the order, or joined Count Dooku and the Separatists. From a corporate perspective, this leaves artistic room for the creation of future "dark" Jedi in comic books, the animated TV series, and the live-action drama.

26. "Of Myth and Men: A Conversation between Bill Moyers and George Lucas on the Meaning of the Force and the True Theology of *Star Wars*," *Time*, April 26, 1999, p. 92.

27. "That's why I hesitate to call the Force God. It's designed primarily to make young people think about the mystery." *Time* 93.

28. The trinity is not a concept universally accepted by all Christians.

29. Dale Pollock, *Skywalking: The Life and Films of George Lucas* (New York: Harmony, 1983), p. 141.

30. See David Brin, "'Star Wars' Despots vs. 'Star Trek' Populists," Salon.com, 29 October 2007. <http://www.salon.com/ent/movies/feature/1999/06/15/brin_main/index.html>.

31. "Adepts learn to harmonize their ki with that of the opponents, so that the aura of the opponent's ki touches on their own. Changes in the flow of an opponent's ki — as when he contemplates attacks or other action — are said to oscillate against the adept's aura, enabling him to read the opponent's movements before they become physically perceptible by other means." Karl F. Friday with Humitake Seki, *Legacies of the Sword: The Kashima-Shinryu and Samurai Martial Culture* (Honolulu, University of Hawai'i Press, 1997), p. 84.

32. Diane Morgan, *The Best Guide to Eastern Philosophy and Religion* (Los Angeles: Renaissance, 2001), p. 162.

33. Howard Reid, *The Way of the Warrior* (London: Eddison/Sadd, 1983), pp. 124, 140; p. 138 for illustration of hand signs.

34. Diane Morgan, *The Best Guide to Eastern Philosophy and Religion* (Los Angeles: Renaissance, 2001), p. 131.

35. The basic difference between the "unifying Force" and the "living Force" can be gleaned from Terry Brooks's novelization of Episode I. Terry Brooks. *Star Wars: Episode I The Phantom Menace* (New York: Lucas, 1999), pp. 137-38.

36. "Chosen One Documentary," *Star Wars Episode III: Revenge of the Sith*, Disc 2, 12:39.

37. Laurent Bouzereau, Star Wars: *The Annotated Screenplays* (New York: Ballantine, 1997), p. 300.

38. "Chosen One Documentary," *Episode III* DVD, Disc 2, Anakin as victim, 3:01; Anakin as hero, 12:39.

39. James Lawler, "The Force Is with *Us:* Hegel's Philosophy of Spirit Strikes Back at the Empire," Star Wars *and Philosophy* (Chicago: Open Court, 2005), pp. 144–56.

40. See Charge #2 in Star Wars *on Trial*— "While claiming mythic significance, *Star Wars* portrays no admirable religious or ethical beliefs." pp. 97–134.

41. Star Wars *and Philosophy*, edited by Kevin S. Decker and Jason T. Eberl, and *The Science of* Star Wars, by Jeanne Cavelos, and *Using the Force*, by Will Brooker are the most academic explorations of *Star Wars*.

42. Terry Brooks, *Star Wars Episode I: The Phantom Menace* (New York: Ballantine Books, 1999), p. 27.

43. Judith Barad, "The Aspiring Jedi's Handbook of Virtue," Star Wars *and Philosophy* (Chicago: Open Court, 2005), pp. 57–68.

44. See "Charge #1: The Politics of *Star Wars* are Anti-democratic and Elitist," Star Wars *on Trial* (Dallas: Benbella, 2006), pp. 81–95.

45. Gordon A. Craig, *The Politics of the Prussian Army 1640–1945* (New York: Oxford University Press, 1964), p. 300.

46. Ryder Windham, Star Wars: *The Ultimate Visual Guide* (New York: DK, 2005), p. 28.

47. John Warry, *Warfare in the Classical World* (New York: St. Martin's, 1980), p. 115.

48. David B. Ralston, *Importing the European Army: The Introduction of European*

Military Techniques and Institutions into the Extra-European World, 1600–1914 (Chicago: University of Chicago Press, 1990), pp. 52–54.

49. Contamine 99.

50. Contamine 150.

51. Dave Lowry's book *Autumn Lightning: The Education of an American Samurai* (Boston: Shambhala, 1985) provides informative and entertaining recounts of his experience with Yagyu training.

52. Daisetsu Suzuki, *Zen and Japanese Culture* (Princeton, NJ: Princeton University Press, 1959, 1989), p. 126.

53. Thomas Cleary, *Soul of the Samurai* (North Claredon, VT: Tuttle, 2005), p. 31.

54. Suzuki 148.

55. Karl F. Friday with Humitake Seki, *Legacies of the Sword: The Kashima-Shinryu and Samurai Martial Culture* (Honolulu: University of Hawai'i Press, 1997), p. 84.

56. Friday 85.

57. George Lucas, "Commentary," *Star Wars Episode III: Revenge of the Sith* DVD, Twentieth Century–Fox, 2005.

58. George Lucas in "Becoming Sidious," Webdoc. *Star Wars Episode III: Revenge of the Sith* DVD, 2005.

59. The ability to hit an opponent with a sword can be explained as the attacker's ability to move faster toward a target or to hit where the defender did not expect an attack. Conversely, a defender may know exactly where an attack will be made but cannot physical move to defend it.

60. The 2007 television program "Secrets of the Samurai," created by the PBS show Nova, shows footage of a swordsman able to cut through an arrow before it can strike him.

61. See David Brin, "'Star Wars' Despots vs. 'Star Trek' Populists," Salon.com. 15 June 1999. <www.salon.com/ent/movies/feature/1999/06/15/brin_main/index.html>.

62. George Lucas, *Star Wars* (New York: Ballantine, 1976), p. 1. Alan Dean Foster is openly acknowledged as the author of the novelization text.

63. Ryder Windham, Star Wars: *The Ultimate Visual Guide* (New York: DK, 2005), p. 31.

64. Windham 42. Another allusion to term limits is found in the Episode II novelization (2002 ed., p. 49) in which Chancellor Palpatine praises Amidala's belief in term limits even though he believes she could have been elected queen for life.

65. R.A. Salatore, *Star Wars Episode II: Attack of the Clones* (New York: Ballantine, 2002), pp. 310–13.

66. George Lucas has clearly indicated in interviews that *Star Wars*, while intended for younger audiences, does have undercurrents that criticize the Republican party in America (he criticizes Nixon's abuse of power and the Vietnam War; the leader of the military-industrial complex Neimoidians—Gunray—is Reagan syllabically reversed). Conservative commentators have also used the *Star Wars* saga to represent their perspective. For conservatives, the "evil empire" refers to the totalitarian regime of the Soviet Union, which President Ronald Reagan referred to in his 1982 speech to the British House of Commons. Ironically, it was Senator Edward Kennedy who later referred to Reagan's Strategic Defense Initiative (SDI), a defense system set in space to destroy incoming intercontinental ballistic missiles before they hit their target, as a "Star Wars" fantasy. Lucas went to court to stop the tendency of governmental officials to use SDI and *Star Wars* interchangeably.

Star Wars references have become so ingrained in the common culture of American discourse that internal references to the saga turn up at all levels. The perpetrators of the Enron scandal in 2001 used references to *Star Wars* in their illegal dealings. Some entities they created include: The Joint Energy Development Investment LP (JEDI LP), Chewco Investments LP, Kenobe Inc., and Obi-1 Holdings LLC. In the Pentagon, military officials referred to Albert Wholstetter (the advocate responsible for the modern emphasis on "discriminating offensive strategies" that relied on the creation of remotely targeted smart bombs) as Yoda because he had a quiet and unassuming personality (Cf. Bacevich 161–62).

Mark Wegierski makes a radical assertion in his article entitled "Reagan: Jedi Knight" that the evil empire was the Soviet Union. (Cf. Mark Wegierski, "Reagan: Jedi Knight," *World*. Worldmag.com. 22 May 1999. <http://www.worldmag.com/world/issue/05-22-99/cover_3.asp>) So broad are the characters and so applicable to any number of political situations that academics assert that *Star Wars* is a "myth," or that the *Star Wars* saga is a parallel of D.W. Griffith's *Birth of a Nation*. (Cf. Charles Ealy, "Understanding *Star Wars*," *Dallas Morning News*, 9 May 1999. <http://dallasmorningnews.com/sunday-reader-nf/reader14.htm>).

Chapter 3

1. Takuan Soho, trans. William Scott Wilson, *The Unfettered Mind* (Tokyo: Kodansha International, 1986), pp. 58–59.
2. Dave Lowry, *Autumn Lightning: The Education of an American Samurai* (Boston: Shambhala, 1985), pp. 5–8.
3. Karl F. Friday with Humitake Seki, *Legacies of the Sword: The Kashima-Shinryu and Samurai Martial Culture* (Honolulu, University of Hawai'i Press, 1997), p. 55.
4. "Takuan was known for fearlessness in his dealings with worldly powers, and this is reflected in his forthright advice to Yagyu Munenori, who was by then sword master to the shogun and chief of the shogun's secret police. Takuan was the Zen teacher of an emperor, shogun, and a number of feudal lords, but he also refused the patronage of certain powerful warlords and retired from the abbacy of the highest ranked Zen monastery in Japan just three days after his debut. After the military government imposed its own regulations on the Zen orders, Takuan was sent into exile for four years for criticizing these rules as inconsistent with the reality of Zen." Munenori Yagyu, trans. Thomas Cleary, *Soul of the Samurai* (North Clarendon, VT: Tuttle, 2005), p. 141.
5. Karl F. Friday insists that a teacher is a "model and guide" and not "lecturer or conveyor of information." "Bugei teachers lead students along the path to mastery of their arts — they do not tutor them." Friday 100.
6. Dale Pollock, *Skywalking* (New York: Harmony, 1983), p. 83.
7. Dave Lowry, *Autumn Lightning* (Boston: Shambhala, 1985), pp. 130–31.
8. Comment made by Greg Angus, Nick Jamilla's personal aikido journal, 1991–95.
9. Eugene Herrigal, *Zen in the Art of Archery* (New York: Vintage, 1999), p. 39.
10. Friday 107–8.
11. Friday 100.

Chapter 4

1. The references to precedents in this chapter offer comparisons of reality to Lucas's fictional universe. Lucas's eclectic approach to the creation of his universe reflects a writer's and director's perspective on the exposition. Almost nowhere is there a one-to-one correlation of a concept that stays consistent with the real world. Instead of saying the Jedi are the Templars of Europe and the Holy Lands, Lucas pulls from both the reality of religious orders of knighthood (Jedi as sword-armed religious servants) and the fictional world of King Arthur (the High Jedi Council arrayed in a circular fashion like the fabled round table) whereever it suited the storyline. Like Tolkien, who publicly resisted the idea that the Free People of Middle-Earth represent the West and the forces of Sauron the Soviet bloc of post–World War II politically divided Europe, Lucas refuses to be termed an allegorist. Lucas's notes and interviews reveal that he rarely attributes particular ideas from reality. While he has mentioned specific influences such as Akira Kurosawa's *Hidden Fortress* — "I was looking for the lowest person on the pecking order [R2 and 3PO], basically like the farmers in *Hidden Fortress* were" (Star Wars *Annotated Screenplays*, p. 9) — there is no mention that Lucas borrowed a specific idea for the Jedi Knights from the Japanese *Sohei* or the Janissaries. The examples in this chapter are *precedents* in that they historically preceded Lucas's treatment of *Star Wars* and are the best instances of the connection between historical warriors and the fictional Jedi Knights.
2. The Catholic catechism says hermits "devote their life to the praise of God and salvation of the world through a stricter separation from the world, the silence of solitude and assiduous prayer and penance" (920). <http://www.vatican.va/archive/catechism/p123a9p4.htm#III>.
3. An Internet source on hermetic life from various faiths can be found at www.hermitary.com.
4. Keith Randell, *The Catholic and Counter Reformations* (London: Hodder & Stoughton, 1990), p. 15.
5. Randell 71–92.
6. G.B. Sansom, *The Western World and*

Japan (Tokyo: Charles E. Tuttle, 1990), pp. 152–64.

7. Muslims, from their perspective, saw invaders from Europe establishing bridgeheads that would eventually lead to their own enslavement or death.

8. Some priests circumvented this rule by using the bludgeoning mace. Others like Pope Julius and Cardinal Richelieu actually carried a sword on their person.

9. Oscar Ratti and Adele Westbrook, *Secrets of the Samurai* (Rutland, VT: Charles E. Tuttle, 1991), p. 138.

10. Karl F. Friday with Humitake Seki, *Legacies of the Sword: The Kashima-Shinryu and Samurai Martial Culture* (Honolulu: University of Hawai'i Press, 1997), p. 121.

11. Ratti and Westbrook 138.

12. Stephen Turnbull, *Japanese Warrior Monks AD 949–1603* (Oxford: Osprey, 2003), pp. 50–51.

13. Turnbull 51.

14. Turnbull 19–20.

15. Bernard Lewis, *Race and Slavery in the Middle East* (Oxford: Oxford University Press, 1994). <http://www.fordham.edu/halsall/med/lewis1.html>.

16. John Keegan, *A History of Warfare* (New York: Vintage, 1993), pp. 32–40.

17. David B. Ralston, "The Reform of the Ottoman Army, 1750–1914," *Importing the European Army: The Introduction of European Military Techniques and Institutions into the Extra-European World, 1600–1914* (Chicago: University of Chicago Press, 1990).

Chapter 5

1. Gunther E. Rothenberg, *The Art of Warfare in the Age of Napoleon* (Bloomington: Indiana University Press, 1978), p. 141.

2. Theresa Urbainczyk, *Sparticus* (London: Bristol Classical, 2004), pp. 19–35, 51–80.

3. A. A. Levin, et al., *Microstructure of a Genuine Damascus Sabre* (Weinheim, Germany: Wiley-Vch Verlag GmbH & Co. KGaA, 2005). <http://www.crystalresearch.com/crt/ab40/905_a.pdf>. 25 November 2007.

4. Leon and Hiroko Kapp and Yoshindo Yoshihara, *The Craft of the Japanese Sword* (Tokyo: Kodansha International, 1987), pp. 29–32.

5. Jeanne Cavelos suggests plasma might be a reasonable substance from which to construct a real lightsaber. Jeanne Cavelos, *The Science of* Star Wars (New York: St. Martin's, 1999), pp. 171–75.

6. The grammar and punctuation of the statement show two independent statements. While the two are related in proximity, the second statement is not contingent on the first. First, a lightsaber has been constructed. Second, Luke's skills are complete. The statement does not say or imply that Luke has created a lightsaber, and *therefore*, his skills are complete, which would indicate that a Jedi's skills are a function of the ability to create a lightsaber. Similarly, Luke's statement at the end of Episode VI when he throws down his lightsaber—"I am a Jedi"—gives further support. If the use of a lightsaber is not required in the creation of a Jedi, then logically it follows that the creation of a lightsaber is not required.

7. Jude Watson, *Jedi Quest: Path to Truth* (New York: Scholastic, 2001), pp. 32–41.

8. George Lucas, *Star Wars* (New York: Ballantine, 1976), p. 79.

9. See <http://www.starwars.com/databank/technology/lightsaber/index.html>. 25 November 2007.

10. A good discussion on the weights of European swords can be found in John Clements's article "What Did Historical Swords Weigh?" <http://www.thearma.org/essays/weights.htm.> 25 November 2007.

11. John Clements, *Medieval Swordsmanship: Illustrated Methods and Techniques* (Boulder, CO: Paladin, 1998), pp. 76–84.

12. Henry de Sainct Didier's *Traicté* (Paris, 1573). See William Gaugler, *History of Fencing: Foundations of Modern European Swordplay* (Bangor, ME: Laureate, 1997), pp. 22–26.

13. Gaugler 50.

14. Of stylistic note is the manner of teaching theatrical fencing with a double-edged sword. Since, for the sake of safety, the quality of theatrical weapons should always be considered suspect, a guard parry should always be received with the edge of the blade so that the force is absorbed by the strength of the steel. A strike on the flat may stress the

blade so much that the defending sword might break in half from a strong slash. Since the theatrical edge is never sharpened, more concern involves flying fragments than chipping an edge of a blade.

15. John Clements, "The Myth of Edge-on-Edge Parrying in Medieval Swordplay," The Association for Renaissance Martial Arts website. 13 November 2007. <http://www.thearma.org/essays/edgemyth.htm>. Also, John Clements, "Edges of Knowledge: Parrying with a Cutting Sword," The Association for Renaissance Martial Arts website. 13 November 2007. <http://www.thearma.org/essays/parry.htm>. "Edge Parrying vs. Flat Parrying" 13 November 2007. <http://swordforum.com/sfu/swordsmanship/parrying.html>.

16. Gaugler 277.

17. Hank Reinhardt, "There Is No 'Best Sword,'" The Association for Renaissance Martial Arts webpage. 13 November 2007. <http://www.thehaca.com/essays/nobest.htm>.

18. H.W.B. Po and F. Po, "Sword" (1911). In *The Encyclopedia Britannica,* 11th Edition, Vol. 26 (Cambridge, England: Cambridge University Press), pp. 269–74.

19. See "Collective Equipment and Uniforms" in Philippe Contamine (trans. Michael Jones), *War in the Middle Ages* (Oxford, England: Basil Blackwell, 1986), pp. 188–92. Also, "Insignia, Uniforms, and Equipment" in Geoffrey Parker, *The Cambridge Illustrated History of Warfare: The Triumph of the West* (Cambridge, England: Cambridge University Press, 1995), pp. 151–52.

20. Victor Davis Hanson, *Ripples of Battle: How Wars of the Past Still Determine How We Fight, How We Live, and How We Think* (New York: Doubleday, 2003), pp. 193–94.

21. Adrian Goldsworthy, *Roman Warfare* (New York: Smithsonian, 2002), pp. 58, 134, 139, 168.

22. Malcolm Vale, *War and Chivalry* (Athens: University of Georgia Press, 1981), p. 105.

23. C.W.C. Oman, *The Art of War in the Middle Ages: A.D. 378–1515* (Ithaca, NY: Cornell University Press, 1953), pp. 126–27.

24. Michael S. Drake, *Problematics of Military Power: Government, Discipline and the Subject of Violence* (London: Frank Cass, 2001), p. 199.

25. For descriptions of medieval shields and techniques employing the shield and sword, see John Clements, *Medieval Swordsmanship: Illustrated Methods and Techniques* (Boulder, CO: Paladin, 1998), pp. 87–178.

26. Philippe Contamine, *War in the Middle Ages* (New York: Basil Blackwell, 1984), p. 177.

27. Laurent Bouzereau, Star Wars*: The Annotated Screenplays* (New York: Ballantine, 1997), p. 278.

28. See Karen Traviss and Ryan Kaufman, "Guide to the Grand Army of the Republic," Star Wars *Insider*, Issue 84, November-December 2005, pp. 24–31.

29. "Pour les 30 000 autres combattants, il s'agirait de hallebardiers et surtout de piquiers, selon une proportion qu'a soine de précise la *Familière institution pour les légionnaires en suivant les ordonnances faites sur ce par le roi composée nouvellement* (Lyon, 1536): "En mille homes (selon l'ordonnance), it doit y avoir 603 piques, 80 hallebardes et 300 arquebuses, n'y étant comptés le capitaine, ses lieutenants, enseignes, fourriers, sergents, tambourins, et fifres, qui sont en tout 17." Philippe Contamine, editor. *Histoire militaire de la France* (Paris: Presses universitaires de France, c.1992–c.1994), p. 251.

30. Translated as "finishers off of the unhorsed."

31. Malcolm Vale, *War and Chivalry* (Athens: University of Georgia Press, 1981), p. 124.

32. J.F. Vergrugger, trans. Samner Willard and S.C.M. Southern, *The Art of Warfare in Western Europe during the Middle Ages* (New York: North-Holland, 1977), pp. 50–52.

33. Vale 124–25.

34. David B. Ralston, *Importing the European Army: The Introduction of European Military Techniques and Institutions into the Extra-European World, 1600–1914* (Chicago: University of Chicago Press, 1990), p. 150.

Chapter 6

1. Peter Diamond, who created the lightsaber fighting in the Original Trilogy, recollects, "George said, 'I've got these laser swords — I don't want broadswords and I

don't want fencing. I want it somewhere in between.'" J.W. Rinzler, *The Making of* Star Wars (New York: Ballantine, 2007), p. 194.

2. Michael D. Coe, et al. *Swords and Hilt Weapons* (New York: Weidenfeld & Nicholson, 1989), pp. 44–50.

3. John Clements, *Renaissance Swordsmanship: The Illustrated Use of Rapiers and Cut-and-Thrust Swords* (Boulder, CO: Paladin, 1997).

4. B.W. Robinson, *The Arts of the Japanese Sword* (London: Faber and Faber, 1961), pp. 16–17.

5. G. Cameron Hurst III, *Armed Martial Arts of Japan* (New Haven & London: Yale University Press, 1998), pp. 17–22.

6. Victor Harris and Nobuo Ogasawara, *Swords of the Samurai* (London: British Museum, 1990), pp. 58–60.

7. Jedi is derived from the Japanese word for "age/period."

8. Hurst 82–100.

9. G. Cameron Hurst III includes a footnote that questions the impact of Zen on Japanese swordsmanship: "Eugen Herrigel, (*Zen in the Art of Archery)*, and D.T. Suzuki, (*Zen and Japanese Culture*), 87–214, are perhaps the two authors most responsible for creating the association of the bugei with Zen. Most subsequent works on the bugei seem to have accepted this association rather uncritically, discussing at length the nature of Zen and why it ought to have appealed to the samurai, but never questioning whether or not it actually *did* have a widespread influence on the bugei prior to modern times. Thus studies like Donn F. Draeger, *Classical Budo,* and Oscar Ratti and Adele Westbrook, *Secrets of the Samurai*—both standard volumes on the shelves of martial arts aficionados—exemplify this epistomological blind spot, while two more recent books, Thomas Cleary, *The Japanese Art of War*, and Winston L. King, *Zen and the Way of the Sword*, virtually reify it, depicting Zen as the heart and soul of samurai martial culture.

Far better perspectives on the intersection of Zen with samurai tradition are provided in E.J. Harrison, *Fighting Spirit*, 140–152; Martin Collcutt, *Five Mountains: The Rinzai Zen Monastic Institution in Medieval Japan*; and G. Cameron Hurst, *The Armed Martial Arts of Japan*. John P. Keenan, "Spontaneity in Western Martial Arts: a Yogacara Critique of Mushin (No Mind)"; Steward McFarlane, "*Mushin*, Morals, and Martial Arts: A Discussion of Keenan's Yogacara Critique"; Keenan, "The Mystique of Martial Arts: A Response to Professor McFarlane"; and McFarlane, "The Mystique of Martial Arts: A Reply to Professor Keenan's Response" offer a lively debate over the role of Zen and other Buddhist and non–Buddhist Eastern religious traditions in Asian martial art." Hurst 201, Footnote #9.

10. Adrenaline causes blood vessels to constrict, thus limiting blood loss; stimulates the production of cortisol, which decreases weakness, fatigue, and loss of resistence; and causes an increase of conversion of proteins to glucose, which helps the musculature system.

11. Mark Ravina, *The Last Samurai: The Life and Battles of Saigo Takamori* (Hoboken, NJ: John Wiley & Sons, 2004).

12. It is interesting to note that in weaponless fights in the movies, punches to the head are routinely made with little obvious trauma. While inflicting a series of concussions seems to fit the expected male pretension of brawling, the fighter intent on killing his opponent ought to strike to the throat where the Adam's apple and trachea are easily crushed.

13. *Hara kiri* is the commoner's term, meaning "belly cutting."

14. Robert F. Evans, *Soldiers of Rome: Praetorians and Legionnaires* (Cabin John, MD: Seven Locks, 1986), p. 27.

15. John Clements, "The Medieval European Knight vs. The Feudal Japanese Samurai?" The Association for Renaissance Martial Arts webpage. 17 November 2007. http://www.thearma.org/essays/knightvs.htm.

Chapter 7

1. Koichi Tohei, *Ki in Daily Life*, rev. ed. (New York: Ki No Kenkyukai H.Q., 2001).

2. Daisetsu Suzuki, *Zen and Japanese Culture* (Princeton: Princeton University Press, 1959, 1989), p. 126.

3. Peter Diamond, online interview (response on cassette tape), 27 August 1999.

4. Susan Wloszczyna, "Christensen on skywalk to 'Star Wars' fame," *USA Today*, 25 October 2001, Virginia ed.: D1.

5. Diamond interview.

6. Dale Pollock, *Skywalking: The Life and Films of George Lucas* (New York: Harmony, 1983) p. 166.

7. Dave Prowse, "Speaking Out about Negativity." Daveprowse.com. 04 January 2002. <http://www.daveprowse.com/editorial.htm>.

8. "The Chosen One" documentary, *Star Wars Episode III: Revenge of the Sith*, Disc 2, (Twentieth Century–Fox, 2005), 2:33.

Chapter 8

1. This convention also applies to individual fights and the flight of missiles across the screen. In order to break from the two initially established camps (and their association of one side of the screen), a clear narrative has to explain the change in perspective. The camera cannot switch from one side of the battlefield to the other without disorienting the audience.

2. William Gaugler, *History of Fencing: Foundations of Modern European Swordplay* (Bangor, ME: Laureate, 1997), p. 54.

3. It is telling of Gillard's personality that he would recruit Jedi from fight clubs. Instead of drawing his talent solely from experienced experts of modern fencing, kendo, or European martial art groups, he chose instead to find brawlers to represent the Jedi at the height of their power.

4. A swordsman cannot use two swords offensively unless he has had specific training in that manner. Contrary to conventional wisdom, an opponent with two swords does not attack with both at the same time. Balancing the two weapons and positioning the body requires that only one sword is used offensively, while the other is in either a defensive or preparatory position. Defensively, the second sword could be used to block an opponent's counterattack. Or, the second sword could be used to deliver a second, but distinct attack after the first. The principal advantage of the two weapons in hand is that one can be used as a holding weapon after blade contact is made, while the other is used to attack an open, unprotected area on the defender. The advantage of two swords is not overwhelming in many respects because the swordsman with the single sword has more power and control with two arms than the single arm; he also has the ability to use his legs to kick or trip because his center of gravity is more controlled; his weapon is held closer to the body and braced by two hands. The two-sword wielder has more blade with which to attack or defend, but both attacks and blocks will be weaker. Parries, especially, if not executed with proper angulation and sufficient positioning so that the energy of an opponent's blow is channeled into the weight of the body, can be easily knocked away with a strong hit.

5. Karl F. Friday with Humitake Seki, *Legacies of the Sword: The Kashima-Shinryu and Samurai Martial Culture* (Honolulu, University of Hawai'i Press, 1997), p. 94.

6. "I love abstraction. All of my student films are like that." George Lucas interviewed by Gavin Smith, "The Genius of the System," *Film Comment*, July/August (2002): 32.

7. The first paragraph about choreography indicates how Yoda's style was partially based on Gillard's Obi-Wan/Qui-Gon versus Maul fight. The second paragraph is a statement that Gillard's choreography already indicated to digital animators where the swords in the Dooku versus Yoda fight would clash. Rob Coleman, "Crouching Yoda, Hidden Dooku," Star Wars *Insider* 61 (2002): 66–69.

8. They are: *Seven Samurai, Yojimbo, Sanjuro, Enter the Dragon, Return of the Dragon, Drunken Master, The Shaolin Temple, Swordsman II, Drunken Master II,* and *Crouching Tiger, Hidden Dragon.* Coleman 67.

9. Barbara Robertson, "Inside Episode III *Star Wars*," *3D World* 66 (July 2006): p. 37.

Bibliography

Amberger, J. Christoph. *The Secret History of the Sword: Adventures in Ancient Martial Arts.* Burbank, CA: Unique Publications, 1999.

Anderson, Kevin J. *The Illustrated* Star Wars *Universe.* New York: Bantam, 1995.

Bacevich, Andrew J. *The New American Militarism: How Americans Are Seduced by War.* Oxford: Oxford University Press, 2005.

Barad, Judith. "The Aspiring Jedi's Handbook of Virtue," Star Wars *and Philosophy.* Chicago: Open Court, 2005.

Black, Jeremy. *Cambridge Illustrated Atlas of Warfare: Renaissance to Revolution.* Cambridge, England: Cambridge University Press, 1996.

Boot, Max. *War Made New: Technology, Warfare, and the Course of History 1500 to Today.* New York: Gotham, 2006.

Bottomley, I., and A. P. Hopson. *Arms and Armor of the Samurai.* New York: Crescent, 1988.

Bouzereau, Laurent. Star Wars*: The Annotated Screenplays.* New York: Ballantine, 1997.

_____, and Jody Duncan. Star Wars*: The Making of* Episode I The Phantom Menace. New York: Ballantine, 1999.

Bresman, Jonathan. *The Art of* Star Wars: Episode I The Phantom Menace. New York: Ballantine Books, 1999.

Brin, David. "'Star Wars' Despots vs. 'Star Trek' Populists," Salon.com. 15 June 1999. www.salon.com/ent/movies/feature/1999/06/15/brin_main/index.html.

_____, and Matthew Woodring Stover. Star Wars *on Trial.* Dallas, TX: Benbella, 2006.

Brooker, Will. *Using the Force: Creativity, Community and* Star Wars *Fans.* New York: Continuum International, 2003.

Brooks, Terry. *Star Wars: Episode I The Phantom Menace.* New York: Ballantine, 1999.

Bryant, Anthony J., and Angus McBride. *Elite Series: The Samurai 200–1500 AD.* London: Osprey, 1991.

Budden, Paul. *Looking at a Far Mountain: A Study of Kendo Kata.* Boston: Tuttle, 2000.

Campbell, Joseph. *The Power of Myth with Bill Moyers.* New York: Doubleday, 1998.

Cavelos, Jeanne. *The Science of* Star Wars. New York: St. Martin's, 1999.

"Chosen One Documentary," *Star Wars Episode III: Revenge of the Sith,* Disc 2 — 12:39.

Cleary, Thomas. *Soul of the Samurai.* North Claredon, VT: Tuttle, 2005.

Clements, John. "Edge Parrying vs. Flat Parrying." 13 November 2007. http://swordforum.com/sfu/swordsmanship/parrying.html.

_____. "Edges of Knowledge: Parrying with a Cutting Sword." The Association for Renaissance Martial Arts website. 13

November 2007. http://www.thearma.org/essays/parry.htm.

_____. "The Medieval European Knight vs. the Feudal Japanese Samurai?" The Association for Renaissance Martial Arts webpage. 17 November 2007. http://www.thearma.org/essays/knightvs.htm

_____. *Medieval Swordsmanship: Illustrated Methods and Techniques.* Boulder, CO: Paladin, 1998.

_____. "The Myth of Edge-on-Edge Parrying in Medieval Swordplay," The Association for Renaissance Martial Arts website. 13 November 2007. http://www.thearma.org/essays/edgemyth.htm.

_____. *Renaissance Swordsmanship: The Illustrated Use of Rapiers and Cut-and-Thrust Swords.* Boulder, CO: Paladin, 1997.

_____. "What Did Historical Swords Weigh?" Accessed 25 November 2007. http://www.thearma.org/essays/weights.htm.

Coe, Michael D., et al. *Swords and Hilt Weapons.* New York: Weidenfeld & Nicolson, 1989.

Coleman, Rob."Crouching Yoda, Hidden Dooku," Star Wars *Insider* 61 (2002): 66–69.

Collier's Encyclopedia. Vol. 2. Crowell Collier and MacMillian, 1967. Armor, pp. 667–77.

Contamine, Philippe. *War in the Middle Ages.* New York: Basil Blackwell, 1984.

_____, ed. *Histoire militaire de la France.* Paris: Presses universitaires de France, c. 1992–c. 1994.

_____, and Olivier Guyotjeannin. *La guerre, la violence et les gens au Moyen Age.* Paris: Edition du CTHS, 1996.

Craig, Gordon A. *The Politics of the Prussian Army 1640–1945.* New York: Oxford University Press, 1964.

Davies, R.W. *Service in the Roman Army.* Edinburgh: Edinburgh University Press, 1989.

Deckers, Kevin S., and Jason T. Eberl, eds. Star Wars *and Philosophy*, Chicago: Open Court, 2005.

Diamond, Peter. Online interview (response on cassette tape), 27 August 1999.

Donohue, John, Ed. *The Overlook Martial Arts Reader: Vol. 2.* Woodstock, NY: Overlook, 2004.

Drake, Michael S. *Problematics of Military Power: Government, Discipline and the Subject of Violence.* London: Frank Cass, 2001.

Duncan, Jody. "Q&A: George Lucas." *Cinefex* 102, July 2005: 57–64.

_____. "Star Wars Episode II: Attack of the Clones: Love and War." *Cinefex* 90, July 2002: 60–119.

_____. "Star Wars Episode II: Revenge of the Sith." *Cinefex* 102, July 2005: 98+.

_____. Star Wars *Mythmaking: Behind the Scenes of* Attack of the Clones. New York: Ballantine, 2002.

_____, Kevin H. Martin, and Mark Cotta Vaz. "Heroes' Journey." *Cinefex* 78, July 1999: 74–145.

Ealy, Charles. "Understanding *Star Wars*," *Dallas Morning News*, 9 May 1999. http://dallasmorningnews.com/sunday-reader-nf/reader14.htm.

Edge, David, and John Miles Paddock. *Arms & Armor of the Medieval Knight.* New York: Crescent, 1988.

Evans, Robert F. *Soldiers of Rome: Praetorians and Legionnaires.* Cabin John, MD: Seven Locks, 1986.

Friday, Karl F., with Humitake Seki. *Legacies of the Sword: The Kashima-Shinryu and Samurai Martial Culture.* Honolulu: University of Hawai'i Press, 1997.

Gaugler, William M. *History of Fencing: Foundations of Modern European Swordplay.* Bangor, ME: Laureate, 1997.

Goldsworthy, Adrian. *Roman Warfare.* New York: Smithsonian, 2002.

Glut, Donald F. *Star Wars: The Empire Strikes Back Illustrated Edition.* New York: Ballantine, 1980.

Hale, J.R. *War and Society in Renaissance Europe, 1450–1620.* Baltimore, MD: John Hopkins University Press, 1985.

Hanson, Victor Davis. *Ripples of Battle: How Wars of the Past Still Determine*

How We Fight, How We Live, and How We Think. New York: Doubleday, 2003.

_____. *The Soul of Battle: From Ancient Times to the Present Day, How Three Great Liberators Vanquished Tyranny*. New York: Free Press, 1999.

_____. *The Western Way of War*. New York: Oxford University Press, 1989.

Harris, Victor, and Nobuo Ogasawara. *Swords of the Samurai*. London: British Museum, 1990.

Henderson, Mary. Star Wars*: The Magic of Myth*. New York: Bantam, 1997.

Herrigel, Eugene. *Zen in the Art of Archery*. New York: Pantheon, 1953.

Hooper, Nicholas, and Matthew Bennett. *The Cambridge Illustrated Atlas of Warfare: The Middle Ages*. Cambridge: Cambridge University Press, 1996.

Hurst, G. Cameron. *Armed Martial Arts of Japan*. New Haven and London: Yale University Press, 1998.

Jenkins, Garry. *Empire Building: The Remarkable, Real-Life Story of* Star Wars (revised and updated edition). Secaucus, NJ: Citadel, 1999.

Jones, Archer. *Art of War in the Western World*. Urbana and Chicago: University of Illinois Press, 1987.

Kahn, James. Star Wars*: Return of the Jedi The Illustrated Edition*. New York: Ballantine, 1983.

Kaminski, Michael. *The Secret History of* Star Wars. Version 2.0. www.thesecrethistoryofstarwars.com, 2007. 09 December 2007.

Kammer, Reinhard. *The Way of the Sword: The Tengu-Geijitsu-Ron of Chozan Shissai*. Boston: Arkana, 1978.

Kaplan, Robert D. *Warrior Politics*. New York: Random House, 2002.

Kapp, Leon, Hiroko Kapp, and Yoshindo Yoshihara. *The Craft of the Japanese Sword*. Tokyo: Kodansha International, 1987.

Keegan, John. *A History of Warfare*. New York: Vintage, 1993.

_____. *The Illustrated Face of Battle*. New York: Viking, 1989.

Keen, Maurice, Ed. *Medieval Warfare: A History*. Oxford: Oxford University Press, 1999.

Kershner, Irvin, dir. *Star Wars: The Empire Strikes Back, Episode VI, Special Edition*, Twentieth Century–Fox, 1980. Videocassette.

Kiyota, Minoru. *The Shambhala Guide to Kendo*. Boston & London: Shambala, 2002.

Köhne, Eckart. *Gladiators and Caesars: The Power of Spectacle in Ancient Rome*. Berkeley: University of California Press, 2000.

Jamilla, Nick. Personal aikido journal, 1991–95. Unpublished.

Lawler, James. "The Force Is with *Us:* Hegel's Philosophy of Spirit Strikes Back at the Empire." Star Wars *and Philosophy*. Chicago: Open Court, 2005.

Leibovitz, Anne. "The Force is Back," *Vanity Fair*. February 1999, pp. 118–29.

Leggett, Trevor. *Zen and the Ways*. Rutland, VT: Charles E. Tuttle, 1987.

Levin, A.A., et al. *Microstructure of a Genuine Damascus Sabre*. Weinheim, Germany: Wiley-Vch Verlag GmbH & Co. KGaA, 2005. http://www.crystalresearch.com/crt/ab40/905_a.pdf.

Lewis, Bernard. *Race and Slavery in the Middle East*. Oxford: Oxford University Press, 1994. http://www.fordham.edu/halsall/med/lewis1.html.

Lowry, Dave. *Autumn Lightning: The Education of an American Samurai*. Boston: Shambhala, 1985.

Lucas, George. "Becoming Sidious" Webdoc. *Star Wars Episode III Revenge of the Sith*. DVD, 2005.

_____. "Commentary," *Star Wars Episode III Revenge of the Sith*. DVD, Twentieth Century–Fox, 2005.

_____. Interview. "The Genius of the System," *Film Comment* July/August (2002): 32.

_____. Interview, MSNBC's *Time & Again*, May 6, 1999.

_____. Interview. Well-rounded.com. 11 May 1999. <http://www.well-rounded.com/movies/lucas_intv.html.

_____. *Star Wars: Episode I The Phantom*

Menace Illustrated Screenplay. New York: Ballantine, 1999.

_____. *Star Wars: From the Adventures of Luke Skywalker.* New York: Ballantine, 1976.

_____, dir. *Star Wars Trilogy: Episodes IV, V, VI, Special Edition*, Twentieth Century–Fox, 2004. DVD.

_____, dir. *Star Wars: The Phantom Menace, Episode I*, Twentieth Century–Fox, 1999. DVD.

_____, dir. *Star Wars: Attack of the Clones, Episode II*, Twentieth Century–Fox, 2002. DVD.

_____, dir. *Star Wars: Revenge of the Sith, Episode III*, Twentieth Century–Fox, 2005. DVD.

Luceno, James. Star Wars*: Cloak of Deception.* New York: Ballantine, 2001.

_____. Star Wars*: Labyrinth of Evil.* New York: Del Rey, 2005.

Lund, Kristin. Star Wars: Episode I *The Complete Guide to the Incredible Locations from* The Phantom Menace. New York: DK, 2000.

Lynn, John A. *Battle: A History of Combat and Culture.* Cambridge, MA: Westview, 2003.

Marquand, Richard, dir. *Return of the Jedi, Episode VI, Special Edition.* Twentieth Century–Fox, 1983. Videocassette.

Mattingly, Garret. *Renaissance Diplomacy.* New York: Dover, 1988 (originally 1955 with Houghton Mifflin).

Meijer, Fik. *Gladiators: History's Most Deadly Sport.* New York: St. Martin's, 2004.

Miller, Jerome. *The Way of Suffering: A Geography of Crisis.* Washington, DC: Georgetown University Press, 1988.

Mol, Serge. *Classical Fighting Arts of Japan: A Complete Guide to Koryu Jujutsu.* New York: Kodansha International, 2001.

Montaigne, Michel de. "That to Think as a Philosopher Is to Learn to Die," translated by George B. Ives. *The Essays of Michel de Montaigne.* New York: Heritage, 1925.

Morgan, Diane. *The Best Guide to Eastern Philosophy and Religion.* Los Angeles: Renaissance, 2001.

Moyers, Bill. "Interview: George Lucas." *Time* 26 April 1999, pp. 90–94.

Musashi, Miyamoto. *A Book of Five Rings.* Translated by Victor Harris. Woodstock, NY: Overlook, 1974.

Oman, C.W.C. *The Art of War in the Middle Ages: A.D. 378–1515.* Ithaca, NY: Cornell University Press, 1953.

Parisi, Paula. "Grand Illusion: The Master of Myth Rewrites History," *Wired.* May 1999: 137–39.

Parker, Geoffrey. *The Cambridge Illustrated History of Warfare: The Triumph of the West.* Cambridge, England: Cambridge University Press, 1995.

_____. *The Military Revolution*, 2nd ed. London: Cambridge University Press, 1996.

Perrin, Noel. *Giving Up the Gun: Japan's Reversion to the Sword, 1543–1879.* Boulder, CO: Shambala, 1979.

Plato. *Great Dialogues of Plato*, trans. W.H.D. Rouse. New York: Mentor, 1956.

Po, H. W. B., and F. Po. "Sword," *The Encyclopedia Britannica.* 11th Edition, Vol. 26, 1911. Cambridge, England: University Press.

Pollock, Dale. *Skywalking: The Life and Films of George Lucas.* New York: Harmony, 1983.

Prowse, Dave. "Speaking Out about Negativity." Daveprowse.com. 4 January 2002. http://www.daveprowse.com/editorial.htm.

Raaflaub, Kurt, and Nathan Rosenstein, eds. *War and Society in the Ancient and Medieval Worlds: Asia, the Mediterranean, Europe, and Mesoamerica.* Cambridge, MA: Harvard University Press, 1999.

Ralston, David B. *Importing the European Army: The Introduction of European Military Techniques and Institutions into the Extra-European World, 1600–1914.* Chicago: University of Chicago Press, 1990.

Randell, Keith. *The Catholic and Counter Reformations.* London: Hodder & Stoughton, 1990.

Ratti, Oscar, and Adele Westbrook. *Secrets*

of the Samurai. Rutland, VT: Charles E. Tuttle, 1991.

Ravina, Mark. *The Last Samurai: The Life and Battles of Saigo Takamori.* Hoboken, NJ: John Wiley & Sons, 2004.

Reid, Howard. *The Way of the Warrior.* London: Century Publishing Co., 1983.

Reinhardt, Hank. "There Is No 'Best Sword.'" The Association for Renaissance Martial Arts webpage. 13 November 2007. http://www.thehaca.com/essays/nobest.htm.

Reynolds, David West. Star Wars: Episode I The Phantom Menace *Incredible Cross-sections.* New York: DK, 1999.

_____. Star Wars: Episode I *The Visual Dictionary.* New York: DK, 1999.

_____. Star Wars: *Incredible Cross-sections.* New York: DK, 1998.

_____. Star Wars: *The Visual Dictionary.* New York: DK, 1998.

Richie, Donald. *The Films of Akira Kurosawa.* Berkeley: University of California Press, 1984.

Rinzler, J. W. *The Making of* Star Wars. New York: Ballantine, 2007.

Robertson, Barbara. "Inside Episode III *Star Wars*," *3D World* 66. July 2006.

Robinson, B.W. *The Arts of the Japanese Sword.* London: Faber and Faber, 1961.

Rothenburg, Gunther E. *The Art of Warfare in the Age of Napoleon.* Bloomington: Indiana University Press, 1978.

Salatore, R.A. *Star Wars Episode II Attack of the Clones.* New York: Ballantine, 2002.

Sansom, G.B. *The Western World and Japan.* Rutland, VT: Charles E. Tuttle, 1990.

Sato, Hiroaki. *The Sword and the Mind.* New York: Overlook, 1988.

Shay, Don. "Return of the Jedi." *Cinefex* 78, July 1999: 15–32.

Shay, Estelle. "Populating Planets." *Cinefex* 78, July 1999: 149–164.

Sidebottom, Harry. *Ancient Warfare: A Very Short Introduction.* Oxford: Oxford University Press, 2004.

Skoss, Diane, ed. *Koryu Bujutsu: Classical Warrior Traditions of Japan.* Berkeley Heights, NJ: Koryu, 1997.

Smith, Bill. Star Wars: *The Essential Guide to Weapons and Technology.* New York: Ballantine, 1997.

Soho, Takuan. *The Unfettered Mind.* Trans. William Scott Wilson. Tokyo and New York: Kodansha International, 1989.

Stevens, Anthony. *The Roots of War and Terror.* New York: Continuum, 2004.

Suzuki, Daisetz. *Zen and Japanese Culture.* Princeton, NJ: Princeton University Press, 1973.

Thompson, Anne. "George Lucas." *Premiere* May 1999, pp. 68–77.

Tohei, Koichi. *Ki in Daily Life.* Revised edition. New York: Ki No Kenkyukai H.Q., 2001.

Traviss, Karen, and Ryan Kaufman. "Guide to the Grand Army of the Republic." Star Wars *Insider*, Issue 84, November–December 2005.

Turnbull, Stephen. *Battles of the Samurai.* London: Arms and Armour, 1987.

_____. *Japanese Warrior Monks AD 949–1600.* Oxford: Osprey, 2003.

_____. *Samurai Warfare.* London: Arms and Armor Books, 1997.

"Unleashing the Force Part 1: The New Beginning." Video. Starwars.com. Released 25 May 2007. <http://www.starwars.com/gaming/videogames/news/tfudoc01.html>.

Urbainczyk, Theresa. *Spartacus.* London: Bristol Classical, 2004.

Vale, Malcolm. *War and Chivalry.* Athens: University of Georgia Press, 1981.

Vaz, Mark Cotta. "Phantom Visions." *Cinefex* 78, July 1999: 39–68.

Vergrugger, J. F. *The Art of Warfare in Western Europe during the Middle Ages.* Trans. Samner Willard and S.C.M. Southern. New York: North-Holland, 1977.

Warry, John. *Warfare in the Classical World.* New York: St. Martin's, 1980.

Watanabe, Tadashige. *Shinkage-ryu Sword Techniques: Traditional Japanese Martial Arts: Volume 1.* Trans. Ronald Balsom. Tokyo: Sugawara Martial Arts Institute, 1993.

Watson, Jude. Star Wars: *Jedi Quest.* New York: Scholastic, 2001.

Wegierski, Mark "Reagan: Jedi Knight," *World*. Worldmag.com. 22 May 1999. http://www.worldmag.com/world/issue/05–22–99/cover_3.asp>.

Windham, Ryder. Star Wars: Episode I The Phantom Menace *Scrapbook*. New York: Random House, 1999.

_____. Star Wars*: The Ultimate Visual Guide*. New York: DK, 2005.

Yagyu, Munenori. *Soul of the Samurai*. Trans. Thomas Cleary. North Clarendon, VT: Tuttle, 2005.

Index